MATHEMATICAL MODELS
OF THE ECONOMY
AND OTHER ESSAYS

MATHEMATICAL
MODELS
OF THE ECONOMY
AND OTHER ESSAYS

by

RICHARD STONE

CHAPMAN AND HALL LTD
11 NEW FETTER LANE LONDON EC4

First published 1970
© Richard Stone 1970
Printed in Great Britain by
Spottiswoode, Ballantyne & Co. Ltd.
London and Colchester
SBN 412 10030 4

FOREWORD

In this volume I have brought together a collection of essays which reflect my interests in the last few years. Most of these essays appeared after the publication of *Mathematics in the Social Sciences*, so that this book can be said to begin where the other left off. The bulk of the collection, sixteen out of the nineteen papers, relates to economics and economic statistics, loosely grouped by subject; the last three papers move into the field of socio-demographic studies.

Paper I surveys briefly the different purposes served by different types of economic model, concluding with a highly condensed summary of the Cambridge Growth Model. This summary, which takes the form of a flow diagram, closes the first stage in the development of the Cambridge model as described in [11]; since it was written, so many non-linearities have been introduced into the model, especially in connection with foreign trade [12], that it is no longer possible to present the solution as a simple diagram.

The next six papers go in pairs. Papers II and III deal with foreign trade and the balance of payments. Papers IV and V deal with various types of inconsistency as they present themselves to the builder of economic models. And papers VI and VII deal with statistical techniques relevant to econometric analysis.

Papers VIII through X relate to the econometrics of consumers' behaviour. I should mention that the section on statistical estimation in paper VIII, though it shows how the results given in this paper were obtained, is now largely out of date as a consequence of recent work by Dr A. Duval at the Geneva branch of the Battelle Institute [19] and by Professor L. Solari at the University of Geneva [56–58].

The largest group, papers XI through XVI, is devoted to national accounting, its origins, its latest developments and its analytical uses. Paper XI has some historical value for anybody interested in the progress of the subject. At the time of writing it, it seemed to me that the international organizations which in the late forties and early fifties had done so much to stimulate and coordinate work on the national accounts had abdicated their role; but this fear proved quite unjustified, since in the following year the major revision of the U.N.'s *System of National Accounts* (SNA) was begun. The results of this revision were published at the end of 1968 [95]. Paper XII, which describes an advanced stage in the revision, was originally presented at the Symposium on National Accounts

v

and Balances held in Warsaw early in 1968 and is reprinted here as a convenient frame of reference for the four papers that follow it. The first of these, paper XIII, compares the SNA with the Material Products System (MPS) used in Russia and the other socialist countries of Eastern Europe and shows how both systems can be derived from the same matrix by applying alternative grouping procedures. The next two papers, XIV and XV, describe some of the analytical uses to which the new SNA can be put. And the last of the group, paper XVI, sets out a treatment of income distribution statistics based on a disaggregation of the sectors distinguished in the SNA.

The last three papers in the book are, as I have said, concerned with the analysis of socio-demographic systems. Paper XVII summarizes a discussion of educational model-building which took place at an O.E.C.D. conference in the spring of 1966. Paper XVIII suggests some statistical and mathematical tools for the analysis of demographic flows. And paper XIX gives the numerical example of the accounting framework proposed for this analysis.

As I emphasized in my earlier book, the user of mathematics will always find many conceptual and technical connections between economics and other disciplines, both within and without the social sciences. Thus, at an elementary level, papers II and XVII illustrate the relevance of ideas derived from control-system engineering to economic and other social problems. Paper XVIII relates socio-demographic models based on transition proportions to economic models based on input–output coefficients and shows that for a socio-demographic system in stationary equilibrium the two models are identical. To many people it might seem more natural to formulate a model based on transition proportions in the language of absorbing Markov chains, as Thonstad, for instance, has done in [46, 84]. However, what seems natural depends on the discipline from which one starts, and it may be helpful to many economists to realise that the fundamental matrix of an absorbing Markov chain is none other than their old friend the matrix inverse of an input–output system, or matrix multiplier. A recognition of this connection makes it possible to draw on either technique as convenient; for example, to introduce a set of price or cost equations into a socio-demographic model so as to link activity levels and budgetary implications in such areas as education or health. I have developed this connection in *Demographic Accounting and Model-Building*, at present in course of publication by the O.E.C.D.

In concluding this foreword there are a number of people I should like to thank. First, Mrs Jane Gunton and my wife for agreeing to the inclusion of paper XIX, which was written jointly with them. Second, Mr H. R. Fisher for allowing me to include his most interesting commentary on paper X. And, finally, the editors of the various journals, conference volumes, etc. in which these essays were first published. The essays are reprinted substantially as they appeared originally, with the exception of paper XV, about half of which has been left out to avoid an unnecessary overlap with paper XII.

RICHARD STONE

Cambridge
January 1970

PLACE AND DATE OF ORIGINAL PUBLICATION

CONTENTS

I
MATHEMATICAL MODELS OF
THE ECONOMY

1. TOY MODELS

Let us begin by setting up a framework for a model of an economy. For simplicity let us consider a closed economy, an economy with no outside world, and let us write down the national accounts for such an economy. There are three of these accounts: one which relates to production, the bringing into being of goods and services; a second which relates to consumption, the using up of goods and services to satisfy the needs of consumers; and a third which relates to accumulation, the withholding of goods for use in the future, either to meet the needs of consumers or to provide the materials or equipment required for production. If we put the monetary incomings into these accounts in the rows of a matrix and their monetary outgoings into the corresponding columns, we can set out the accounting framework for any given time period in the form

0	ϵ	$\dot{\omega}$
μ	0	0
0	σ	0

The first row and column pair of this matrix relates to production. The revenue comes from: the sale of goods for consumption, ϵ; and the sale of goods for capital purposes, shown here as $\dot{\omega}$, the change in the capital stock, ω. The whole of this revenue is paid out as income, μ, to those who take part in production. This income provides the revenue for the second account and is either spent on consumption goods or it is saved. This saving, σ, provides the revenue for the third account and, in fact, exactly pays for capital expenditures, $\dot{\omega}$.

Since, by definition, accounts balance, this system provides three identities connecting the four variables, ϵ, $\dot{\omega}$, μ and σ. Two of these identities are independent and so for a determinate system we need two additional equations. These we should expect to take the form of assumptions about the real world and, since we are dealing with an economic

2

example, to express some aspect either of the behaviour of consumers or of the techniques of production.

In the case of consumers, we can reasonably suppose that the amount they save (and therefore the amount they consume) depends partly on their income and partly on their wealth, ω. Thus we might write

$$\sigma = \beta\mu - \alpha\omega \tag{1}$$

where α and β are positive constants less than one, since consumption is likely to respond positively to both income and wealth.

In the case of producers, we can reasonably suppose that an increase in output requires additional capital expenditure. If the capital expenditure needed is proportional to the increase in income (or output), we can write

$$\dot{\omega} = \kappa\dot{\mu} \tag{2}$$

where κ is a positive constant. If to (1) and (2) we add the identity

$$\sigma \equiv \dot{\omega} \tag{3}$$

we obtain a determinate model connecting σ, μ and ω. Having solved this system of equations, we can readily calculate ϵ since

$$\epsilon \equiv \mu - \sigma \tag{4}$$

Let us now consider the behavioural and technical equations, (1) and (2), separately under conditions of constant exponential growth in income. If income is given by

$$\mu = \mu_0 e^{\rho\theta} \tag{5}$$

then it follows from (1) and (3) that

$$\sigma = \left[\frac{\beta\mu_0}{\alpha+\rho} - \omega_0\right]\alpha e^{-\alpha\theta} + \frac{\beta\rho\mu_0}{\alpha+\rho}e^{\rho\theta} \tag{6}$$

The first term in (6), the transient, approaches zero with increasing θ. If we ignore this term, we can see from (5) and (6) that the ratio of saving to income tends to

$$\frac{\sigma}{\mu} = \frac{\beta\rho}{\alpha+\rho} \tag{7}$$

By dividing (2) by μ and using (5), we see that

$$\frac{\dot{\omega}}{\mu} = \kappa\rho \tag{8}$$

and from (3), (7) and (8) it follows that

$$\rho = (\beta/\kappa) - \alpha \tag{9}$$

unless it is equal to zero. With ρ as in (9) it follows from (7) that

$$\frac{\sigma}{\mu} = \beta - \alpha\kappa \tag{10}$$

This model, for all its simplicity, does provide some insight into the process of economic growth and, moreover, squares approximately with the facts. If we set $\alpha = 0.05$, $\beta = 0.25$ and $\kappa = 3$, we see that $\rho = 0.033$ and $\sigma/\mu = 0.10$. In other words an economy of the very simple kind assumed in the model and in which behaviour and technology are characterized by the values of α, β and κ just given, would tend to grow at an instantaneous rate of 3·3 per cent and would tend to save 10 per cent of its income. All these numbers are reasonably characteristic of this country at the present time.

At the same time this toy model leaves an enormous amount out of the picture. Demographic changes, the size of the labour force and the structure of skills possessed by this labour force were never even mentioned. The diversity of production and the need of different branches for different materials, labour and capital equipment were ignored. Nothing was said about finance, prices or foreign trade. In this imaginary economy, social attitudes, with the exception of the attitude to spending and saving, play no part and no explicit role is assigned to technical change; yet, in the world we know, attitudes to innovation, mobility, restrictive practices and countless other matters are important, and the same is true of new discoveries and inventions, which make possible new products and new processes.

2. PREDICTION AND PLANNING

Before I discuss the means whereby at least some of these over-simplifications might be removed, I should like to say something about the purposes that models of the economy can serve. Apart from insight, which I have mentioned, we should undoubtedly like to gain understanding of the way in which the economy works. But, in addition, we usually have an eye to the future and build models either to enable us to predict or to enable us to plan. By prediction I mean calculating the values of the variables that are likely to be realized in the future, usually on the tacit assumption that the methods of operating the economy will remain virtually unchanged. By planning I mean a conscious effort to change the predicted outcome by changing the operating conditions. The two aims are, of course, different but the information needed to carry them out largely overlaps. This can be illustrated with the help of the toy model of the preceding section.

The basis for prediction is provided by solving the system of equations consisting of (1), (2) and (3). The result is

$$\mu = \frac{\alpha(\omega_0 - \kappa\mu_0) + \sigma_0 e^{\rho\theta}}{\beta - \alpha\kappa} \tag{11}$$

$$\omega = \frac{\beta(\omega_0 - \kappa\mu_0) + \kappa\sigma_0 e^{\rho\theta}}{\beta - \alpha\kappa} \tag{12}$$

and

$$\sigma = \sigma_0 \, e^{\rho\theta} \tag{13}$$

where ρ is given by (9). Thus if we know the initial values μ_0, ω_0 and σ_0, and the parameters α, β and κ, we can predict the values of μ, ω and σ at any future time, θ.

The amount of planning we can do with a model as simple as this is very limited. If, however, we are interested in the rate of growth of the economy, we can see from (9) that this rate can only be changed by increasing β or by reducing α or κ. The relative effectiveness of these different possibilities can be measured by calculating the elasticity of the growth rate, ρ, with respect to α, β and κ. Thus

$$\frac{\partial \rho}{\partial \alpha} \cdot \frac{\alpha}{\rho} = -\frac{\alpha\kappa}{\beta - \alpha\kappa} \tag{14}$$

$$\frac{\partial \rho}{\partial \beta} \cdot \frac{\beta}{\rho} = \frac{\beta}{\beta - \alpha\kappa} \tag{15}$$

and

$$\frac{\partial \rho}{\partial \kappa} \cdot \frac{\kappa}{\rho} = -\frac{\beta}{\beta - \alpha\kappa} \tag{16}$$

These calculations show that a given proportionate increase in β would have the same effect on the growth rate as the same proportionate reduction in κ. The same proportionate reduction in α would necessarily have a smaller effect since, in a growing economy, $\beta > \alpha\kappa$. The effort required to bring about these different effects would indicate a course of action for the planner.

Thus we see that in prediction we need to know the initial state of the system and the numerical values of its parameters. In planning we need to know at least the numerical value of the parameters and the cost of changing them. This is true if our aim is unambiguous, as in the above example. If we are in doubt about our aim, vacillating, for example, between the desire for faster growth and the desire for a more favourable balance of payments, we must assign rates of substitution to these aims so that we can calculate how far to give up one in order to obtain a little more of the other.

3. LARGE-SCALE MODELS

By building large-scale models we can represent the economy in greater detail and so can remove some of the oversimplifications inseparable from toy models. This in itself is an interesting exercise. But there are other factors as well that lead us to increase the size and scope of models. In the first place, policy-making requires some attention to detail; and this is true whether we are concerned with short-term policies to avoid fluctuations in economic activity or with long-term policies for faster growth. In the second place, model-building requires detailed knowledge of a kind which can only be obtained from people engaged on practical tasks and such information is inevitably fairly specific; the practical world knows little about total production or even about the total production of capital goods, but individuals can always be found in it who know a great deal about the production of coal or ships or rubber tyres. In the third place, the system we are modelling does not respect professional distinctions between economic and social influences and requires us to come to grips with many factors, especially social factors, which are not represented at all in small economic models.

How then to start on enlarging the size and scope of a model? If we look round the world at the various attempts that are being made [80], we can see that practice varies enormously depending on the purpose the model is intended to serve, the information available in the country concerned, the particular interests of the group building the model, the resources available to them and so on. As a result some models go further in particular directions, others in others. At this stage it is too early to generalize and the best I can do is to give a single example of work on a large-scale model based on my own experience.

4. THE CAMBRIDGE GROWTH MODEL: A SUMMARY

The main purpose of this model is to examine the possibilities of realizing certain broad economic aims in this country and the problems that such an endeavour would be likely to raise. It is assumed that most people would like their standard of living to be as high and to rise as fast as is compatible with meeting a number of other aims such as avoiding excessive hours of work and an excessive rate of adaptation, maintaining ideals of liberty and social justice and, incidentally, making adequate provision for that regrettable necessity defence expenditure. Accordingly, we have started our work with assumptions about the level of public and private spending for consumption in 1970 and its rate of growth thereafter and with assumptions about future export possibilities. We have also postulated that from 1970 onwards our foreign transactions should show a small favourable balance. Given these aims and a few others of less importance, our first step has been to ask what levels of output in the different branches of production and what levels of capital expenditure would be compatible with our assumptions, what inputs would be required by each branch, what amount of imports would be possible and how this amount would be distributed over different products. The initial solution at this stage raises further problems: what steps should be taken to enable the labour force to produce the total output required; or to stimulate sufficient saving to finance domestic capital expenditure as well as a favourable balance of payments. The next stages, on which we have been working for some time but which are not yet integrated with the first stage, are designed to examine these problems. Eventually, the results of successive stages will react back on the first: partly by showing some of the blocks that would have to be removed if our aims were to be met; and partly by causing us to revise our ideas on various matters, such as relative costs and prices in the future.

This is not the place to attempt a detailed account of our work. For those interested, a description is being built up gradually in a series of publications entitled *A Programme for Growth* [6–11]. In this paper I shall concentrate on the first stage, on the calculations we have actually made. The two steps involved at this stage are set out in two diagrams which I have already made use of in [70]. With the help of the notes I shall now give, these diagrams will, I hope, be self-explanatory.

(*a*) *Conventions and symbols.* With two exceptions, capital letters denote matrices. The exceptions are: the shift operator, E, and the difference operator, Δ. For example, $E\mu\,(1970) \equiv \mu\,(1971)$, and $\Delta \equiv E - 1$.

Small italic letters denote column vectors; with the addition of a prime superscript, they denote row vectors. The letter i denotes the unit vector. Small italic letters surmounted by a circumflex accent denote diagonal matrices; the only exception to this is the unit matrix, which is denoted by the familiar I.

Small greek letters denote scalars.

With one exception, the boxes, whatever their shape, contain variables. The exception is the octagon in the second diagram which contains a 1, indicating the constant terms in a particular set of functions.

With two exceptions, the expressions along the arrows premultiply the variables from whose boxes the arrows emerge: for example, $e = Ce^*$. The exceptions are: the non-linear relationships connecting e^* with μ and p (and Ee^* with $E\mu$ and Ep) in which, of necessity, the variables μ and p (and $E\mu$ and Ep) also appear; and the row summations connecting r with R^* (and Er with ER^*) in which the i's are postmultipliers.

(*b*) *Dates and valuation.* All variables not preceded by E or Δ relate to 1970. Those preceded by E relate to 1971. Those preceded by Δ relate to the change from 1970 to 1971, which is assumed to remain constant thereafter.

All variables are reckoned at 1960 prices.

(*c*) *Diagram 1: data processing.* This diagram shows how a number of initial assumptions and starting values (enclosed in octagons) are processed to provide the main exogenous variables (enclosed in circles) of diagram 2.

DIAGRAM 1   DATA PROCESSING

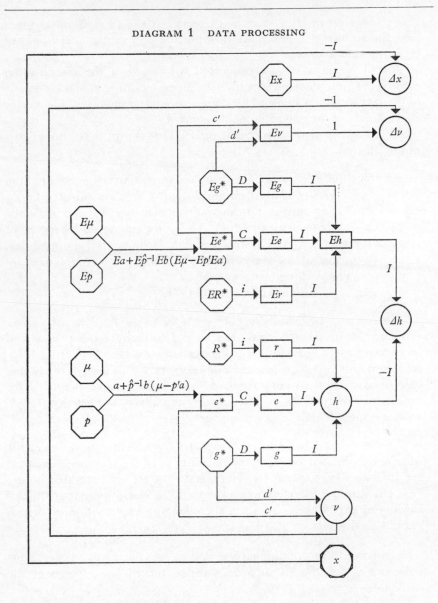

(*i*) *Private consumers' demands for goods and services.* Total consumers' expenditure in 1970, μ, is fixed as an aim and combined with the price vector, p, to give the quantities of consumers' goods and services (forty categories), the elements of e^*. The relationship shown implies that consumers buy certain basic quantities of each good or service, the elements of a, and spread any remaining money over the different goods and services in certain proportions, the elements of b. The parameters a and b, which change gradually from year to year, are estimated from data covering the period 1900–1960. Some changes (not shown in the diagram) are made to the projections in the light of recent developments.

The elements of e^* are converted by means of the classification converter C into demands for industrial commodities, e, and by means of the ratios c' into a demand for complementary imports, v. The vector e forms part of exogenous home demand, h.

The same calculations are made for 1971, as shown in the upper part of the diagram.

(*ii*) *Government demands for public purposes.* Government spending intentions for 1967–68 have been published. These are adjusted to our classification of government purposes (twelve categories) and projected to 1970 to give the elements of g^*. These are converted by means of the classification converter D into demands for industrial commodities, g, and by means of the ratios d' into a demand for complementary imports, v. The vector g forms part of h.

The same calculations are made for 1971.

(*iii*) *Industrial demands for the replacement of fixed assets.* These estimates are based on normal life-spans of different classes of asset and on the average investment in these assets one life-span back from 1970. Replacements, R^*, are worked out industry by industry (thirty-one categories) and then summed over industries to give demands for industrial commodities, r. The vector r completes our estimates of h.

The same calculations are made for 1971.

(*iv*) *Foreign demands for British exports.* These demands, the elements of x, are estimated commodity by commodity (thirty-one categories) for 1970 and 1971, partly by reference to the trends suggested by the N.E.D.C., partly by reference to the trend in world trade in manufactures, and partly by reference to the changing composition of British exports in the past.

The outcome of this preliminary work is to provide the main exogenous variables, h, v, x, Δh, Δv and Δx, needed for the next stage in the calculations.

(*d*) *Diagram 2: the circuit of commodity balances.* This diagram shows how we use the exogenous variables just mentioned (enclosed in circles) and a constant value of the balance of trade, β (enclosed in an octagon), to estimate the total demand for commodities and the levels of domestic output and of competitive imports needed in 1970 to meet this demand. The missing, endogenous, elements of demand which we must calculate for this purpose are: industrial demands for the extension of fixed assets

DIAGRAM 2   THE CIRCUIT OF COMMODITY BALANCES

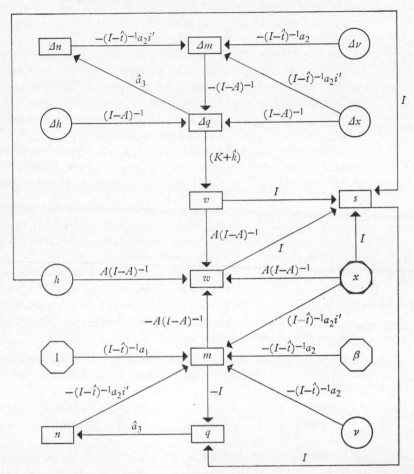

and for additions to stocks, and industrial demands for intermediate inputs.

(*i*) *Industrial demand for the extension of fixed assets and additions to stocks.* These demands, the elements of the vector *v*, shown in the upper part of the diagram, depend on the increase in output levels, Δq. This increase must be sufficient to meet Δh and Δx plus the indirect demands for intermediate product to which they give rise, except in so far as any of these demands are met by an increase in competitive imports, Δm. On the assumption that the balance of trade, β, is held constant, that is $\Delta\beta = 0$, then Δm depends on Δx and Δv plus the change in complementary imports into production, Δn.

In the diagram, the elements of Δn are shown as proportional to the corresponding elements of Δq, the factors of proportionality being the elements of a_3. The elements of Δm are defined inclusive of customs duties, the rates of which are the elements of t. The elements of Δm before duty are proportional to $i'\Delta x - i'\Delta n - \Delta v$, the factors of proportionality being in this case the elements of a_2.

The calculation of Δm provides the missing elements in the calculation of Δq. The parameters required are the current input–output coefficients, the elements of A, which measure the amount of each commodity needed directly to produce one unit of each commodity. The matrix multiplier $(I - A)^{-1} \equiv I + A + A^2 + \dots$ measures the direct and indirect requirements per unit of each commodity output.

Industrial extensions and additions to stocks, v, are derived from Δq. The parameters required are the capital input–output coefficients for extensions, the elements of K, and the stock-output ratios, the elements of k.

(*ii*) *Industrial demand for intermediate inputs.* These demands, the elements of w, depend positively on h, v and x and negatively on m (competitive imports). To calculate w we need all the terms in the matrix multiplier except the first, which is equivalent to multiplying $(I - A)^{-1}$ by A. The determination of m is similar to the determination of Δm except that we must allow for two additional factors: a possibly non-zero value of the balance of trade, β; and the intercepts, a_1, as well as the slopes, a_2, of the competitive import functions.

(*iii*) *Total supplies and domestic outputs.* The remaining relationships shown in the diagram are accounting identities. Total commodity supplies, s, are equal to total commodity demands, $h + v + w + x$; and domestic outputs, q, are equal to total commodity supplies, s, less competitive imports, m.

(*e*) *Variables, equations, degrees of freedom.* The diagrams on the preceding pages give a clear picture of the model as it has been developed and programmed so far. As further stages are completed, it will be necessary to add further diagrams and to modify the present ones to allow for feedback from the later stages. For example, with the help of production functions it will be possible to build up estimates of future prices (from future costs) and so modify the initial values of p (and Ep) which so far we have taken at their 1960 values.

But though the structure of the model may be clear, it may still be difficult to get a proper appreciation of its size, despite the fact that the sizes of the various categories have been given, and of its determinateness. These questions can, however, easily be settled by the accounting method, based on the identity: number of variables equals number of equations plus number of degrees of freedom.

The account for diagram 1 is as follows:

Exogenous variables (μ, $E\mu$, p, Ep, g^*, Eg^*, R^*, ER^*, x, Ex)		Assumptions (μ, $E\mu$, p, Ep, g^*, Eg^*, R^*, ER^*, x, Ex)	2090
	2090	Identities:	
Endogenous variables (e^{**}, Ee^{**}, e^*, Ee^*, e, Ee, g, Eg, r, Er, h, Eh, Δh, v, Ev, Δv, Δx)		arithmetical (e^*, Ee^*, r, Er, h, Eh, Δh, Δv, Δx)	267
	473	accounting	0
		Equalities (e^{**}, Ee^{**}, e, Ee, g, Eg, v, Ev)	206
		Degrees of freedom	0
Total	2563	Total	2563

In this account, the variables are divided into exogenous and endogenous. The exogenous variables are determined by what I call assumptions but this does not mean that the values are necessarily chosen arbitrarily. In the case of μ, the total amount to be spent at 1960 prices on goods and services by private consumers, the value chosen is arbitrary; but in the case of g^*, government expenditures on goods and services, it is not, being based on stated government intentions. In all these cases, however, we are free to consider alternative figures and, since the thirty million arithmetical operations needed to solve the system of equations represented by both diagrams take about one hundred seconds computing time, the examination of many alternatives is a practical possibility.

The endogenous variables are determined by equations (identities or equalities). In the present case there are no degrees of freedom since the model is determinate.

The account for diagram 2 is as follows:

Exogenous variables (h, Δh, v, Δv, x, Δx, β)	127	Assumptions: derived from the preceding stage (h, Δh, v, Δv, x, Δx)	126
		made at this stage (β)	1
Endogenous variables (Δn, Δm, Δq, v, n, m, w, s, q)	279	Identities: arithmetical (s)	31
		accounting (q)	31
		Equalities (Δn, Δm, Δq, v, n, m, w)	217
		Degrees of freedom	0
Total	406	Total	406

The total number of endogenous variables in the two accounts is 752. These are connected by 329 identities and 423 equalities. We can thus see that the model consists of 423 independent endogenous variables connected by an equal number of equations that are not identities.

By simply counting symbols we find that 1753 independent parameters are involved in diagram 1 and 2077 in diagram 2, making 3830 in all. These numbers are, however, considerably inflated by zero values. The same can be said of the number of exogenous variables in diagram 1; for example, since most commodities are not capital goods, the majority of entries in R^* and ER^*, which contribute 1922 out of the total of 2090, are zero.

5. CONCLUSION

I have tried in this paper to give some examples of the use of mathematics in the building of economic models. The mathematics in my examples are extremely simple but are probably fairly representative of one aspect of the use of mathematics by economists. Examples of the use of much more advanced methods could easily be found, but to set these all out in an orderly way would carry us far beyond the limits of a single paper.

II

OUR UNSTABLE ECONOMY: CAN PLANNING SUCCEED?

As economic models become more complex, and have a greater empirical content, to make them applicable to the real world, the answers to general questions become less possible. The economist may need, therefore, to shift his ground from the general to the particular, and to follow the methods and the experience of the engineer.

R. G. D. ALLEN, *Mathematical Economics* (1956)

1. INTRODUCTION

Since the last war the total output of the British economy has grown a little faster and shown rather more stability than it did in the years between the wars. But, even so, it has not grown very fast and it has not been very stable. As soon as production begins to pick up and a new upward movement is getting under way, it is found necessary to damp it down in order to protect our foreign reserves and the value of the pound. God save the quid becomes the popular cry. Recently we have seen the melancholy sight of our first attempts at planning for faster growth nipped in the bud by our failure to control economic instability. No one can claim that this is an easy thing to do, but experience suggests that we may not be going about it in the right way and certainly that we should learn all we can from any discipline with a better record at regulation and control.

Controlling an economy is often likened to driving a car. Clearly there is something in this analogy, since each involves the regulation of a complex system, but it does not go very far. Without any understanding of neurology, of the engineering principles embodied in car design and road construction or of cybernetics, most people can learn by experience after a little instruction, in which none of the above subjects is ever mentioned, to drive and to cope more or less adequately with most of the situations they are ever likely to meet. If they have accidents it is regrettable but it does not bring travel by road to an end. By contrast, success in controlling an economy cannot be achieved in this intuitive, trial and error, way; and failure to control instability does make nonsense of planning for growth. A better analogy with the control of an economy would be the control of an industrial plant, where success can only be expected from a knowledge of the dynamics of the plant and from the ability to devise and install a control device which will achieve a number of aims.

This is the theme of my talk this evening. It is not very original but perhaps sufficiently novel to bear a little reiteration.

Before we can design the means of controlling a system, we need to understand how the system works. Our knowledge must be quantitative because successful design depends on the structure of the system, on the strength of the responses of its various parts to the factors that influence them and on the delays and time-lags to which these responses are subject. On the basis of this knowledge we must build a model of the economic system and use this model to explore possible means of control. The model will be complex, representable by a system of non-linear difference or differential equations of a high order. We must use every device available to us to simplify the model by cutting out inessentials so that, with the help of a computer, we can explore by simulation methods the probable effects of alternative methods of control. By these means we may hope to design a control mechanism that is reasonably efficient without having to live through the periodic disturbances that are damaging alike to our economic performance, to our prestige abroad and even to our social cohesion.

At the present time these ideas are in the air. They have been expounded in recent years by a number of distinguished writers in this country, notably Goodwin, Phillips and Tustin. What is now needed is a determined effort to get empirical work going on a sufficient scale and to use the results of this work in policy making. Without such a systematic approach it is difficult to see how our present mistakes can be avoided. It takes more than alchemy to split the atom.

In order to indicate the importance of systematic study, I shall now present a very simple example and show that, even in such a case, considerable care is needed in designing a satisfactory control system. I shall also show that even when the system has been stabilized it does not at all follow that its performance is optimal. However, there is little point in talking about optimality until stability has been achieved.

The obvious criticism of my example is that the real world is so hopelessly complicated that the method I am suggesting could never be applied. That it is difficult I should agree but I am very suspicious of statements about impossibility. In the present case they seem to overlook the advances that have been made in the last generation in economic statistics, econometrics, control-system engineering and computers. So I shall conclude by sketching out a programme of research which I think would be practicable with the knowledge we already possess.

2. A SIMPLE EXAMPLE

Consider an economy characterized by the following relationships:

$$q_d = h + x - m \tag{1}$$

$$q_s = \frac{\theta}{D + \theta} q_d \qquad (2)$$

$$h = \alpha + \beta q_s + \gamma D q_s \qquad (3)$$

$$m = \mu q_s \qquad (4)$$

$$x = \text{a constant} \qquad (5)$$

The symbol q_d denotes the demand for output and, from (1), this is composed of home demand, h, export demand, x, less imports, m. The symbol q_s denotes the supply of output which, from (2), adjusts itself to demand at speed θ. In (2), D denotes the differential operator, d/dt, and $1/\theta$ is the time constant of the adjustment process. From (3), home demand is composed of three elements: a constant term α, a term which is proportional to q_s with coefficient β and a term which is proportional to Dq_s with coefficient γ. From (4), imports are proportional to q_s with coefficient μ; and from (5), export demand is an exogenous constant.

By making the necessary substitutions it is easy to see that q_s is characterized by the following first-order differential equation.

$$\left[D + \frac{\theta(1 - \beta + \mu)}{1 - \theta\gamma} \right] q_s = \frac{\theta(\alpha + x)}{1 - \theta\gamma} \qquad (6)$$

Thus q_s will vary around the value

$$\frac{\alpha + x}{1 - \beta + \mu}$$

but whether or not its variation will be stable depends on the sign of the coefficient of q_s on the left-hand side of (6). If the coefficient $\theta(1 - \beta + \mu)/(1 - \theta\gamma)$ is positive, q_s will return to the value $(\alpha + x)/(1 - \beta + \mu)$ if disturbed from this value. On the other hand, if $\theta(1 - \beta + \mu)/(1 - \theta\gamma)$ is negative, q_s will depart from the value $(\alpha + x)/(1 - \beta + \mu)$ if, initially, it has a different value. If the initial value exceeds the stable value, q_s will increase without limit; if the initial value falls short of the stable value, q_s will decrease without limit. In either case, the movement of q_s is given by the solution of (6), namely

$$q_s = \frac{\alpha + x}{1 - \beta + \mu} + \left[q_{s0} - \frac{\alpha + x}{1 - \beta + \mu} \right] e^{-\frac{\theta(1 - \beta + \mu)}{1 - \theta\gamma} t} \qquad (7)$$

where q_{s0} denotes the initial value of q_s, e denotes the base of natural logarithms and t denotes time.

The stability of q_s depends on the values of the parameters in the coefficient of q_s in (6) or, what is the same thing, in the exponent of e

in (7). If we put $\beta = 0\cdot8$, $\gamma = 2$ and $\mu = 0\cdot2$, we can express this critical coefficient, b say, in terms of θ. Thus for stability, we must have

$$b = \frac{0\cdot4\theta}{1 - 2\theta} > 0 \tag{8}$$

and so, since θ is essentially positive, we must have

$$\theta < 0\cdot5 \tag{9}$$

It follows that q_s will only be stable if θ is small, that is if supply adjusts rather slowly to demand. If θ is large, that is if supply adjusts quickly to demand, q_s will be unstable.

To start with, let us suppose that θ is small so that q_s is stable. It does not follow from this that the whole system is stable. If we put $x = 20$, q_s will tend to return to a value of

$$2\cdot5\alpha + 50$$

and this will only be an equilibrium value if it is equal to $x/\mu = 100$, that is if $\alpha = 20$. If $\alpha > 20$, imports will exceed exports at the stable value of q_s and foreign reserves will decline without limit; correspondingly, if $\alpha < 20$ they will increase without limit. In either case reserves are unstable.

One way to stabilize the whole system would be to wait until reserves had reached a critically low level and then remove sufficient purchasing power from the system to cause q_s to fall to a level at which $0\cdot2\, q_s < 20$. At this level of q_s, reserves would increase and, if the excess purchasing power were kept out of the system, q_s would remain constant and reserves would increase continually. At some point, a safe level of reserves would be reached and, if the excess purchasing power were then restored to the system, q_s would rise to its original level and reserves would start to fall. If purchasing power were removed again when reserves had reached their critical level, q_s would again fall and reserves would improve. Under this regime, reserves would rise steadily and fall steadily between their critical and safe levels and q_s would be for a certain period alternately above and below its stable value.

This is a simple example of on–off control analogous to the thermostat of a domestic heating system. Something in the system is unstable, in the present case the level of reserves, and the method used to remove this instability induces oscillations in all the variables of the system, in output as well as in reserves. The system is stable in the sense that it does not explode or collapse, but it is oscillatory. The parallel with our stop–go policy in economic affairs is all too plain.

A good control mechanism may not be able to avoid regular oscillations altogether but it ought to be able to keep such oscillations to a tolerable amplitude. Accordingly, it should be possible to find a better alternative to stop–go. Since the unstable element is the level of reserves, it seems natural to try the effect of using this level as the control variable. Let us therefore add to (1) a variable, g say, and let us define the control function by the relationship

$$g = \sigma \frac{(x - m)}{D} \tag{10}$$

which implies that purchasing power is introduced into or removed from the system in proportion to the level of reserves above some arbitrary level.

With this addition to the system, the differential equation for q_s is now of the second order and takes the form

$$\left[D^2 + \frac{\theta(1 - \beta + \mu)}{1 - \theta\gamma}D + \frac{\theta\mu\sigma}{1 - \theta\gamma}\right]q_s = \frac{\theta\sigma x}{1 - \theta\gamma} \tag{11}$$

or, in standard form,

$$(D^2 + bD + c)\,q_s = A \tag{12}$$

In this system, q_s will vary around the value

$$\frac{A}{c} = \frac{x}{\mu} \tag{13}$$

and so the stable value of q_s will also be an equilibrium value for the system since, when it is achieved, $m = x$ and reserves do not change either up or down.

A necessary condition for the stability of this system is that $b > 0$. Thus we see, by comparing (11) with (6), that this stabilization policy will not render q_s stable if it was not so originally. We saw above that the stability of q_s in the original model depended on θ being small, that is on supply adjusting itself sluggishly to demand. This is not a very realistic assumption and so it is not very likely that the policy just considered would in fact have the desired results.

The control variable g in (10) is proportional to the integral of the balance of payments above an arbitrary level. We could try the effect of choosing a control function which depended on the level and the derivative of the balance of payments as well as on its integral. Let us therefore add a variable, g^* say, to (1) and define the control function by the relationship

$$g^* = \frac{\sigma(x - m)}{D} + \pi(x - m) + \rho D(x - m) \tag{14}$$

where π and ρ as well as σ are constants.

With this form of control function, the differential equation for q_s is again of the second order, namely

$$\left\{D^2 + \frac{\theta[1 - \beta + \mu(1 + \pi)]}{1 + \theta(\rho\mu - \gamma)}D + \frac{\theta\mu\sigma}{1 + \theta(\rho\mu - \gamma)}\right\}q_s = \frac{\theta\sigma x}{1 + \theta(\rho\mu - \gamma)} \tag{15}$$

which, with $\theta = 1$ and the values already given for β, γ and μ, can be written as

$$\left[D^2 + \frac{\pi + 2}{\rho - 5}D + \frac{\sigma}{\rho - 5}\right]q_s = \frac{5\sigma x}{\rho - 5} \tag{16}$$

From (15) we see that q_s will vary around the equilibrium value $(x/\mu) = 5x$ as before. From (16) we see that we are now in a position to ensure the stability of q_s. A necessary condition for this stability is that $(\pi + 2)/(\rho - 5)$ be positive. This result can be achieved either by making $\pi > -2$ and $\rho > 5$ or by making $\pi < -2$ and $\rho < 5$. If we choose the first alternative we must make $\sigma > 0$ and if we choose the second we must make $\sigma < 0$, since to avoid a positive root in (16) we must ensure that $\sigma/(\rho - 5)$ is positive. To avoid oscillations we must ensure that $(\pi + 2)^2/(\rho - 5) > 4\sigma$.

Thus, in principle, we can stabilize both output and reserves and we can avoid even damped oscillations in doing so. In practice we shall probably have to contend with difficulties that I have not considered; there may be limits to the strength of the responses, that is to the magnitude of π, ρ and σ; and these responses are likely to be subject to a time-lag or delay. The effect of introducing exponential lags or delays into (14) can readily be examined but would lead to equations that cannot suitably be introduced into a general discussion of the subject.

A further point which is worth noting is that all we have done is to introduce into (1) a variable g^* depending on the control variable $x - m$. The terms in the control function (14) have not been assigned between h and m nor between the components of h, consumption and investment. As far as stabilization is concerned, such an assignment is irrelevant, although it does of course affect the variables concerned.

Once we have worked out the most suitable values of π, ρ and σ, we have, in a sense, solved the control problem as far as this simple model is concerned. But if we think about what we have done it becomes apparent that we have only hit on a particular solution of the problem implied by the original model. The trouble all arose because the stable level of q_s might imply a cumulative loss of reserves. Even if the original first-order differential equation (6) for q_s were not stable, we have seen from (15) that we could stabilize it and at the same time ensure that, at the stabilized value, reserves would not change. But at what level have we stabilized output? At the level x/μ. There is no reason to think that this is the maximum level of output of which the economy is capable; it is simply the level which ensures a zero balance of payments and therefore stable reserves.

We can now see clearly the plight of this simple economy, which has much in common with the plight of our own economy. If it is to be stable it may have to accept a level of output lower than it could achieve, with consequent unemployment, open or disguised. Any attempt to increase output above this level destabilizes the system by causing a cumulative loss of reserves unless, at the same time, something is done to change the structure of the system. In my simple example, in which it is assumed that export demand is fixed, there is only one change in structure that will help: a reduction in the ratio of imports to output. Unless, somehow or other, this can be achieved, maximum output is incompatible with stability.

Accordingly, we might concentrate on a different means of control which forced imports into an acceptable relationship with exports. This does not imply either a free exchange rate or quantitative restrictions on imports; it could be achieved by introducing an import currency which importers would be free to bid for and by fixing the amount of such currency in each period by reference to past export performance. In terms of the model, (4) would be replaced by, say,

$$m = \frac{\eta}{D+\eta} x \qquad (17)$$

that is to say, imports would follow exports with speed η. In this case the differential equation for q_s takes the form

$$\left\{ D^2 + \left[\eta + \frac{\theta(1-\beta)}{1-\theta\gamma} \right] D + \frac{\eta\theta(1-\beta)}{1-\theta\gamma} \right\} q_s = \frac{\eta\theta\alpha}{1-\theta\gamma} \qquad (18)$$

Thus q_s now varies around a value of $\alpha/(1-\beta)$, the value appropriate to a closed economy. If q_s is stable, there is no danger of reserves disappearing because of the high value of α. This is not to say either that α will necessarily be high enough to ensure full employment or that difficulties would not arise if α were so high that the ratio of imports to output had to be cut drastically. It shows simply the need to control α and μ so as to maximize output subject to the stability of the reserves. This brings us to adaptive control methods in which our aim is to control one or more parameters of the system rather than one or more of its variables.

For q_s to be stable it is necessary that the coefficient of Dq_s on the left-hand side of (18) should be positive; and this condition can always be met, in principle, by increasing η, the speed of adjustment of imports to exports. But it is also necessary that the coefficient of q_s itself should be positive; and this depends, with the numerical values given above, on a sluggish response of supply to demand ($\theta < 0\cdot5$). If this condition is violated it cannot be imposed by any of the control devices that have been considered.

I do not propose to pursue this example any further. Its aim has simply been to show the necessity of understanding the dynamics of a system we are trying to control, even if that system is a very simple one. It is not enough to choose some plausible indicator in terms of which to regulate the system and then to act quickly and forcibly. If we do this without attending to the responses and time lags of the system itself we may easily cause regular oscillations or even increase instability. The road to hell is paved with good intentions.

3. PRESENT KNOWLEDGE AND FUTURE RESEARCH

In economics, use is made of models of very different degrees of complexity. The range extends from toy models, of the kind exemplified in the preceding section, which contain few, highly-aggregated variables, to large models, particularly models of industrial interdependence, in which the variables are numbered in hundreds if not in thousands. In between there are medium-sized models, containing perhaps fifty to a hundred variables, which combine dynamic forms of relationship with some degree of disaggregation. A model of this kind would provide a good starting point for analysing the problems which we are discussing this evening. Probably it would be wise to start off with a modest version of the model and gradually develop it in the light of sensitivity analysis.

For this purpose a great deal of statistical information and econometric results are available for Britain. Several models, in varying degrees relevant to the present investigation, have already been built and many aspects of economic life, such as consumers' behaviour, import and export demand and stockbuilding, have been studied intensively. It would not therefore be a question of starting from scratch on the formidable task of data processing and economic modelling.

There are, however, several areas in which our present knowledge is inadequate. One of these relates to the time constants in various adjustment processes. We know, for example, that the structure of response through a chain of distributors and stockholders may convert a comparatively stable demand by final consumers into an oscillating supply by producers. We can see this happening in some cases and we can also see that commonsense stabilizing devices, such as the contra-cyclical timing of advertising expenditures, may in practice act as destabilizers because the structure of lagged responses around the production–consumption loop is not properly understood. But information of this kind has not been collected systematically. It would, however, be possible to introduce some reasonable estimates of time lags into a model and then test the sensitivity of the solution to the values of these estimates. In this way it might be possible to show that only in a limited number of cases was it worth while to obtain more accurate information.

A second area, which is important for present purposes, relates to stocks of materials and equipment. In general, a system with adequate stocks will behave quite differently from a system with inadequate stocks since it will have a greater capacity to absorb temporary fluctuations in supply or demand. In this case, only a limited amount of information is available: regular estimates are made of the gross stock of equipment in the main branches of production and of stocks of materials, work in progress and finished goods held in various parts of the economy.

The building of a model is only a first step. A non-linear model of even moderate size presents very great difficulties of analysis. It is therefore necessary to simplify it partly by linearization, where this can be done without destroying the essential characteristics of the model, and partly by modifying certain connections in the model which contribute only minor transients to the solution. This is a matter in which control-system engineers have much more experience than economists have and it is for this reason in particular that I greatly welcome the willingness of Professor J. F. Coales to collaborate with me in investigating control problems in a model of the British economy.

This second step provides a simplified model which can be handled computationally with the equipment at present available. I say 'handled computationally' because there is no question of handling it in any other way. As long as economists concentrate their attention on small models capable of yielding analytical, general solutions, they will continue to produce results which are better suited to the lecture hall than to the government or business office.

The third step is to use the simplified model to investigate the dynamic properties of the system with particular reference to questions of stability and oscillation. Only if we have at least a rough idea of these properties can we profitably move on to the final step.

The final step is to design a control system which will render our economy stable and leave us free to work for other desirable aims without the constant fear of a major upset. The design of a control system depends partly on the dynamical characteristics of the system to be controlled and partly on the instruments of control that are available in practice. An important feature of this design is that all regulations should be simple and predictable. The system that is being controlled must be free to make its plans with as little dislocation as possible. The purpose of a control system is to render the system stable in all foreseeable circumstances and this purpose is largely defeated by arbitrary, *ad hoc* changes. No doubt in an economic context it is impossible to design a self-regulating mechanism that never needs to be touched but it should be possible to improve substantially on the present performance of our economic regulators.

4. CONCLUSION

I have tried to make out a case for mounting a major intellectual attack on the problem of economic instability by methods which are still ignored by many influential economists to say nothing of administrators and politicians. If we could stop devoting all our efforts to the moment and recognize that difficult problems remain with us until they are solved, I think we should get on better. If we wait for the problem of economic instability to be solved by commonsense trial and error, we may well wait for centuries and in the meantime destroy ourselves. Such things have happened in history.

III

FOREIGN TRADE AND FULL EMPLOYMENT: AN INPUT–OUTPUT ANALYSIS

1. INTRODUCTION

A country whose balance of payments is habitually adverse may try to meet its predicament in various ways. It may solicit gifts from other countries, reduce its foreign commitments, sell its assets abroad or contract loans from the rest of the world. Whatever may be said for or against such policies, one thing is fairly certain: they are palliatives and can provide only a temporary solution of the underlying problem. Sooner or later the country, like the overwhelming majority of individuals, will have to get its spending in balance with its income. This means that it will have to export more in relation to its imports than is its wont; and it can try to do this by a mixture of export expansion and import saving.

However, if nothing else were to change, any mixture would require more domestic output either to produce the additional exports or to replace the imports saved. If the country were initially in a state of full employment, this increase in domestic output would only be possible if domestic final demand were correspondingly reduced.

Given specific proposals for export expansion or import saving, input–output analysis can be used to work out the pattern of domestic output levels compatible with these proposals, with the observed behaviour of consumers and with the need to hold constant the primary inputs into the productive system as a whole. These calculations, which can take into account indirect effects, would give at least an approximate measure of the shifts in resources implied by the proposals. If these implications were acceptable, the problems of policy would be, first, to devise means of bringing about the changes and, second, to convince the public that the inconveniences and sacrifices involved are the price of their survival as members of an economically independent community.

2. THE FRAMEWORK OF THE ANALYSIS

An important development in input–output analysis has taken place in recent years: the separation of product flows between domestic outputs and imports [20, 55, 87: 1968]. This development enables us to write the flow equations for outputs and imports as

$$
\begin{bmatrix} q \\ \cdots \\ m \end{bmatrix} = \begin{bmatrix} A_h & \vdots & 0 \\ \cdots & \vdots & \cdots \\ A_m & \vdots & 0 \end{bmatrix} \begin{bmatrix} q \\ \cdots \\ m \end{bmatrix} + \begin{bmatrix} h + x - m_f \\ \cdots \\ m_f \end{bmatrix}
$$

$$
= \begin{bmatrix} I - A_h & \vdots & 0 \\ \cdots & \vdots & \cdots \\ - A_m & \vdots & I \end{bmatrix}^{-1} \begin{bmatrix} h + x - m_f \\ \cdots \\ m_f \end{bmatrix}
$$

$$
= \begin{bmatrix} (I - A_h)^{-1} & \vdots & 0 \\ \cdots & \vdots & \cdots \\ A_m(I - A_h)^{-1} & \vdots & I \end{bmatrix} \begin{bmatrix} h + x - m_f \\ \cdots \\ m_f \end{bmatrix} \tag{1}
$$

In this equation, a single, all-embracing commodity classification is applied both to outputs and to imports. The symbols q, h, x, m and m_f denote, respectively, the vectors of domestic outputs, domestic final demands, exports, total imports, and imports of final goods and services; A_h and A_m denote matrices of partial input-output coefficients relating to domestically produced inputs and to imported inputs, respectively; and I denotes the unit matrix.

From the first row of (1) we can see that

$$
q = (I - A_h)^{-1}(h + x - m_f) \tag{2}
$$

Since the elements of m_f are components of the elements of h, (2) enables us to express domestic outputs in terms of domestically produced final demands without any explicit reference to imports.

From the second row of (1) we can see that

$$
m = A_m(I - A_h)^{-1}(h + x - m_f) + m_f
$$
$$
= A_m q + m_f \tag{3}
$$

Since $A_m q$ represents intermediate imports, (3) simply states that total imports are equal to intermediate imports plus final imports.

From (2) and (3) we can easily derive the conventional flow equation for domestic outputs. Thus

$$
q = A_h q + h + x - (m - A_m q)
$$
$$
= (I - A_h - A_m)^{-1}(h + x - m)
$$
$$
= (I - A)^{-1}(h + x - m) \tag{4}
$$

since $A_h + A_m \equiv A$.

As they stand, these equations are insufficient for our purpose, since they do not show us, when we change x or m, how to change h so as to hold total primary inputs constant. The way to do this can be seen by combining with (4) the corresponding price equation, bearing in mind that, with flows measured in money units, all prices are unity: $p \equiv i$. This price equation can be written as

$$i = A'i + f \tag{5}$$

where the elements of the vector f denote the value of primary inputs per unit of output. By combining (4) and (5) we can see that

$$f'q = i'(h + x - m) \tag{6}$$

and so, if $f'q$ is to remain constant, it follows that

$$i'\Delta h = -i'\Delta(x - m) \tag{7}$$

or, in other words, the sum of the changes in domestic final demands must be equal, but opposite in sign, to the sum of the changes in net exports.

We shall now consider how h depends on $i'h$. For present purposes we shall assume a very simple form of dependence, namely that

$$h = a + b(i'h) \tag{8}$$

from which it follows that

$$\Delta h = bi'\Delta h \tag{9}$$

where $i'a = 0$ and $i'b = 1$.

Finally, we must consider how the elements of m_f are related to the corresponding elements of h and x. Here we shall assume that

$$m_f = \hat{c}h + \hat{d}x \tag{10}$$

where $\hat{c}$ and $\hat{d}$ denote diagonal matrices constructed from the factors of proportionality, the vectors c and d.

3. THE ANALYSIS

In this section we shall consider three possibilities: the expansion of exports, the saving of imports and a mixture of the two. The analysis is essentially similar in all three cases, but the expansion of exports is in some ways the simplest and so we shall discuss it first.

(*a*) *Export expansion.* In this case, none of the coefficients is changed, the initial position of the system is therefore irrelevant and we can work entirely with changes from that position. The equations for Δq and Δm take the form

$$\begin{bmatrix} \Delta q \\ \cdots \\ \Delta m \end{bmatrix} = \begin{bmatrix} A_{11} & \vdots & 0 \\ \cdots & \vdots & \cdots \\ A_{21} & \vdots & I \end{bmatrix} \left\{ \begin{bmatrix} B_{11} \\ \cdots \\ B_{21} \end{bmatrix} \Delta m + \begin{bmatrix} C_{11} \\ \cdots \\ C_{21} \end{bmatrix} \Delta x \right\} \tag{11}$$

where

$$A_{11} = (I - A_h)^{-1} \tag{12}$$

$$A_{21} = A_m(I - A_h)^{-1} \tag{13}$$

$$B_{11} = (I - \hat{c}) bi' \tag{14}$$

$$B_{21} = \hat{c} bi' \tag{15}$$

$$C_{11} = [I - (I - \hat{c}) bi' - \hat{d}] \tag{16}$$

$$C_{21} = -\hat{c} bi' + \hat{d} \tag{17}$$

From the second row of (11) we can see that

$$\Delta m = (A_{21} B_{11} + B_{21}) \Delta m + (A_{21} C_{11} + C_{21}) \Delta x$$
$$= [I - (A_{21} B_{11} + B_{21})]^{-1} (A_{21} C_{11} + C_{21}) \Delta x \tag{18}$$

and from the first row of (11) we can see that

$$\Delta q = A_{11} B_{11} \Delta m + A_{11} C_{11} \Delta x$$
$$= A_{11}\{B_{11}[I - (A_{21} B_{11} + B_{21})]^{-1} (A_{21} C_{11} + C_{21}) + C_{11}\} \Delta x \tag{19}$$

Since Δx is given by the programme of export expansion, it is a comparatively simple matter to calculate Δm and Δq. By adding these vectors to m and q respectively we obtain the solution to our problem. With this additional information there is no difficulty in calculating all the elements of a new input–output matrix which can be compared in every detail with the original one.

(b) *Import saving.* This case is a little more complicated. In the first place, $\Delta x = \{0, 0, \ldots, 0\}$ and so we cannot obtain a unique value of Δm from an equation like (18). In the second place, the programme of import saving changes some of the coefficients in A_h, A_m, c and d. Suppose, for instance, that our programme requires that we cease to import product j and that we replace this type of import by an increased domestic production of j. In respect of intermediate demand, this implies that we add the jth row of A_m to the jth row of A_h, thus forming a new matrix, A_h^* say; and at the same time replace A_m by a new matrix, A_m^* say, in which all the elements in the jth row are zero. In respect of final demand, we must form new vectors, c^* and d^* say, in which the jth elements are zero.

With $\Delta x = \{0, 0, \ldots, 0\}$, we can write

$$\begin{bmatrix} q + \Delta q \\ \cdots \\ m + \Delta m \end{bmatrix} = \begin{bmatrix} A_{11}^* & \vdots & 0 \\ \cdots & \vdots & \cdots \\ A_{21}^* & \vdots & I \end{bmatrix} \left(\begin{bmatrix} B_{11}^* \\ \cdots \\ B_{21}^* \end{bmatrix} \Delta m + \begin{bmatrix} C_{11}^* \\ \cdots \\ C_{21}^* \end{bmatrix} h + \begin{bmatrix} D_{11}^* \\ \cdots \\ D_{21}^* \end{bmatrix} x \right) \tag{20}$$

where

$$A_{11}^* = (I - A_h^*)^{-1} \tag{21}$$

$$A_{21}^* = A_m^*(I - A_h^*)^{-1} \tag{22}$$

$$B_{11}^* = (I - \hat{c}^*) bi' \tag{23}$$

$$B_{21}^* = \hat{c}^* bi' \tag{24}$$

$$C_{11}^* = (I - \hat{c}^*) \tag{25}$$

$$C_{21}^* = \hat{c}^* \tag{26}$$

$$D_{11}^* = (I - \hat{d}^*) \tag{27}$$

$$D_{21}^* = \hat{d}^* \tag{28}$$

From the second row of (20) we can see that

$$(m + \Delta m) = (A_{21}^* B_{11}^* + B_{21}^*) \Delta m + (A_{21}^* C_{11}^* + C_{21}^*) h + (A_{21}^* D_{11}^* + D_{21}^*) x \tag{29}$$

whence

$$\Delta m = [I - (A_{21}^* B_{11}^* + B_{12}^*)]^{-1} [(A_{21}^* C_{11}^* + C_{21}^*) h + (A_{21}^* D_{11}^* + D_{21}^*) x - m] \tag{30}$$

And from the first row of (20) we can see that

$$(q + \Delta q) = A_{11}^* (B_{11}^* \Delta m + C_{11}^* h + D_{11}^* x) \tag{31}$$

which, on being combined with (30), gives Δq in terms of the known vectors h, x, m and q.

(c) *The combination of the two programmes.* In this case $\Delta x \neq \{0, 0, \ldots, 0\}$, and so it might seem possible to go back to method (a). This, however, is not so because the coefficients have changed as a consequence of the programme of import saving. We must, therefore, use method (b), adding appropriate terms in Δx. With these additions we can write

$$\begin{bmatrix} q + \Delta q \\ \cdots \\ m + \Delta m \end{bmatrix} = \begin{bmatrix} A_{11}^* & \vdots & 0 \\ \cdots & \vdots & \cdots \\ A_{21}^* & \vdots & I \end{bmatrix} \left\{ \begin{bmatrix} B_{11}^* \\ \cdots \\ B_{21}^* \end{bmatrix} \Delta m + \begin{bmatrix} C_{11}^* \\ \cdots \\ C_{21}^* \end{bmatrix} h + \begin{bmatrix} D_{11}^* \\ \cdots \\ D_{21}^* \end{bmatrix} x + \begin{bmatrix} E_{11}^* \\ \cdots \\ E_{21}^* \end{bmatrix} \Delta x \right\} \tag{32}$$

where

$$E_{11}^* = -(I - \hat{d}^*) bi' \tag{33}$$

$$E_{21}^* = -\hat{d}^* bi' \tag{34}$$

and the remaining coefficients are the same as in (20). Equation (32) can be solved in the same manner as (20), since Δx is given by the programme of export expansion.

4. A COMPARISON OF THE RESULTS

In the preceding section the calculations required by the different programmes were set out as simply as possible, with the consequence that the results are not very easy to compare. However, it is not difficult to show that two programmes can only differ in their effect on domestic production if they imply different vectors of net exports.

Consider first a programme of export expansion. Since for this programme we know that $\Delta h_a = -\Delta(x_a - m_a)$, we can write

$$q_a = A_h q_a + h_o + x_o - m_{fo} + (I - bi') \Delta(x_a - m_a) + \Delta(m_a - m_{fa})$$
$$= A q_a + h_o + x_o - m_o + (I - bi') \Delta(x_a - m_a) \tag{35}$$

where the suffix o denotes an initial value and the suffix a denotes a final value obtained with a programme of type (a).

A similar result can be obtained from a programme of import saving. Since $A_h^* + A_m^* = A_h + A_m = A$, we can write

$$q_b = A_h^* q_b + h_o + x_o - m_{fo} + (I - bi')\Delta(x_b - m_b) + \Delta(m_b - m_{fb})$$
$$= A q_b + h_o + x_o - m_o + (I - bi')\Delta(x_b - m_b) \tag{36}$$

where the suffix b denotes a final value obtained from a programme of type (b). Thus $q_a = q_b$ if and only if $\Delta(x_a - m_a) = \Delta(x_b - m_b)$ or, equivalently, if and only if $(x_a - m_a) = (x_b - m_b)$. These vectors are not, of course, known initially, and have to be determined by the methods of the preceding section.

5. A NUMERICAL EXAMPLE

It may be useful to illustrate numerically the methods described in section 3 above. Only methods (a) and (b) will be considered, since method (c) is simply an extension of method (b).

Table 1 below gives a rearranged and condensed version of table 19 in the 1968 edition of the official Blue Book, *National Income and Expenditure* [87]. In it the British productive system is divided into three branches: metals, engineering, and the rest.

TABLE 1

A SUMMARY TRANSACTIONS MATRIX FOR BRITAIN, 1963

(*£ million*)

Outputs		Inputs					Total
		Intermediate input			Final input		
		Metals	Eng.	Other	Dom.	Exports	
Domestic outputs	Metals	0	757	667	18	281	1 723
	Engineering	124	0	1 425	2 046	1 257	4 852
	Other	516	1 225	9 633	23 384	4 014	38 772
Imports	Metals	181	65	49	−8	0	287
	Engineering	0	65	102	268	0	435
	Other	114	107	2 911	1 834	262	5 228
Primary resources		788	2 633	23 985	2 851	0	30 257
Total		1 723	4 852	38 772	30 393	5 814	81 554

It can be seen from table 1 that engineering imports amounted in 1963 to £435 million. The two cases considered for illustration are: (a) the expansion of engineering exports by £435 million; and (b) the replacing of the £435 million of engineering imports by an equal amount of domestic production. In each case, domestic final demand is reduced so that the total input of primary resources into the productive system as a whole remains unchanged.

(a) *Export expansion.* In this case we have

$$A_{11} = (I - A_h)^{-1}$$

$$= \begin{bmatrix} 1 \cdot 00000 & -0 \cdot 15602 & -0 \cdot 01720 \\ -0 \cdot 07197 & 1 \cdot 00000 & -0 \cdot 03675 \\ -0 \cdot 29948 & -0 \cdot 25247 & 0 \cdot 75155 \end{bmatrix}^{-1}$$

$$= \begin{bmatrix} 1 \cdot 02150 & 0 \cdot 16734 & 0 \cdot 03157 \\ 0 \cdot 08958 & 1 \cdot 02718 & 0 \cdot 05228 \\ 0 \cdot 43714 & 0 \cdot 41175 & 1 \cdot 36073 \end{bmatrix} \tag{37}$$

$$A_{21} = A_m(I - A_h)^{-1}$$

$$= \begin{bmatrix} 0 \cdot 10505 & 0 \cdot 01340 & 0 \cdot 00126 \\ 0 & 0 \cdot 01340 & 0 \cdot 00263 \\ 0 \cdot 06616 & 0 \cdot 02205 & 0 \cdot 07508 \end{bmatrix} \begin{bmatrix} 1 \cdot 02150 & 0 \cdot 16734 & 0 \cdot 03157 \\ 0 \cdot 08958 & 1 \cdot 02718 & 0 \cdot 05228 \\ 0 \cdot 43714 & 0 \cdot 41175 & 1 \cdot 36073 \end{bmatrix}$$

$$= \begin{bmatrix} 0 \cdot 10906 & 0 \cdot 03186 & 0 \cdot 00574 \\ 0 \cdot 00235 & 0 \cdot 01484 & 0 \cdot 00428 \\ 0 \cdot 10238 & 0 \cdot 06464 & 0 \cdot 10541 \end{bmatrix} \tag{38}$$

$$B_{11} = (I - \hat{e})bi'$$

$$= \begin{bmatrix} 1 \cdot 80000 & 0 & 0 \\ 0 & 0 \cdot 88418 & 0 \\ 0 & 0 & 0 \cdot 92727 \end{bmatrix} \begin{bmatrix} 0 \cdot 00040 & 0 \cdot 00040 & 0 \cdot 00040 \\ 0 \cdot 08400 & 0 \cdot 08400 & 0 \cdot 08400 \\ 0 \cdot 91560 & 0 \cdot 91560 & 0 \cdot 91560 \end{bmatrix}$$

$$= \begin{bmatrix} 0 \cdot 00072 & 0 \cdot 00072 & 0 \cdot 00072 \\ 0 \cdot 07427 & 0 \cdot 07427 & 0 \cdot 07427 \\ 0 \cdot 84901 & 0 \cdot 84901 & 0 \cdot 84901 \end{bmatrix} \tag{39}$$

$$B_{21} = \hat{e}bi'$$

$$= \begin{bmatrix} -0 \cdot 80000 & 0 & 0 \\ 0 & 0 \cdot 11582 & 0 \\ 0 & 0 & 0 \cdot 07273 \end{bmatrix} \begin{bmatrix} 0 \cdot 00040 & 0 \cdot 00040 & 0 \cdot 00040 \\ 0 \cdot 08400 & 0 \cdot 08400 & 0 \cdot 08400 \\ 0 \cdot 91560 & 0 \cdot 91560 & 0 \cdot 91560 \end{bmatrix}$$

$$= \begin{bmatrix} -0 \cdot 00032 & -0 \cdot 00032 & -0 \cdot 00032 \\ 0 \cdot 00973 & 0 \cdot 00973 & 0 \cdot 00973 \\ 0 \cdot 06659 & 0 \cdot 06659 & 0 \cdot 06659 \end{bmatrix} \tag{40}$$

$C_{11} = [I - (I - \hat{e})bi' - \hat{d}]$

$$= \begin{bmatrix} 1\cdot00000 & 0 & 0 \\ 0 & 1\cdot00000 & 0 \\ 0 & 0 & 0\cdot93873 \end{bmatrix} - \begin{bmatrix} 0\cdot00072 & 0\cdot00072 & 0\cdot00072 \\ 0\cdot07427 & 0\cdot07427 & 0\cdot07427 \\ 0\cdot84901 & 0\cdot84901 & 0\cdot84901 \end{bmatrix}$$

$$= \begin{bmatrix} 0\cdot99928 & -0\cdot00072 & -0\cdot00072 \\ -0\cdot07427 & 0\cdot92573 & -0\cdot07427 \\ -0\cdot84901 & -0\cdot84901 & 0\cdot08972 \end{bmatrix} \tag{41}$$

$C_{21} = -\hat{e}bi' + \hat{d}$

$$= \begin{bmatrix} 0\cdot00032 & 0\cdot00032 & 0\cdot00032 \\ -0\cdot00973 & -0\cdot00973 & -0\cdot00973 \\ -0\cdot06659 & -0\cdot06659 & -0\cdot06659 \end{bmatrix} + \begin{bmatrix} 0 & 0 & 0 \\ 0 & 0 & 0 \\ 0 & 0 & 0\cdot06127 \end{bmatrix}$$

$$= \begin{bmatrix} 0\cdot00032 & 0\cdot00032 & 0\cdot00032 \\ -0\cdot00973 & -0\cdot00973 & -0\cdot00973 \\ -0\cdot06659 & -0\cdot06659 & -0\cdot00532 \end{bmatrix} \tag{42}$$

If these values are substituted into (18) and (19), we obtain, for $\Delta x = \{0 \quad 435 \quad 0\}$,

$\Delta m = [I - (A_{21}B_{11} + B_{21})]^{-1}(A_{21}C_{11} + C_{21})\Delta x$

$$= \begin{bmatrix} 1\cdot00856 & 0\cdot00856 & 0\cdot00856 \\ 0\cdot01769 & 1\cdot01769 & 0\cdot01769 \\ 0\cdot19686 & 0\cdot19686 & 1\cdot19686 \end{bmatrix} \begin{bmatrix} 0\cdot10207 & 0\cdot02487 & -0\cdot00161 \\ -0\cdot01212 & -0\cdot00038 & -0\cdot01045 \\ -0\cdot05857 & -0\cdot09631 & -0\cdot00073 \end{bmatrix} \begin{bmatrix} 0 \\ 435 \\ 0 \end{bmatrix}$$

$$= \begin{bmatrix} 10\cdot55189 \\ -0\cdot38299 \\ -47\cdot98298 \end{bmatrix} \tag{43}$$

and

$\Delta q = A_{11}(B_{11}\Delta m + C_{11}\Delta x)$

$$= \begin{bmatrix} 1\cdot02150 & 0\cdot16734 & 0\cdot03157 \\ 0\cdot08958 & 1\cdot02718 & 0\cdot05228 \\ 0\cdot43714 & 0\cdot41175 & 1\cdot36073 \end{bmatrix} \left\{ \begin{bmatrix} -0\cdot02723 \\ -2\cdot80850 \\ -32\cdot10462 \end{bmatrix} + \begin{bmatrix} -0\cdot31320 \\ 402\cdot69000 \\ -369\cdot32000 \end{bmatrix} \right\}$$

$$= \begin{bmatrix} 53\cdot9 \\ 389\cdot7 \\ -381\cdot7 \end{bmatrix} \tag{44}$$

With this information it is possible to fill in a new transactions matrix taking into account the expansion of exports. Only one figure is missing: the element at the intersection of the row for primary resources and the column for domestic final input. This element, which represents indirect taxes debited directly to domestic final buyers, can be obtained from table 1 above as $2851/27542 = 0\cdot10351$ times the sum of the remaining elements in the column for domestic final input.

The new transactions matrix is set out in table 2 below. It will be noticed that the total input of primary resources into the productive system is the same as in table 1: $811 + 2845 + 23750 = 788 + 2633 + 23985 = 27406$.

TABLE 2   THE TRANSACTIONS MATRIX MODIFIED
TO ALLOW FOR EXPORT EXPANSION

(£ million)

Output		Inputs					Total
		Intermediate input			Final input		
		Metals	Eng.	Other	Dom.	Exports	
Domestic outputs	Metals	0	818	660	18	281	1 777
	Engineering	128	0	1 411	2 011	1 692	5 242
	Other	532	1 323	9 538	22 983	4 014	38 390
Imports	Metals	188	70	48	−8	0	298
	Engineering	0	70	102	263	0	435
	Other	118	116	2 881	1 803	262	5 180
Primary resources		811	2 845	23 750	2 802	0	30 208
Total		1 777	5 242	38 390	29 872	6 249	81 530

(b) *Import saving.* In this case we have

$$A^*_{11} = (I - A^*_h)^{-1}$$

$$= \begin{bmatrix} 1\cdot00000 & -0\cdot15602 & -0\cdot01720 \\ -0\cdot07197 & 0\cdot98660 & -0\cdot03938 \\ -0\cdot29948 & -0\cdot25247 & 0\cdot75155 \end{bmatrix}^{-1}$$

$$= \begin{bmatrix} 1\cdot02190 & 0\cdot16986 & 0\cdot03229 \\ 0\cdot09203 & 1\cdot04265 & 0\cdot05675 \\ 0\cdot43812 & 0\cdot41795 & 1\cdot36252 \end{bmatrix} \tag{45}$$

$$A^*_{21} = A^*_m(I - A^*_h)^{-1}$$

$$= \begin{bmatrix} 0\cdot10505 & 0\cdot01340 & 0\cdot00126 \\ 0 & 0 & 0 \\ 0\cdot06616 & 0\cdot02205 & 0\cdot07508 \end{bmatrix} \begin{bmatrix} 1\cdot02190 & 0\cdot16986 & 0\cdot03229 \\ 0\cdot09203 & 1\cdot04265 & 0\cdot05675 \\ 0\cdot43812 & 0\cdot41795 & 1\cdot36252 \end{bmatrix}$$

$$= \begin{bmatrix} 0\cdot10914 & 0\cdot03234 & 0\cdot00587 \\ 0 & 0 & 0 \\ 0\cdot10254 & 0\cdot06561 & 0\cdot10569 \end{bmatrix} \tag{46}$$

$B_{11}^* = (I - \hat{c}^*)\, bi'$

$$= \begin{bmatrix} 1\cdot80000 & 0 & 0 \\ 0 & 1\cdot00000 & 0 \\ 0 & 0 & 0\cdot92727 \end{bmatrix} \begin{bmatrix} 0\cdot00040 & 0\cdot00040 & 0\cdot00040 \\ 0\cdot08400 & 0\cdot08400 & 0\cdot08400 \\ 0\cdot91560 & 0\cdot91560 & 0\cdot91560 \end{bmatrix}$$

$$= \begin{bmatrix} 0\cdot00072 & 0\cdot00072 & 0\cdot00072 \\ 0\cdot08400 & 0\cdot08400 & 0\cdot08400 \\ 0\cdot84901 & 0\cdot84901 & 0\cdot84901 \end{bmatrix} \tag{47}$$

$B_{21}^* = \hat{c}^*\, bi'$

$$= \begin{bmatrix} -0\cdot80000 & 0 & 0 \\ 0 & 0\cdot00000 & 0 \\ 0 & 0 & 0\cdot07273 \end{bmatrix} \begin{bmatrix} 0\cdot00040 & 0\cdot00040 & 0\cdot00040 \\ 0\cdot08400 & 0\cdot08400 & 0\cdot08400 \\ 0\cdot91560 & 0\cdot91560 & 0\cdot91560 \end{bmatrix}$$

$$= \begin{bmatrix} -0\cdot00032 & -0\cdot00032 & -0\cdot00032 \\ 0 & 0 & 0 \\ 0\cdot06659 & 0\cdot06659 & 0\cdot06659 \end{bmatrix} \tag{48}$$

$C_{11}^* = (I - \hat{c}^*)$

$$= \begin{bmatrix} 1\cdot80000 & 0 & 0 \\ 0 & 1\cdot00000 & 0 \\ 0 & 0 & 0\cdot92727 \end{bmatrix} \tag{49}$$

$C_{21}^* = \hat{c}^*$

$$= \begin{bmatrix} -0\cdot80000 & 0 & 0 \\ 0 & 0\cdot00000 & 0 \\ 0 & 0 & 0\cdot07273 \end{bmatrix} \tag{50}$$

$D_{11}^* = (I - \hat{d}^*)$

$$= \begin{bmatrix} 1\cdot00000 & 0 & 0 \\ 0 & 1\cdot00000 & 0 \\ 0 & 0 & 0\cdot93873 \end{bmatrix} \tag{51}$$

$D_{11}^* = \hat{d}^*$

$$= \begin{bmatrix} 0 & 0 & 0 \\ 0 & 0 & 0 \\ 0 & 0 & 0\cdot06127 \end{bmatrix} \tag{52}$$

If these values are substituted into (30) and (31), we obtain

$\Delta m = [I - (A_{21}^* B_{11}^* + B_{21}^*)]^{-1} [(A_{21}^* C_{11}^* + C_{21}^*)\, h + (A_{21}^* D_{11}^* + D_{21}^*)\, x - m]$

$$= \begin{bmatrix} 1\cdot00898 & 0\cdot00898 & 0\cdot00898 \\ 0 & 1\cdot00000 & 0 \\ 0\cdot19491 & 0\cdot19491 & 1\cdot19491 \end{bmatrix} \left\{ \begin{bmatrix} -0\cdot60356 & 0\cdot03234 & 0\cdot00545 \\ 0 & 0 & 0 \\ 0\cdot18457 & 0\cdot06561 & 0\cdot17073 \end{bmatrix} \right.$$

$$\begin{bmatrix} 10 \\ 2\,314 \\ 25\,218 \end{bmatrix} + \begin{bmatrix} 0\cdot10914 & 0\cdot03234 & 0\cdot00551 \\ 0 & 0 & 0 \\ 0\cdot10254 & 0\cdot06561 & 0\cdot16048 \end{bmatrix} \begin{bmatrix} 281 \\ 1\,257 \\ 4\,276 \end{bmatrix} - \left. \begin{bmatrix} 287 \\ 435 \\ 5\,228 \end{bmatrix} \right\}$$

$$= \begin{bmatrix} 10\cdot5 \\ -435\cdot0 \\ -47\cdot9 \end{bmatrix} \tag{53}$$

and

$$(q + \Delta q) = A_{11}^*(B_{11}^* \Delta m + C_{11}^* h + D_{11}^* x)$$

$$= \begin{bmatrix} 1 \cdot 02190 & 0 \cdot 16986 & 0 \cdot 03229 \\ 0 \cdot 09203 & 1 \cdot 04265 & 0 \cdot 05675 \\ 0 \cdot 43812 & 0 \cdot 41795 & 1 \cdot 36252 \end{bmatrix} \left\{ \begin{bmatrix} -0 \cdot 3 \\ -39 \cdot 7 \\ -401 \cdot 1 \end{bmatrix} + \begin{bmatrix} 18 \cdot 0 \\ 2\,314 \cdot 0 \\ 23\,384 \cdot 0 \end{bmatrix} + \begin{bmatrix} 281 \cdot 0 \\ 1\,257 \cdot 0 \\ 4\,013 \cdot 9 \end{bmatrix} \right\}$$

$$= \begin{bmatrix} 1\,777 \\ 5\,241 \\ 38\,391 \end{bmatrix} \tag{54}$$

With this information it is possible to fill in a new transactions matrix taking into account the saving of imports. This is done in table 3 below.

TABLE 3   THE TRANSACTIONS MATRIX MODIFIED
TO ALLOW FOR IMPORT SAVING

(£ million)

Outputs		Inputs					Total
		Intermediate input			Final input		
		Metals	Eng.	Other	Dom.	Exports	
Domestic outputs	Metals	0	818	660	18	281	1 777
	Engineering	128	70	1 512	2 274	1 257	5 241
	Other	532	1 323	9 539	22 983	4 014	38 391
Imports	Metals	188	70	48	−8	0	298
	Engineering	0	0	0	0	0	0
	Other	118	116	2 881	1 803	262	5 180
Primary resources		811	2 844	23 751	2 802	0	30 208
Total		1 777	5 241	38 391	29 872	5 814	81 095

6. A COMPARISON OF THE NUMERICAL RESULTS

A comparison of tables 2 and 3 suggests the following comments.

First, granted that in table 2 more engineering products are being exported and that in table 3 correspondingly less are being imported, the two tables are virtually identical. This is to be expected, since in the present example the net export vectors derived from the two programmes are the same in round numbers.

4

Second, in both cases the improvement in the balance of trade exceeds the improvement directly aimed at in the respective programmes. This is due to the reduction in domestic final demand needed to ensure a constant input of primary resources into the productive system as a whole. The analysis could be adapted to yield a given improvement in the balance of trade. If this were done in the present instance, with the direct effect on the balance of trade given by the two programmes as the final target, domestic final demands would rise and net exports would fall.

Third, a comparison of either table with table 1 shows that the domestic outputs of metals and engineering products rise and that of other products falls. In particular, the output of engineering products rises by between 8 and 9 per cent. Typically, it would be impossible to increase the output of a single branch of industry by so much in a short time. The example, however, is an extreme one in which the programmes are wholly concentrated on a single industry.

7. CONCLUSION

The analysis set out in this paper provides a means of examining the consequences of specific proposals for export expansion and import saving under conditions in which primary resources are being fully used, so that if some branches of production are to expand, others must contract. Since the analysis is based on the techniques of input–output rather than programming, it cannot indicate a best course of action; it can only provide an approximate knowledge of the consequences of alternative courses of action for those who have to choose between different policies. Such an analysis may be useful, however, because if advantage is to be taken of market opportunities abroad or of the possibilities of import substitution at home, consideration must be given to their repercussions on the capacities of industries and to the restraints they are likely to impose on domestic final buyers.

IV
CONSISTENT PROJECTIONS IN MULTI-SECTOR MODELS

1. INTRODUCTION

This paper is concerned with two issues: what do we mean by consistency, and how can we attain it in projections made from multi-sector models. I propose to discuss these questions in terms of a specific model [6], in which a distinction is made between long-term problems and transitional problems of adaptation. This will enable me to give specific illustrations of the various points I want to make, but will not, I think, detract appreciably from the generality of what I have to say. Indeed, most of my remarks are independent of the degree of aggregation and so apply as much to highly aggregated models as to highly disaggregated ones.

2. CONSISTENT WITH WHAT?

It is usual to talk of consistency in a rather restricted sense to mean, simply, that certain identities must be satisfied by the input and output of the model. This is certainly important, but I want to discuss consistency in an altogether wider sense, to include consistency with everything we know, everything we expect, and everything we desire to achieve.

Having put the question on so broad a footing, it is difficult to divide it up into a convenient set of exclusive and exhaustive classes. The best I have been able to do is to formulate the following seven classes of consistency.

(a) Consistency with arithmetic identities.
(b) Consistency with accounting identities.
(c) Consistency with what we know about past behaviour and technology.
(d) Consistency with what we expect about future behaviour and technology.
(e) Consistency with transitional possibilities.
(f) Consistency with all aspects of the problem.
(g) Consistency with all our long-term aims.

Let me now give examples of these different kinds of consistency.

(*a*) *Consistency with arithmetic identities.* This is the simplest case. It requires, for example, that we should not use price and quantity index-numbers that do not multiply out to the change in value, and that we should not produce estimates of the components of consumers' expenditure that do not add up to the total of this expenditure.

The second example shows that we must formulate an acceptable set of consumption functions that are additive if we want to embed these functions in a complete model. If we start off with a non-additive set of functions we immediately involve ourselves in a contradiction unless we add on a feedback device which will eliminate the discrepancy. But then the original set plus the feedback device constitute an additive set. If the set with which we start is nearly additive for all outcomes of the model, the feedback device can be regarded as a convenient and fairly harmless form of error control. But if the feedback device is doing any real work in allocating expenditure to different products, it is dangerous because it is most unlikely that it and the original set of functions together constitute an economically acceptable set of demand functions. If they do, well and good; but it is probably better to make a direct approach to the formulation of additive functions.

What I have just said means that we must be careful in introducing into complete models forms of demand function which are otherwise convenient and promising. An obvious example is the system of log-normal integral Engel curves described by Aitchison and Brown [2, 3]. These curves take account of the phenomenon of saturation and give a very good fit. They are approximately additive in the neighbourhood of the average values observed, but depart more and more from additivity as we move away from these values.

(*b*) *Consistency with accounting identities.* This requires that we should begin and end with a complete set of accounts for the economic system which balance [7]. On the input side the difficulty arises from the fact that the compilers of social accounts frequently leave a residual error or statistical discrepancy which shows the extent to which they have been unable to balance income and expenditure, or unallocated items which show the extent to which they have been unable to quantify all industrial inputs and outputs. No doubt these residuals are left in the accounts from good motives: the wish to show no more than the data allow. But residuals are in fact an infernal nuisance to the model-builder, who has to contrive to get rid of them with far less information than is available to the compilers of the original accounts. It would be a great help to model-builders if accounts could be published without residuals. Since allowances are usually made for many uncertain items, such as understatement of income, which must be quite large, it seems pointless not to go the whole hog and publish fully adjusted accounts. Specific knowledge and common sense could be helped by statistical techniques as suggested in [62, pp. 160–3].

On the output side we have to ensure that the calculated totals of incomings and outgoings all balance. This can always be done by choosing forms of relationship which do not contradict the accounting identities, as in simple input–output models, or by leaving sufficient variables otherwise undetermined so that these identities are effective. For example, our growth model automatically generates a national income equal to the national expenditure, and the saving of each sector, which in the aggregate is equal to net domestic investment plus foreign lending and capital transfers, is determined as the residual item on the income account of each sector. Thus a pattern of required saving emerges. We intend before long to start work on a financial circuit in the model which will provide, among other things, a pattern of the supply of saving. We shall then be faced with a possible discrepancy between the supply of and demand for saving, which could be treated in various ways: (i) it could be fed back to modify the parameters of the saving functions so that the supply would equal the demand; or (ii) we could leave one saving ratio, the central government's, undetermined and balance the remaining accounts by tax changes.

(c) Consistency with what we know about past behaviour and technology. This requires that the relationships we use to connect the variables of a model should, when applied to the past, give a good description of it. It might be thought that we are always likely to meet this kind of consistency fairly well, because the parameters in our relationships will usually be estimated from econometric studies of the past. This conclusion does not follow, however, because we may restrict ourselves to a limited amount of past information, say post-war time-series. If we find that the parameters derived from these series could not account for pre-war observations or for observations based on family budgets, we may either ignore these facts or try to rationalize our findings by saying that behaviour has changed or that time-series and cross-sections cannot be compared. But these are dangerous arguments, and a belief in them must weaken our faith in projections. Accordingly, we should try to take account of as much past information as possible.

This question can be illustrated by the analysis of private consumers' behaviour used in our growth model [6, 67, 76, VIII]. Its main features are that total expenditure and each price appear in each demand equation, and that the coefficients in these equations change systematically through time, thus taking account of gradual changes in consumers' responses. The analysis is based on time-series covering the years 1900 through 1960. It does not make use of cross-section data, and we may ask if it is compatible with such data. This question is not an easy one to answer

for a variety of reasons: long- and short-term elasticities may be different
and we may not be quite sure what we are measuring by either method;
a fairly sophisticated technique is required to extract expenditure elasticities from budgets unconfounded with the effects of family composition.
However, on a simple and partial check our model comes out well. In
1938, budgets [2, 83] show a total expenditure elasticity for food of 0·6
in contrast with a figure of 0·3 in 1960 [90]. To this degree of accuracy
our model gives identical results. For clothing, the figures are 1·1 for 1938
[50] and 1·4 for 1953 [22]. Again to this degree of accuracy our model
gives identical results. We are now embarking on a systematic comparison
of elasticities which will probably result in a combination of the two
sources to provide maximum likelihood estimates on the lines suggested
by Durbin [17].

Before we leave this subject, it is worth noting that reliable time-series
of elasticities can help in making projections in another way. If we accept
the log-normal integral Engel curves proposed by Aitchison and Brown
[2, 3], we can use elasticities combined with real consumption-levels to
yield estimates of saturation-levels at different dates. If we apply this idea
to the two examples of the preceding paragraph, we find that in the case
of food the saturation-level has remained constant over the last half-
century. What has happened over this period is that the average consumer
has risen from 51 per cent of his saturation-level for food in 1913 to 86
per cent of it in 1960. In the case of clothing, on the other hand, the position
is quite different; since 1938 the implied saturation-level for clothing has
almost doubled. At present, conclusions such as these must be regarded
as speculative; if they could be firmly established they would provide a
valuable guide in making demand projections.

(d) *Consistency with what we expect about future behaviour and technology.*
In making projections it is not enough to know that our relationships give
a good approximation to the past; we must also feel that they give a good
approximation to the future. Where we can measure changing parameters,
as in the case of the demand functions I have just been talking about,
and check them against an alternative source of information, we may feel
reasonably confident. But we are often not in this comparatively happy
position. In estimating input–output relationships, for example, we do not
have a long series of comparable observations; typically we have one or,
perhaps, two tables relating to the more or less distant past. How are we
to get from this information to an input–output table for the future?

The methods we have used in connection with our growth model are
a combination of direct investigation and mathematical deduction [8]. In
the early stages of our work we have had to rely mainly on the projection
of past input–output coefficients by means of row and column multipliers.
Thus we first estimate from past data row and column multipliers so that

an input–output coefficient in period 1, $_1a_{jk}$ say, can be estimated from the corresponding coefficient in period 0 by a relationship of the form $_1a_{jk} = r_j {}_0a_{jk} s_k$, where r_j and s_k are multipliers relating respectively to row j and column k of the input–output matrix. If this matrix is of order n, there are $2n - 1$ independent multipliers to be estimated.

If, now, we wish to calculate $_2a_{jk}$, where the interval between the future year 2 and year 1 is the same as the interval between year 1 and year 0, we take as our initial estimate $_2a_{jk} = r_j {}_1a_{jk} s_k$. This amounts to projecting the movements of the coefficients along exponential trends. We then examine the results of this procedure and consider in each case whether the results seem plausible in the light of our limited industrial knowledge. For example, we find a fairly general tendency to substitute oil or electricity for coal and to substitute plastics for wood and metalware. Again, we find that in agriculture there is a tendency for machinery maintenance to rise but for the consumption of petroleum products to fall. At first sight this is not very plausible, but further investigation shows that it is in fact compatible with trends in fuel economy in internal combustion engines combined with a shift to less highly processed fuels. As a final example, the projection of past trends suggests a fairly rapid increase in the proportion of petroleum products in the fuel inputs into electricity generation. At first sight this seems plausible, but further investigation shows that the generators now in production or planned for the near future will in fact damp out this trend in the years immediately ahead.

The method just described is applied only in cases where we cannot make more direct estimates of individual coefficients. For example, we have annual estimates of coal used in coke ovens, where coal is a raw material rather than a fuel. These figures show that the coal input per unit of coke output has been virtually constant for a number of years. Had we been forced in this case to rely on the general mathematical method of projection, we should have underestimated the future value of this coefficient.

By these means we can make estimates of future input–output coefficients which embody whatever knowledge the compilers may possess. The next step is to widen this knowledge by discussing the results with the different industries and thus to improve the estimates both of base-year and future coefficients. We have already been able to apply this method in the case of several industries, and expect to be able to apply it on a much wider scale in the future.

(e) Consistency with transitional possibilities. The model I have in mind in the illustrations given in this paper is a long-term growth model which abstracts, in the first instance, from transitional problems of adaptation. It draws a picture of a future year in which there is so much demand for consumption and exports and in which provision must be made for such

and such increases in industrial capacity and for an assigned surplus in foreign trade. In doing this, we assume that the necessary plant and industrial skills have already been acquired.

The point of such a model is to help in deciding the rate of growth to aim at in the long run. Having taken a provisional decision on this subject, which involves among other things an assumption about the level of consumption achieved in the future year, we can next ask how the economy could best move from where it is now to where it would like to be at the end of the transitional period, that is, in the above future year. One could go about this problem in several ways; the method we contemplate at present [68] involves maximizing consumption over the transitional period subject to known initial stocks and minimum terminal stocks and subject also to a constraint on the path of consumption which will either prevent it from falling below its initial level or will prevent it from falling below a given minimum level. This problem can be put in the form of a linear programme, though in practice it is necessary to use dynamic programming methods so that it can be solved step by step, that is to say, year by year. The result of this calculation is a detailed picture of the economy in each year of the transitional period.

Once we have these pictures we are likely to modify our ideas about the state of the economy that we should like to see at the end of the transitional period. For example, we may find that while the programme enables us to attain the desired consumption-level and future growth of capacity at the end of the transitional period, it does so by holding consumption as low as possible in the early stages of the transitional period and then allows it to go up with a rush at the very end. As a consequence the time-path of consumption may show stagnation, followed by a sharp rise, followed at the end of the transitional period by the long-term rate of growth originally decided on. Such a time-path would not be very desirable and would suggest a modification of the original long-term programme. An obvious possibility would be to reduce the level of consumption at the outset of the long-term programme in the belief that this would lead to a smoother and therefore more acceptable time-path.

It may be thought that to speak of an inconsistency between long-term aims and transitional possibilities is a mistake which shows only that the speaker has not got his ideas straight. In principle, this is probably true, and, indeed, my friend Alan Brown has suggested a form of programme in which the economy is carried to a preassigned growth as quickly as possible subject to the same kind of restrictions on the path of consumption that I mentioned earlier. By altering the preassigned rate we can observe the resulting course of consumption. In practice, however, this method is difficult to follow if we move away from simple and not very realistic models of technology and behaviour.

(*f*) *Consistency with all aspects of the problem.* We are now moving into an area where we can hardly expect to obtain complete success. A model is an abstraction, and the best we can hope for in the early stages of building one is that we have succeeded in identifying and giving an approximate form to the main elements in the situation. Even so, we are likely to formulate only some of these and to assume that the others will somehow come out in the wash.

I can give two examples of this from the present stage of our growth model. This model relates essentially to the real side of the economy and treats the financial side in a comparatively summary way. Since it is set in an accounting framework, we can be sure that spending plus saving will always equal income and that investment will always equal saving. But at present there are no financial relationships in the model and so we cannot demonstrate that the community would want to do the amount of saving required, still less that financial investors would want to take up the particular collection of financial claims, securities, mortgages, and so on, that would emerge from the real activity. As a consequence, financing problems have no effect whatsoever on the outcome.

The justification for this kind of omission is that one has to start somewhere and cannot do everything at once. In a preliminary calculation for 1970 which we undertook recently [75], we found that, assuming a growth rate for consumption of 3 per cent per head in the 1960s and of 4 per cent per head thereafter, saving in 1970 would have to be 14 per cent of income compared with the 12 per cent it was in 1960. It would be interesting to know whether this increase was likely to come about naturally or whether it would involve changes in dividend or fiscal policy. As I said before, we intend to study this side of the economy in the near future.

My second example concerns the supply of skills. In economic discussions it is usual to consider the amount of investment, which enables us to introduce the new equipment required for new techniques, and also the form that the new assets will take: will they be the products of construction, mechanical engineering, the electronics industry, or what? It is not so usual to ask the corresponding question about labour: will the future labour force possess the skills that the new techniques require? Yet it is fairly obvious that if the required skills are not available in the right quantities, the adoption of new techniques which depend on these skills will be slowed down, perhaps to a point where the growth rate we want will be unachievable.

In our model we began by treating labour as homogeneous, and have only recently extended it so that we can use it to discuss the supply of and demand for skills [75]. This means that we must make the whole system of education and training, including apprenticeship and retraining, an integral part of the model. The demand for different skills in the future depends on the level of activity in different industries and the kinds of technique they employ; the supply of skills depends on the system of education and training coupled with the birth and death characteristics of the population. If the supply of skills which would emerge 'naturally' in the future does not correspond with the demand, we must change the system of education and training unless we want the discrepancy, as it emerges, to slow down the introduction of new techniques.

How best to make these changes is a difficult question. At its simplest the problem can be formulated as follows. The elements of the education and training matrix show the proportion of those in a given age-group and of a certain educational level who are so trained that in the following year they pass into the next-highest educational group. This information, combined with data on specific birth and death rates, leads to a transition matrix connecting next year's population with this year's. The dominant characteristic vector of this matrix shows the ultimate distribution of skills which will be supplied if present conditions remain unchanged. To meet future demands for skills we need a different transition matrix whose dominant characteristic vector corresponds to these demands. We must therefore alter the original transition matrix, subject to conditions about the rate of convergence and the cost of the change. Such conditions are needed to enable us to choose a good solution out of the large number of possible ones.

It is one thing to formulate a problem, quite another to reach a quantitative solution. In this area the amount of suitable, processed data is very small. It is for this reason that we, like other builders of economic models, began by treating labour as homogeneous and are only now beginning to tackle the problem of the supply of and demand for skills.

(g) *Consistency with all our long-term aims.* In the preceding subsection I considered problems that would have to be solved if the projections from the model were to become reality, but whose manner of solution did not form part of the original model. I come now to my last class of problems: those which from a 'purely economic' point of view do not have to be solved, though for other reasons we should probably dislike solutions that did not take account of them. I can illustrate what I mean by two kinds of problem that we have thought about but so far not worked on in connection with our growth model.

Like most other model-builders, we treat households as a single sector of our model; as a consequence we can say nothing about the distribution of income between households. We could try to examine this problem by subdividing households and treating each category as a separate sector in the model. We should then need relationships which showed how income flowed into different categories of household, and we should have to elaborate our consumption functions so that they related to each class of household and not simply to the average consumer. Within this set-up we could study two kinds of problem that at present are outside our grasp. First, what difference would be made to the pattern of consumption and, therefore, of production if the distribution of incomes was changed radically; second, what would have to be done by way of changes in taxes and transfers if we did not like the distribution of incomes that emerged from our calculations.

My second example relates to the regional aspect of economic development. With a national model there is no specification of the region in which any activity takes place. In Britain we have observed for many decades a drift to the South with its attendant problems of depressed areas, sprawling towns, and a general reduction in aesthetic and cultural amenities. In principle, a national model could be decomposed into a set of regional models and so one could examine locative problems and thus frame a plan that did not require all solutions to these to come out in the wash. In practice, most of the data needed to do this for a set of twelve regions are available for Britain in unprocessed form, but the job of putting all this information together is beyond the powers of the group at present working on the national model. By a great co-operative effort it would be possible to set up multi-sector models on the lines proposed in [63], and from these we could learn a great deal. The main part missing would be information on trade between pairs of regions. Even here something could be done. With the development of operational research, firms are putting more and more effort into the solution of transport problems. If we could combine such information with Leontief's distinction between locally produced and nationally traded goods [34], we could probably make quite an impact on the economics of location.

3. PROJECTIONS, PLANNING, AND PREDICTIONS

Any particular model will meet the different requirements of consistency in different degrees. We may reasonably hope to meet these requirements in cases (a) and (b). In case (c) we may hope to do a fairly good job in the sense that the relationships we use accord with a wide range of information about the past. In case (d) there is certainly a lot that can be done with the co-operation of industrial experts who spend their lives facing similar problems in their own limited fields. The position in case (e) depends on the stage that the model has reached; with our model we are on the point of getting results from a transitional programme which will be used to revise the initial conditions of the long-term programme. In cases (f) and (g) there will always be more to do as we try to make our models cover a wider area of economic and social life. In the meantime we must accept the fact that, with our best endeavours, there are aspects of life which our model does not handle. There is nothing to be ashamed of in all this, nor any ground for just criticism. Models are an aid to decision-taking, all the better for being as complete as possible, but they do not take the decisions.

The outcome of such a model I call a projection: a possible picture of our economic future as detailed and complete as we can make it. In the early stages, many things are assumed to come out in the wash, and we can only work to diminish their number.

Prediction is quite a different matter: it represents an attempt to say what is actually likely to happen. If we are to pass from a projection to a prediction, we must narrow the range of possibilities down to the most probable. Unless we regard the economy as a piece of mechanism which operates systematically and largely independently of the actions of society, we cannot narrow down the range without considering how society will wish to act and how far it has the administrative arrangements to carry its wishes into effect [65].

This means that before we make predictions we need an agreed plan. Paradoxical as it may seem, agreement to accept the outcome of *laissez-faire* meets this need. Since nowadays there is obviously no agreement on this point, it is necessary to formulate a plan and the administrative arrangements for carrying it out; and the plan and the arrangements must have the acceptance of society.

The philosophy which guides our work on economic growth should now be clear. We believe that by building a model with the help of many other people we can demonstrate possibilities and throw light on the problems of achieving different aims. We believe that this kind of work is indispensable in paving the way for a fruitful, consistent, and realistic discussion of economic policy, which alone can lead to a practical and acceptable plan. The predictions that we are interested in can be made only after a plan has been accepted.

V

INPUT–OUTPUT PROJECTIONS: CONSISTENT PRICES AND QUANTITY STRUCTURES

1. INTRODUCTION

Input–output projections, such as those given in [11], are often made entirely in terms of quantities without any explicit reference to price movements. These quantities are usually measured in £'s worth at base-year prices rather than in ordinary physical units such as tons, gallons or square yards. With these units the price of each product and each factor of production is 1. If we denote by A_{00}^* and B_{00}^* respectively our estimates of the intermediate and primary input–output coefficient matrices for the base year (year 0) measured at base-year prices, it is clear that

$$(A_{00}^{*'} + B_{00}^{*'})i = i \tag{1}$$

where i denotes the unit vector. If the corresponding matrices for the projection year (year 1), also measured at base-year prices, are denoted by A_{01}^* and B_{01}^*, it is equally clear that, in general,

$$(A_{01}^{*'} + B_{01}^{*'})i \neq i \tag{2}$$

In many cases some or all of the rows of B_{01}^* are left unmeasured and $B_{01}^{*'}i$ is measured residually as $(I - A_{01}^{*'})i$ so that the inequality in (2) is replaced by an equality. If this is done, a completely balanced table can be constructed for the projection year given an estimate of the vector of final demand, e_{01}^* say. The vector of outputs, q_{01}^* say, is given by $(I - A_{01}^*)^{-1} e_{01}^*$, the matrix of intermediate inputs is given by $A_{01}^* \hat{q}_{01}^*$ and the matrix of primary inputs is given by $B_{01}^* \hat{q}_{01}^*$, where the circumflex accents denote diagonal matrices constructed from the vectors that they surmount. These estimates form a completely balanced accounting system since, on the assumption made,

$$\begin{aligned} q_{01}^* &= A_{01}^* q_{01}^* + e_{01}^* \\ &= \hat{q}_{01}^*(A_{01}^{*'} + B_{01}^{*'})i \end{aligned} \tag{3}$$

We have seen, however, that this assumption, which affects the second row of (3), is not generally justified so that the coherence of the system based on (3) is spurious. In order to construct a truly coherent system we must estimate the price relatives connecting year 1 with year 0. If we use symbols without asterisks to denote true values and if we denote by p_{01} and f_{01} respectively the price vectors for products and factors, then the truly coherent system corresponding to (3) can be expressed as follows.

First, if we remove the asterisks from the first row of (3) and premultiply by $\hat{p}_{01}$, we can write

$$\hat{p}_{01} q_{01} = (\hat{p}_{01} A_{01} \hat{p}_{01}^{-1}) \hat{p}_{01} q_{01} + \hat{p}_{01} e_{01} \tag{4}$$

or, shifting our unit of measurement to the £'s worth at the prices of the projection year,

$$q_{11} = A_{11} q_{11} + e_{11} \tag{5}$$

Second, corresponding to the second row of (3), we have

$$\hat{p}_{01} q_{01} = \hat{p}_{01} \hat{q}_{01} (\hat{p}_{01}^{-1} A'_{01} \hat{p}_{01} + \hat{p}_{01} B'_{01} \hat{f}_{01}) i \tag{6}$$

which implies that

$$p_{01} = (A'_{01} p_{01} + B'_{01} f_{01}) \tag{7}$$

Again, shifting our unit of measurement as above, we can write in place of (6)

$$q_{11} = \hat{q}_{11} (A'_{11} + B'_{11}) i \tag{8}$$

Thus, in order to construct a coherent system for the projection year, we find it necessary to introduce the prices of that year as well as the quantities. But if we form initial estimates, p_{01}^* and f_{01}^*, of p_{01} and f_{01}, we are likely to find that the resulting system is not coherent because the initial estimates of prices are not consistent with the initial estimates of the quantity structure, A_{01}^* and B_{01}^*.

The purpose of this paper is to show how adjustments can be made which will yield a coherent system. It has much in common with the paper presented by Fontela and Duval [21] to the Fourth International Conference on Input–Output Techniques. The technique of solution, the adjustment of conditioned observations by the method of least squares, is common to both papers, but here the problem is somewhat differently formulated and consideration is given to the possibility of adjusting the structure of quantities as well as to that of adjusting prices and to a compromise between these two methods.

2. METHODS OF ADJUSTMENT

Suppose that we make initial estimates p_{01}^* and f_{01}^* in addition to A_{01}^*, B_{01}^* and e_{01}^*. There are then three types of adjustment we can make: (a) we can accept the initial estimates of A_{01}^* and B_{01}^* (I shall not consider here any change in e_{01}^*) and allow the whole adjustment to fall on p_{01}^* and f_{01}^*; (b) we can accept the initial estimates of p_{01}^* and f_{01}^* and allow the whole adjustment to fall on A_{01}^* and B_{01}^*; and (c) we can adopt some compromise between the extremes (a) and (b).

Method (a). In this case we have to ensure that (7) holds not only for the true values, p_{01} and f_{01}, but also for the adjusted estimates, p_{01}^{**} and f_{01}^{**} say. Since there are an unlimited number of vectors, $y_{01}^{**} = \{p_{01}^{**} : f_{01}^{**}\}$ say, which would satisfy this constraint it is necessary to make a choice, and the method proposed here is to choose that vector which is as near as possible to the initial estimate, y_{01}^* say. We thus seek the best linear unbiased estimator, y_{01}^{**}, derivable from y_{01}^*, of the true price vector y_{01} subject to the constraint

$$[(I - A_{01}^{*\prime}) \vdots -B_{01}^{*\prime}] y_{01} = \{0, 0, \ldots, 0\} \tag{9}$$

The solution, provided by the classical method of adjusting conditioned observations [62], is given by

$$y_{01}^{**} = [I - V^* G'(GV^*G')^{-1}G] y_{01}^*$$
$$= H y_{01}^* \tag{10}$$

say, where V^* is the variance matrix of y_{01}^* and $G = [(I - A_{01}^{*\prime}) \vdots - B_{01}^{*\prime}]$, that is, the constraint matrix in (9).

It will be noticed that H is an idempotent matrix, that is to say $H^\theta = H$. Thus $H y_{01}^{**} = H^2 y_{01}^* = y_{01}^{**}$. Also had y_{01}^* been a compatible price vector which balanced the set of accounts, premultiplication by H would have left it unchanged.

Nothing has been said about the means to be used in estimating y_{01}^* and so no prescription can be given for estimating the variances and covariances which form the elements of V^*. In practice it would almost certainly be necessary to estimate the elements of V^* subjectively bearing in mind the sources and methods used in estimating the elements of y_{01}^*. If we were willing to increase or reduce any element of y_{01}^* by the same amount independently of the other elements in the interests of producing a balanced set of accounts, then we could put $V^* = I$. As can be seen from (10) the estimates of the elements of V^* need only be approximated up to a scalar multiplier.

Method (b). In this case we can use the same technique as in (a) but the problem is a much larger one since there are far more elements in the matrix $\{A_{01}^* : B_{01}^*\}$ than in the vector y_{01}^*. Perhaps the simplest way of expressing the adjustment mechanism in this case is to start with a vector, x_{01}^* say, whose elements consist of the outputs of each branch of production followed by the inputs into that branch arranged in order. These elements are derived from e_{01}^* using A_{01}^* and B_{01}^*. They have to be adjusted subject to two sets of constraints: (i) each output minus the intermediate use of that output must equal the corresponding element of e_{01}^*; and (ii) the sum of the inputs into each branch of production when multiplied by the corresponding element of y_{01}^* must equal the output of that branch multiplied by the corresponding element of p_{01}^*. These constraints which operate on the true values, x_{01}^* say, can be written in the form

$$Jx_{01} = \{e_{01}^* : 0\}$$
$$= k \tag{11}$$

say. The adjusted estimates, x_{01}^{**} say, are then given by

$$x_{01}^{**} = x_{01}^* - U^* J'(JU^*J')^{-1}(Jx_{01}^* - k) \tag{12}$$

where U^* denotes the variance matrix of x_{01}^*. Equation (12) gives the vector closest to x_{01}^* which satisfies the constraints and any attempt to adjust x_{01}^{**} by the method used to adjust x_{01}^* leaves it unchanged.

Method (c). In this case we take a weighted average of the results of methods (a) and (b), the weights, λ and $1 - \lambda$ say ($0 \leqslant \lambda \leqslant 1$), reflecting our confidence in our ability to project quantity structures and prices respectively.

If we use method (a) we obtain estimates of (4) and (6) given by

$$\hat{p}_{01}^{**} q_{01}^* = (\hat{p}_{01}^{**} A_{01}^* \hat{p}_{01}^{**-1}) \hat{p}_{01}^{**} q_{01}^* + \hat{p}_{01}^{**} e_{01}^* \tag{13}$$

and

$$\hat{p}_{01}^{**} q_{01}^* = \hat{p}_{01}^{**} \hat{q}_{01}^* (\hat{p}_{01}^{**-1} A_{01}^{*\prime} \hat{p}_{01}^{**} + \hat{p}_{01}^{**-1} B_{01}^{*\prime} f_{01}^{**}) i \tag{14}$$

If we use method (b) the corresponding equations are

$$\hat{p}_{01}^* q_{01}^{**} = (\hat{p}_{01}^* A_{01}^{**} \hat{p}_{01}^{*-1}) \hat{p}_{01}^* q_{01}^{**} + \hat{p}_{01}^* e_{01}^* \tag{15}$$

and

$$\hat{p}_{01}^* q_{01}^{**} = \hat{p}_{01}^* \hat{q}_{01}^{**} (\hat{p}_{01}^{*-1} A_{01}^{**\prime} \hat{p}_{01}^* + \hat{p}_{01}^{*-1} B_{01}^{**\prime} f_{01}^*) i \tag{16}$$

From method (a) we can set up a consistent accounting matrix, S_{11a}^{**} say, and from method (b) we can set up a corresponding matrix, S_{11b}^{**} say. We can then form our final estimate, S_{11}^{**} say, as

$$S_{11}^{**} = \lambda S_{11a}^{**} + (1 - \lambda) S_{11b}^{**} \tag{17}$$

If we wanted to retain our original units of quantity, £'s worth at base-year prices, we should have to decide how best to decompose the elements of S_{11}^{**} into price and quantity components. But if we shift our units of quantity to £'s worth at prices in the projection year, the question does not arise.

3. A NUMERICAL EXAMPLE

The foregoing procedure will now be illustrated by a simple numerical example involving only three branches and two factors of production. Let us assume that

$$A_{01}^* = \begin{bmatrix} 0 \cdot 4 & 0 \cdot 3 & 0 \cdot 2 \\ 0 \cdot 2 & 0 \cdot 2 & 0 \cdot 1 \\ 0 \cdot 1 & 0 \cdot 1 & 0 \cdot 1 \end{bmatrix} \tag{18}$$

$$B_{01}^* = \begin{bmatrix} 0\cdot2 & 0\cdot3 & 0\cdot4 \\ 0\cdot1 & 0\cdot1 & 0\cdot2 \end{bmatrix} \tag{19}$$

It will be noticed that $(A_{01}^{*\prime} + B_{01}^{*\prime})i = i$, a constraint frequently imposed though it is in no way essential to the calculation that follows. Further, let us assume that

$$e_{01}^* = \{2 \quad 5 \quad 1\} \tag{20}$$

$$y_{01}^* = \{1\cdot10 \quad 1\cdot15 \quad 1\cdot05 \quad 1\cdot25 \quad 0\cdot95\} \tag{21}$$

$$V^* = U^* = I \tag{22}$$

and

$$\lambda = 0\cdot5 \tag{23}$$

Let us now apply the three methods of adjustment to this example.

Method (a). In this case

$$G = \begin{bmatrix} 0\cdot6 & -0\cdot2 & -0\cdot1 & -0\cdot2 & -0\cdot1 \\ -0\cdot3 & 0\cdot8 & -0\cdot1 & -0\cdot3 & -0\cdot1 \\ -0\cdot2 & -0\cdot1 & 0\cdot9 & -0\cdot4 & -0\cdot2 \end{bmatrix} \tag{24}$$

$$H = \begin{bmatrix} 0\cdot208817 & 0\cdot212824 & 0\cdot207724 & 0\cdot248893 & 0\cdot121741 \\ 0\cdot212824 & 0\cdot218654 & 0\cdot211235 & 0\cdot271118 & 0\cdot086169 \\ 0\cdot207724 & 0\cdot211235 & 0\cdot206766 & 0\cdot242832 & 0\cdot131443 \\ 0\cdot248893 & 0\cdot271118 & 0\cdot242832 & 0\cdot471136 & -0\cdot233980 \\ 0\cdot121741 & 0\cdot086169 & 0\cdot131443 & -0\cdot233980 & 0\cdot894627 \end{bmatrix} \tag{25}$$

$$y_{01}^{**} = \{1\cdot11933 \quad 1\cdot12811 \quad 1\cdot11693 \quad 1\cdot20718 \quad 0\cdot92845\} \tag{26}$$

and

$$S_{11a}^{**} = \begin{bmatrix} 3\cdot926 & 2\cdot964 & 0\cdot686 & 2\cdot239 \\ 1\cdot978 & 1\cdot991 & 0\cdot346 & 5\cdot641 \\ 0\cdot979 & 0\cdot986 & 0\cdot343 & 1\cdot117 \\ 2\cdot117 & 3\cdot196 & 1\cdot481 & 0 \\ 0\cdot814 & 0\cdot819 & 0\cdot569 & 0 \end{bmatrix} \tag{27}$$

The last two rows of S_{11a}^{**} relate to the two factors of production. The sum of the elements in these two rows is equal (apart from rounding-off errors) to the sum of the elements in the last column which relates to final demand.

By dividing the entries in the first three columns of (27) by the corresponding column sum, we obtain

$$A_{11a}^{**} = \hat{p}_{01}^{**} A_{01}^* \hat{p}_{01}^{**-1}$$

$$= \begin{bmatrix} 0\cdot398 & 0\cdot292 & 0\cdot201 \\ 0\cdot206 & 0\cdot204 & 0\cdot097 \\ 0\cdot095 & 0\cdot096 & 0\cdot094 \end{bmatrix} \tag{28}$$

and

$$B_{11a}^{**} = \hat{f}_{01}^{**} B_{01}^{*} \hat{p}_{01}^{**-1}$$

$$= \begin{bmatrix} 0\cdot219 & 0\cdot326 & 0\cdot444 \\ 0\cdot082 & 0\cdot082 & 0\cdot163 \end{bmatrix} \tag{29}$$

Method (*b*). In this case

$$J = \begin{bmatrix} 1 & -1 & 0 & 0 & 0 & 0 \\ 0 & 0 & -1 & 0 & 0 & 0 \\ 0 & 0 & 0 & -1 & 0 & 0 \\ 1\cdot10 & -1\cdot10 & -1\cdot15 & -1\cdot05 & -1\cdot25 & -0\cdot95 \\ 0 & 0 & 0 & 0 & 0 & 0 \\ 0 & 0 & 0 & 0 & 0 & 0 \end{bmatrix}$$

$$\begin{matrix} 0 & -1 & 0 & 0 & 0 & 0 \\ 1 & 0 & -1 & 0 & 0 & 0 \\ 0 & 0 & 0 & -1 & 0 & 0 \\ 0 & 0 & 0 & 0 & 0 & 0 \\ 1\cdot15 & -1\cdot10 & -1\cdot15 & -1\cdot05 & -1\cdot25 & -0\cdot95 \\ 0 & 0 & 0 & 0 & 0 & 0 \end{matrix}$$

$$\begin{matrix} 0 & -1 & 0 & 0 & 0 & 0 \\ 0 & 0 & -1 & 0 & 0 & 0 \\ 1 & 0 & 0 & -1 & 0 & 0 \\ 0 & 0 & 0 & 0 & 0 & 0 \\ 0 & 0 & 0 & 0 & 0 & 0 \\ 1\cdot05 & -1\cdot10 & -1\cdot15 & -1\cdot05 & -1\cdot25 & -0\cdot95 \end{matrix} \tag{30}$$

$$x_{01}^{*} = \{8\cdot7682 \quad 3\cdot5073 \quad 1\cdot7536 \quad 0\cdot8768 \quad 1\cdot7536 \quad 0\cdot8768$$
$$8\cdot8253 \quad 2\cdot6476 \quad 1\cdot7651 \quad 0\cdot8825 \quad 2\cdot6476 \quad 0\cdot8825$$
$$3\cdot0660 \quad 0\cdot6132 \quad 0\cdot3066 \quad 0\cdot3066 \quad 1\cdot2264 \quad 0\cdot6132\} \tag{31}$$

$$k_{01} = \{2 \quad 5 \quad 1 \quad 0 \quad 0 \quad 0\} \tag{32}$$

$$x_{01}^{**} = \{8\cdot777 \quad 3\cdot498 \quad 1\cdot732 \quad 0\cdot871 \quad 1\cdot691 \quad 0\cdot829$$
$$8\cdot797 \quad 2\cdot686 \quad 1\cdot793 \quad 0\cdot922 \quad 2\cdot639 \quad 0\cdot876$$
$$3\cdot083 \quad 0\cdot593 \quad 0\cdot273 \quad 0\cdot290 \quad 1\cdot151 \quad 0\cdot556\} \tag{33}$$

and

$$S_{11b}^{**} = \begin{bmatrix} 3\cdot848 & 2\cdot955 & 0\cdot652 & 2\cdot200 \\ 1\cdot992 & 2\cdot062 & 0\cdot314 & 5\cdot750 \\ 0\cdot915 & 0\cdot968 & 0\cdot305 & 1\cdot050 \\ 2\cdot114 & 3\cdot299 & 1\cdot439 & 0 \\ 0\cdot788 & 0\cdot832 & 0\cdot528 & 0 \end{bmatrix} \tag{34}$$

By dividing the entries in the first three columns of (34) by the corresponding column sum, we obtain

$$A_{11b}^{**} = \hat{p}_{01}^{*} A_{01}^{**} \hat{p}_{01}^{*-1}$$

$$= \begin{bmatrix} 0 \cdot 400 & 0 \cdot 298 & 0 \cdot 200 \\ 0 \cdot 202 & 0 \cdot 200 & 0 \cdot 101 \\ 0 \cdot 100 & 0 \cdot 099 & 0 \cdot 100 \end{bmatrix} \tag{35}$$

and

$$B_{11b}^{**} = \hat{f}_{01}^{*} B_{01}^{**} \hat{p}_{01}^{*-1}$$

$$= \begin{bmatrix} 0 \cdot 216 & 0 \cdot 321 & 0 \cdot 432 \\ 0 \cdot 083 & 0 \cdot 082 & 0 \cdot 166 \end{bmatrix} \tag{36}$$

Method (c). Since the results in (27) and (34) are not very different and since those in (28) and (29) are very close to those in (35) and (36), it follows that the compromise solution cannot depart very much from either of the original ones. In fact

$$S_{11}^{**} \equiv \tfrac{1}{2}(S_{11a}^{**} + S_{11b}^{**})$$

$$= \begin{bmatrix} 3 \cdot 887 & 2 \cdot 960 & 0 \cdot 669 & 2 \cdot 220 \\ 1 \cdot 985 & 2 \cdot 027 & 0 \cdot 330 & 5 \cdot 696 \\ 0 \cdot 947 & 0 \cdot 977 & 0 \cdot 324 & 1 \cdot 084 \\ 2 \cdot 116 & 3 \cdot 248 & 1 \cdot 460 & 0 \\ 0 \cdot 801 & 0 \cdot 826 & 0 \cdot 549 & 0 \end{bmatrix} \tag{37}$$

whence

$$A_{11}^{**} = \begin{bmatrix} 0 \cdot 399 & 0 \cdot 295 & 0 \cdot 201 \\ 0 \cdot 204 & 0 \cdot 202 & 0 \cdot 099 \\ 0 \cdot 097 & 0 \cdot 097 & 0 \cdot 097 \end{bmatrix} \tag{38}$$

and

$$B_{11}^{**} = \begin{bmatrix} 0 \cdot 217 & 0 \cdot 324 & 0 \cdot 438 \\ 0 \cdot 082 & 0 \cdot 082 & 0 \cdot 165 \end{bmatrix} \tag{39}$$

The results set out in (38) and (39) can be compared with the best, though necessarily inconsistent, estimates that could have been made without using an adjustment procedure. If we denote these estimates by A_{11}^{*} and B_{11}^{*}, we can write

$$A_{11}^{*} = \hat{p}_{01}^{*} A_{01}^{*} \hat{p}_{01}^{*-1}$$

$$= \begin{bmatrix} 0 \cdot 400 & 0 \cdot 287 & 0 \cdot 210 \\ 0 \cdot 209 & 0 \cdot 200 & 0 \cdot 110 \\ 0 \cdot 095 & 0 \cdot 091 & 0 \cdot 100 \end{bmatrix} \tag{40}$$

$$B_{11}^{*} = \hat{f}_{01}^{*} B_{01}^{*} \hat{p}_{01}^{*-1}$$

$$= \begin{bmatrix} 0 \cdot 227 & 0 \cdot 326 & 0 \cdot 476 \\ 0 \cdot 086 & 0 \cdot 083 & 0 \cdot 181 \end{bmatrix} \tag{41}$$

and

$$(A_{11}^{*\prime} + B_{11}^{*\prime})i = \{1 \cdot 017 \quad 0 \cdot 987 \quad 1 \cdot 077\} \tag{42}$$

Equation (42) provides a measure of the inconsistency of the unadjusted estimates; and a comparison of (38) and (39) with (40) and (41) shows the extent of individual discrepancies. These run as high as five to ten per cent and are particularly noticeable in the final column of both matrices and in the first row of the second matrix.

4.　SOME COMMENTS ON THE METHOD

The problem discussed in this paper is well known to input–output analysts and usually shows itself most strikingly in the estimates of value added in different branches of production when account is taken of changing quantity coefficients but not of changing prices. The method of solution proposed is not an arbitrary one but represents an attempt to use systematically what impressions we possess about the reliability and interdependence of our necessarily imperfect initial estimates. It can readily be admitted that, in economics, our original estimates cannot in any strict sense be said to be unbiased, as they should be for the adjustment procedure to be firmly based, and that we may not be able to make very good estimates of the elements of the variance matrices, V^* and U^*. To the extent that these criticisms are important our adjustments will be imperfect; but what are the alternatives? Either to accept the inconsistent picture given by our initial estimates; or to attempt an adjustment 'by hand'; or to wait until we have really accurate data which do not need adjustment.

Experience shows that the first alternative is likely to produce misleading results, particularly in the case of totals expressed in money, like value added. The second alternative is hardly practicable; if it were, we could make consistent initial estimates. And the third alternative is never likely to be realized since, in the context of projections, it means that we have accurate information not only about the past and present but also about the future.

It seems difficult, therefore, to resist the use of adjustment procedures such as are proposed here either on the ground that the problem they are designed to solve is unimportant or on the ground that simpler methods are ready to hand. There remains the question of how difficult the proposed methods would be to apply in a practical situation. A number of points are relevant here.

First, in estimating a variance matrix it would seem best to start by putting it equal to I and then work through the improvements that could be made to this assumption. The first step would be to consider the variances of the estimates. Generally speaking one would expect relatively small items to have relatively small variances, but some small items might be very badly estimated (and some large items might be very well estimated) so that their variances would be larger (or smaller) than the idea of a uniform coefficient of variation would suggest. The second step would be to consider the covariance of the estimates. In some cases one might want the adjustments to two or more items to tend in the same direction, in other cases to tend in opposite directions. These wishes could be realized by inserting positive or negative entries in the off-diagonal cells of the variance matrices. Since the ratio of covariances to variances is $(\nu - 1)/2:1$ for a system of ν estimates, it is probably best to try to incorporate only strong and clear connections in the matrix and to ignore all weak or doubtful ones.

Second, computing problems are likely to be quite serious. For example with ν branches and μ factors of production, V^* is of order $\nu + \mu$ and U^* is of order $\nu(\nu + \mu + 1)$. Fortunately, however, these matrices do not have to be inverted. The inverses that appear in (10) and (12) are of the same order as the number of constraints, that is ν and 2ν respectively. If covariances are largely ignored V^* and U^* will be very sparse; if they are ignored completely the non-zero elements in V^* and U^* will be $\nu + \mu$ and $\nu(\nu + \mu + 1)$ respectively.

Third, a lack of price uniformity may, in practice, increase the size of the matrices beyond what has just been stated. In the methods proposed it is assumed that all products and all factors have uniform prices. In practice product prices may not be uniform: different buyers may buy a different product mix from a given branch and particular buyers, such as foreigners, may pay prices substantially different from those paid by others. To some extent these problems can be overcome either by adopting a relatively homogeneous basis of valuation such as factor costs or basic values [95] or by treating sales to particular classes of buyer, such as foreigners, as separate commodities. In the case of primary inputs, lack of price uniformity may require either disaggregation, recognizing for example several kinds of labour, or the treatment of the bundle of inputs used in different branches under the general heading of capital as separate inputs. Carried to the limit this would mean that instead of there being a single primary input called capital there would be as many forms of this input as there were branches of production.

Fourth, the size of the matrices that may have to be manipulated makes it worth while to consider whether there may not be a simpler, partial solution, especially in the case of method (*b*). Reflection shows that such a solution can be obtained as a weighted average of two extreme assumptions: (i) that the quantity adjustments are to be carried out by applying a set of multipliers to the rows of A_{01}^* and B_{01}^*; and, alternatively, (ii) that they are to be carried out by applying a set of multipliers to the columns of A_{01}^* and B_{01}^*. In case (i) we replace the original coefficient matrices by $\hat{r}_1^{**} A_{01}^*$ and $\hat{r}_2^{**} B_{01}^*$; and in case (ii) we replace them by $A_{01}^* \hat{s}_1^{**}$ and $B_{01}^* \hat{s}_1^{**}$. The elements of $r^{**} = \{r_1^{**} : r_2^{**}\}$ represent a reassessment of the substitution possibilities of different inputs; the elements of s_1^{**} represent a reassessment of the size of the basket of inputs needed by each branch of production to produce a unit of output.

The assumptions of this method of adjustment are essentially those that lie behind the RAS method [8, 64]. It is well known that this method gives good results only if certain elements, which do not fit in with the assumption of uniform row and column multipliers, are treated separately. The following description of the partial adjustment procedures ignores this complication.

In the case of the row multipliers, $r^* = i$ and we seek the best linear unbiased estimator, r^{**}, of the true vector r which is closest to r^* subject to the constraint $Li = p_{01}^*$. This estimator takes the form

$$r^{**} = i - W^* L'(LW^* L')^{-1} (Li - p_{01}^*) \tag{43}$$

where W^* denotes the variance matrix of r^* and

$$L = [A_{01}^{*'} \hat{p}_{01}^* : B_{01}^{*'} \hat{f}_{01}^*] \tag{44}$$

In the case of the column multipliers, it is also true that $s_1^* = i$ but there is now a unique value of s_1^{**} which produces a balanced set of accounts. This value is given by

$$\hat{s}_1^{**-1} i = \hat{p}_{01}^{*-1} (A_{01}^{*'} p_{01}^* + B_{01} f_{01}^*) \tag{45}$$

An application of these partial methods to the numerical example of the preceding section yields, with $W^* = I$,

$$r^{**} = \{0\cdot73891 \quad 1\cdot62592 \quad 0\cdot96550 \quad 1\cdot05024 \quad 0\cdot38928\} \tag{46}$$

This result compares with the average row multipliers, $\bar{r}^{**}$ say, which can be calculated from the complete quantity adjustment given in (12), namely

$$\bar{r}^{**} = \{1\cdot002 \quad 0\cdot993 \quad 1\cdot008 \quad 0\cdot974 \quad 0\cdot953\} \tag{47}$$

Further,

$$s_1^* = \{0\cdot98214 \quad 1\cdot01321 \quad 0\cdot92920\} \tag{48}$$

and this result compares with the average column multipliers, $\bar{s}_1^{**}$ say, which can be calculated from the complete quantity adjustment, namely

$$\bar{s}_1^{**} = \{0\cdot982 \quad 1\cdot014 \quad 0\cdot928\} \tag{49}$$

The difference between (46) and (47) and the similarity between (48) and (49) stand out. The complete quantity adjustment is not a RAS process and the treatment of the variance matrices in all these examples is purely formal. In this example we should apparently give a negligible weight to the reassessment of the substitution effects and almost a full weight to the reassessment of the productivity effects; but it is hard to see how we could have known this in advance.

$$(52)$$

$$
U^{***} =
\begin{bmatrix}
0{\cdot}69 & 0{\cdot}31 & 0{\cdot}10 & 0{\cdot}09 & 0{\cdot}10 & 0{\cdot}07 & 0{\cdot}03 & 0{\cdot}19 & -0{\cdot}03 & -0{\cdot}03 & -0{\cdot}05 & -0{\cdot}04 & 0{\cdot}03 & 0{\cdot}18 & -0{\cdot}03 & -0{\cdot}03 & -0{\cdot}05 & -0{\cdot}04 \\
0{\cdot}31 & 0{\cdot}49 & -0{\cdot}10 & -0{\cdot}10 & -0{\cdot}18 & -0{\cdot}03 & -0{\cdot}19 & -0{\cdot}19 & 0{\cdot}03 & 0{\cdot}03 & 0{\cdot}05 & 0{\cdot}04 & -0{\cdot}03 & -0{\cdot}18 & 0{\cdot}03 & 0{\cdot}03 & 0{\cdot}05 & 0{\cdot}04 \\
0{\cdot}10 & -0{\cdot}10 & 0{\cdot}59 & -0{\cdot}14 & -0{\cdot}18 & -0{\cdot}12 & 0{\cdot}18 & 0{\cdot}12 & -0{\cdot}18 & 0{\cdot}07 & 0{\cdot}10 & 0{\cdot}08 & -0{\cdot}03 & 0{\cdot}08 & -0{\cdot}23 & 0{\cdot}03 & 0{\cdot}05 & 0{\cdot}04 \\
0{\cdot}09 & -0{\cdot}09 & -0{\cdot}14 & 0{\cdot}61 & -0{\cdot}14 & -0{\cdot}11 & -0{\cdot}03 & 0{\cdot}07 & 0{\cdot}03 & -0{\cdot}23 & 0{\cdot}05 & 0{\cdot}04 & 0{\cdot}19 & 0{\cdot}11 & 0{\cdot}08 & -0{\cdot}19 & 0{\cdot}09 & 0{\cdot}07 \\
0{\cdot}10 & -0{\cdot}10 & -0{\cdot}13 & -0{\cdot}14 & 0{\cdot}64 & -0{\cdot}27 & -0{\cdot}05 & 0{\cdot}10 & 0{\cdot}05 & 0{\cdot}05 & -0{\cdot}14 & -0{\cdot}10 & -0{\cdot}05 & 0{\cdot}10 & 0{\cdot}05 & 0{\cdot}05 & -0{\cdot}14 & -0{\cdot}10 \\
0{\cdot}07 & -0{\cdot}07 & -0{\cdot}12 & -0{\cdot}11 & -0{\cdot}27 & 0{\cdot}79 & -0{\cdot}04 & 0{\cdot}07 & 0{\cdot}04 & 0{\cdot}04 & -0{\cdot}10 & -0{\cdot}08 & -0{\cdot}04 & 0{\cdot}08 & 0{\cdot}04 & 0{\cdot}04 & -0{\cdot}10 & -0{\cdot}08 \\
0{\cdot}03 & -0{\cdot}19 & 0{\cdot}18 & -0{\cdot}03 & -0{\cdot}05 & -0{\cdot}04 & 0{\cdot}68 & 0{\cdot}10 & 0{\cdot}32 & 0{\cdot}10 & 0{\cdot}10 & 0{\cdot}08 & 0{\cdot}03 & 0{\cdot}18 & 0{\cdot}03 & 0{\cdot}03 & 0{\cdot}03 & 0{\cdot}04 \\
0{\cdot}19 & -0{\cdot}19 & 0{\cdot}12 & 0{\cdot}07 & 0{\cdot}10 & 0{\cdot}07 & 0{\cdot}10 & 0{\cdot}60 & -0{\cdot}10 & -0{\cdot}13 & -0{\cdot}15 & -0{\cdot}11 & -0{\cdot}03 & -0{\cdot}03 & -0{\cdot}23 & 0{\cdot}05 & 0{\cdot}04 & 0{\cdot}04 \\
-0{\cdot}03 & 0{\cdot}03 & -0{\cdot}18 & 0{\cdot}03 & 0{\cdot}05 & 0{\cdot}04 & 0{\cdot}32 & -0{\cdot}10 & 0{\cdot}68 & -0{\cdot}10 & -0{\cdot}10 & -0{\cdot}08 & -0{\cdot}03 & -0{\cdot}18 & 0{\cdot}03 & 0{\cdot}05 & 0{\cdot}03 & 0{\cdot}04 \\
-0{\cdot}03 & 0{\cdot}03 & 0{\cdot}07 & -0{\cdot}23 & 0{\cdot}05 & 0{\cdot}04 & 0{\cdot}10 & -0{\cdot}13 & -0{\cdot}10 & 0{\cdot}61 & -0{\cdot}14 & -0{\cdot}10 & 0{\cdot}19 & 0{\cdot}12 & 0{\cdot}08 & -0{\cdot}19 & 0{\cdot}09 & 0{\cdot}07 \\
-0{\cdot}05 & 0{\cdot}05 & 0{\cdot}10 & 0{\cdot}05 & -0{\cdot}14 & -0{\cdot}10 & 0{\cdot}10 & -0{\cdot}15 & -0{\cdot}10 & -0{\cdot}14 & 0{\cdot}64 & -0{\cdot}27 & -0{\cdot}05 & 0{\cdot}10 & 0{\cdot}05 & 0{\cdot}05 & -0{\cdot}14 & -0{\cdot}10 \\
-0{\cdot}04 & 0{\cdot}04 & 0{\cdot}08 & 0{\cdot}04 & -0{\cdot}10 & -0{\cdot}08 & 0{\cdot}08 & -0{\cdot}11 & -0{\cdot}08 & -0{\cdot}11 & -0{\cdot}27 & 0{\cdot}79 & -0{\cdot}04 & 0{\cdot}08 & 0{\cdot}04 & 0{\cdot}04 & -0{\cdot}10 & -0{\cdot}08 \\
0{\cdot}03 & -0{\cdot}03 & -0{\cdot}03 & 0{\cdot}19 & -0{\cdot}05 & -0{\cdot}04 & 0{\cdot}03 & -0{\cdot}03 & -0{\cdot}03 & 0{\cdot}19 & -0{\cdot}05 & -0{\cdot}04 & 0{\cdot}69 & 0{\cdot}09 & 0{\cdot}31 & 0{\cdot}10 & 0{\cdot}09 & 0{\cdot}07 \\
0{\cdot}18 & -0{\cdot}18 & 0{\cdot}08 & 0{\cdot}11 & 0{\cdot}10 & 0{\cdot}08 & 0{\cdot}18 & -0{\cdot}03 & -0{\cdot}18 & 0{\cdot}12 & 0{\cdot}10 & 0{\cdot}08 & 0{\cdot}09 & 0{\cdot}58 & -0{\cdot}15 & -0{\cdot}09 & -0{\cdot}15 & -0{\cdot}11 \\
-0{\cdot}03 & 0{\cdot}03 & -0{\cdot}23 & 0{\cdot}08 & 0{\cdot}05 & 0{\cdot}04 & 0{\cdot}03 & -0{\cdot}23 & 0{\cdot}03 & 0{\cdot}08 & 0{\cdot}05 & 0{\cdot}04 & 0{\cdot}31 & -0{\cdot}15 & 0{\cdot}60 & -0{\cdot}10 & -0{\cdot}15 & -0{\cdot}12 \\
-0{\cdot}03 & 0{\cdot}03 & 0{\cdot}03 & -0{\cdot}19 & 0{\cdot}05 & 0{\cdot}04 & 0{\cdot}03 & 0{\cdot}05 & 0{\cdot}05 & -0{\cdot}19 & 0{\cdot}05 & 0{\cdot}04 & 0{\cdot}10 & -0{\cdot}09 & -0{\cdot}10 & 0{\cdot}69 & -0{\cdot}09 & -0{\cdot}07 \\
-0{\cdot}05 & 0{\cdot}05 & 0{\cdot}05 & 0{\cdot}09 & -0{\cdot}14 & -0{\cdot}10 & 0{\cdot}03 & 0{\cdot}04 & 0{\cdot}03 & 0{\cdot}09 & -0{\cdot}14 & -0{\cdot}10 & 0{\cdot}09 & -0{\cdot}15 & -0{\cdot}15 & -0{\cdot}09 & 0{\cdot}64 & -0{\cdot}27 \\
-0{\cdot}04 & 0{\cdot}04 & 0{\cdot}04 & 0{\cdot}07 & -0{\cdot}10 & -0{\cdot}08 & 0{\cdot}04 & 0{\cdot}04 & 0{\cdot}04 & 0{\cdot}07 & -0{\cdot}10 & -0{\cdot}08 & 0{\cdot}07 & -0{\cdot}11 & -0{\cdot}12 & -0{\cdot}07 & -0{\cdot}27 & 0{\cdot}79
\end{bmatrix}
$$

Fifth and last, in section 3 a variance matrix was found to be an essential element in the adjustment procedure; for example, U^* is the variance matrix of x^*. But it is also of interest to work out the variance matrix U^{**} of x^{**} which takes into account not only our subjective impressions but also the constraints. This adjusted variance matrix is given by

$$U^{**} = U^* - U^*J'(JU^*J')^{-1}JU^* \qquad (50)$$

Thus, in the examples of section 3,

$$V^{**} = H \qquad (51)$$

as given in (25) and U^{**} is given in (52) on the preceding page.

5. CONCLUSIONS

I have tried to show how the well-known method of adjusting conditioned observations by the method of least squares can be applied to the problem of making consistent input–output projections. The method is designed to make the best use of the kind of information likely to be available and might not be needed if our data were more plentiful and our powers of analysis greater than they actually are. The method is simple and the difficulties associated with it are mainly practical. It is only through applications that we can expect to test its worth.

VI

MODELS FOR SEASONAL ADJUSTMENT

1. INTRODUCTION

The existence of seasonal variations presents a recurring problem to those engaged in the analysis and interpretation of monthly, quarterly and other series which are recorded regularly through the year. Many procedures have been suggested [39] for extracting a normal seasonal movement from a set of observations and the practical problem is not so much to find a new method as to make a rational choice in any particular instance among the methods already available. What would be more useful, however, is not just a single cut and dried method but a strategy which permitted the often complicated phenomenon of seasonality to be explored and analysed as expeditiously as possible.

In this paper an attempt is made to provide such a strategy. In doing this a number of considerations must be kept in mind.

First, one must try to discover whether, in a particular series, there is evidence of systematic seasonal variation. This variation may be changing or constant.

Second, since very little is usually known, at least in the case of economic series, of the ultimate causes of seasonal variation, it seems best to begin by inquiring into the significance of the differences between seasonal trends and seasonal means without attempting to ascribe these differences to particular causes.

Third, when this has been done, a more searching analysis of causes is desirable, if only for the reason that seasonal influences do not operate with perfect uniformity year after year. Thus, for example, in this country January tends to be relatively cold and dark, but not equally so in all years.

Fourth, in the interests of mechanizing the process of seasonal adjustment, one should, if possible, adopt a procedure which does not normally have regard to exceptional influences believed to be at work in particular years. It is obvious, for example, that the General Strike of 1926 produced quite abnormal movements in many economic series and, on this account, 1926 does not, in many cases, provide much evidence on normal seasonal movements. If data were available for a very large number of years, the appearance from time to time of even striking abnormalities would be of little significance. But in practice economic data are frequently available for a generation or less and in these circumstances it seems desirable to ignore information which is disturbed by an event such as a general strike.

It does not seem equally desirable, however, to extend this kind of reasoning on the ground that there are exceptional influences at work in almost every period. Although this is likely to be the case, it is doubtful whether any substantial gain can be expected from a subjective *a priori* adjustment of the series to be analysed which goes beyond the omission of certain years when highly disturbing influences are known to have been at work.

These considerations suggest the following general procedure or strategy.

(*a*) The analysis of seasonal variations should be based on an explicit stochastic model.

(*b*) This model should relate the series to be analysed to certain dummy variables with the object of detecting significant differences between seasonal trends and seasonal means. At this first stage of the investigation the object of the analysis should be to assign the series under investigation to one of three classes, as follows:

(i)   Significant differences among seasonal trends. This class requires a uniformly changing seasonal adjustment.

(ii) No significant difference between seasonal trends but a significant difference between seasonal means adjusted for trend. This class requires a constant seasonal adjustment.

(iii) No significant difference between seasonal means adjusted for trend. No seasonal adjustment can properly be applied to members of this class.

(*c*) After stage (*b*) has been carried out, consideration should be given to particular causal influences. This can be done by introducing into the model series for the chosen causal influences orthogonalized with respect to seasonal trends and means. This will provide an acceptable test of significance and the additional adjustment associated with specific causes can be added to that derived at stage (*b*). The specific causes may be continuous variables such as temperature and rainfall or discrete variables which denote, for example, the presence or absence of moveable feasts such as Easter.

2.   THE SIMPLEST MODEL

If there is no trend in the series to be analysed, the first question to be answered is whether or not there is a significant difference between seasonal means. The model in this case can be written in the form

$$y_{st} = \alpha + b_s + e_{st}$$

$$= c_s + e_{st} \tag{1}$$

say, where y_{st} denotes the element of the series to be analysed which occurs in season s of year t, α denotes the true mean of the whole series,

b_s denotes the excess over α of the true mean for season s, and e_{st} denotes a disturbance which by hypothesis is independently distributed with zero mean and constant variance. If the sum of squares $\sum_s \sum_t e_{st}^2$ is minimized subject to the condition that $\sum_s b_s = 0$, then the estimators, $\bar{\alpha}, \bar{b}_s$ and $\bar{c}_s$, of α, b_s and c_s are

$$\bar{c}_s = \sum_t y_{st}/\nu$$

$$= \bar{y}_s \tag{2}$$

where ν is the number of years for which observations are available and $\bar{y}_s$ is the mean of the observation for season s. Given the $\bar{c}_s$, then $\bar{\alpha}$ is given by

$$\bar{\alpha} = \sum_s \bar{c}_s/\mu$$

$$= \sum_s \sum_t y_{st}/\mu\nu$$

$$= \bar{y} \tag{3}$$

where μ is the number of seasons into which each year is divided and $\bar{y}$ is the general mean of the observations. The estimator $\bar{b}_s$ is given by

$$\bar{b}_s = \bar{c}_s - \bar{\alpha}$$

$$= \bar{y}_s - \bar{y} \tag{4}$$

from (2) and (3).

This simple model can readily be expressed in matrix notation which, while not needed in the present case, will be found convenient in more complicated cases. Thus (1) can be written in the form

$$y = i\alpha + Sb + e$$

$$= S(i_\mu \alpha + b) + e$$

$$= Sc + e \tag{5}$$

where α has the same meaning as in (1), i and i_μ denote, respectively, the unit vector with $\mu\nu$ and with μ elements, y, b and e denote vectors the elements of which are y_{st}, b_s and e_{st}, and S denotes a matrix of type $\mu\nu \times \mu$ which contains the unit matrix of order μ repeated ν times.

Corresponding to (2), the least-squares estimator of c is

$$\bar{c} = (S'S)^{-1}S'y \tag{6}$$

and since, by definition, $\bar{c}$ must satisfy the relationship

$$\bar{c} = i_\mu \bar{\alpha} + \bar{b} \tag{7}$$

and $\bar{b}$ must satisfy the condition

$$i_\mu' \bar{b} = 0 \tag{8}$$

it follows that

$$\bar{\alpha} = (i_m' i_m)^{-1} i_m' \bar{c}$$
$$= (i' i)^{-1} i' y \tag{9}$$

corresponding to (3), since

$$(S' S)^{-1} \equiv I_\mu / \nu \tag{10}$$

and

$$S i_\mu \equiv i \tag{11}$$

Finally, corresponding to (4), there results, on combining (6), (7) and (9),

$$\bar{b} = [I_\mu - i_\mu (i_\mu' i_\mu)^{-1} i_\mu'] (S' S)^{-1} S' y$$
$$= (S' S)^{-1} S' [I - i(i' i)^{-1} i'] y \tag{12}$$

which is equivalent to saying that $\bar{b}$ is equal to the set of seasonal means adjusted for the general mean.

3. A TEST OF SIGNIFICANCE FOR THE SIMPLEST MODEL

An adjustment for seasonality should be made only if there is a significant variation associated specifically with seasons. This will be the case if the variance of the seasonal means about the general mean is sufficiently large compared with the variance of the observations each taken about its seasonal mean. The information required for deciding this question is obtained by dividing the sum of squares of the observations into three independent parts, one associated with the mean value of the series, one associated with the deviations of seasonal means about the general mean and one associated with the deviations of the actual observations about their respective seasonal means. This information is conveniently assembled in the familiar table for the analysis of variance as follows.

ANALYSIS OF VARIANCE FOR MODEL $(1) = (5)$

	Degrees of freedom	Sums of squares	
		Suffix notation	Matrix notation
1. Mean value	1	$\mu \nu \bar{y}^2$	$y'[i(i' i)^{-1} i'] y$
2. Between seasons	$\mu - 1$	$\nu \sum_s (\bar{y}_s - \bar{y})^2$	$y'[S(S' S)^{-1} S' - i(i' i)^{-1} i'] y$
3. Within seasons	$\mu(\nu - 1)$	$\sum_s \sum_t (y_{st} - \bar{y}_s)^2$	$y'[I - S(S' S)^{-1} S'] y$
4. Total	$\mu \nu$	$\sum_s \sum_t y_{st}^2$	$y'[I] y$

Variance estimators corresponding to the sums of squares shown in the table are obtained by dividing the latter by their respective degrees of freedom. On the assumption that the e_{st} are normally distributed, a test for the significance of the variance between seasons can be obtained from the ratio of the mean square between seasons to the mean square within seasons, since on the null hypothesis that $b = \{0, 0, \ldots, 0\}$, this ratio, being the ratio of two independent estimates of the same population variance, has an F-distribution with $\mu - 1$ and $\mu(\nu - 1)$ degrees of freedom.

4. THE INTRODUCTION OF TRENDS INTO THE MODEL

The model which has so far been considered was introduced in order to illustrate the procedures involved in the simplest possible case. In practice it is not likely to be of much value, since there will usually be a trend in the series under investigation or, at least, this possibility will have to be considered. For, if there is a trend in the series, the means for seasons which occur later in the year will tend to be systematically different from those which occur earlier. In order to isolate the seasonal component in the differences between the seasonal means it is necessary to allow for the trend in the series. With the addition of a linear trend term the model takes the form

$$y = Sc + t\lambda + e \tag{13}$$

where the vector t denotes the numbers $1, \ldots, \mu\nu$ each with the mean of the series, $(\mu\nu + 1)/2$, subtracted.

Model (13) would probably be reasonably satisfactory in many practical cases. It will not, however, be considered in detail here because it does not allow for the possibility that the seasonal pattern may be changing, in the sense that the observations for different seasons have significantly different trends. This possibility can be introduced by replacing the vector t in (13) by the matrix T where

$$T = \hat{t}S \tag{14}$$

In (14) $\hat{t}$ is a diagonal matrix constructed from the vector t so that T is related to t in a manner similar to that in which S is related to i. The model now becomes

$$\begin{aligned} y &= i\alpha + Sb + t\lambda + Tm + e \\ &= S(i_\mu \alpha + b) + T(i_\mu \lambda + m) + e \\ &= Sc + Tn + e \end{aligned} \tag{15}$$

If $m = \{0, \ldots, 0\}$, then (15) reduces to (13); if in addition $\lambda = 0$, then (15) reduces to (5). If

$$M = [I - S(S'S)^{-1}S'] \tag{16}$$

and

$$N = [I - T(T'T)^{-1}T'] \tag{17}$$

then the estimators $\bar{c}$, $\bar{n}$, $\bar{\alpha}$, $\bar{b}$, $\bar{\lambda}$ and $\bar{m}$ of the parameters c, n, α, b, λ and m in (15) are given by

$$\bar{c} = (S' \, NS)^{-1} \, S' \, Ny \tag{18}$$

$$\bar{n} = (T' \, MT)^{-1} \, T' \, My \tag{19}$$

$$\bar{\alpha} = (i'_\mu \, i_\mu)^{-1} \, i'_\mu \, \bar{c} \tag{20}$$

$$\bar{b} = \bar{c} - i_\mu \, \bar{\alpha} \tag{21}$$

$$\bar{\lambda} = (i'_\mu \, i_\mu)^{-1} \, i'_\mu \, \bar{n} \tag{22}$$

$$\bar{m} = \bar{n} - i_\mu \, \bar{\lambda} \tag{23}$$

5. A TEST OF SIGNIFICANCE FOR MODEL (15)

With model (15) it is possible to test whether the hypothesis of a constant seasonal pattern is justified by the observations. This can be done by means of an analysis of covariance [32] as set out in the following table.

ANALYSIS OF COVARIANCE FOR MODEL (15)

Variance	Degrees of freedom	Sums of squares
1. General mean	1	$y'[i(i'\,i)^{-1}\,i']y$
2. General trend	1	$y'[t(t'\,t)^{-1}\,t']y$
3. Between seasonal means	$\mu - 1$	$y'[S(S'\,S)^{-1}\,S' + Mt(t'\,Mt)^{-1}\,t'\,M$ $\quad - i(i'\,i)^{-1}\,i' - t(t'\,t)^{-1}\,t']y$
4. Between seasonal trends	$\mu - 1$	$y'[MT(T'\,MT)^{-1}\,T'\,M - Mt(t'\,Mt)^{-1}\,t'\,M]y$
5. Residual	$\mu(\nu - 2)$	$y'[I - S(S'\,S)^{-1}\,S' - MT(T'\,MT)^{-1}\,T'\,M]y$
6. Total	$\mu\nu$	$y'[I]y$

The significance of the difference between seasonal trends can be tested by calculating the variance ratio obtained from rows 4 and 5 of the table since, on the usual assumptions, this ratio has the F-distribution with the degrees of freedom shown. If the null hypothesis, that there is no significant difference between seasonal trends, is rejected, then there is evidence of a systematically changing seasonal pattern and adjustment should be made for this. It should be recognized that such a state of affairs is abnormal, in the sense that systematic change of this kind cannot be expected to persist indefinitely.

If no significant difference is found in the seasonal trends, then the sums of squares and degrees of freedom shown in rows 4 and 5 of the table should be combined to form a new estimate of the residual variance with which to compare the variance attributable to differences between seasonal means (apart from trend effects) associated with row 3 of the table. If in this case the null hypothesis is rejected, then the series should be adjusted for a constant seasonal variation as given by the elements of the vector $\bar{b}$. If this hypothesis is not rejected then no seasonal adjustment can usefully be made.

The analysis just described permits the assignment of the series to one of the three classes referred to under (*b*) in the introduction.

6. TRANSFORMATIONS OF VARIABLES

The vector y with elements y_{st} has so far only been described as the series to be analysed; thus, for example, it might represent a monthly series of coal production or of retail prices. If in fact y had this meaning, then the models considered in the preceding sections would lead to an analysis of seasonal variations in absolute terms. In many cases, however, it may seem more plausible to consider the hypothesis of a constant (or systematically changing) relative seasonal variation. This can be achieved, in the case of essentially positive series, by defining y as the series obtained by taking the logarithms of the original series. In a similar way it may be desired to analyse the deviations (absolute or relative) from a moving average rather than the series as originally given. In such a case y may be defined as the series of deviations and whichever model is considered appropriate may be applied to this transformed series.

Thus considerations relating to the kind of hypothesis about seasonality provide one reason for transforming the dependent variable. A second reason for doing this is provided by considerations of efficient estimation.

The variables contained in the matrices S and T are not stochastic variables but are fixed and so can give rise to no difficulty from the standpoint of least-squares estimation. There is, however, another problem to be faced from this point of view, namely that the disturbances, e_{st}, in the model should be independently distributed with zero mean and constant variance. Given the more or less oscillatory character of many economic time series, it is to be expected that the assumption of the serial independence of the disturbances would rarely be plausible in economic applications if the dependent variable in the model were either the original series or its logarithms. The assumption of serial independence would frequently be much more plausible if the dependent variable took the form of the first differences of the original series or of its logarithms. The use of moving averages might also be expected to be helpful from this point of view.

The first-difference model can be applied as follows. If the elements of a vector z are the first differences of the elements of y, then this model can be written in the form

$$z = Sc^* + Tn^* + e \tag{24}$$

The parameters b and c in (15) are related to c^* in (24) as follows. Let Q denote a matrix of order μ, as in (12) above, which when applied to a vector, removes from each element the mean of the elements of the vector. Thus

$$Q = [I_\mu - i_\mu (i'_\mu i_\mu)^{-1} i'_\mu] \tag{25}$$

Let P denote a matrix of order μ with units in the subdiagonal and zer o elsewhere. Then

$$\begin{aligned} b &= Qc \\ &= Q(I - P)^{-1} Qc^* \\ &= Rc^* \end{aligned} \tag{26}$$

say, where R is the simple circulant matrix

$$R = \begin{bmatrix} r_1 & r_\mu & r_{\mu-1} & \cdots & r_2 \\ r_2 & r_1 & r_\mu & \cdots & r_3 \\ r_3 & r_2 & r_1 & \cdots & r_4 \\ \vdots & \vdots & \vdots & & \vdots \\ r_\mu & r_{\mu-1} & r_{\mu-2} & \cdots & r_1 \end{bmatrix} \tag{27}$$

with $r_\theta = (\mu - 2\theta + 1)/2\mu$; $\theta = 1, 2, \ldots, \mu$.

In a similar way, m and n in (15) are related to n^* in (24). If (24) is believed to be a more appropriate model than (15), and this belief can to some extent be tested empirically by reference to the serial correlation in the observed residuals, then b should be estimated by combining (24) and (26) and not directly from (15).

7. A TEST OF SIGNIFICANCE FOR MODEL (24)

No new problems are involved in the estimation of the parameters in (24). In this case, however, the test of significance is slightly different from, and indeed somewhat simpler than, that appropriate to (15). The form of the analysis of covariance may be set out as shown opposite.

The terminology used in this table is appropriate to first differences and needs some reinterpretation if it is to be compared with the corresponding analysis for (15). A non-zero mean in first differences implies a linear trend in the original series. The variance estimates derived from rows 3 and 4 of the table can be compared in order to test the null hypothesis that there is no difference in the seasonal trends. If this hypothesis is sustained, then rows 3 and 4 can be combined to produce a new variance estimate with which the estimate from row 2 can be compared in order

ANALYSIS OF COVARIANCE FOR MODEL (24)

Variance	Degrees of freedom	Sums of squares
1. General mean	1	$z'[i(i'i)^{-1}i']z$
2. Between seasonal means	$\mu - 1$	$z'[S(S'S)^{-1}S' - i(i'i)^{-1}i']z$
3. Trends	μ	$z'[MT(T'MT)^{-1}T'M]z$
4. Residual	$\mu(\nu - 2)$	$z'[I - S(S'S)^{-1}S' - MT(T'MT)^{-1}T'M]z$
5. Total	$\mu\nu$	$z'[I]z$

to test the null hypothesis of no differences between seasons apart from trend effects. Thus, again, the series can be assigned to its appropriate class.

8.   THE INTRODUCTION OF SPECIFIC CAUSAL FACTORS

So far no attempt has been made to test the effect of introducing specific influences on the pattern of seasonality, since it seems best to do this after the preliminary classification has been made. This implies that specific influences are introduced in a form in which they are orthogonalized with respect to S and T, so that it is only the additional variation associated with them that comes into the analysis. If F^* denotes a matrix the columns of which contain the values of particular factors over the period of observation, then the component, F say, of F^* orthogonal to S and T can be written as

$$F = [I - S(S'S)^{-1}S' - MT(T'MT)^{-1}T'M]F^* \tag{28}$$

Thus the final model takes the form

$$y = Sc + Tn + Fr + e \tag{29}$$

where r is a vector of parameters and, as before, the adjusted series, y^* say, is given by

$$y^* = \bar{\alpha}i + \bar{\lambda}t + e$$
$$= y - S\bar{b} - T\bar{m} - F\bar{r} \tag{30}$$

where $\bar{\alpha}$, $\bar{b}$, $\bar{\lambda}$, $\bar{m}$ and $\bar{r}$ are the least-squares estimators of α, b, λ, m and r. Equation (30) is written on the assumption that there is a significant difference between seasonal trends. If this is not the case, the term $T\bar{m}$ must be included in y^*.

The elements to be found in the columns of F^* are illustrated by the following examples. If F_1^* denotes a column of F^* introduced to test

6

whether there is a significant variation associated with the presence of Easter, then the elements of F_1^* will be unity in any season which contains Easter and otherwise zero. Similarly, the influence of rainfall can be introduced by including a column, F_2^* say, the elements of which are observations on rainfall. If rainfall is to be introduced in such a way that it can have a different influence in each season, then F_2^* must be replaced by μ columns, each of which shows the rainfall level in a particular season and contains zeros in all other seasons.

The analysis of variance will immediately show whether or not the variables in F taken together make a significant contribution to the residual variance of the preliminary analysis. A further analysis of this contribution is possible in terms of the significance of individual elements in r. The correct procedure at this point must depend, to some extent, on what is known about the phenomena being investigated. For example, if the monthly index of industrial production is investigated over the post-war years it will be found that production in August tends to fall relatively over time, probably as a consequence of the extension of holidays with pay which are taken mainly in that month. The amount of holidays with pay under collective agreements is known only on an annual basis but this variable could be included in F^* for August or, separately, for any other month. If the analysis were restricted to a period when holidays with pay were rising steadily it is to be expected that their influence on production would already have been largely accounted for in the differential trend for August, that is by the August component of T. The holidays-in-August component of F might therefore appear not significant. However, the influence of additional holidays cannot continue at the same strength indefinitely and if, therefore, it were thought that the spread of holidays with pay was in fact responsible for the differential trend of August in the preliminary analysis, it would be appropriate to retain the holidays-in-August component in F in making adjustments for future years. Indeed it is just such factors as this that must be suspected if significant differences are found in the trends for seasons in the preliminary analysis.

9. THE STANDARD ERRORS OF THE ESTIMATORS OF MODEL (29)

Model (29) can be written in a more compact and, for present purposes, more convenient notation, as follows:

$$y = [S \vdots T \vdots F] \begin{bmatrix} c \\ \cdots \\ n \\ \cdots \\ r \end{bmatrix} + e$$

$$= [X_1 \vdots X_2 \vdots X_3] \begin{bmatrix} h_1 \\ \cdots \\ h_2 \\ \cdots \\ h_3 \end{bmatrix} + e \qquad (31)$$

say. In this notation the least-squares estimator of h, $\bar{h}$ say, is given by

$$\bar{h} = (X' X)^{-1} X' y \qquad (32)$$

and the variance matrix, $V(\bar{h})$ say, of $\bar{h}$ is given by

$$V(\bar{h}) = \sigma^2 (X' X)^{-1} \qquad (33)$$

where σ^2 is the variance of the elements of e. The estimator of this variance matrix, $\bar{V}(\bar{h})$ say, is given by replacing σ^2 by an estimator, $\bar{\sigma}^2$ say, based on the observations, of the usual form

$$\bar{\sigma}^2 = e' e / (\mu \nu - \kappa) \qquad (34)$$

where e is the vector of residuals from the regression equation and κ is the number of elements in h. Written in partitioned form, $\bar{V}(\bar{h})$ is given by

$$\bar{V} \begin{bmatrix} \bar{h}_1 \\ \cdots \\ \bar{h}_2 \\ \cdots \\ \bar{h}_3 \end{bmatrix} = \bar{\sigma}^2 \begin{bmatrix} C_{11} \vdots C_{12} \vdots 0 \\ \cdots \vdots \cdots \vdots \cdots \\ C_{21} \vdots C_{22} \vdots 0 \\ \cdots \vdots \cdots \vdots \cdots \\ 0 \vdots 0 \vdots C_{33} \end{bmatrix} \qquad (35)$$

where C_{ij} is the matrix in the ijth partition of $(X' X)^{-1}$.

The estimators $\bar{\alpha}$, $\bar{b}$, $\bar{\lambda}$, $\bar{m}$ and $\bar{r}$ are related in a simple way to $\bar{h}_1$, $\bar{h}_2$ and $\bar{h}_3$. If y represents the original series or its logarithms, then

$$\begin{bmatrix} \bar{\alpha} \\ \cdots \\ \bar{b} \\ \cdots \\ \bar{\lambda} \\ \cdots \\ \bar{m} \\ \cdots \\ \bar{r} \end{bmatrix} = \begin{bmatrix} (i'_\mu i_\mu)^{-1} i'_\mu \vdots 0 & \vdots 0 \\ \cdots \cdots \cdots \cdots \vdots \cdots \cdots \vdots \cdots \\ Q & \vdots 0 & \vdots 0 \\ \cdots \cdots \cdots \cdots \vdots \cdots \cdots \vdots \cdots \\ 0 & \vdots (i'_\mu i_\mu)^{-1} i'_\mu \vdots 0 \\ \cdots \cdots \cdots \cdots \vdots \cdots \cdots \vdots \cdots \\ 0 & \vdots Q & \vdots 0 \\ \cdots \cdots \cdots \cdots \vdots \cdots \cdots \vdots \cdots \\ 0 & \vdots 0 & \vdots I \end{bmatrix} \begin{bmatrix} \bar{h}_1 \\ \cdots \\ \bar{h}_2 \\ \cdots \\ \bar{h}_3 \end{bmatrix} \qquad (36)$$

or, more compactly,

$$\bar{g} = K' \bar{h} \qquad (37)$$

The estimator of the variance matrix of $\bar{g}$, $\bar{V}(\bar{g})$ say, is given by

$$\bar{V}(\bar{g}) = \bar{\sigma}^2 [K'(X' X)^{-1} K] \qquad (38)$$

Thus, for example,

$$\bar{V}(\bar{b}) = \bar{\sigma}^2 \underset{\sim}{Q} C_{11} \underset{\sim}{Q} \qquad (39)$$

since $\underset{\sim}{Q}$ is a symmetric matrix.

These relationships are readily adapted to specific models such as the first-difference model (24). If this model is used it can be seen that $\overline{V}(\overline{b})$ takes the form

$$\overline{V}(\overline{b}) = \overline{\sigma}^2 \, RC_{11} \, R \tag{40}$$

in view of (26).

If, in a first-difference model, it is found that there is a significant difference associated with seasonal means adjusted for trend but no significant difference associated with trends, then it is possible to test the hypothesis that there is no difference between consecutive values of y adjusted for seasonal variation. To do this it is necessary to compare the adjusted difference, $\overline{z}_{st}$ say, with the appropriate element of $\overline{V}(\overline{b})$, where

$$\overline{b} = Q\overline{c} \tag{41}$$

and $\overline{V}(\overline{b})$ has the same form as (39) with $\overline{\sigma}^2$ the estimator of the residual variance (including the variance associated with trends) in the first-difference model.

10. A TEST OF THE BASIC MODEL: CONSUMERS' EXPENDITURE, 1948–1954

Quarterly estimates of consumers' expenditure at 1948 prices are available from the beginning of 1948 to 1954. In analysing these data, the original series was first transformed to logarithms, since it seemed more appropriate to consider seasonal differences in proportionate rather than in absolute terms. The following three different versions of the basic model were considered:

(i) y denotes the logarithms of the original series;
(ii) y denotes the first differences of the logarithms of the original series;
(iii) y denotes the deviations of the logarithms of the original series from a two quarters' moving average of a four quarters' moving average.

In each case there was evidence of a constant seasonal pattern but not of a uniformly changing seasonal pattern. The values of the seasonal constants and of Durbin and Watson's d-statistic [18] for the three models are set out below.

	Original series (i)	First differences (ii)	Moving average (iii)
I	0·940	0·944	0·943
II	0·989	0·989	0·990
III	1·022	1·018	1·020
IV	1·053	1·051	1·049
d	0·49	1·94	2·18

The values of the seasonal patterns are in this case very similar. Models (ii) and (iii) are to be preferred to model (i) on the d-test for serial correlation in the residuals, since their residuals do not show evidence of serial correlation while those of model (i) do.

11. THE SIGNIFICANCE OF SEASON-TO-SEASON CHANGES IN THE FIRST-DIFFERENCE MODEL

If $\overline{V}(\overline{b})$ is estimated for model (ii), it is found that

$$\overline{V}(\overline{b}) = \begin{bmatrix} 0 \cdot 000007020 \\ 0 \cdot 000007020 \\ 0 \cdot 000006828 \\ 0 \cdot 000006828 \end{bmatrix} \tag{42}$$

From these values, the corresponding standard errors of the elements of $\overline{b}$ can readily be calculated and the antilogarithms of these values are in each case approximately 1·006. If two standard errors are taken, the antilogarithms are approximately 1·012. Thus a change in the seasonally adjusted series of total consumers' expenditure between consecutive quarters must differ by at least 1·2 per cent from the level of the earlier quarter if it is to be judged significantly different from zero on this test.

12. SEASONAL VARIATIONS IN THE COMPONENTS OF CONSUMERS' EXPENDITURE

In the following example the total of consumers' expenditure is subdivided into twelve component series. Model (ii), that is (24) of section 6 above, was used to analyse these series. The following table shows the seasonal constants in all cases and the year-to-year changes in these constants in the four cases in which these changes are significant.

Commodity group	Constant component of seasonal variation				Year-to-year change in seasonal variation			
	I	II	III	IV	I	II	III	IV
Food	0·958	0·982	1·031	1·030	—	—	—	—
Beer					0·996	1·004	0·997	1·003
Other drink	0·943	0·855	0·916	1·353	—	—	—	—
Tobacco	0·953	0·998	1·053	0·999	—	—	—	—
Housing	0·974	1·022	1·006	0·999	0·998	1·002	1·000	0·999
Fuel and light	1·214	0·964	0·815	1·049	1·002	1·003	0·999	0·996
Household goods	0·972	0·959	0·950	1·129	—	—	—	—
Footwear	0·819	1·090	0·967	1·159	—	—	—	—
Clothing	0·914	1·034	0·909	1·164	—	—	—	—
Travel	0·832	1·040	1·264	0·913	—	—	—	—
Entertainment	1·028	0·969	1·023	0·980	—	—	—	—
Other	0·918	0·986	1·053	1·049	1·002	0·999	0·998	1·002

With this more detailed analysis a second estimate can be made of the seasonally adjusted series for total consumers' expenditure by adding up the adjusted values for the twelve components. By this means a slightly smoother series is obtained. The implied seasonal patterns for the extreme years, 1948 and 1954, are compared with the constant pattern derived from the analysis of total expenditure in the following table.

	Analysis of total	Analysis based on components	
	1948–1954	1948	1954
I	0·944	0·943	0·948
II	0·989	0·990	0·994
III	1·018	1·030	1·013
IV	1·051	1·046	1·059

13. A TEST FOR SERIAL CORRELATION IN THE RESIDUALS OF THE COMPONENT SERIES

It was shown in section 9 that a first-difference model was satisfactory for consumers' expenditure as a whole in the sense that there was no evidence of serial correlation in the observed residuals. In the case of the components, however, two cases must be distinguished. The first arises where there is evidence of significant differences among seasonal trends. In this case the analysis decomposes into a separate analysis for each season and, with the small number of years available, it does not seem worth while to investigate serial correlation.

The second case arises in the remaining eight analyses, in all of which significant constant seasonal variations were found. If the d-test is applied in these cases, it is found that the null hypothesis is sustained in one case, rejected in one case and that the test is indeterminate in the remaining six cases. Fortunately, as has been pointed out by Durbin and Watson [18], it is comparatively simple in the kind of application made here to calculate the variance ratio, F. When this is done for the six doubtful cases it is found that there is no evidence of serial correlation in any of them. From this point of view, therefore, the first-difference model is satisfactory in seven out of eight cases. The results of the tests are brought together in the following table. A single asterisk indicates that the test is inconclusive at the five per cent level of significance; a double asterisk indicates that the null hypothesis, of no serial correlation, is rejected at the 5 per cent level. The notation used is that of Durbin and Watson. In calculating F on the basis of $\mu = 4$ and $\nu = 6$ it is found that $p = 11 \cdot 0225$

and that $q = 12 \cdot 1458$. The table of F is entered with $2q = 24$ and $2p = 22$ degrees of freedom.

Commodity group	d	$F = p(4 - d)/qd$
Food	1·63*	1·32
Other drink	2·79*	0·40
Tobacco	2·35*	0·64
Household goods	1·62*	1·33
Footwear	1·37*	1·81
Clothing	2·33	—
Travel	2·58*	0·50
Entertainment	3·31**	—

14. SUMMARY AND CONCLUSION

This paper contains a brief account of a general method of analysing seasonal variations which can be extended to take account of a wide range of hypotheses about the nature and causes of seasonal variation. The characteristics of this method can be summarized as follows.

First, the models on which the analysis rests are all based on explicit stochastic considerations. Subject to the usual assumptions, the method leads to efficient estimates of the seasonal constants and other parameters and to valid tests of significance.

Second, the first stage in the analysis is descriptive rather than explanatory. It consists of assigning the series to be analysed to one of three classes according as it exhibits no seasonality, a constant seasonality or a systematically changing seasonality. This is accomplished by regression analysis on dummy variables accompanied by an appropriate analysis of covariance.

Third, it is believed that, as a rule, the stochastic term in the model will adequately represent the effect of particular influences operating at different periods and, if this is correct, little is likely to be gained by attempting an *a priori* adjustment of the data in the light of the history of the period. It is recognized, however, that periods will occasionally be encountered when conditions are so abnormal that the observations in these periods are useless and should be discarded.

Fourth, the series to be investigated may have to be transformed before analysis, for one of two kinds of reason. An example of the first kind is that the hypothesis made about seasonality is believed to be more appropriate in relative than in absolute form; if so, the logarithms of the observations rather than the observations themselves should appear as the dependent variable in the analysis. An example of the second kind is that the efficiency of a simple estimation procedure may be substantially increased if the original series is replaced by its first differences.

Fifth, considerable importance attaches to choosing a form of the model which is efficient for estimation purposes. It seems likely that the first-difference model will frequently prove satisfactory, at least in applications to economic time series, but this must depend to some extent on the frequency of the observations.

Sixth, it may be sufficient to stop at the descriptive analysis just outlined. If desired, however, this analysis can be extended to admit the testing of the effect of specific influences and so may take on, in part, a causal character. This is done by testing whether hypothetical specific influences contribute significantly to the residual variance arising from the descriptive analysis. Care in interpreting the results will sometimes be needed with short time series since specific influences may appear as little more than trends and so their effect will already have been largely taken into account in the descriptive analysis. However, it will often be a simple matter to discover when this danger is present.

VII

A GENERALIZATION OF THE
THEOREM OF FRISCH AND WAUGH

1. INTRODUCTION

In [23] Frisch and Waugh showed that in estimating regression constants by the method of least squares it is a matter of indifference whether linear trends are first removed from the determining variables or whether the number of these variables is increased by the addition of time. The purpose of this note is to show that in this context time may be replaced by any subset of determining variables.

2. THE GENERALIZED THEOREM

Consider the linear regression equation

$$y = [X_r \vdots X_s] \begin{bmatrix} b_r \\ \cdots \\ b_s \end{bmatrix} + e \tag{1}$$

in which y is a vector whose elements are the observed values of the dependent variable; X_r is a matrix with r columns each of which contains the observed values of one of the determining variables in the first subset; X_s is a matrix with s columns each of which contains the observed values of one of the determining variables in the second subset; b_r and b_s with r and s elements respectively are vectors of constants; and e is a vector of disturbances. Let b_r^* denote the regression estimator of b_r, derived from (1) by the method of least squares.

Now consider the linear regression equation connecting X_r and X_s, which may be written as

$$X_r = X_s A + U \tag{2}$$

where A, of type $s \times r$, is a matrix of constants and U is a matrix of disturbances and is of type $n \times r$ if there are n sets of observations. Let A^* denote the regression estimator of A obtained by the method of least squares.

Finally let $Z = X_r - X_s A^*$ and consider the linear regression equation

$$y = Zc + v \tag{3}$$

where c is a vector of r constants and v is a vector of disturbances. Let c^* denote the regression estimator of c obtained by the method of least squares.

Then the theorem states that $b_r^* = c^*$.

3. A PROOF OF THE THEOREM

From (1):

$$\begin{bmatrix} b_r^* \\ \cdots \\ b_s^* \end{bmatrix} = \begin{bmatrix} X_r' X_r & \vdots & X_r' X_s \\ \cdots & \vdots & \cdots \\ X_s' X_r & \vdots & X_s' X_s \end{bmatrix}^{-1} \begin{bmatrix} X_r' y \\ \cdots \\ X_s' y \end{bmatrix}$$

$$= \begin{bmatrix} E & \vdots & F \\ \cdots & \vdots & \cdots \\ G & \vdots & H \end{bmatrix}^{-1} \begin{bmatrix} X_r' y \\ \cdots \\ X_s' y \end{bmatrix} \tag{4}$$

say. From the Frobenius-Schur relationship [4], the inverse on the right-hand side of (4) can be written in the form

$$\begin{bmatrix} J^{-1} & \vdots & -J^{-1} F H^{-1} \\ \cdots & \vdots & \cdots \\ -H^{-1} G J^{-1} & \vdots & (I + H^{-1} G J^{-1} F) H^{-1} \end{bmatrix}$$

where I denotes the unit matrix and $J = E - F H^{-1} G$. Thus

$$\begin{aligned} b &= J^{-1}(X_r' y) - J^{-1} F H^{-1}(X_s' y) \\ &= [(X_r' X_r) - (X_r' X_s)(X_s' X_s)^{-1}(X_s' X_r)]^{-1} \\ &\quad \times [(X_r' y) - (X_r' X_s)(X_s' X_s)^{-1}(X_s' y)] \\ &= (X_r' M X_r)^{-1}(X_r' M y) \end{aligned} \tag{5}$$

where $M = [I - X_s(X_s' X_s)^{-1} X_s']$.

From (2),

$$A^* = (X_s' X_s)^{-1}(X_s' X_r) \tag{6}$$

and so

$$\begin{aligned} Z &= X_r - X_s A^* \\ &= M X_r \end{aligned} \tag{7}$$

so that

$$\begin{aligned} c^* &= (Z' Z)^{-1}(Z' y) \\ &= [(X_r' M')(M X_r)]^{-1}(X_r' M y) \\ &= (X_r' M X_r)^{-1}(X_r' M y) \end{aligned} \tag{8}$$

since M is symmetric and idempotent, that is $M = M' = M^2$. A comparison of (5) and (8) completes the proof.

VIII

MODELS FOR DEMAND PROJECTIONS

1. INTRODUCTION

Prasanta Chandra Mahalanobis has enlivened so many branches of research in the course of his scientific life that a contributor to this volume has a large number of possibilities to choose from. The topic I have selected spans two of these branches: national economic planning and the analysis of consumers' behaviour. Consumption is the principal purpose of all economic activity, and it is largely to diminish the gap between technical limits and 'natural' achievements in respect of consumption and its rate of growth that national economic planning is gaining ground all over the world. In drawing up a plan, therefore, a necessary ingredient is a budget of future consumption and we do not need to be fanatical champions of consumers' sovereignty to agree that in drawing up this budget we should take account of probable demands in the future situation.

The models I shall now describe are based on experience with British data, to which they have been applied in [74, 76] with some success. Thanks to the initiative and perseverence of Mahalanobis, the Indian National Sample Survey must by now have accumulated sufficient information to make an application to India practicable. Moreover, it should enable this to be done in an extended form which, by treating different income groups separately, would make it possible to discuss the quantitative effects of future redistributions of income.

In the following section I discuss the approach to demand studies which seems to me most relevant to problems of national planning, listing the factors we must take into account if our models are to help the planner and emphasizing the need for a comprehensive picture of future demand, simple to start with but capable of elaboration as knowledge and experience grow. In section 3 I describe a series of interrelated models which provide the basis for the analysis of consumption in our present work on British economic growth [6]; in section 4 I take up the question of statistical estimation; and in section 5 I give some results from our first attempt to use one of the models for demand projections. The paper ends with a brief conclusion and a list of works cited.

2. STRATEGY AND TACTICS

By the strategy of demand analysis I mean the assessment of what influences on demand we ought to consider and of what form these influences should take in our model. By the tactics of demand analysis I mean the course we ought to follow in passing from an analysis of broad classes, such as food or clothing, to successively finer analyses of their components. Let us begin by looking at these two kinds of problem.

(*a*) *Strategy*. We should, I think, try to take account of the following sets of influences.

(*i*) *Income and prices*. These are the determining variables of classical demand theory. In introducing income we should remember that there is such a thing as saturation, and that at different times and in different places consumers will be much nearer it for some goods than for others. In Britain, for example, the average consumer is nearer to saturation for bread and cereals than he is for meat, and nearer for television sets than he is for motor-cars. In introducing prices we should remember that a change in one price, other things being equal, affects in principle all demands and not simply the demand for the good whose price has changed.

(*ii*) *Tastes*. This kind of variable, so important in the real world, is assumed constant in classical demand theory and for that reason the theory forms an insufficient basis for empirical demand analysis. It is not merely that new goods are continually being introduced, with consequent uncertainty as to their acceptance by consumers. The demand for old goods may change radically: in Britain the taste for alcohol has declined and that for tobacco risen over the last hundred years.

(*iii*) *Adaptation*. Classical demand theory implies that adaptations to a change in circumstances are instantaneous. In fact they are not, particularly in the case of durable goods the acquisition of which frequently faces the consumer with a financing problem. This question may not be of the first importance in making long-term projections, especially in a country where durable goods form a small item in the consumers' budget. It assumes importance either where durable goods form a large item or where we are interested not only in the position five or ten years hence but also in the path by which this position is approached.

(*iv*) *The distribution of income*. The classical theory of demand is largely concerned with the individual consumer and has little to say on the problem of aggregation. In practice it is usual to include in demand analysis a single income variable, the mean of the income distribution. In our work on British economic growth we have not, as yet, gone further than this, but it would be possible to treat households in different ranges of income separately. This would make it possible to discuss the quantitative effects of income redistribution, which may be of particular interest in the context of Indian planning.

(b) *Tactics.* Our ultimate aim is to analyse demand in as much detail as possible. But even if we had data on the fine structure of demand we should almost certainly find it difficult to obtain a consistent picture of changing demand patterns if we were to analyse commodities one at a time. I suggest, therefore, that we should approach our ultimate aim in stages: first, analysing the main categories of demand such as food, clothing, housing, transport, etc.; second, analysing the main components of these categories such as cereals, meat, fats, vegetables and so on in the case of food; and, finally, analysing the elements of the main components such as bread, flour, biscuits, cakes, cereal products and so on in the case of cereals. By this means we may hope to keep the whole picture in focus and ensure that at each stage our estimates are consistent, a point which is important for realistic planning, where components must add up to totals.

3. SOME COMPUTABLE MODELS

In economics, as in other subjects, we may look to models either for insight or for usable, quantitative results. To be usable, a model must satisfy three criteria: it must provide an acceptable approximation to the process we are studying; it must be capable of application with existing data or data which could be collected for the purpose; and it must be computable, that is, it must be of such a form that its parameters can be estimated by a reasonably objective and efficient method. Economists, who all too often concern themselves exclusively with insight, are apt to relax if their model passes the first test; for the user of their results, the second and third are equally indispensable.

With this in mind I shall now develop a particular model of demand which I have elsewhere [59] called the linear expenditure system. Despite its simplicity it can easily be modified to give a reasonable approximation to the pattern of demand and therefore provides a good point of departure.

(a) *The simple linear expenditure system.* In matrix notation, the equation of this system can be written in the form

$$\hat{p}e = b\mu + Bp \tag{1}$$

In (1), e denotes a vector of quantities demanded, p denotes a vector of the corresponding commodity prices, and $\hat{p}$ denotes a diagonal matrix formed from p so that $\hat{p}e$ denotes a vector of expenditures. The symbol $\mu \equiv p'e$ (in which the prime indicates transposition) denotes total expenditure and b and B denote respectively a vector and a matrix of parameters. If total expenditure is divided between ν commodity groups, then the vectors have ν elements and the matrix is of order ν. Equation (1) expresses the theory that each element of expenditure is a homogeneous linear function of total expenditure and of each of the elements of the price vector.

The number of elements in b and B together are $\nu(\nu + 1)$. However, these cannot all be independent. If we premultiply (1) by the unit row vector, $i' \equiv [1, 1, \ldots, 1]$, we should obtain μ on the right-hand side. Thus $i'b = 1$ and $i'B = [0, 0, \ldots, 0]$. This reduces the number of independent constants to be estimated to $(\nu^2 - 1)$.

This is still a large number: if $\nu = 10$ there are 99 constants to be estimated. Moreover, if we tried to estimate them with the amount of information usually available we could be certain that the results would be highly implausible. The way to overcome this difficulty is to introduce further restrictions on the parameters, and the obvious one is to require that the matrix of elasticities of substitution be symmetric. As applied to the individual consumer, this is the Slutsky condition. It is not strictly applicable to the average consumer because of differences in individual preferences and possible changes in the distribution of income; but I shall ignore this objection. In this case, as shown in [59], B must satisfy the relationship

$$B\hat{p}(I - ib') = (I - bi')\hat{p}B' \qquad (2)$$

If B is to be independent of p, this means that

$$B = (I - bi')\hat{c} \qquad (3)$$

where c denotes a vector of constants. So, with this simplification, the number of independent constants to be estimated is reduced to $2\nu - 1$: with $\nu = 10$ this means 19 constants in place of the 99 mentioned above. Naturally, this simplification is bought at a price: how high this price is, we shall see in a moment.

By combining (1) and (3) we can write

$$\hat{p}e = b\mu + (I - bi')\hat{c}p$$

$$= \hat{p}c + b(\mu - p'c) \qquad (4)$$

We can now see clearly the theory of consumers' behaviour which this system of equations represents and we can interpret the parameters b and c. According to (4), consumers buy quantities, the elements of c, at the current prices and the total cost of this expenditure is $p'c$. The money they have left over, $\mu - p'c$, they devote to the different commodities in proportion to the elements of b. Thus the elements of c can be interpreted as purchases to which the average consumer is committed and the elements of b can be interpreted as the proportions in which he devotes his uncommitted expenditure to the different commodities.

It has been shown elsewhere [59, 62, 78] that this model has a number of properties, some useful, some restrictive. The more important of these are as follows.

(i) The model is associated [24, 54] with an ordinal utility function of the form

$$v = \phi \left[\prod_{\zeta=1}^{\nu} (e_\zeta - c_\zeta)^{b_\zeta} \right] \tag{5}$$

where v denotes total utility and ϕ denotes an arbitrary monotonic function. Thus v is a function of a geometric average of the excesses of actual purchases over the corresponding committed quantities.

(ii) The model is associated [33] with a constant-utility index-number of the cost of living, μ_1^*/μ_0, where μ_1^* takes the form

$$\mu_1^* = p_1'c + (\mu_0 - p_0'c)\pi_b \tag{6}$$

In (6), π_b is a geometric average of the price ratios (period 1 divided by period 0) with the elements of b as weights. Thus the amount of money the average consumer must have in period 1 to enable him to obtain the same utility as in period 0 is equal to the cost of the committed quantities valued at the prices of period 1 plus the uncommitted expenditure of period 0 changed by a geometric index of the price ratios.

(iii) The model can handle only a set of competing commodity groups; it cannot allow for complementary or inferior groups [59].

(iv) The Engel curves connecting e with μ for fixed values of the other variables are linear with intercept $c_\zeta - b_\zeta(p'c)/p_\zeta$ and slope b_ζ/p_ζ.

(v) The ordinary price-quantity demand curves connecting e_ζ with p_ζ for fixed values of the other variables are hyperbolae. With positive c_ζ they cannot be elastic.

(b) *A price-sensitive variant.* The above model takes account only of total expenditure and the price situation. Experience shows that committed expenditure is a large part of the total so that the quantities demanded are not very sensitive to prices. For large commodity groups this is plausible, but clearly it would not be satisfactory in handling a set of close substitutes such as different brands of a given product or the demands for a given product from different sources of supply. In both these cases it seems reasonable to assume a fairly stable commitment to purchase a given amount of the product in total, but one would expect the allegiance to a particular brand or source to be sensitive to relative prices.

If we return to (2) we can see that this kind of situation can be accommodated in the model. The symmetry of this equation would not be affected if we replaced $\hat{c}$ in (3) by $\hat{c} + \hat{p}D$ where $D = D'$. In this case we should replace (4) by

$$\hat{p}e = b\mu + (I - bi')(\hat{c} + \hat{p}D)p$$
$$= \hat{p}(c + Dp) + b[\mu - (c' + p'D)p] \tag{7}$$

The addition of D without any further restrictions than the condition of symmetry would add $\nu(\nu+1)/2$ parameters to the system, making in all $(\nu^2 + 5\nu - 2)/2$ or, with $\nu = 10$, 74. Some simplification is therefore desirable, and one might approach the problem as follows.

Let us consider D as made up of three components: a constant scalar, λ say, which represents the importance of price differences in effecting substitutions; a scalar, varying from year to year, which ensures the correct dimensionality of D, say the inverse of the weighted arithmetic average of prices, $i'c/p'c$; and a set of elements which reflect the transfer potential between the brands or sources. For example, with three commodities we might write

$$D = \frac{\lambda i' c}{p' c} \begin{bmatrix} -c_1(c_2 + c_3) & c_1 c_2 & c_1 c_3 \\ c_2 c_1 & -c_2(c_1 + c_3) & c_2 c_3 \\ c_3 c_1 & c_3 c_2 & -c_3(c_1 + c_2) \end{bmatrix} \tag{8}$$

where $c = \{c_1 c_2 c_3\}$. In this form D is not only symmetric but $Di = D'i = \{0\,0\,0\}$. Thus, if $p_1 = p_2 = p_3$, the term Dp in (7) disappears and we return to (4). If p_1 rises in relation to p_2 and p_3, then the first element of Dp is negative and the second and third elements are positive and together equal in magnitude but opposite in sign to the first element. Thus the effect of a rise in p_1 relative to p_2 and p_3 is to transfer part of the total existing commitment from brand or source 1 to brands or sources 2 and 3. At the same time there is a change in uncommitted expenditure, but this is likely to be small.

This variant involves only one additional parameter, giving 20 in all for $\nu = 10$. I have not experimented with this model but I think it might be useful in analysing the demand for a product which may come from many sources such as home production and imports from different regions abroad.

(c) *The introduction of changes in tastes.* Let us now return to the model set out in (4). Bearing in mind the meaning of b and c it is to be expected that these parameters will change over time, mainly because a rising standard of living will lead to higher levels of commitments and to a redistribution of uncommitted expenditure over the different commodities. This is an important aspect of changes in taste and can be represented by making b and c functions of predetermined variables. In the simplest case we can make them functions of time, in which case for year θ we have

$$b_\theta = b^* + b^{**} \theta \tag{9}$$

and

$$c_\theta = c^* + c^{**} \theta \tag{10}$$

If b and c in (4) are replaced by the expressions in (9) and (10), we have $2(2\nu - 1)$ independent constants, or 38 if $\nu = 10$. The reason is that in (9) the additivity condition $p'c \equiv \mu$ requires that $i'b^* = 1$ and $i'b^{**} = 0$.

As indicated in [76], this model works reasonably well and could be made to work better if the linear trends in (9) and (10) were replaced by more complicated trends. It is a simple matter to introduce quadratic trends and this will allow for tendencies to accelerate or decelerate. Such a modification yields a better fit but is not ideal, since an accelerating trend can hardly continue indefinitely and a decelerating trend can hardly be expected to become negative. Positively skewed sigmoid trends would probably be best from an economic point of view but I do not know how these could be fitted.

(d) A link with budget studies. In [76], the model consisting of (4), (9) and (10) was used to analyse consumers' expenditure in Britain, divided into eight groups, over the period 1900–1960. Fourteen war years were omitted and so $8 \times 47 = 376$ observations were available to determine $2 \times 15 = 30$ independent constants.

Had regular budget studies been available over the period, an attempt could have been made to obtain from them extraneous estimates of the b_θ. We can see from (4), (9) and (10) that the elasticity at time θ, $H_{\zeta\theta}$ say, of expenditure on commodity ζ with respect to total expenditure, is given by

$$H_{\zeta\theta} = \frac{\partial(p_{\zeta\theta} e_{\zeta\theta})}{\partial \mu_\theta} \cdot \frac{\mu_\theta}{p_{\zeta\theta} e_{\zeta\theta}}$$

$$= \frac{b_{\zeta\theta} \mu_\theta}{p_{\zeta\theta} e_{\zeta\theta}}$$

$$= \frac{\partial e_{\zeta\theta}}{\partial \mu_\theta} \cdot \frac{\mu_\theta}{e_{\zeta\theta}} \tag{11}$$

From (11) we see that $H_{\zeta\theta}$ is equal to the ratio of the proportion of uncommitted expenditure devoted to commodity ζ at time θ divided by the proportion of total expenditure devoted to that commodity at the same time. We also see that the expenditure elasticity and the quantity elasticity are equal. If therefore we had estimates of $H_{\zeta\theta}$ we could obtain extraneous estimates of $b_{\zeta\theta}$ from the relationship

$$b_{\zeta\theta} = H_{\zeta\theta} \frac{p_{\zeta\theta} e_{\zeta\theta}}{\mu_\theta} \tag{12}$$

In this way we should use the time series to determine only the 2ν parameters necessary to estimate the c_θ. Alternatively, we might attempt a set of maximum likelihood estimates using time series and budgets together [17].

I mention these possibilities because the National Sample Survey might provide the means of applying in India the model obtained by combining (4), (9) and (10). Without long, comparable series one could not base this

7

model solely on annual data. But if the b_θ can be obtained from cross-section data, even ten years should provide enough information to form usable estimates of the c_θ.

That this possibility is worth serious consideration is exemplified by the following example taken from [76]. In Britain a large budget study was conducted in 1938 and, in the case of food, comparable data are also available for several postwar years. Estimates of the elasticity of food expenditure with respect to total expenditure derived from (11) are set out in the following table and compared with the independent estimates derived from budget studies.

TABLE 1   TOTAL EXPENDITURE ELASTICITIES FOR FOOD
IN BRITAIN

Year	$b_{\zeta\theta}$	$\dfrac{p_{\zeta\theta}e_{\zeta\theta}}{\mu_\theta}$	Elasticities from: model	budgets
1900	0·314	0·327	0·96	—
1938	0·166	0·292	0·57	0·59
1955	0·100	0·343	0·29	0·30
1960	0·080	0·309	0·26	0·25

Budget estimates for 1938, reached by different methods, can be found in [3, 83]. Those for 1955 and 1960 are taken from [90]. These results are striking, partly for the close agreement between the two sets of estimates and partly for the ability of the time-series model to show a strong downward trend in the elasticity although the proportion of total expenditure devoted to food was comparatively constant. The explanation of this phenomenon is that committed purchases of food were gradually rising through time while the proportion of uncommitted expenditure devoted to food was falling.

(e) *A disaggregated model.* So far, I have only considered models which relate to the average consumer. In Britain the available time series relate to consumers as a whole and are subdivided only by commodity. But in India, with the National Sample Survey, it is presumably possible to obtain the necessary data for many subgroups of the population: rich and poor, urban and rural, etc. In this way, a very full analysis of consumers' behaviour would be possible.

In deriving Engel curves at different times from budgets it seems best to use a sigmoid curve. For Britain we have obtained good results with the log-normal integral curve proposed in [3]. This curve has a saturation level which is related in a simple way to the consumption and corresponding elasticity at any point on the curve. With regular information from budgets, it is possible to form a time series of saturation levels; from the above relationship it is possible to do this without budget data, as the following example shows.

TABLE 2   FOOD SATURATION IN BRITAIN

(£ 1938 *per head*)

Year	Observed food expenditure	Proportion of saturation	Implied saturation
1900	21·3	0·39	54·7
1913	21·7	0·51	42·6
1924	23·9	0·59	40·5
1938	27·4	0·65	42·2
1950	31·5	0·78	40·7
1960	34·7	0·86	40·4

The most striking feature of this table is the comparative constancy of the saturation level from 1913 onwards. Even the small movements of this level may be economically determined: the relatively high level in 1938, for example, is associated with a relatively low level of food prices. The comparatively high saturation level in 1900 may be due to the less accurate information for the past or to the very simple trends in the parameters b and c which obviously could not be expected to continue indefinitely. On the other hand it may represent a real effect, since it is not hard to imagine a fall in Britain in the notion of what constitutes a desirable amount of food, between the nineteenth and twentieth centuries.

The table is also interesting from the point of view of welfare. A community becomes better off as what it has approximates what it wants. This may happen either because what it has remains constant and what it wants declines or because what it wants remains constant and what it has rises. We see both tendencies at work in Britain in the last two generations.

The figures are also enlightening for the planner. It would be a mistake to regard these indirect estimates of saturation levels as accurate and immutable but at least they tell us something about what people want but do not have.

(*f*) *A model of adaptation.* Let us now return to the simple model of equation (4) and ask how it can be generalized to take account of the fact that adjustments to changing circumstances cannot always be carried out quickly but must, in some cases, be spread over several years. This version of the model is based on [81] and has been developed in [61, 78]. The treatment here is brief but, I hope, sufficient.

We start by dividing the purchases of each commodity into two parts: consumption denoted by an element of u and net investment denoted by an element of v. Thus

$$e \equiv u + v \tag{13}$$

where $e_\zeta = u_\zeta$ and $v_\zeta = 0$ if ζ denotes a perishable good. Consumption is defined by a reducing-balance depreciation formula, so that

$$u \equiv \hat{n}^{-1} s + \hat{m}^{-1} e \tag{14}$$

where s denotes a vector of written-down stocks at the beginning of the year, $\hat{n}^{-1}$ is a diagonal matrix of depreciation rates and $\hat{m}^{-1}$ is a diagonal matrix whose elements depend on n. If ζ denotes a perishable good, then $s_\zeta = 0$ and $n_\zeta = m_\zeta = 1$. If on the other hand ζ denotes a durable good, then $s_\zeta \geqslant 0$ and $1 < n_\zeta < m_\zeta$. Equation (14) thus defines consumption as the depreciation on the initial written-down stock plus the depreciation on the purchases of the year. If these purchases take place uniformly, then it can be shown [81] that

$$m_\zeta = \sum_{\theta=1}^{\infty} (1/\theta n_\zeta^\theta) \bigg/ \sum_{\theta=2}^{\infty} (1/\theta n_\zeta^\theta) \tag{15}$$

an expression which converges rapidly to $2n_\zeta - 1/3$ as n_ζ increases.

Adaptation is allowed for by relating net investment to the difference between the initial stock, s, and a desired stock, s^*, at present unspecified. If the relationship is in all cases one of proportionality then we can write

$$v = \hat{r}(s^* - s) \tag{16}$$

where r_ζ is the proportion of the discrepancy $s_\zeta - s_\zeta$ which is removed in a year, and so can be interpreted as an adjustment rate.

In equilibrium, consumption, u^*, is proportional to the stock, s^*, and net investment, v^*, equals 0. Accordingly,

$$u^* = (1 - \hat{m}^{-1})^{-1} \hat{n}^{-1} s^* = \hat{k} s^* \tag{17}$$

say. By combining (14), (16) and (17), we can see that

$$u = \hat{r}^* u^* + (I - \hat{r}^*) \hat{k} s \tag{18}$$

where $r^* \equiv \hat{n} \hat{m}^{-1} r$. It can be shown [81] that

$$\lim_{n_\zeta \to 1} k_\zeta s_\zeta = E^{-1} e_\zeta \tag{19}$$

where $E^\theta e_\zeta(\tau) \equiv e_\zeta(\tau + \theta)$. Thus the whole system can be written as

$$u = \hat{r}^* u^* + (I - \hat{r}^*) x \tag{20}$$

and so

$$e = \hat{r}^* \hat{m} u^* + (I - \hat{r}^* \hat{m}) x = \hat{r} \hat{n} u^* + (I - \hat{r} \hat{n}) x \tag{21}$$

where $x_\zeta = [m_\zeta / n_\zeta (1 - m_\zeta)] s_\zeta$ if ζ is durable and $x_\zeta = E^{-1} e_\zeta$ if ζ is perishable.

The final step is to replace u^* in (20) and (21) by an observable expression. Thus let

$$\hat{p}u^* = b\mu + (I - bi')\hat{c}p \tag{22}$$

so that

$$\hat{p}u = \hat{r}^* b\mu + \hat{r}^*(I - bi')\hat{c}p + (I - \hat{r}^*)\hat{p}x \tag{23}$$

from (20) and (22), and

$$\hat{p}e = \hat{r}\hat{n}b\mu + \hat{r}\hat{n}(I - bi')\hat{c}p + (I - \hat{r}\hat{n})\hat{p}x \tag{24}$$

from (21) and (22).

This model enables us to distinguish between long and short-term responses. Thus from (22) and (24),

$$\frac{\partial e}{\partial \mu} = \hat{r}\hat{n}\frac{\partial u^*}{\partial \mu} \tag{25}$$

and so, if $\hat{r}\hat{n} = I$, the vector of short-term responses is equal to the vector of long-term responses and, in fact, we have returned to the model given by (4). But any component of $\hat{r}n$, say $r_\zeta n_\zeta$, may be $\leqq 1$, and so the corresponding short-term response may be $\leqq$ the long-term response.

Given n, the model expressed by (24) involves $3\nu - 1$ parameters. As we shall see in the next section, the adding-up theorem can no longer ensure that $i'b = 1$ when the parameters are fitted by the simple method of least squares and so it is necessary to introduce an undetermined multiplier to ensure that this condition is fulfilled.

(*g*) *The analysis of subgroups.* In principle there is no limit to the number of groups among which total consumption is divided in any of the preceding models provided that each group is a substitute for every other. In practice, however, it may be impossible to carry out the calculations involved if the number of groups is large and so it may be necessary to analyse first the main groups and then their components. This can be done because the linear expenditure system is decomposable, as can be seen in what follows.

Consider a group, j say, of the complete system. The equation for this group can be written as

$$\hat{p}_j e_j = \hat{p}_j c_j + b_j(\mu - p'c) \tag{26}$$

where the suffix j denotes that the vector to which it is attached contains elements relating only to group j. If we premultiply (26) by i' we obtain

$$p'_j e_j = \mu_j = p'_j c_j + i'b_j(\mu - p'c) \tag{27}$$

so that

$$\mu - p'c = (i'b_j)^{-1}(\mu_j - p'_j c_j) \tag{28}$$

If we substitute for $\mu - p'c$ from (28) into (26) we obtain

$$\hat{p}_j e_j = \hat{p}_j c_j + b_j(i'b_j)^{-1}(\mu_j - p'_j c_j) \tag{29}$$

From an analysis of the main groups we can obtain estimates of $i'b_j$ and $i'c_j$. From an analysis of the components of group j we can obtain estimates of c_j and $b_j(i'b_j)^{-1}$. We can thus estimate b and c for the whole system.

(h) *A link with the consumption function.* The linear expenditure system enables us to relate expenditure on individual categories to total expenditure. If we could relate total expenditure to disposable income, that is income after taxes, we could relate expenditure on individual categories to disposable income. Following [82] I shall now show how this can be done in a way which links up with recent developments of the consumption function.

Let us denote real expenditure by ϵ, real disposable income by ρ and real wealth by ω; and let us divide each of these into a permanent and a transient component, denoted respectively by the suffixes 1 and 2. These components are not observable, but I shall make the assumption that a change in the permanent component of income is a constant proportion, λ say, of the excess of this year's observed income over last year's permanent component. I shall also make an identical assumption for wealth. Thus

$$\varDelta^* \rho_1 = \lambda(\rho - E^{-1}\rho_1) \tag{30}$$

and

$$\varDelta^* \omega_1 = \lambda(\omega - E^{-1}\omega_1) \tag{31}$$

where the operator E has the same meaning as before and $\varDelta^* \equiv (1 - E^{-1})$.

Let us now assume that the permanent component of expenditure, ϵ_1, is a homogeneous linear function of the permanent components of income and wealth,

$$\epsilon_1 = \alpha_1 \omega_1 + \beta_1 \rho_1 \tag{32}$$

say, and that the transient component of expenditure, ϵ_2, is a homogeneous linear function of the transient component of income,

$$\epsilon_2 = \beta_2 \rho_2 \tag{33}$$

From (30) through (33) it follows that

$$\epsilon = \alpha_1 \omega_1 + \beta_1 \rho_1 + \beta_2 \rho_2$$
$$= \alpha_1 \lambda \omega + \beta_1 \lambda \rho + \beta_2 (1 - \lambda)\varDelta^* \rho + (1 - \lambda) E^{-1} \epsilon \tag{34}$$

In (34), ϵ is expressed in terms of observable variables and the parameters can be estimated without ambiguity.

Let us denote the consumers' price index by $\pi = \mu_1^*/\mu_0$ in the symbolism of subsection (a.ii) above, and let us identify total committed expenditure,

$p'c$, with the permanent component of expenditure expressed in money terms, $\pi\epsilon_1$. Then

$$p'c = \pi\epsilon_1 = \pi(\alpha_1\omega_1 + \beta_1\rho_1)$$

$$= \pi\lambda\left[\alpha_1 \sum_{\theta=0}^{\infty}(1-\lambda)^\theta E^{-\theta}\omega + \beta_1 \sum_{\theta=0}^{\infty}(1-\lambda)^\theta E^{-\theta}\rho\right] \qquad (35)$$

from (30) through (32). We can now rewrite (4) as

$$\hat{p}e = \hat{p}c + b[\pi(\epsilon - \epsilon_1)] = \hat{p}c + b(\pi\epsilon_2) \qquad (36)$$

This is equivalent to saying that the expenditure on each class of commodity is a homogeneous linear function of the price index of that class and of the current value of the transient component of total expenditure. In this formulation, the elements of b and c can be estimated from a set of simple regressions on two variables. If (35) holds, then these estimates satisfy the constraint $i'b = 1$.

From (36) we can express the expenditure on each class in terms of prices and of the current values of present and past incomes. Thus

$$\hat{p}e = \hat{p}c + \pi\alpha_2 b\left[(1-\lambda)\rho - \sum_{\theta=1}^{\infty}(1-\lambda)^\theta E^{-\theta}\rho\right] \qquad (37)$$

I do not know how this model works out in practice beyond the fact that, for Britain, (34) seems to give fairly satisfactory results.

4. STATISTICAL ESTIMATION

The models we are using in our present work on the British economy are those given by (4), (9) and (10) on the one hand and by (24) on the other. In both cases the parameters can be estimated by an iterative two-stage least-squares procedure. In the first case the adding-up theorem ensures that the constraint $i'b = 1$ is satisfied; in the second case it does not. I will now give a proof of the adding-up theorem and then describe the two methods of estimation.

Nicholson [40] propounded an adding-up theorem of considerable value in regression analysis. In its general form, this theorem states that if a set of variables subject to a linear constraint is made to depend linearly on one of their numbers and on any other variables whatsoever, then the least-squares regression estimator will be such that the linear constraint is satisfied by the regression estimates which will equal the true value in the case of the included variable.

This theorem can be proved as follows. Let Y, of type $\tau \times (\nu + 1)$ denote a set of τ observations on $\nu + 1$ variables such that

$$Ya = \{0, 0, \ldots, 0\} \qquad (38)$$

where a is a vector of $\nu + 1$ constants. As an example, consider the regression on total expenditure of expenditures on individual groups of commodities. If the first column of Y represents total expenditure and the remaining columns represent group expenditures, then $a = \{-1, 1, \ldots, 1\}$ indicating that the group expenditures add up to the total. If the variables in Y are regressed on a set of variables in X, we can write the regression equation as

$$Y = XB + W \tag{39}$$

where B is a matrix of regression coefficients and W is a matrix of disturbances. The regression estimator, B^*, obtained by the method of least squares, is

$$B^* = (X'X)^{-1} X' Y \tag{40}$$

Estimates for any period θ can be written as

$$Y_\theta^{*'} = X_\theta' B^* \tag{41}$$

where $Y_\theta^{*'}$ and X_θ' are row vectors whose elements are the values for period θ of the variables appearing in Y and X. Substituting for B^* from (40) into (41) and post-multiplying by a, we obtain

$$Y_\theta^{*'} a = X_\theta'(X'X)^{-1} X' Ya = 0 \tag{42}$$

from (38). Thus the regression estimates satisfy the same constraint as the observations. If the first column of Y, total expenditure in the example, is the same as the first column of X, then the first column of B^* is $\{1, 0, \ldots, 0\}$ and so the constraint is satisfied by the true value of total expenditure and the regression estimates of its components.

Let us now turn to the two estimation procedures, which I shall call method 1 and method 2.

Method 1. The problem is to estimate the parameters b^*, b^{**}, c^* and c^{**} in the model given by (4), (9) and (10). We begin by guessing values of b^* and b^{**} which I shall denote by b_0^* and b_0^{**}. We then form a vector of type $\nu \times 1$, y_θ say, as follows

$$y_\theta \equiv \hat{p}_\theta e_\theta - (b_0^* + \theta b_0^{**}) \mu_\theta \tag{43}$$

We also form a matrix of order ν, Y_θ say, as follows

$$Y_\theta \equiv [I - (b_0^* + \theta b_0^{**}) i'] \hat{p}_\theta \tag{44}$$

Apart from a random element, y_θ and Y_θ are connected by the relationship

$$y_\theta = [Y_\theta \vdots \theta Y_\theta] \begin{bmatrix} c^* \\ \cdots \\ c^{**} \end{bmatrix} \tag{45}$$

If we now define

$$y \equiv \{y_1, y_2, \ldots, y_\tau\} \tag{46}$$

and
$$Y \equiv \{Y_1, Y_2, \ldots, Y_\tau\} \tag{47}$$

we can write, apart from a random element,

$$y = Xg \tag{48}$$

where $X \equiv [Y \vdots \theta Y]$ and $g \equiv \{c^* \vdots c^{**}\}$. The least-squares estimator, g_1, of g is

$$g_1 = (X'X)^{-1} X'y \tag{49}$$

Given g, we can form a vector of type $\nu \times 1$, w_θ say, as follows

$$w_\theta \equiv \hat{p}_\theta[e_\theta - (c_1^* + \theta c_1^{**})] \tag{50}$$

and a matrix of order ν, W_θ say, as follows

$$W_\theta \equiv [\mu_\theta - \hat{p}_\theta'(c_1^* + \theta c_1^{**})] I \tag{51}$$

It will be noticed that W_θ is a scalar matrix. Apart from a random element, w_θ and W_θ are connected by the relationship

$$w_\theta = [W_\theta \vdots \theta W_\theta] \begin{bmatrix} b^* \\ \cdots \\ b^{**} \end{bmatrix} \tag{52}$$

so that if we define

$$w \equiv \{w_1, w_2, \ldots, w_\tau\} \tag{53}$$

and

$$W \equiv \{W_1, W_2, \ldots, W_\tau\} \tag{54}$$

we can write, apart from a random element,

$$w = Zh \tag{55}$$

where $Z \equiv [W \vdots \theta W]$ and $h \equiv \{b^* \vdots b^{**}\}$. The least-square estimator, h_1, of h is

$$h_1 = (Z'Z)^{-1} Z'w \tag{56}$$

Given h, we can return to (45), replace b_0^* and b_0^{**} by b_1^* and b_1^{**} and calculate the next approximation $g_2 \equiv \{c_2^* \vdots c_2^{**}\}$ of g. If we continue in this way until the estimates cease to change, we shall have reached a solution.

In estimating h, since W_θ is a diagonal matrix, the system of equations breaks down into ν separate equations. At the same time the adding-up theorem ensures that $i'b^* = 1$ and $i'b^{**} = 0$ for the estimated values of b^* and b^{**}. In estimating g, on the other hand, since Y_θ is not a diagonal matrix, the ν equations all contribute to giving a single, average estimator of g.

This method is laborious and probably impracticable without electronic computing equipment. The example in [76] involved eight consumption groups observed in each of forty-seven years. Twelve complete cycles were needed to obtain a reasonable degree of convergence and the number of operations involved was of the order of twelve million. Some of the results have been given above. We are now working on a variant with quadratic trends which seems likely to give even better results. The computing scheme is essentially the same as that set out above.

Two main problems have to be faced in applying this method. First, we have assumed that b_0^* is equal to the vector of average expenditures on the different commodity groups and that $b_0^{**} = 0$. Our test of sufficient convergence is that $i'|\Delta c^*| \leqslant 10^{-4}$ and since we stop the calculations when this condition is satisfied, we cannot be certain that the process really is converging to values close to our final estimates though we may be fairly confident that the process does in fact converge [72]. In two-dimensional problems it is often found that convergence requires that the initial estimates lie in a certain region. Sometimes it is possible to specify this region. I do not know of any results which would be helpful in the present case.

Second, in applying simple, rather than generalized, least squares, it is necessary to assume the usual scalar variance matrix for the disturbances. This is not very plausible since some commodity groups are much smaller than others and, as time goes on, prices rise and recent expenditure levels are substantially larger than those of the past. The results, however, do not indicate markedly bad fits for small groups or for early periods and, accordingly, we have not so far attempted a generalized treatment.

Method 2. The problem here is to estimate the elements of r, b and c in (24), it being assumed that the elements of n are given. Since the adding-up theorem cannot help us in this case we must impose the condition that $i'b = 1$.

We begin by guessing values of r and b, which I shall denote by r_0 and b_0. We then form a vector of type $\nu \times 1$, y_θ say, as follows

$$y_\theta \equiv \hat{p}_\theta[e_\theta - (I - \hat{r}_0 \hat{n}) x_\theta] - \hat{r}_0 \hat{n} b_0 \mu_\theta \tag{57}$$

We also form a matrix of order ν, X_θ say, as follows

$$X_\theta \equiv \hat{r}_0 \hat{n}(I - b_0 i') \hat{p}_\theta \tag{58}$$

As with method 1, let $y \equiv \{y_1, y_2, \dots, y_\tau\}$ and let $X \equiv \{X_1, X_2, \dots, X_\tau\}$. Then apart from a random element we can write

$$y = Xc \tag{59}$$

whence the least-squares estimator, c_1 say, of c is

$$c_1 = (X'X)^{-1} X'y \tag{60}$$

Now let us define

$$w_\theta \equiv \hat{p}_\theta(x_\theta - c_1) \tag{61}$$

$$Z_\theta \equiv (\mu_\theta - p'_\theta c_1) I \tag{62}$$

and

$$\hat{z}_\theta \equiv \hat{n}^{-1} \hat{p}_\theta (\hat{x}_\theta - \hat{e}_\theta) \tag{63}$$

Also, let $w \equiv \{w_1, w_2, \ldots, w_\tau\}$, $Z \equiv \{Z_1, Z_2, \ldots, Z_\tau\}$ and $\hat{z} = \{\hat{z}_1, \hat{z}_2, \ldots, \hat{z}_\tau\}$. Then apart from a random element we can write

$$w = [Z \vdots \hat{z}] \begin{bmatrix} b \\ \cdots \\ \hat{r}^{-1} i \end{bmatrix} \tag{64}$$

and this must be solved subject to $i'b = 1$. If λ denotes an undetermined multiplier, the normal equations are

$$\begin{bmatrix} Z'w \\ \cdots \\ \hat{z}w \\ \cdots \\ 1 \end{bmatrix} = \begin{bmatrix} Z'Z \vdots Z'\hat{z} \vdots i \\ \cdots \vdots \cdots \vdots \cdots \\ \hat{z}Z \vdots \hat{z}^2 \vdots 0 \\ \cdots \vdots \cdots \vdots \cdots \\ i' \vdots 0 \vdots 0 \end{bmatrix} \begin{bmatrix} b \\ \cdots \\ \hat{r}^{-1} i \\ \cdots \\ \lambda \end{bmatrix} \tag{65}$$

from which the required estimates can be made. If we now replace r_0 and b_0 by r_1 and b_1 in (59), we can calculate the next approximation, c_2 say, of c. As before, we continue until the successive estimates cease to change.

This method is subject to much the same comments as method 1: it gives interesting results but it is laborious and converges slowly. No doubt the slow convergence is at least partly due to the general interdependence of economic phenomena coupled with the small samples which the analyst of economic time series is forced to work with. If cross-section data could be combined with time series in estimating the parameters of these models, the procedure would not only be greatly simplified but much less information would be required from the time series.

5. AN EXAMPLE OF DEMAND PROJECTIONS

The models and methods I have been describing have been developed for use in a model of economic growth which has been described in [6] and is being elaborated in further papers in the same series. I shall now describe the method of demand projection and illustrate it by some provisional results for 1970, set out in greater detail in [76].

In using the model consisting of (4), (9) and (10) for purposes of projection, five steps are involved.
(i)   We calculate b_θ and c_θ for $\theta = 10$, that is for 1970.
(ii) We calculate p_θ for $\theta = 10$. Eventually these prices will emerge as shadow prices worked out in the general model, but those shown below are simply the result of extrapolating exponential trends fitted to data for 1950 through 1960.
(iii) We calculate μ_{10}^* from

$$\mu_{10}^* = p_{10}' c_{10} + (\mu_0 - p_0' c_{10}) \pi_{b_{10}} \tag{66}$$

This equation is the same as (6) with b and c put at their 1970 values. Accordingly, μ_{10}^{*} represents the amount of money which would be needed by the average consumer of 1970, faced initially with the total expenditure and price structure of 1960, to feel equally well off under the price conditions of 1970.

(iv) We calculate $\mu_{10} = \mu_{10}^{*}e^{10\rho}$ where ρ denotes the instantaneous rate of growth in real consumption per head that we wish to consider between 1960 and 1970.

(v) We calculate e_{10} from (4), replacing b, c, p and μ by b_{10}, c_{10}, p_{10} and μ_{10}.

The original calculations were made with eight commodity groups including two very small ones, communications and entertainment. I have here reduced the number to six, combining communications with transport and entertainment with other. The results could be presented in many ways; here I shall select three of them.

Table 3 shows the change from 1970 in the average consumption of each of the six groups of commodities for different values of ρ.

TABLE 3   PROJECTED CONSUMPTION LEVELS FOR BRITAIN
IN 1970

(*Observed levels in* 1960 = 1·00)

	$\hat{e}_0^{-1}e_{10}$ for different values of ρ		
Commodity groups	0·020	0·030	0·040
Food	1·10	1·11	1·13
Clothing	1·43	1·72	2·04
Household	1·25	1·40	1·56
Transport and communication	1·39	1·67	1·98
Drink and tobacco	1·14	1·23	1·34
Other	1·34	1·54	1·76
Total	1·24	1·39	1·54

We can see from this table that the projections for food and for drink and tobacco are well below the average but that food hardly rises at all with ρ, whereas drink and tobacco rise considerably. At the same time the category 'household' almost exactly keeps pace with the average. Finally, the remaining three categories start above the average and rise more than it does.

Table 4 shows the composition of consumption and of expenditure in 1970 for different values of ρ compared with the composition in 1960.

In this table, the consumption figures are expenditures valued throughout at 1938 prices. The left-hand side of the table shows quite marked

TABLE 4   COMPOSITION OF CONSUMPTION AND EXPENDITURE IN
BRITAIN: 1960 AND 1970

(*Percentages*)

Commodity groups	Consumption				Expenditure			
		1970 for different values of ρ				1970 for different values of ρ		
	1960	0·020	0·030	0·040	1960	0·020	0·030	0·040
Food	29·4	26·0	23·7	21·6	30·9	31·0	28·5	26·2
Clothing	9·8	11·3	12·1	12·9	10·0	9·4	10·1	10·9
Household	23·4	23·6	23·6	23·7	21·0	22·1	22·4	22·6
Transport and communication	12·5	14·0	15·1	16·1	10·7	13·2	14·3	15·3
Drink and tobacco	9·7	8·9	8·7	8·4	13·2	9·6	9·4	9·2
Other	15·1	16·3	16·9	17·3	14·2	14·7	15·3	15·8
Total	100·0	100·0	100·0	100·0	100·0	100·0	100·0	100·0

shifts in the proportions, especially for high values of ρ. The percentages on the right-hand side show smaller shifts between 1960 and 1970; indeed for $\rho = 0·020$, approximately the normal peace-time growth rate over the last half century, the two sets of figures are very similar except that the positions of the transport group and the drink and tobacco group are interchanged. The total expenditure elasticities vary slightly with ρ and would also vary if the assumption about relative prices were changed. In the case of food, this elasticity, on the assumptions made, works out at about 0·15 in 1970.

These results should be regarded as little more than an illustration. The price projections are crude, nothing more in fact than extrapolations of past trends designed to make this illustration possible. The trends in b and c are linear, the simplest possible form. No attempt has yet been made to subdivide the commodity groups into components or to discuss the results obtained with producers or distributors. Nevertheless I think these first results justify the use and development of the models described in this paper and suggest that they might fruitfully be applied to other countries as well as to Britain.

6.   CONCLUSIONS

In concluding this description of our work on demand projections, I should like to explain the links with other forms of demand analysis and the way in which I think it should be developed and used.

First, the models I have described are intended to give a plausible approximation to the changing pattern of demand, in which account is taken both of responses to income and prices and also of changes in tastes. A recognition that relationships do change seems to me essential in econometric work designed to help in planning our future. Indeed it is essential to all econometric work which aspires to being more than a numerical branch of economic history.

Second, the models are intended to be used in conjunction with a general model of economic growth which deals with such matters as production, accumulation and foreign trade as well as with consumption. The emphasis is, therefore, on consistency and manageability. No doubt, for certain commodities better approximations could be achieved, but the range that could be covered in this way is limited and it would be impossible to build a general model of consumption out of them. At present there is a need for broad, comprehensive models and for detailed studies of individual components. We must try to find methods of combining them.

Finally, results of the kind presented here, even if greatly elaborated and improved, should be regarded primarily as a basis for discussion with people of practical experience who may be able to bring additional knowledge to bear on conclusions which, with our best endeavours, are based on simple assumptions and general tendencies. We need not despair on this account. Each part of the practical world knows far more about its little corner than we do, but it does not possess a general picture and, by itself, has no means of reaching one. The task of the econometrician, in my opinion, is first to work out a detailed quantitative statement of future demand, supply or whatever it may be, in a form in which outside knowledge can be brought to bear on it, and then to reconstruct a coherent statement after the initial coherence has been destroyed by outside criticism.

IX

CONSUMERS' WANTS AND EXPENDITURES: A SURVEY OF BRITISH STUDIES, 1945–1961*

1. INTRODUCTION

The purpose of this paper is to give a brief survey of information about consumers' wants and expenditures in Britain, accompanied by a full bibliography. This is a very large subject, and I have therefore confined myself mainly to statistical and econometric studies undertaken since the war and have only considered theoretical writings if they are associated with empirical work. The resulting paper is, accordingly, little more than a systematic introduction to the bibliography; it provides an account of sources of information and of topics studied but it does not provide even a summary of the results obtained.

2. DATA: TIME SERIES

(*a*) *Up to 1938.* For the years 1900–1938, data on consumers' prices, quantities and expenditures are given in the series of *Studies in the National Income and Expenditure* edited by Stone. For the period 1900–1919, estimates made by Prest and Adams were given in [*152*]. For the period 1920–1938, estimates for food, drink and tobacco, rent, rates and water charges, and fuel and light, made by Stone and others, were given in [*245*]. Estimates for the remaining categories over these years will appear in a forthcoming volume [*243*] by Stone and Rowe. All these studies contain a detailed account of sources and methods and [*245*] also contains a large number of econometric analyses. Consistent series at current and constant prices for the main categories over the whole period have been compiled from these sources and carried forward to 1955 with the help of official sources (see (*b*) below). These will appear in Mitchell and Deane's *Abstract of Historical Statistics* [*131*]. In [*94*] Jefferys and Walters brought together existing estimates of the main categories of income and expenditure from 1870 to 1952.

* *Note:* In this paper the numbers in square brackets refer to the paper's own bibliography on pp. 107–20.

(*b*) *1938 to date*. For the period since 1938, detailed estimates of prices, quantities and expenditures have been made by the Central Statistical Office. The basic source is the annual *Blue Book* on national income and expenditure [260] which appears each year about September. The sources and methods used in compiling these estimates are given in [261, 282] which should, however, be supplemented by the notes in the later *Blue Books*. Provisional summary estimates are given each year in a White Paper [262] which accompanies the Budget. Quarterly information is given in *Economic Trends* [258]. Some of this information can also be found in the *Annual Abstract of Statistics* [257] and in the *Monthly Digest of Statistics* [259] which also contain series relating to many individual commodities. Reference should also be made to the quarterly Bulletin of the London and Cambridge Economic Service [156] and the National Institute's *Economic Review* [137]. Data for the war years, now somewhat out of date, were published in the *Statistical Digest of the War* [263].

3. DATA: CROSS-SECTION SURVEYS

It is convenient to consider official, university and commercial surveys separately and, at this point, to refer to the very thorough treatment of social survey technique by Moser in [135] and to the account of this branch of research given by Abrams in [1].

(*a*) *Official surveys*. Under this heading reference is made to the National Food Survey, the Ministry of Labour Surveys and the Social Survey.

(*i*) *The National Food Survey*. This survey was started in 1940, and results to 1949 were described in [265]. Since 1952 the Ministry of Agriculture, Fisheries and Food has organized a continuous survey of food purchases and expenditure with the intention of obtaining representative data from the entire population living in households in Great Britain. A sample of 10 000 households is taken each year, and each household submits a complete record of food expenditure and purchases for one week. Detailed analyses of these surveys are published each year [264] in which the households are analysed by such factors as region, social class, household composition and income. In each annual report there is usually some analysis of special interest: in the reports for 1957 and 1958 income elasticities were given for about one hundred foods and in the report for 1958 own-price elasticities for the same foods were given, using the method described by Brown [19].

(*ii*) *The Ministry of Labour Surveys*. Following the recommendations of the Cost of Living Advisory Committee, the Ministry of Labour and National Service carried out a complete expenditure survey of the population living in British households in 1953–1954. This survey covered some 12 000 households, each of which submitted complete records of household and personal expenditures covering consecutive periods of four weeks spread evenly over twelve months. Full analyses of this survey were published in [267], though their present relevance is reduced because of rationing and other restraints due to supply difficulties during the survey period. This survey has been followed up since 1957 by a continuous survey conducted on the same lines, but at the rate of only 4000 households a year [283].

In concluding this section it may be mentioned that details of the Ministry of Labour's 1937–1938 survey, the publication of which was suspended during the war, were published in [266] and more fully as Part III of [150] by Prais and Houthakker.

(*iii*) *The Social Survey.* This official survey unit, which started work during the war, has conducted a very large number of surveys many of which are relevant to the study of consumers' wants and expenditures. Sometimes the results of a survey are published, sometimes they appear, along with other material, in a report issued by the department which commissioned the survey and sometimes they are simply combined with other sources and not made available separately. Information on methods and results can be found in [66] by Gray and Corlett, in [136] by Moss and in [99] by Kemsley and Nicholson. The role of these surveys in making the official estimates of consumers' expenditure is indicated in [261, 282].

(*b*) *University surveys.* Under this heading reference is made to the Oxford Savings Surveys, the Cambridge Survey, the work on low-cost diets carried out over a period of some twenty years by Schulz and some other small surveys.

(*i*) *The Oxford Savings Surveys.* During the 1950s a number of surveys, concerned mainly with income, saving and expenditure on durable goods, were conducted at the Institute of Statistics at Oxford. These are described in a number of papers by Lydall [116–124] and in his book [126]. Other aspects of these important surveys were described by Erritt and Nicholson [46], Hill [78, 80], Hill, Klein and Straw [81], Klein [101, 102], Klein, Straw and Vandome [105], Klein and Vandome [106], Lydall and Dawson [127], and Straw [246, 247].

(*ii*) *The Cambridge Survey.* In 1953–1954 a number of sample surveys were conducted at the Department of Applied Economics, which were intended to provide data for the construction of a set of social accounts of Cambridgeshire. Various aspects of the enquiry into household income and expenditure have been set out by Cole in [27], Cole and Utting in [29, 269, 270] and Utting in [268]. A second enquiry, conducted at Cambridge, into the income, expenditure and saving of old people is described by Cole in [28].

8

(*iii*) *Other surveys*. First among these is the work of Schulz on low-cost diets. These investigations, which form a link with the earlier work of Rowntree on the human needs of labour, have been conducted over a period of some twenty years and have been published in a series of papers [*162–212*] in the *Bulletin of the Oxford Institute of Statistics*. Second, a small-scale survey of consumer expenditure was described by Bellamy and Bowen in [*8*]. Finally, two surveys on the expenditure patterns of students have been published: one, relating to Glasgow, by Pattison in [*144*]; the other, relating to Glasgow and Birmingham, by Harper in [*71*].

(*c*) *Commercial surveys*. A large volume of commercial market research is carried out in Britain, but its results are not generally available to the independent research worker. This is true both of the *ad hoc* enquiries commissioned by individual firms and organizations and of a number of continuous panel enquiries covering both private households and retail outlets.

Reference may be made here to a number of readership surveys [*90, 91, 100, 143, 252*] and to various papers [*2, 39, 42, 43, 216, 274*] relating to market research. In 1950 a new edition of Harrison and Mitchell's *The Home Market* appeared [*74*]. In the last few years the Market Research Society has put out a small duplicated magazine called *Commentary* [*129*]. An organization called Technical Planning Ltd. at present puts out a magazine entitled *Market Research* [*250*].

4. DATA: MISCELLANEOUS

This section is devoted to various sources of information which do not fit conveniently into sections 2 and 3 above.

(*a*) *The development of retail trading*. For a number of years an enquiry was directed by Jefferys at the National Institute of Economic and Social Research into the current conditions and historical development of retail trading in Britain. The results are published in [*93, 95*].

(*b*) *Royal Statistical Society: special reprint series*. For a number of years a series of articles was published in the Society's Journal (Series A) describing the sources and nature of statistical information in some special field. Examples with particular relevance to the present paper are contained in [*6, 36, 38, 112, 128, 145, 219, 275, 276*]. The whole series was brought together in two volumes entitled *The Sources and Nature of the Statistics of the United Kingdom* [*158*].

(*c*) *Other papers, mainly descriptive*. A number of quite disconnected papers are listed below under commodity headings: housing, Bowley [*11*],

Burchardt [24], Moos [133], Nixon [142]; clothing, Ross [157], Wadsworth [273]; durable goods, Dawson [37], Knox [108]; television, Emmett [45]; cinemas, Browning and Sorrell [22]; reading habits, Stuart [248]; newspapers, Wadsworth [272]; transport, Menzler [130], Rudd [159]; doctors and medicine, Gray and Cartwright [64, 65]; life assurance, Johnston and Murphy [97]; saving, Preston [153, 154], Saunders [161].

(d) Which? and the Consumers' Association. This association is an independent, non-profit-making organization that was established to help the consumer by making factual, unbiased information about goods and services available to all. Since the autumn of 1957 it has published its findings in Which? [30]. Apart from the results of various physical and engineering tests, this magazine provides information about the characteristics of different varieties, for example makes of beer, together with the price of a standard quantity of each variety.

5. ANALYSES: TOPICS

(a) Income elasticities and Engel curves. These elasticities have been studied both from time series and from household surveys. This section is concerned with two topics: the form of the Engel curve and the distinction between short- and long-term elasticities.

In [139] Nicholson made a detailed study of working-class expenditure in 1937–1938 using parabolic Engel curves. In [249] Stuvel and James showed, in analysing the demand for food in Holland by means of linear and log-linear Engel curves, that the behaviour of the rich was better approximated by the linear form and that the behaviour of the poor was better approximated by the log-linear form. In [85, 86] Houthakker discussed the form of the Engel curve. In [147] Prais experimented with a number of forms and reached the conclusion that no one form was suitable in all cases: these results were incorporated in [150]. In [4] Aitchison and Brown showed that a log-normal integral form was sufficiently flexible to represent all the commodity groups they studied; these results were also incorporated in [5]. In [58] Fisk showed that a log-logistic form could be substituted for the log-normal integral. This result is not surprising since, in the terminology of biological assay, the last two forms arise from the method of probits and the method of logits. In [233] Stone remarked that a log-logistic Engel curve coupled with an exponential growth of income would give rise to a logistic growth of consumption over time. These last-mentioned forms are of particular interest since the income-elasticity of demand falls from ∞ to 0 as income rises from 0 to ∞. Thus every good starts as a luxury and ends, with rising income, as a necessity. The extension of this analysis to inferior goods (negative income-elasticity) was discussed in [5].

In [240] Stone and Rowe set out a dynamic model of demand which leads to estimates of the short- and long-term elasticities. They found that their long-term elasticities tended to approximate to estimates from survey data and that the short-term elasticities were larger or smaller than the long-term ones according as the ratio of the rate of consumers' adjustment to the depreciation rate is $\leqq 1$; further developments of this model are given in [230, 241, 242, 244]. In [237] Stone and Croft-Murray combined the above dynamic model with Stone's linear expenditure system [226] to provide estimates of short- and long-term income and price elasticities having certain properties of consistency. This model, which gives rise to interesting problems of statistical estimation, is further described and elaborated in [234].

(b) *Price elasticities.* Most of the models described in this paper lead to estimates of price elasticity. For example, in [245] Stone and others gave distributions of the price elasticities of the components of food expenditure and showed that they followed a theoretically acceptable pattern, the own-price substitution elasticities being all effectively negative and the cross elasticities showing more substitutes than complements. In [82] Hirsch brought together estimates for different commodities from a large number of sources. In [237] Stone and Croft-Murray gave estimates of a price substitution matrix which satisfies the Slutsky condition. In [19] Brown showed how the analysis of covariance can be used to extract price elasticities from monthly data on prices and quantities. His detailed analysis of individual foods has been reworked in the reports of the National Food Survey Committee [264], issued in 1960 and 1961.

(c) *Quality elasticities.* With increasing income, a family's expenditure on a particular category of goods tends to rise faster than the corresponding quantity: in other words they improve the quality of what they buy. This effect, the difference between expenditure and quantity elasticities, has been studied by Theil in [251], by Houthakker in [84, 85] and by Houthakker and Prais in [87, 150].

(d) *Changes in tastes and new commodities.* It has usually been the practice to introduce a residual trend into analyses with time series so as to allow for gradual changes in consumers' tastes. In [151] Prest showed that if this is done over a long period, a large part of the observed variation in consumption may come to be attributed to a dummy variable: time. In [50] Farrell showed that part of this residual variation can be attributed to real variables (income and prices) if the demand functions are made irreversible, so that the effect of a rise in a real variable is different from the effect of a corresponding fall. In [288] Stone suggested means whereby the characteristics of the goods available in different periods could be put on a more homogeneous basis and so improve index-number comparisons. In [225] Stone showed the effect of the kind of change discussed here over a period of fifty years but did not apply the method of systematically changing parameters described in [226]. In [230, 237, 240] Stone and others have shown how changes in tastes can in principle be introduced into the dynamic model. Ironmonger has considered a demand model in which utility is a function of wants and these wants are satisfied by goods, the connection being of a possibly changing, technical character. In this way analytical expression can be given to the changing character of goods: tinned and packaged food helps to save labour as well as to provide nutrition. He has also proposed a model on linear programming lines which should prove very useful in dealing with new commodities. Interesting work on the analysis of new commodities has been undertaken in Cambridge by Bain [279, 280] and by Pyatt [281].

The question of tastes, in the sense of discrimination, has been studied from a psychological point of view as, for example, in the work of Bliss [10], Ehrenberg and Shewan [44], Gridgeman [67, 68] and Harper [72, 73].

(e) *Adjustment problems.* Traditional demand analysis is based on a static model of consumers' behaviour in which consumers adjust immediately to changes in circumstances. In fact this is not always true, and in [240] Stone and Rowe set out a dynamic model in which the equilibrium, not the actual, demand is governed by a static equation. This model was originally designed for the analysis of durable goods but can also be applied to perishable goods. It is a true generalization of static demand functions since it reduces to them if the parameters take suitable values. Applications and developments can be found in [230, 234, 237, 241, 242, 244]. The dynamics of consumers' behaviour were discussed by Vandome in [271].

(f) *Family composition and equivalent adult scales.* One of the problems considered by Nicholson in [139] was the expenditure attributable to additional members of the family. This question was also studied by Henderson in [75, 76, 77], by Hajnal and Henderson in [70] and by Kemsley in [98]. In [148] Prais developed an iterative method of computing specific equivalent adult scales and this problem is also discussed in [150]. In [17] Brown set out the interesting consequences of applying the log-normal integral Engel curve to the study of food expenditure in households of different composition. In [12] Brennan and in [59] Forsyth described further studies of the relationship between family size and family expenditure.

(g) *The life cycle.* Income and family responsibility vary with age and the relationship of income to age varies greatly between occupations. This problem, which complicates the analysis of cross-section data, has been studied in [*125*] by Lydall and in [*55*] by Fisher (see also the comment in [*132*]).

(*h*) *The influence of assets.* The importance of the existing stock as a determinant of demand is usually recognized in studies of the demand for durable goods, as in the studies of cars by Farrell in [*52*] and by Cramer in [*33*], and in the dynamic model described in [*240*]. In [*31*] Cramer recast the theory of demand in terms of stocks, in [*32*] he investigated ownership elasticities mainly by reference to Dutch data and in [*35*] he examined a model of the demand for durable goods with the help of data from the 1953 Oxford Savings Survey.

(*i*) *Social class differentials.* In [*245*] Stone and others fitted constant-elasticity Engel curves to data for working-class and middle-class households, allowing for a proportionate difference in their levels of expenditure. In [*150*] this problem was further examined by Prais and Houthakker.

(*j*) *Regional differences.* Even in a relatively homogeneous country like Britain there are noticeable regional differences in income levels. In [*85*] Houthakker and in [*150*] Prais and Houthakker examined certain aspects of regional differences in consumption levels and in [*235*] Stone gave a regional accounting matrix for 1948 based on the unpublished work of Deane.

(*k*) *Rationing and restrictions.* Rationing puts constraints on consumers' choice and in [*255*] the effects of rationing on demand elasticities was investigated by Tobin and Houthakker. In [*88*] they made estimates of the free demand for rationed foods and their work was further discussed and elaborated in [*40, 89, 238*].

(*l*) *Interdependent preferences.* In [*150*] a model involving the interdependence of consumers' preferences was given by Prais and Houthakker following the work of Johnson [*96*].

(*m*) *Forecasting.* Reference has been made, in (*k*) above, to papers on forecasting the free demand for rationed foods, and a brief discussion of forecasting market demand was given by Stone in [*229*]. Although many forecasts of demand must have been made in this period, the number published and discussed are remarkably few. For the purpose of forecasting, the interest of the work outlined in this paper lies mainly in two developments.

The first is that the analytical developments discussed above provide insights into the quantitative importance of many factors which influence the structure of demand. This means that we are improving our understanding of the factors that influence demand and consequently, though there are still unsolved problems and also new situations brought about by the changing character of the goods available, that we are improving our ability to foresee the changing demand patterns of the future. Though inter-country comparisons are only in their infancy, the interesting results obtained, for example, by Clark [26] and by Gilbert and others [62] are noteworthy.

The second is the development of general models of the economic process which are designed specifically to look into the future. In [227] Stone set out a simple national accounting model which was intended to introduce some technical and behavioural constraints into the short term forecasting process known as national budgeting. The statistical aspects of this type of model have been examined by Briggs in [13, 14]. In [107] Klein and others have set out an altogether more sophisticated model, somewhat in the spirit of Tinbergen's econometric model-building, which makes use of quarterly data over the postwar period. In [232] Stone outlined a new model designed to work out the implications of different assumed rates of growth in aggregate consumption. These models are highly ambitious since they make great demands on data, on formulations that must be empirically manageable of all the main relationships in the economic process, and on computing. But by providing a framework of possible economic developments they should assist the making of realistic forecasts of demands for individual categories of consumption good.

6. ANALYSES: COMMODITIES

The object of this section is to indicate the entries in the bibliography which contain analyses of the demand for particular goods. Sources of information have already been dealt with in sections 2, 3 and 4 above.

(a) *Food.* In [245] Stone and others gave analyses for a large number of foods and groups of foods based on annual time series over the years 1920 to 1938 and on family budgets relating to 1937–1939. Earlier reports on this work are contained in [220, 222, 223, 224]. In [150] Prais and Houthakker studied many aspects of the demand for food with the aid of the budgets for 1937–1939. Earlier reports on various aspects of this work are contained in [84, 85, 86, 147, 148]. In [4, 5] Aitchison and Brown gave the empirical results of their log-normal integral Engel curve in which several groups of food are shown separately. This work was based on working-class budgets for 1937–1938. The corresponding analysis by Fisk was given in [58]. Other budgetary analyses of food were given by Nicholson in [139], Quenouille in [155] and Brown in [16, 17]. A budgetary analysis of food in Holland was given by Stuvel and James in [249]. A demand function for food in the United States was given by Tobin in [253]. Inter-country analyses of the demand for food were given by Clark in [26] and by Gilbert and others in [62]. An analysis of the demand for potatoes was given by Lomax in [113]. An analysis of the demand for fish was given by Gorman in [63]. Analyses of the demand for citrus fruits were given by Smyth and Mace in [217] and by Brown and Bain in [20]. A detailed analysis of price elasticities based on short period time series was given by Brown in [19]. Food appeared as a single group in the systems of equations used by Stone and Croft-Murray in [237] and by Leser in [111].

(b) *Drink and tobacco.* In [245] Stone and others gave demand analyses for the components of this group. In [241] Stone and Rowe gave analyses for beer, other alcoholic drinks and tobacco based on postwar time series and compared these results with those based on prewar time series and on budgets. As is well known, budgets are an unreliable source for these items of expenditure and so, while they appeared in some analyses based on budgets, no further reference to these analyses will be made here.

(c) *Housing.* Owing largely to the operation of rent restriction, it is particularly difficult in Britain to study this form of expenditure from time series. It is included however in the major analyses based on budgets [5, 150].

(d) *Fuel and light.* Items in this group are analysed, mainly from time series, in [241, 245] and from budgets in [5, 150]. In [83] Houthakker studied various aspects of the consumption of electricity.

(e) *Clothing.* Analyses for this group were given by Lomax in [114], Bartlett in [7], Stone and Rowe in [240, 241] and Stone and Croft-Murray in [237]. Budgetary analyses were given in [5, 150]. An analysis of the colonial demand for cotton goods was made by Lomax in [115].

(f) *Durable goods.* Analyses for furniture and furnishings and for radio and electrical goods were given by Stone and Rowe in [240, 241, 242, 244]. An analysis for cars was given by Stone and Croft-Murray in [237]. A study of major durables based on the Oxford Savings Survey was given by Cramer in [35]. Other budgetary analyses were given in [5, 150].

(g) *Other goods and services.* Analyses of these items are mainly to be found in studies based on budgets [5, 150]. An analysis of the demand for petrol was given by Cramer in [34].

(h) *Total consumption and saving*. Studies of the aggregate consumption, or saving, function were made by Stone and Rowe in [239], by Klein in [103] and by Fisher in [55]. The last-mentioned study, which used the Oxford Savings Survey to examine various hypothesis, was commented on by a number of writers [56, 60, 61, 69, 79, 104, 132, 160, 256]. Studies based on American data were made by Tobin in [254] and by Brumberg in [23]. A comparison of personal saving in Britain and America was made by Lansing and Lydall in [110]. Spending patterns in Britain and America were discussed by Wright in [278]. An Engel-type demand curve for cash was given by Spraos in [218].

7. ANALYSES: STATISTICAL METHODS

(a) *Regression analysis of time series*. In [245] Stone and others discussed the main problems, serial correlation, errors in variables and in equations, and multicollinearity, which arise when one or other of the assumptions of the basic method of least squares is not satisfied. A fairly full account of work up to 1953 is given there. In recent years the stream of papers on these subjects has continued but, since they belong to the general methodology of statistics, they will not be noticed here. The following sections deal with specific topics having particular relevance to the analysis of demand.

(b) *Covariance analysis*. The use of this technique, which may be regarded as a branch of regression analysis involving dummy variables, in the analysis of family budgets is exemplified in the work of Quenouille [155] and of Stuvel and James [249]. Its use in the analysis of monthly time series is exemplified in the work of Brown [19]. A theoretical paper by Brown [18] is unfortunately only available in mimeographed form.

(c) *Seasonal variations*. In [228] Stone set out a method of analysing time series according to the nature of their seasonal variation which makes use of regression methods and the analysis of variance and covariance.

(d) *Extraneous estimators*. In principle, models can be developed for the joint analysis of data from budgets and time series. In practice, however, as in Stone and others [245], it is more usual to estimate, say, the income elasticity from budgets and use this as an 'extraneous estimator' in an analysis of time series. The properties of such estimators have been set out by Durbin in [41] and, following him, by Stone and others in [245]. Further comments on this method were given by Kuh and Meyer in [109].

(e) *Grouping problems*. It is frequently necessary to use grouped observations in the analysis of family budgets, and many of the problems encountered were discussed by Prais and Aitchison in [149].

(*f*) *Heteroscedasticity.* Given the wide range of observations available in budget studies, the least-squares assumption that errors are distributed with constant variance can hardly be expected to hold. Estimation with heteroscedastic errors was discussed by Prais in [*146*], Prais and Aitchison in [*149*] and Fisher in [*54*]. Another aspect of heteroscedasticity was considered by Aitchison and Brown in [*3*].

(*g*) *Systems of equations.* This heading is used to cover two quite different topics. First, 'simultaneous equation' methods have been relatively little used in Britain for demand analysis. Examples of supply and demand models have already been mentioned [*7, 237*]. Interesting applications, not however to the analysis of consumers' demand in Britain, can be found in the work of Morgan and Corlett [*134*], Bergstrom [*9*] and Fisher [*57*]. Second, models which have as their aim the simultaneous analysis of a complete set of demand equations call for special methods of estimation. A method appropriate to the static version of the linear expenditure system was given by Stone in [*226*] and this was further considered by Stone, Aitchison and Brown in [*236*]. A method for the dynamic version of this system was given by Stone in [*234*] though this has now been superseded by a method, not yet published, which enables a constraint to be put on the sum of the marginal propensities to consume individual commodities. The estimation of the parameters in Leser's system is described in [*111*].

(*h*) *Additivity and aggregation.* It is often desirable to choose a form of function and a method of estimation which ensure that some additive constraint is satisfied. This problem was raised by Nicholson in [*139*] and further discussed by Worswick, Champernowne and Nicholson in [*25, 140, 141, 277*]. A number of aggregation problems in demand analysis were discussed by Farrell in [*51*] and by Stone and others in [*245*].

(*i*) *Equivalent adult scales.* The derivation of specific scales from behavioural relationships was discussed by Prais in [*148*]. The use of electronic equipment for this and other computing problems was described by Brown, Houthakker and Prais in [*21*].

(*j*) *Probits and logits.* In estimating the parameters of sigmoid Engel curves, use is made of methods developed for purposes of biological assay. A general account of these methods is given by Finney in [*53*]. For application to demand analysis, reference should be made to Aitchison and Brown [*4, 5*] and Fisk [*58*].

(*k*) *Programming.* Reference has already been made to the as yet unpublished work of Ironmonger on a method of handling new commodities by means of linear programming methods. An application to the classical least-cost-diet problem was given by Brown in [*15*]. More recent researches by Brown have shown that the highly unrealistic diets which tend to result from an unconstrained application of this method can be radically improved if a weight constraint is put on the diet. The results of a computing programme which traces the curve connecting least-cost and least-weight diets has not yet been published. Some calculations on least-cost diets were given by Newman in [138].

(l) *Factor analysis.* Reference has already been made to the work of Harper [73] on the use of factor analysis in examining complex data on foods and to the work of Gorman on the demand for fish [63]. The use of this method to reduce a large number of series, such as price series, to a small number of independent forms of variation, or to provide weights with which to combine indicators which cannot be combined by value, would seem to be very promising, but the only applications of factor analysis to income and expenditure data seem to be those given by Stone in [221, 231].

8. BIBLIOGRAPHY

This section is devoted to a brief description of three general bibliographies and to a list of works cited.

(a) *General bibliographies.* The International Association for Research in Income and Wealth has from time to time issued in mimeographed form a world-wide annotated bibliography on all topics of interest to the Association. These issues are subsequently collated to cover one or more years and published [92]. So far six printed volumes have appeared, covering publications from 1937 to 1954.

As part of the Royal Statistical Society's bibliographies on mathematical statistics, a group at Cambridge assisted in compiling a bibliography of applications to economics covering the years 1943–1950. These were published by Scott in [213, 214].

Recently, the Food and Agriculture Organization of the United Nations has started to publish an annotated bibliography on demand analysis and projections [47, 48] and a list of institutions dealing with these subjects [49].

(b) *A list of works cited.* Below is a list of the 283 works cited by number in this paper.

1. ABRAMS, Mark Alexander. *Social Surveys and Social Action.* Contemporary Science Books. London, 1951.
2. ABRAMS, Mark Alexander. Technical problems in the I.P.A. readership survey. *The Incorporated Statistician*, vol. 8, no. 2, 1958, pp. 55–66.
3. AITCHISON, J., and J. A. C. BROWN. An estimation problem in quantitative assay. *Biometrika*, vol. 41, pts. 3 and 4, 1954, pp. 338–43.

4. AITCHISON, J., and J. A. C. BROWN. A synthesis of Engel curve theory. *The Review of Economic Studies*, vol. XXII, 1954–1955, pp. 35–46.

5. AITCHISON, J., and J. A. C. BROWN. *The Lognormal Distribution*. Cambridge University Press, 1957.

6. ANON. U.K. tobacco statistics. *Journal of the Royal Statistical Society, Series A (General)*, vol. 113, pt. 4, 1950, pp. 487–508.

7. BARTLETT, M. S. A note on the statistical estimation of supply and demand relations from time series. *Econometrica*, vol. 16, no. 4, 1948, pp. 323–29.

8. BELLAMY, Joyce, and Ian BOWEN. A survey of consumer expenditure. *Yorkshire Bulletin of Economic and Social Research*, vol. 2, no. 1, 1950, pp. 31–62.

9. BERGSTROM, A. R. An econometric study of supply and demand for New Zealand's exports. *Econometrica*, vol. 23, no. 3, 1955, pp. 258–76.

10. BLISS, C. I. Some statistical aspects of preference and related tests. *Applied Statistics*, vol. 9, no. 1, 1960, pp. 8–19.

11. BOWLEY, Marian. The housing statistics of Great Britain. *Journal of the Royal Statistical Society, Series A (General)*, vol. 113, pt. 3, 1950, pp. 396–411.

12. BRENNAN, T. Household structure and family income. *Scottish Journal of Political Economy*, vol. II, no. 2, 1955, pp. 157–62.

13. BRIGGS, F. E. A. On problems of estimation in Leontief models. *Econometrica*, vol. 25, no. 3, 1957, pp. 444–55.

14. BRIGGS, F. E. A. The estimation of regression equations when the independent variables are otherwise related to the dependent variables. *Metroeconomica*, vol. XII, no. 2–3, 1960, pp. 39–57.

15. BROWN, J. A. C. Minimum cost diets. *Ferranti Conference on Linear Programming*, London, 1954 (mimeographed).

16. BROWN, J. A. C. The consumption of food in relation to household composition and income. *Econometrica*, vol. 22, no. 4, 1954, pp. 444–60.

17. BROWN, J. A. C. Economics, nutrition and family budgets. *Proceedings of the Nutrition Society*, vol. 14, no. 1, 1955, pp. 63–70.

18. BROWN, J. A. C. *On the use of covariance technique in demand analysis*. FAO/ECE Study Group on the Demand for Agricultural Products, 1958 (mimeographed).

19. BROWN, J. A. C. Seasonality and elasticity of the demand for food in Great Britain since derationing. *Journal of Agricultural Economics*, vol. XIII, no. 3, 1959, pp. 228–39.

20. BROWN, J. A. C., and A. D. BAIN. Trends in the consumption of citrus fruit in the United Kingdom. *Journal of Agricultural Economics*, vol. XIII, no. 4, 1960, pp. 446–56.

21. BROWN, J. A. C., H. S. HOUTHAKKER, and S. J. PRAIS. Electronic computation in economic statistics. *Journal of the American Statistical Association*, vol. 48, 1953, pp. 414–28.

22. BROWNING, H. E., and A. A. SORRELL. Cinemas and cinema-going in Great Britain. *Journal of the Royal Statistical Society, Series A (General)*, vol. 117, pt. 2, 1954, pp. 133–70.

23. BRUMBERG, R. E. An approximation to the aggregate saving function. *The Economic Journal*, vol. LXVI, no. 261, 1956, pp. 68–72.

24. BURCHARDT, F. A. Working-class housing at economic rents. *Bulletin of the Oxford Institute of Statistics*, vol. 7, no. 4 and 5, 1945, pp. 91–6.

25. CHAMPERNOWNE, D. G. The general form of the adding-up criterion: a rejoinder. *Journal of the Royal Statistical Society, Series A (General)*, vol. 120, pt. 4, 1957, pp. 457–8.

26. CLARK, Colin. World supply and requirements of farm products. *Journal of the Royal Statistical Society, Series A (General)*, vol. 117, pt. 3, 1954, pp. 263–96.

27. COLE, Dorothy E. Field work in sample surveys of household income and expenditure. *Applied Statistics*, vol. V, no. 1, 1956, pp. 49–61.

28. COLE, D. E. The income, expenditure and saving of old people households in Cambridgeshire. *Proceedings of the Fourth Congress, International Association of Gerontology*, 1957.

29. COLE, D. E., and J. E. G. UTTING. Estimating expenditure, saving and income from household budgets (with discussion). *Journal of the Royal Statistical Society, Series A (General)*, vol. 119, pt. 4, 1956, pp. 371–98.

30. CONSUMERS' ASSOCIATION LTD. *Which?* Consumers' Association Ltd., London, since autumn 1957, now monthly.

31. CRAMER, J. S. A dynamic approach to the theory of consumer demand. *The Review of Economic Studies*, vol. XXIV, 1957, pp. 73–86.

32. CRAMER, J. S. Ownership elasticities of durable consumer goods. *The Review of Economic Studies*, vol. XXV, 1957–1958, pp. 87–96.

33. CRAMER, J. S. The depreciation and mortality of motor-cars. *Journal of the Royal Statistical Society, Series A (General)*, vol. 121, pt. 1, 1958, pp. 18–59.

34. CRAMER, J. S. Private motoring and the demand for petrol. *Journal of the Royal Statistical Society, Series A (General)*, vol. 122, pt. 3, 1959, pp. 334–47.

35. CRAMER, J. S. *A Statistical Model of the Ownership of Major Consumer Durables with an Application to some Findings of the 1953 Oxford Savings Survey.* Cambridge University Press, 1962.

36. DANIEL, G. H. Electricity and gas statistics. *Journal of the Royal Statistical Society, Series A (General)*, vol. 113, pt. 4, 1950, pp. 509–30.

37. DAWSON, R. F. F. Ownership of cars and certain durable household goods. *Bulletin of the Oxford Institute of Statistics*, vol. 15, no. 5, 1953, pp. 177–91.

38. DEANE, Marjorie. United Kingdom publishing statistics. *Journal of the Royal Statistical Society, Series A (General)*, vol. 114, pt. 4, 1951, pp. 468–89.

39. DOWNHAM, J. S., and J. A. P. TREASURE. Market research and consumer durables. *The Incorporated Statistician*, vol. 7, no. 3, 1956, pp. 108–17.

40. DOWNIE, J. A note on the demand for food. *The Economic Journal*, vol. LXII, no. 248, 1952, pp. 936–9.

41. DURBIN, J. A note on regression when there is extraneous information about one of the coefficients. *Journal of the American Statistical Association*, vol. 48, no. 264, 1953, pp. 799–808.

42. EHRENBERG, A. S. C. The pattern of consumer purchases. *Applied Statistics*, vol. 8, no. 1, 1959, pp. 26–41.

43. EHRENBERG, A. S. C. A study of some potential biases in the operation of a consumer panel. *Applied Statistics*, vol. 9, no. 1, 1960, pp. 20–7.

44. EHRENBERG, A. S. C., and J. M. SHEWAN. A reliability study of sensory assessments. *Applied Statistics*, vol. 8, no. 3, 1959, pp. 186–95.

45. EMMETT, B. P. The television audience in the United Kingdom. *Journal of the Statistical Society, Series A (General)*, vol. 119, pt. 3, 1956, pp. 284–311.

46. ERRITT, M. J., and J. L. NICHOLSON. The 1965 Savings Survey. *Bulletin of the Oxford Institute of Statistics*, vol. 20, no. 2, 1958, pp. 113–52.

47. F.A.O. *Bibliography on Demand Analysis and Projections: 1959.* Mimeographed, Rome, 1959.

48. F.A.O. *Bibliography on Demand Analysis and Projections: 1960 Supplement.* Mimeographed, Rome, 1960.

49. F.A.O. *Institutions dealing with Demand Analysis and Projections.* Mimeographed, Rome, 1960.

50. FARRELL, M. J. Irreversible demand functions. *Econometrica*, vol. 20, no. 2, 1952, pp. 171–86.

51. FARRELL, M. J. Some aggregation problems in demand analysis. *The Review of Economic Studies*, vol. XXI, 1953–1954, pp. 193–203.

52. FARRELL, M. J. The demand for motor-cars in the United States. *Journal of the Royal Statistical Society, Series A (General)*, vol. 117, pt. 2, 1954, pp. 171–201.

53. FINNEY, D. J. *Probit Analysis: A Statistical Treatment of the Sigmoid Response Curve.* Cambridge University Press, 1947, second edition 1952.

54. FISHER, G. R. Maximum likelihood estimators with heteroscedastic errors. *Review of the International Statistical Institute*, vol. XXV, no. 1–3, 1957, pp. 1–4.

55. FISHER, Malcolm R. Explorations in savings behaviour. *Bulletin of the Oxford Institute of Statistics*, vol. 18, no. 3, 1956, pp. 201–77.

56. FISHER, Malcolm R. A reply to the critics. *Bulletin of the Oxford Institute of Statistics*, vol. 19, no. 2, 1957, pp. 179–99.

57. FISHER, M. R. A sector model—the poultry industry of the U.S.A. *Econometrica*, vol. 26, no. 1, 1958, pp. 37–66.

58. FISK, P. R. Maximum likelihood estimation of Tornqvist demand equations. *The Review of Economic Studies*, vol. XXVI, 1958–1959, pp. 33–50.

59. FORSYTH, F. G. The relationship between family size and family expenditure. *Journal of the Royal Statistical Society, Series A (General)*, vol. 123, pt. 4, 1960, pp. 367–97.

60. FRIEDMAN, Milton. Savings and the balance sheet. *Bulletin of the Oxford Institute of Statistics*, vol. 19, no. 2, 1957, pp. 125–36.

61. FRIEND, Irwin. Some conditions of progress in the study of savings. *Bulletin of the Oxford Institute of Statistics*, vol. 19, no. 2, 1957, pp. 165–70.

62. GILBERT, Milton, and associates. *Comparative National Products and Price Levels.* O.E.E.C., Paris, 1958.

63. GORMAN, W. M. *The Demand for Fish: an Application of Factor Analysis.* University of Birmingham, Faculty of Commerce and Social Science Series A, no. 6, 1960 (mimeographed).

64. GRAY, P. G., and A. CARTWRIGHT. Choosing and changing doctors. *The Lancet*, no. 265, 1953, pp. 1308–9.

65. GRAY, Percy G. and Ann CARTWRIGHT. Who gets the medicine ? *Applied Statistics*, vol. 3, no. 1, 1954, pp. 19–28.

66. GRAY, P. G., and T. CORLETT. Sampling for the Social Survey. *Journal of the Royal Statistical Society, Series A (General)*, vol. 113, pt. 2, 1950, pp. 150–206.

67. GRIDGEMAN, Norman T. A tasting experiment. *Applied Statistics*, vol. 5, no. 2, 1956, pp. 106–12.

68. GRIDGEMAN, Norman T. Statistics and taste testing. *Applied Statistics*, vol. 9, no. 2, 1960, pp. 103–12.

69. HAAVELMO, Trygve. Econometric analysis of the Saving Survey data. *Bulletin of the Oxford Institute of Statistics*, vol. 19, no. 2, 1957, pp. 145–9.

70. HAJNAL, J., and A. M. HENDERSON. The economic position of the family. *Papers of the Royal Commission on Population*, vol. V, H.M.S.O., London, 1950.

71. HARPER, J. Ross. Student income and expenditure in the universities of Glasgow and Birmingham: a comparative survey. *Scottish Journal of Political Economy*, vol. IV, no. 3, 1957, pp. 194–206.

72. HARPER, Roland. Fundamental problems in the subjective appraisal of foodstuffs. *Applied Statistics*, vol. 4, no. 3, 1955, pp. 145–61.

73. HARPER, Roland. Factor analysis as a technique for examining complex data on foodstuffs. *Applied Statistics*, vol. 5, no. 1, 1956, pp. 32–48.

74. HARRISON, G., and F. C. MITCHELL. *The Home Market: 1950 Edition*. Allen and Unwin, London, 1950.

75. HENDERSON, A. M. The cost of a family. *The Review of Economic Studies*, vol. XVII, 1949–1950, pp. 127–48.

76. HENDERSON, A. The cost of children, part I. *Population Studies*, vol. III, no. 1, 1949, pp. 130–50.

77. HENDERSON, A. The cost of children, part II and III. *Population Studies*, vol. IV, no. 3, 1950, pp. 267–98.

78. HILL, T. P. Incomes, savings and net worth: the Savings Surveys of 1952–1954. *Bulletin of the Oxford Institute of Statistics*, vol. 17, no. 2, 1955, pp. 129–72.

79. HILL, T. P. Expectations and consumer behaviour. *Bulletin of the Oxford Institute of Statistics*, vol. 19, no. 2, 1957, pp. 137–44.

80. HILL, T. P. A pilot survey of incomes and savings. *Bulletin of the Oxford Institute of Statistics*, vol. 22, no. 2, 1960, pp. 131–42.

81. HILL, T. P., L. R. KLEIN, and K. H. STRAW. The Savings Survey 1953: response rates and reliability of data. *Bulletin of the Oxford Institute of Statistics*, vol. 17, no. 1, 1955, pp. 89–126.

82. HIRSCH, W. Z. A survey of price elasticities. *The Review of Economic Studies*, vol. XIX, 1951–1952, pp. 50–60.

83. HOUTHAKKER, H. S. Some calculations on electricity consumption in Great Britain. *Journal of the Royal Statistical Society, Series A (General)*, vol. 114, pt. 3, 1951, pp. 359–71.

84. HOUTHAKKER, H. S. Compensated changes in quantities and qualities consumed. *The Review of Economic Studies*, vol. XIX, 1951–1952, pp. 155–64.

85. HOUTHAKKER, H. S. The econometrics of family budgets. *Journal of the Royal Statistical Society, Series A (General)*, vol. 115, pt. 1, 1952, pp. 1–28.

86. HOUTHAKKER, H. S. La forme des courbes d'Engel. *Cahiers du Séminaire d'Econométrie*, no. 2, 1953, pp. 59–66.

87. HOUTHAKKER, H. S., and S. J. PRAIS. Les variations de qualité dans les budgets de famille. *Economie appliquée*, vol. V, no. 1, 1952, pp. 65–78.

88. HOUTHAKKER, H. S., and J. TOBIN. Estimates of the free demand for rationed foodstuffs. *The Economic Journal*, vol. LXII, no. 245, 1952, pp. 103–18.

89. HOUTHAKKER, H. S., and J. TOBIN. A note on the demand for food: a rejoinder. *The Economic Journal*, vol. LXII, no. 248, 1952, p. 939.

90. HULTON PRESS LTD. *The Hulton Readership Survey 1953*. The Hulton Press, London, 1953. A similar report was issued in 1954.

91. INSTITUTE OF PRACTITIONERS IN ADVERTISING. *The National Readership Survey – 1954 Edition*. I.P.A., London, 1954.

92. INTERNATIONAL ASSOCIATION FOR RESEARCH IN INCOME AND WEALTH. *Bibliography on Income and Wealth*. Bowes and Bowes, London: vol. I (1937–1947) 1952; vol. II (1948–1949) 1953; vol. III (1950) 1953; vol. IV (1951) 1954; vol. V (1952) 1955; vol. VI (1953–1954) 1958.

93. JEFFERYS, James B. *Retail Trading in Great Britain 1850–1950*. Cambridge University Press, 1954.

94. JEFFERYS, James B., and Dorothy WALTERS. National income and expenditure of the United Kingdom, 1870–1952. *Income and Wealth, Series V*, Bowes and Bowes, London, 1955.

95. JEFFERYS, James B., and others. *The Distribution of Consumer Goods*. Cambridge University Press, 1950.

96. JOHNSON, Harry G. The effects of income-redistribution on aggregate consumption with interdependence of consumers' preferences. *Economica,* new series, vol. XIX, no. 74, 1952, pp. 131–47.

97. JOHNSTON, J., and G. M. MURPHY. The growth of life assurance in U.K. since 1880. *The Manchester School,* vol. XXV, no. 2, 1957, pp. 107–82.

98. KEMSLEY, W. F. F. Estimating individual expenditure from family totals. *Applied Statistics,* vol. 1, 1952, pp. 192–201.

99. KEMSLEY, W. F. F., and J. L. NICHOLSON. Some experiments in methods of conducting family expenditure surveys. *Journal of the Royal Statistical Society, Series A (General),* vol. 123, pt. 3, 1960, pp. 307–28.

100. KEMSLEY PRESS LTD. *A Survey of Certain Aspects of Newspaper Readership in the North of England.* Kemsley Press Ltd., London, 1954.

101. KLEIN, L. R. Patterns of savings: the surveys of 1953 and 1954. *Bulletin of the Oxford Institute of Statistics,* vol. 17, no. 2, 1955, pp. 173–214.

102. KLEIN, L. R. Major consumer expenditure and the ownership of durable goods. *Bulletin of the Oxford Institute of Statistics,* vol. 17, no. 4, 1955, pp. 387–414.

103. KLEIN, L. R. The British propensity to save. *Journal of the Royal Statistical Society, Series A (General),* vol. 121, pt. 1, 1958, pp. 60–96.

104. KLEIN, L. R., and N. LIVIATAN. The significance of income variability on savings behaviour. *Bulletin of the Oxford Institute of Statistics,* vol. 19, no. 2, 1957, pp. 151–60.

105. KLEIN, L. R., K. H. STRAW, and Peter VANDOME. Savings and finances of the upper income classes. *Bulletin of the Oxford Institute of Statistics,* vol. 18, no. 4, 1956, pp. 291–319.

106. KLEIN, L. R., and Peter VANDOME. Sampling errors in the Savings Surveys. *Bulletin of the Oxford Institute of Statistics,* vol. 19, no. 1, 1957, pp. 85–95.

107. KLEIN, L. R., and others. *An Econometric Model of the United Kingdom.* Basil Blackwell, Oxford, 1961.

108. KNOX, F. Some international comparisons of consumers' durable goods. *Bulletin of the Oxford Institute of Statistics,* vol. 21, no. 1, 1959, pp. 31–8.

109. KUH, Edwin, and John R. MEYER. How extraneous are extraneous estimates ? *The Review of Economics and Statistics,* vol. XXXIX, no. 4, 1957, pp. 380–93.

110. LANSING, John B., and Harold LYDALL. An Anglo-American comparison of personal saving. *Bulletin of the Oxford Institute of Statistics,* vol. 22, no. 3, 1960, pp. 225–58.

111. LESER, C. E. V. Commodity group expenditure functions for the United Kingdom, 1948–1957. *Econometrica,* vol. 29, no. 1, 1961, pp. 24–32.

112. LEVER BROTHERS and UNILEVER LTD. Oils and fats statistics. *Journal of the Royal Statistical Society, Series A (General),* vol. 113, pt. 3, 1950, pp. 376–95.

113. LOMAX, K. S. The demand for potatoes. *The Manchester School,* vol. XVIII, no. 2, 1950, pp. 175–6.

114. LOMAX, K. S. Analysis of demand and supply in textiles. *The Manchester School,* vol. XVI, no. 1, 1948, pp. 46–65.

115. LOMAX, K. S. Colonial demand for cotton goods. *Yorkshire Bulletin of Economic and Social Research,* vol. 4, no. 1, 1952, pp. 67–71.

116. LYDALL, H. F. A pilot survey of incomes and savings. *Bulletin of the Oxford Institute of Statistics,* vol. 13, no. 9, 1951, pp. 257–91.

117. LYDALL, H. F. Personal income in Oxford. *Bulletin of the Oxford Institute of Statistics,* vol. 13, no. 11 and 12, 1951, pp. 379–98.

118. LYDALL, H. F. Liquid asset holdings in Oxford. *Bulletin of the Oxford Institute of Statistics*, vol. 14, no. 3, 1952, pp. 97–115.

119. LYDALL, H. F. Personal saving and its determinants in the light of the Oxford survey. *Bulletin of the Oxford Institute of Statistics*, vol. 14, no. 7, 1952, pp. 197–230.

120. LYDALL, H. F. National survey of personal incomes and savings. *Bulletin of the Oxford Institute of Statistics*, vol. 14, no. 11 and 12, 1952, pp. 369–92.

121. LYDALL, H. F. National survey of personal incomes and savings. *Bulletin of the Oxford Institute of Statistics*, vol. 15, no. 2 and 3, 1953, pp. 35–84.

122. LYDALL, H. F. National survey of personal incomes and savings. *Bulletin of the Oxford Institute of Statistics*, vol. 15, no. 6 and 7, 1953, pp. 193–236.

123. LYDALL, H. F. National survey of personal incomes and savings. *Bulletin of the Oxford Institute of Statistics*, vol. 15, no. 10 and 11, 1953, pp. 341–401.

124. LYDALL, H. F. The methods of the Savings Survey. *Bulletin of the Oxford Institute of Statistics*, vol. 16, no. 7 and 8, 1954, pp. 197–244.

125. LYDALL, Harold. The life cycle in income, saving and asset ownership. *Econometrica*, vol. 23, no. 2, 1955, pp. 131–50.

126. LYDALL, H. F. *British Incomes and Savings*. Blackwell, Oxford, 1955.

127. LYDALL, H. F., and R. F. F. DAWSON. Household income, rent and rates. *Bulletin of the Oxford Institute of Statistics*, vol. 16, no. 4, 1954, pp. 97–129.

128. LYLE, Philip. The sugar industry. *Journal of the Royal Statistical Society, Series A (General)*, vol. 113, pt. 4, 1950, pp. 531–43.

129. MARKET RESEARCH SOCIETY. *Commentary*. Distributed to members of the Market Research Society approximately half yearly. No. 4 appeared in the winter of 1960–1961.

130. MENZLER, F. A. A. London and its passenger transport system. *Journal of the Royal Statistical Society, Series A (General)*, vol. 113, pt. 3, 1950, pp. 299–345.

131. MITCHELL, Brian, and Phyllis DEANE. *Abstract of Historical Statistics of Great Britain*. Cambridge University Press, 1962.

132. MODIGLIANI, Franco, and Albert K. ANDO. Tests of the life cycle hypothesis of savings. *Bulletin of the Oxford Institute of Statistics*, vol. 19, no. 2, 1957, pp. 99–124.

133. MOOS, S. Estimates of housing needs. *Bulletin of the Oxford Institute of Statistics*, vol. 7, no. 13, 1945, pp. 218–26.

134. MORGAN, D. J., and W. J. CORLETT. The influence of price in international trade. *Journal of the Royal Statistical Society, Series A (General)*, vol. 114, pt. 3, 1951, pp. 307–58.

135. MOSER, C. A. *Survey Methods in Social Investigation*. Heinemann, London, 1958.

136. MOSS, L. Sample surveys and the administrative process. *UNESCO International Social Science Bulletin*, vol. 5, 1953, pp. 482–94.

137. NATIONAL INSTITUTE OF ECONOMIC AND SOCIAL RESEARCH. *Economic Review*. National Institute, London, bi-monthly.

138. NEWMAN, Peter. Some calculations on least-cost diets using the simplex method. *Bulletin of the Oxford Institute of Statistics*, vol. 17, no. 3, 1955, pp. 303–20.

139. NICHOLSON, J. L. Variations in working class family expenditure. *Journal of the Royal Statistical Society, Series A (General)*, vol. 112, pt. 4, 1949, pp. 359–418.

140. NICHOLSON, J. L. The general form of the adding-up criterion. *Journal of the Royal Statistical Society, Series A (General)*, vol. 120, pt. 1, 1957, pp. 84–5.

9

141. NICHOLSON, J. L. A reply to [25] above. *Journal of the Royal Statistical Society, Series A (General)*, vol. 120, pt. 4, 1957, p. 458.

142. NIXON, J. W. On the size, constitution and housing standards of households in England and Wales, 1931 and 1951. *Review of the International Statistical Institute*, vol. 20, no. 2–3, 1952, pp. 135–47.

143. ODHAMS PRESS LTD. *The Buying Habits and Purchasing Power of 'Daily Herald' Readers.* Odhams Press, London, 1953.

144. PATTISON, J. S. Expenditure of Glasgow University students. *Bulletin of the Oxford Institute of Statistics*, vol. 15, no. 5, 1953, pp. 163–76.

145. PETERSON, A. W. The statistics of gambling. *Journal of the Royal Statistical Society, Series A (General)*, vol. 115, pt. 2, 1952, pp. 199–218.

146. PRAIS, S. J. A note on the heteroscedastic errors in regression analysis. *Review of the International Statistical Institute*, vol. XXI, no. 1–2, 1953, pp. 28–9.

147. PRAIS, S. J. Non-linear estimates of the Engel curves. *The Review of Economic Studies*, vol. XX, no. 2, 1953, pp. 87–104.

148. PRAIS, S. J. The estimation of equivalent-adult scales from family budgets. *The Economic Journal*, vol. LXIII, no. 252, 1953, pp. 791–810.

149. PRAIS, S. J., and J. AITCHISON. The grouping of observations in regression analysis. *Review of the International Statistical Institute*, vol. XXII, no. 1–3, 1954, pp. 1–22.

150. PRAIS, S. J., and H. S. HOUTHAKKER. *The Analysis of Family Budgets.* Cambridge University Press, 1955.

151. PREST, A. R. Some experiments in demand analysis. *The Review of Economics and Statistics*, vol. XXXI, no. 1, 1949, pp. 35–49.

152. PREST, A. R., assisted by A. A. ADAMS. *Consumers' Expenditure in the United Kingdom, 1900–1919.* Cambridge University Press, 1954.

153. PRESTON, Esme. Personal savings through institutional channels. *Bulletin of the Oxford Institute of Statistics*, vol. 12, no. 9, 1950, pp. 243–60.

154. PRESTON, Esme. Personal savings through institutional channels 1949 and 1950. *Bulletin of the Oxford Institute of Statistics*, vol. 13, no. 9, 1951, pp. 294–304.

155. QUENOUILLE, M. H. An application of least squares to family diet surveys. *Econometrica*, vol. 18, no. 1, 1950, pp. 27–44.

156. REDDAWAY, W. B. (editor). London and Cambridge Economic Bulletin. *The Times Review of Industry*. The Times Publishing Co., London, monthly. The Bulletin appears quarterly.

157. ROSS, K. H. Working class clothing consumption, 1937–1938. *Journal of the Royal Statistical Society, Series A (General)*, vol. 109, pt. 2, 1948, pp. 145–60.

158. ROYAL STATISTICAL SOCIETY. *The Sources and Nature of the Statistics of the United Kingdom.* Oliver and Boyd, Edinburgh and London: vol. I, 1952; vol. II, 1957.

159. RUDD, Ernest. Estimates of expenditure on road transport in Great Britain. *Journal of the Royal Statistical Society, Series A (General)*, vol. 115, pt. 2, 1952, pp. 179–98.

160. SARGAN, J. D. The danger of over-simplification. *Bulletin of the Oxford Institute of Statistics*, vol. 19, no. 2, 1957, pp. 171–8.

161. SAUNDERS, C. T. Some problems in the estimation of personal savings and investment. *The Review of Economic Studies*, vol. XXII, 1954–1955, pp. 109–28.

162. SCHULZ, T. Working-class income and household expenditure. *Bulletin of the Oxford Institute of Statistics*, vol. 7, no. 2, 1945, pp. 17–30.

163. SCHULZ, T. Food expenditure and nutrition. *Bulletin of the Oxford Institute of Statistics*, vol. 7, no. 3, 1945, pp. 37–55.

164. SCHULZ, T. Sales of groceries in 1943 and 1944. *Bulletin of the Oxford Institute of Statistics*, vol. 7, no. 6 and 7, 1945, pp. 116–23.

165. SCHULZ, T. Inexpensive family diets; April 1945. *Bulletin of the Oxford Institute of Statistics*, vol. 7, no. 8, 1945, pp. 129–37.

166. SCHULZ, T. Proper nutrition at low cost. *Bulletin of the Oxford Institute of Statistics*, vol. 7, no. 17, 1945, pp. 291–302.

167. SCHULZ, T. Income and household expenditure of working-class families with children. Part I. Income and expenditure on non-food items. *Bulletin of the Oxford Institute of Statistics*, vol. 8, no. 2, 1946, pp. 29–43.

168. SCHULZ, T. Income and household expenditure of working-class families with children. Part II. Outlay on food and nutrition. *Bulletin of the Oxford Institute of Statistics*, vol. 8, no. 3, 1946, pp. 61–80.

169. SCHULZ, T. Grocery sales and rationing. *Bulletin of the Oxford Institute of Statistics*, vol. 8, no. 4, 1946, pp. 97–107.

170. SCHULZ, T. Low cost family diets and individual nutrition. *Bulletin of the Oxford Institute of Statistics*, vol. 8, no. 6, 1946, pp. 178–89.

171. SCHULZ, T. Inexpensive family diets in November, 1946. *Bulletin of the Oxford Institute of Statistics*, vol. 8, no. 12, 1946, pp. 375–87.

172. SCHULZ, T. Working class income and household expenditure. *Bulletin of the Oxford Institute of Statistics*, vol. 9, no. 5, 1947, pp. 133–69.

173. SCHULZ, T. Feeding a family: inexpensive family diets in April 1947. *Bulletin of the Oxford Institute of Statistics*, vol. 9, no. 6, 1947, pp. 183–95.

174. SCHULZ, T. Consumption of groceries and rationing. *Bulletin of the Oxford Institute of Statistics*, vol. 9, no. 8, 1947, pp. 261–73.

175. SCHULZ, T. Food and energy. Some nutritional aspects of rationing. *Bulletin of the Oxford Institute of Statistics*, vol. 10, no. 2, 1948, pp. 53–66.

176. SCHULZ, T. Consumption of groceries. *Bulletin of the Oxford Institute of Statistics*, vol. 10, no. 4, 1948, pp. 105–16.

177. SCHULZ, T. A family diet of low cost. *Bulletin of the Oxford Institute of Statistics*, vol. 10, no. 5, 1948, pp. 129–39.

178. SCHULZ, T. Family expenditure in 1947. Part I. Income and outlay. *Bulletin of the Oxford Institute of Statistics*, vol. 10, no. 11, 1948, pp. 353–72.

179. SCHULZ, T. Family expenditure in 1947. Part II. Outlay on food nutritional intake. *Bulletin of the Oxford Institute of Statistics*, vol. 10, no. 12, 1948, pp. 401–23.

180. SCHULZ, T. Nutrition at low cost. *Bulletin of the Oxford Institute of Statistics*, vol. 11, no. 1, 1949, pp. 9–17.

181. SCHULZ, T. A 'human needs' diet. *Bulletin of the Oxford Institute of Statistics*, vol. 11, no. 6, 1949, pp. 149–62.

182. SCHULZ, T. 'Human needs' diet from 1936 to 1949. *Bulletin of the Oxford Institute of Statistics*, vol. 11, no. 10, 1949, pp. 307–25.

183. SCHULZ, T. A 'human needs' diet, November 1949. *Bulletin of the Oxford Institute of Statistics*, vol. 11, no. 12, 1949, pp. 382–88.

184. SCHULZ, T. Working class household expenditure in 1948. *Bulletin of the Oxford Institute of Statistics*, vol. 12, no. 3, 1950, pp. 81–98.

185. SCHULZ, T. Food expenditure and nutrition in 1948. *Bulletin of the Oxford Institute of Statistics*, vol. 12, no. 4, 1950, pp. 99–108.

186. SCHULZ, T. A 'human needs' diet in spring 1950. *Bulletin of the Oxford Institute of Statistics*, vol. 12, no. 5, 1950, pp. 127–37.

187. SCHULZ, T. 'Human needs' of a single person. *Bulletin of the Oxford Institute of Statistics*, vol. 12, no. 6, 1950, pp. 159–66.

188. SCHULZ, T. A 'human needs' diet in November 1950. *Bulletin of the Oxford Institute of Statistics*, vol. 13, no. 1, 1951, pp. 17–22.

189. SCHULZ, T. Family expenditure in 1949. Part I. *Bulletin of the Oxford Institute of Statistics,* vol. 13, no. 4, 1951, pp. 128–40.

190. SCHULZ, T. Family expenditure in 1949. Part II. *Bulletin of the Oxford Institute of Statistics,* vol. 13, no. 5, 1951, pp. 141–50.

191. SCHULZ, T. A 'human needs' diet in April, 1951. *Bulletin of the Oxford Institute of Statistics,* vol. 13, no. 6, 1951, pp. 173–77.

192. SCHULZ, T. Household expenditure in France and England. *Bulletin of the Oxford Institute of Statistics,* vol. 13, no. 8, 1951, pp. 229–42.

193. SCHULZ, T. A 'human needs' diet in November 1951. *Bulletin of the Oxford Institute of Statistics,* vol. 13, no. 11 and 12, 1951, pp. 367–71.

194. SCHULZ, T. Working-class food consumption from 1942 to 1949. *Bulletin of the Oxford Institute of Statistics,* vol. 14, no. 2, pp. 33–44.

195. SCHULZ, T. A 'human needs' diet in April, 1952. *Bulletin of the Oxford Institute of Statistics,* vol. 14, no. 6, 1952, pp. 177–81.

196. SCHULZ, T. The cost of inexpensive nutrition before and after the war. *Bulletin of the Oxford Institute of Statistics,* vol. 14, no. 7, 1952, pp. 231–44.

197. SCHULZ, T. A 'human needs' diet in November, 1952. *Bulletin of the Oxford Institute of Statistics,* vol. 14, no. 11 and 12, 1952, pp. 423–9.

198. SCHULZ, T. A 'human needs' diet: April, 1953. *Bulletin of the Oxford Institute of Statistics,* vol. 15, no. 6 and 7, 1953, pp. 249–54.

199. SCHULZ, T. A 'human needs' diet: autumn 1953. *Bulletin of the Oxford Institute of Statistics,* vol. 15, no. 12, 1953, pp. 421–35.

200. SCHULZ, T. A 'human needs' diet: spring 1954. *Bulletin of the Oxford Institute of Statistics,* vol. 16, no. 4, 1954, pp. 130–6.

201. SCHULZ, T. The means of subsistence: income from earnings and from assistance, 1935–1953. *Bulletin of the Oxford Institute of Statistics,* vol. 17, no. 2, 1955, pp. 215–38.

202. SCHULZ, T. A 'human needs' diet: spring 1955. *Bulletin of the Oxford Institute of Statistics,* vol. 17, no. 2, 1955, pp. 239–40.

203. SCHULZ, T. A 'human needs' diet: autumn 1955. *Bulletin of the Oxford Institute of Statistics,* vol. 18, no. 1, 1956, pp. 87–93.

204. SCHULZ, T. A 'human needs' diet: spring 1956. *Bulletin of the Oxford Institute of Statistics,* vol. 18, no. 2, 1956, pp. 195–7.

205. SCHULZ, T. A 'human needs' diet: autumn 1956. *Bulletin of the Oxford Institute of Statistics,* vol. 18, no. 4, 1956, pp. 387–9.

206. SCHULZ, T. A 'human needs' diet: spring 1957. *Bulletin of the Oxford Institute of Statistics,* vol. 19, no. 3, 1957, pp. 285–7.

207. SCHULZ, T. A 'human needs' diet: autumn 1957. *Bulletin of the Oxford Institute of Statistics,* vol. 20, no. 1, 1958, pp. 107–12.

208. SCHULZ, T. The problem of adequate nutrition. *Bulletin of the Oxford Institute of Statistics,* vol. 20, no. 3, 1958, pp. 305–17.

209. SCHULZ, T. A 'human needs' diet: autumn 1958. *Bulletin of the Oxford Institute of Statistics,* vol. 21, no. 1, 1959, pp. 55–8.

210. SCHULZ, T. Inexpensive nutrition before and after the war. *Bulletin of the Oxford Institute of Statistics,* vol. 21, no. 2, 1959, pp. 121–8.

211. SCHULZ, T. Nutrition at different income levels. *Bulletin of the Oxford Institute of Statistics,* vol. 22, no. 2, 1960, pp. 143–50.

212. SCHULZ, T., and D. E. FIELD. A 'human needs' diet: autumn 1954, *Appendix:* 'Human needs' diets in Northern Ireland. *Bulletin of the Oxford Institute of Statistics,* vol. 16, no. 11 and 12, 1954, pp. 363–71.

213. SCOTT, A. D. Bibliography of applications of mathematical statistics to economics, 1943–1949. *Journal of the Royal Statistical Society, Series A (General),* vol. 114, pt. 3, 1951, pp. 372–93.

214. SCOTT, A. D. Bibliography of applications of mathematical statistics to economics: supplement for 1950. *Journal of the Royal Statistical Society, Series A (General)*, vol. 116, pt. 2, 1953, pp. 177–85.

215. SEERS, Dudley, The working-class share in pre-war consumption. *Bulletin of the Oxford Institute of Statistics*, vol. 10, no. 6, 1948, pp. 181–94.

216. SHANKLEMAN, Eric. Measuring the readership of newspapers and magazines. *Applied Statistics*, vol. 4, no. 3, 1955, pp. 183–94.

217. SMYTH, R. L., and David MACE. Some aspects of the marketing of South African oranges in Great Britain. *Yorkshire Bulletin of Economic and Social Research*, vol. 8, no. 2, 1956, pp. 89–108.

218. SPRAOS, John. An Engel-type curve for cash. *The Manchester School*, vol. XXV, no. 2, 1957, pp. 183–9.

219. STEDMAN JONES, W. D. Food statistics. *Journal of the Royal Statistical Society, Series A (General)*, vol. 16, pt. 1, 1953, pp. 57–84.

220. STONE, Richard. The analysis of market demand. *Journal of the Royal Statistical Society*, vol. 108, pts. 3 and 4, 1945, pp. 1–98.

221. STONE, Richard. On the interdependence of blocks of transactions. *Supplement to the Journal of the Royal Statistical Society*, vol. IX, no. 1–2, 1947, pp. 1–45.

222. STONE, Richard. The analysis of market demand: an outline of methods and results. *Review of the International Statistical Institute*, vol. 16, no. 1–4, 1948, pp. 23–35.

223. STONE, Richard. *The Role of Measurement in Economics*. Cambridge University Press, 1951.

224. STONE, Richard. The demand for food in the United Kingdom before the war. *Metroeconomica*, vol. III, no. 1, 1951, pp. 8–27.

225. STONE, Richard. The way the money went. *The Times*, 25 and 26 February 1954.

226. STONE, Richard. Linear expenditure systems and demand analysis: an application to the pattern of British demand. *The Economic Journal*, vol. LXIV, no. 255, 1954, pp. 511–27.

227. STONE, Richard. Transaction models with an example based on the British national accounts. *Boletin del Banco Central de Venezuela*, April 1955 (in Spanish). *Accounting Research*, vol. VI, no. 3, 1955, pp. 1–24.

228. STONE, Richard. *Quantity and Price Indexes in National Accounts*. O.E.E.C., Paris, 1956.

229. STONE, Richard. Market forecasting and the family income. *The Times Review of Industry*, vol. 13, no. 153 (new series), 1959, pp. 6 and 9.

230. STONE, Richard. A dynamic model of demand (in Polish). *Przeglad Statystyczny*, vol. 7, no. 3, 1960, pp. 255–70. (English version, Department of Applied Economics reprint series, no. 167).

231. STONE, Richard. A comparison of the economic structure of regions based on the concept of distance. *Journal of Regional Science*, vol. 2, no. 2, 1960, pp. 1–20.

232. STONE, Richard. An econometric model of growth: the British economy in ten years time. *Discovery*, vol. XXII, no. 5, 1961, pp. 216–19.

233. STONE, Richard. Population mathematics, demand analysis and investment planning (in Polish). *Przeglad Statystyczny*, vol. 8, no. 2, 1961, pp. 127–36. (English version, Department of Applied Economics reprint series, no. 176).

234. STONE, Richard. *Input-Output and National Accounts*. O.E.E.C., Paris, 1961.

235. STONE, Richard. Social accounts at the regional level: a survey. In *Regional Economic Planning: Techniques of Analysis*. O.E.E.C., Paris, 1961.

236. STONE, Richard, J. AITCHISON and J. A. C. BROWN. Some estimation problems in demand analysis. *The Incorporated Statistician*, vol. 5, no. 4, 1955, pp. 165–77.

237. STONE, Richard, and Giovanna CROFT-MURRAY. *Social Accounting and Economic Models*. Bowes and Bowes, London, 1959.

238. STONE, Richard, and S. J. PRAIS. Forecasting from econometric equations: a further note on derationing. *The Economic Journal*, vol. LXIII, no. 249, 1953, pp. 189–95.

239. STONE, Richard, and D. A. ROWE. Aggregate consumption and investment functions for the household sector considered in the light of British experience. *Nationalekonomisk Tidsskrift*, vol. 94, pts. 1 and 2, 1956, pp. 1–32.

240. STONE, Richard, and D. A. ROWE. The market demand for durable goods. *Econometrica*, vol. 25, no. 3, 1957, pp. 423–43.

241. STONE, Richard, and D. A. ROWE. Dynamic demand functions: some econometric results. *The Economic Journal*, vol. LXVIII, no. 270, 1958, pp. 256–70.

242. STONE, Richard, and D. A. ROWE. The durability of consumers' durable goods. *Econometrica*, vol. 28, no. 2, 1960, pp. 407–16.

243. STONE, Richard, and D. A. ROWE. *The Measurement of Consumers' Expenditure and Behaviour in the United Kingdom, 1920–1938*. Vol. II, Cambridge University Press, 1966.

244. STONE, Richard, and D. A. ROWE. Hire-purchase and the demand for durable goods. (To be published).

245. STONE, Richard, and others. *The Measurement of Consumers' Expenditure and Behaviour in the United Kingdom, 1920–1938*. Vol. I, Cambridge University Press, 1954.

246. STRAW, K. H. The Savings Surveys and official sources: a reconciliation of estimates of personal income. *Bulletin of the Oxford Institute of Statistics*, vol. 17, no. 3, 1955, pp. 283–302.

247. STRAW, K. H. Consumers' net worth: the 1953 Savings Survey. *Bulletin of the Oxford Institute of Statistics*, vol. 18, no. 1, 1956, pp. 1–59.

248. STUART, A. Reading habits in three London boroughs. *Journal of Documentation*, vol. 8, no. 1, 1952, pp. 33–49.

249. STUVEL, G., and S. F. JAMES. Household expenditure on food in Holland. *Journal of the Royal Statistical Society, Series A (General)*, vol. 113, pt. 1, 1950, pp. 59–80.

250. TECHNICAL PLANNING LTD. *Market Research*. The third issue appeared in October 1960.

251. THEIL, H. Quality, prices and budget enquiries. *The Review of Economic Studies*, vol. XIX, 1951–1952, pp. 129–47.

252. THRIFT, H. J. The Newspaper Society regional readership survey. *The Incorporated Statistician*, vol. 9, no. 4, 1959, pp. 115–37.

253. TOBIN, James. A statistical demand function for food in the U.S.A. *Journal of the Royal Statistical Society, Series A (General)*, vol. 113, pt. 2, 1950, pp. 113–49.

254. TOBIN, James. Relative income, absolute income and saving. *Money, Trade and Economic Growth*, The Macmillan Co., New York, 1951, pp. 135–56.

255. TOBIN, J., and H. S. HOUTHAKKER. The effects of rationing on demand elasticities. *The Review of Economic Studies*, vol. XVIII, no. 3, 1951, pp. 1–14.

256. TOBIN, James, and Harold WATTS. An evaluation of the tests. *Bulletin of the Oxford Institute of Statistics*, vol. 19, no. 2, 1957, pp. 161–4.

257. U.K. CENTRAL STATISTICAL OFFICE. *Annual Abstract of Statistics*. H.M.S.O., London, annually.

258. U.K. CENTRAL STATISTICAL OFFICE. *Economic Trends.* H.M.S.O., London, monthly.
259. U.K. CENTRAL STATISTICAL OFFICE. *Monthly Digest of Statistics.* H.M.S.O., London, monthly.
260. U.K. CENTRAL STATISTICAL OFFICE. *National Income and Expenditure.* H.M.S.O., London, annually.
261. U.K. CENTRAL STATISTICAL OFFICE. *National Income Statistics: Sources and Methods.* H.M.S.O., London, 1956.
262. U.K. CENTRAL STATISTICAL OFFICE. *Preliminary Estimates of National Income and Expenditure.* H.M.S.O., London, annually.
263. U.K. CENTRAL STATISTICAL OFFICE. *Statistical Digest of the War.* H.M.S.O. and Longmans Green and Co., London, 1951.
264. U.K. MINISTRY OF AGRICULTURE, FISHERIES AND FOOD. *Domestic Food Consumption and Expenditure.* Annual Reports of the National Food Survey Committee, H.M.S.O., London, annually since 1952.
265. U.K. MINISTRY OF FOOD. *The Urban Working Class Household Diet, 1940 to 1950.* H.M.S.O., London, 1951.
266. U.K. MINISTRY OF LABOUR AND NATIONAL SERVICE. *Weekly Expenditure of Working-Class Households in the United Kingdom in 1937–1938.* Mimeographed, 1949.
267. U.K. MINISTRY OF LABOUR AND NATIONAL SERVICE. *Report of an Enquiry into Household Expenditure in 1953–1954.* H.M.S.O., London, 1957.
268. UTTING, J. E. G. Sample surveys for household income and expenditure information. *Schweizerische Zeitschrift für Volkswirtschaft und Statistik,* vol. 90, no. 3, 1954, pp. 1–8.
269. UTTING, J. E. G., and Dorothy COLE. Sample surveys for the social accounts of the household sector. *Bulletin of the Oxford Institute of Statistics,* vol. 15, no. 1, 1953, pp. 1–24.
270. UTTING, J. E. G., and Dorothy COLE. Sampling for social accounts: some aspects of the Cambridgeshire Survey. *Bulletin of the International Statistical Institute,* vol. XXXIV, pt. 2, 1954, pp. 301–28.
271. VANDOME, Peter. Aspects of the dynamics of consumer behaviour. *Bulletin of the Oxford Institute of Statistics,* vol. 20, no. 1, 1958, pp. 65–105.
272. WADSWORTH, A. P. Newspaper circulations, 1800–1954. *Transactions of the Manchester Statistical Society,* 1954–1955.
273. WADSWORTH, H. E. Utility cloth and clothing scheme. *The Review of Economic Studies,* vol. XVI, 1949–1950, pp. 82–101.
274. WADSWORTH, Robert N. The experience of a user of a consumer panel. *Applied Statistics,* vol. 1, 1952, pp. 169–78.
275. WEATHERBURN, J. R. Clothing statistics. *Journal of the Royal Statistical Society, Series A (General),* vol. 115, pt. 3, 1952, pp. 424–9.
276. WILSON, Ross. The Scotch whisky industry. *Journal of the Royal Statistical Society, Series A (General),* vol. 118, pt. 3, 1955, pp. 345–62.
277. WORSWICK, G. D. N., and D. G. CHAMPERNOWNE. A note on the adding-up criterion. *The Review of Economic Studies,* vol. XXII, 1954–1955, pp. 57–60.
278. WRIGHT, Leslie C. Spending patterns in U.K. and U.S. *Scottish Journal of Political Economy,* vol. VI, no. 1, 1959, pp. 71–7.

Addendum: The following publications referred to in the text have appeared after the above list was compiled.

279. BAIN, A. D. The growth of demand for new commodities. *Journal of the Royal Statistical Society, Series A (General)*, vol. 126, pt. 2, 1963, pp. 285–99.

280. BAIN, A. D. *The Growth of Television Ownership in the United Kingdom.* Cambridge University Press, 1964.

281. PYATT, F. Graham. *Priority Patterns and the Demand for Household Durable Goods.* Cambridge University Press, 1964.

282. U.K. CENTRAL STATISTICAL OFFICE. *National Accounts Statistics: Sources and Methods.* H.M.S.O., London, 1968.

283. U.K. MINISTRY OF LABOUR. *Family Expenditure Survey.* H.M.S.O., London, periodically from 1961.

X

SPENDING AND SAVING IN RELATION TO INCOME AND WEALTH

1. INTRODUCTION

In this paper I shall describe some new calculations with a model of aggregate spending (or saving) which has been applied in Britain over the last five years [66, 82] and has given reasonably satisfactory results. By this I do not mean simply that it gives a good approximation to what is observed; in addition, it does this in a plausible way which is helpful in studying both the transient and the steady-state aspects of aggregate spending and saving.

The numerical results given below will be of interest to many readers only as illustrations of a model that could be applied in other countries. Apart from these specific results, the paper is also concerned with a general problem that econometricians have always to face: the problem arising from the conflict between a theoretically satisfying formulation of a relationship and the simplifications imposed by lack of data. The line taken here is that strenuous efforts should be made to work with relationships that are theoretically satisfying even if this means that a certain amount of statistical crudity and conceptual rigidity has to be tolerated. This attitude cannot be stated as an overriding principle; in any economic endeavour it is the balance of advantage that must be sought. Nevertheless, it may be better on occasions to make bricks without straw than to forego the temporary building that can be made out of them.

2. THE MAIN FEATURES OF THE MODEL

Before I set out the model explicitly, let us consider some of its main features which lead to the kind of problem just mentioned. First, a great deal of work on the aggregate consumption function has concentrated on income, or income-like explanatory variables, to the exclusion of wealth. This is clearly not plausible at the micro-level, but it is not very plausible at the macro-level either. Income does not bear a constant relationship to wealth at all times and places, and so it cannot be regarded as a proxy for wealth. This lack of correspondence is likely to show up over the trade cycle and even more forcibly in more abnormal circumstances. For example, after a war in which production has increased, consumption has been cut back and the war effort has been financed in large part from private saving, the community is likely to find itself with more wealth in relation to its income than usual. At the same time it will have a great desire to spend on the many goods and services that were in short supply during the war. Just because it has accumulated an abnormal amount of wealth, it can afford an abnormal amount of expenditure. It is not surprising in these circumstances if for a time the personal sector spends more than its disposable income. By doing so, however, it will tend to reduce its wealth in relation to its income and so reach a point where it again has a motive for saving. The general proposition that emerges from this example is that whereas we should expect more income to be accompanied by more spending and more saving, we should expect more wealth to be accompanied by more spending and less saving. This proposition probably commands general assent, but it can be pointed out that there is hardly a country in the world that regularly collects data on personal or private wealth. As a result the econometrician has no series for wealth to put into his regression analysis. However, he might be willing to accept as a proxy a series of accumulated saving added to a base figure of wealth. If the calculations were made at constant prices, this device should at least give a first approximation, though it would not take account of capital gains and losses. In normal circumstances, the resulting series would look very much like a trend and so merely introducing a residual trend would achieve much the same statistical results. But this is not true from an analytical point of view. The statement that the rate of change of wealth (saving) is a function of income and wealth leads to conclusions that cannot be extracted from the statement that the rate of change of wealth is a function of income and time.

Second, following Friedman, there seem to be good reasons for distinguishing the permanent component of income from the corresponding transient component. The same is probably true of wealth. It is not plausible that a change in income or wealth which is expected to persist will have the same effect on spending and saving as a corresponding windfall change. The difficulty in making this distinction is that the components cannot be observed or, at any rate, that they are not observed. It is necessary, therefore, to relate the unobservable components to something that can be observed and then to carry out an algebraic manipulation which will clear the unobservable components out of the regression equation. In the model described below it is assumed that this year's permanent component is a weighted average of this year's total and last year's permanent component. In order to carry out the algebraic manipulation, it is necessary to assume that the weights in this weighted average are the same for income and wealth. Something is gained but only at the cost of a certain rigidity which one would rather not accept.

Third, there can be little doubt that different kinds of income recipient respond differently to changes in their income. For example, it used to be commonly assumed that the whole of wage income was spent, so that all saving came out of income from property. This is undoubtedly an exaggeration but, nevertheless, some difference in response is to be expected. The difficulty in this case is that while we can form series of different types of income payment, we cannot divide spending or saving correspondingly. What we can discover, therefore, is how total spending is affected by changes in the different components of different types of income payment. In doing this it is necessary, in the formulations adopted here, to use the same weights in defining the permanent components not only for income and wealth but also for different types of income. In spite of this rigidity, the results obtained are of considerable interest.

Finally, there is the question, already mentioned, of capital gains and losses. This is another case in which we cannot, as yet, appeal to direct observations. If we are to do anything, therefore, about this question we must again resort to a device. We could, for example, see whether the model would be improved by assuming that the community continually revalues its wealth in the light of the current rate of return on it.

In the following section I shall describe how all these problems can be handled; but, when it comes to applications, I shall deal only with the first three. So far, I have made no calculations involving revaluations.

3. THE MODEL

Let us begin by introducing four variables: disposable income, μ; wealth (or net worth), ω; expenditure, ϵ; and saving, σ. These variables relate to a sector of the economy; they can be thought of as relating to the personal sector though, as we shall see, the model can also be applied to the company sector. The permanent components of income and wealth are denoted respectively by μ_1 and ω_1; and the corresponding transient components are denoted by μ_2 and ω_2. Income from wages and small transfers is denoted by μ_a; other income by μ_b.

If expenditure is also divided into components, it is assumed that each is a homogeneous linear function of the corresponding components of wealth and income. That is,

$$\epsilon_1 = \alpha_1 \omega_1 + \beta_1 \mu_1 \tag{1}$$

and

$$\epsilon_2 = \alpha_2 \omega_2 + \beta_2 \mu_2 \tag{2}$$

where α_1, β_1, α_2 and β_2 are constants. From (1) and (2), the equation for total expenditure, ϵ, is

$$\begin{aligned}
\epsilon &= \epsilon_1 + \epsilon_2 \\
&= \alpha_1 \omega_1 + \beta_1 \mu_1 + \alpha_2 \omega_2 + \beta_2 \mu_2 \\
&= \alpha_2 \omega + \beta_2 \mu + (\alpha_1 - \alpha_2) \omega_1 + (\beta_1 - \beta_2) \mu_1
\end{aligned} \tag{3}$$

since $\omega \equiv \omega_1 + \omega_2$ and $\mu \equiv \mu_1 + \mu_2$.

As already mentioned, the permanent components of wealth and income are assumed to be weighted averages of wealth or income in the current year and their permanent components in the preceding year. That is,

$$\omega_1 = \lambda\omega + (1-\lambda)E^{-1}\omega_1 \tag{4}$$

and

$$\mu_1 = \lambda\mu + (1-\lambda)E^{-1}\mu_1 \tag{5}$$

where λ is a constant and E is an operator which advances or retards the variable to which it is applied. Since $E^\theta\mu(\tau) \equiv \mu(\tau+\theta)$, the application of E^{-1} to a variable denotes its value in the preceding year.

By combining (3), (4) and (5) we obtain

$$\epsilon = [\alpha_1\lambda + \alpha_2(1-\lambda)]\omega + [\beta_1\lambda + \beta_2(1-\lambda)]\mu$$
$$+ (\alpha_1 - \alpha_2)(1-\lambda)E^{-1}\omega_1 + (\beta_1 - \beta_2)(1-\lambda)E^{-1}\mu_1 \tag{6}$$

and by multiplying (3) by $(1-\lambda)E^{-1}$ we obtain

$$(1-\lambda)E^{-1}\epsilon = \alpha_2(1-\lambda)E^{-1}\omega + \beta_2(1-\lambda)E^{-1}\mu$$
$$+ (\alpha_1 - \alpha_2)(1-\lambda)E^{-1}\omega_1 + (\beta_1 - \beta_2)(1-\lambda)E^{-1}\mu_1 \tag{7}$$

Thus, from (7), we can replace the unobservable terms in (6) by lagged values of observable variables and write

$$\epsilon = [\alpha_1\lambda + \alpha_2(1-\lambda)]\omega + [\beta_1\lambda + \beta_2(1-\lambda)]\mu$$
$$- \alpha_2(1-\lambda)E^{-1}\omega - \beta_2(1-\lambda)E^{-1}\mu + (1-\lambda)E^{-1}\epsilon$$
$$= \alpha_1\lambda\omega + \alpha_2(1-\lambda)\Delta^*\omega + \beta_1\lambda\mu + \beta_2(1-\lambda)\Delta^*\mu + (1-\lambda)E^{-1}\epsilon \tag{8}$$

where $\Delta^* \equiv (1-E^{-1})$ denotes the backward first-difference operator.

It will be noticed that the five constants α_1, α_2, β_1, β_2 and λ are all identified in (8). However, the variables on the right-hand side of (8) are closely related and if, as in the present applications, wealth is measured as accumulated saving, so that $\Delta^*\omega \equiv E^{-1}\sigma$, it follows that

$$\mu - \Delta^*\mu - \Delta^*\omega - E^{-1}\epsilon \equiv 0 \tag{9}$$

Thus we cannot hope to estimate all the parameters in (8); the term in at least one of the variables in (9) must be left out. In earlier papers [66, 82], already referred to, the transient component of wealth was omitted. In the notation of (8), this is equivalent to leaving out the term in $\Delta^*\omega$. We shall see in the following section that this term is indeed the obvious candidate for omission since all attempts to introduce it lead to absurd results, that is to an apparent negative influence of transient wealth on spending.

With the qualification that has just been made, (8) can be regarded as the basic equation of the model. In all the applications made, the variables are expressed at constant prices, the price index-number used to deflate each variable being that appropriate to consumers' goods and services.

Nevertheless, in a growing economy, the dependent variable still shows a considerable upward trend and so, for regression purposes, it may be advisable to work either with differences or with ratios. In the applications of the next section, two transformations are made: one to give the first difference in expenditure; a second to give the ratio of saving to income. The first transformation is obtained by subtracting $E^{-1}\epsilon$ from both sides of (8) to give

$$\Delta^*\epsilon = \alpha_1\lambda\omega + \alpha_2(1-\lambda)\Delta^*\omega + \beta_1\lambda\mu + \beta_2(1-\lambda)\Delta^*\mu - \lambda E^{-1}\epsilon \quad (10)$$

The second transformation is obtained by using the identity $\mu \equiv \epsilon + \sigma$ to give

$$\frac{\sigma}{\mu} = (1-\beta_1\lambda) - \beta_2(1-\lambda)\frac{\Delta^*\mu}{\mu} - \alpha_1\lambda\frac{\omega}{\mu} - \alpha_2(1-\lambda)\frac{\Delta^*\omega}{\mu} - (1-\lambda)\frac{E^{-1}\epsilon}{\mu} \quad (11)$$

In either case the structural constants can be estimated unequivocally from the regression constants. They should be approximately the same in the two formulations, and we shall see in the following section that this is in fact the case.

We come now to the problem of dividing income into two parts, μ_a and μ_b, where $\mu_a + \mu_b \equiv \mu$. If, as in Britain, this is the only variable that can be so divided, then it is necessary to assume that α_1, α_2 and λ are the same for each type of income recipient. On these assumptions, (10) and (11) become, respectively,

$$\Delta^*\epsilon = \alpha_1\lambda\omega + \alpha_2(1-\lambda)\Delta^*\omega + \beta_{1a}\lambda\mu_a + \beta_{1b}\lambda\mu_b$$
$$+ \beta_{2a}(1-\lambda)\Delta^*\mu_a + \beta_{2b}(1-\lambda)\Delta^*\mu_b - \lambda E^{-1}\epsilon \quad (12)$$

and

$$\frac{\sigma}{\mu} = (1-\beta_{1a}\lambda)\frac{\mu_a}{\mu} + (1-\beta_{1b}\lambda)\frac{\mu_b}{\mu} - \beta_{2a}(1-\lambda)\frac{\Delta^*\mu_a}{\mu} - \beta_{2b}(1-\lambda)\frac{\Delta^*\mu_b}{\mu}$$
$$- \alpha_1\frac{\lambda\omega}{\mu} - \alpha_2(1-\lambda)\frac{\Delta^*\omega}{\mu} - (1-\lambda)\frac{E^{-1}\epsilon}{\mu} \quad (13)$$

Before we turn to the question of revaluations, referred to in the preceding section, there is one additional variable that ought to be introduced: government measures to influence the level of spending. Largely through an attempt to maintain the value of the £ in the face of continuous wage and price inflation, the government has manipulated a number of financial and fiscal instruments, hire-purchase and credit conditions, interest rates and taxation, partly with the object of restraining or encouraging spending. It would be interesting to construct a sophisticated indicator of the movement of these influences, but in this and the earlier papers referred to, their combined movement is represented by the percentage down-payment on the hire-purchase of radio and electrical goods. As we shall see, even this imperfect indicator has a significant influence on spending and saving.

This indicator, ξ say, is introduced into the model as follows. If ξ^* denotes the normal level of this indicator then it is assumed that ξ^* is related to ξ in exactly the same way that ω_1 and μ_1 are related to ω and μ in (4) and (5). That is,

$$\xi^* = \lambda\xi + (1 - \lambda)E^{-1}\xi^* \tag{14}$$

where the constant λ has the same value as in (4) and (5), a further rigidity. To the right-hand side of (2), a further term is added: $\delta(\xi - \xi^*)$, where δ is a constant. The result of this is to introduce a term $\delta(1 - \lambda)\varDelta^*\xi$ into (10) and (12) and a corresponding term $-\delta(1 - \lambda)\varDelta^*\xi/\mu$ into (11) and (13). Again, in each case, the value of δ can be estimated from the regression analysis.

This brings us to the question of revaluations (capital gains and losses) which introduce difficulties somewhat different from those encountered so far. In developing the model to this point, I have defined wealth as accumulated savings. The introduction of revaluations means that these should also be included in the concept of wealth, which should now be given a different symbol, say ω^*. Thus

$$\omega^* \equiv E^{-1}(\omega^* + \sigma + \rho) \tag{15}$$

where ρ denotes revaluations. Our former concept of wealth might now be taken as corresponding to permanent wealth, that is,

$$\omega_1^* = E^{-1}(\omega^* + \sigma) \tag{16}$$

and so we should have

$$\omega_2^* = E^{-1}\rho \tag{17}$$

that is, transient wealth equals last year's revaluations.

Since, for the present, we have no means of measuring ρ directly, we must find some indirect method of measurement if we are to make any use of the foregoing equations. One method would be to connect revaluations to wealth by the relationship

$$\rho = \frac{(\mu_b - \mu_b^*)}{\mu_b^*}\omega^*$$
$$= \gamma\mu_b - \omega^* \tag{18}$$

where $\gamma = \omega^*/\mu_b^*$, that is to say the reciprocal of the normal income, μ_b^*, associated with wealth, ω^*. Equation (18) implies that wealth is revalued each year in such a way that the actual income obtained from it in the year appears normal in relation to the new value. I realize that μ_b as previously defined is not exactly appropriate in this context, but it does not seem worth while, in this case, to introduce a new symbol.

It follows from (15) and (18) that

$$\omega^* = E^{-1}(\gamma\mu_h + \sigma) \tag{19}$$

Let us now see what happens if we try to introduce these ideas into the basic equation. We have already seen that it is impossible to introduce all the variables into the final equation and that the obvious candidate for omission is the transient component of wealth. Let us, therefore, start from the equation

$$\begin{aligned}
\epsilon &= \alpha_1 \omega_1^* + \beta_1 \mu_1 + \beta_2 \mu_2 \\
&= \alpha_1 \gamma E^{-2} \mu_b + \alpha_1(E^{-2} + E^{-1})\sigma + \beta_2 \mu + (\beta_1 - \beta_2)\mu_1
\end{aligned} \tag{20}$$

Any attempt to remove μ_1 from this equation by the method of substitution which led to (8) yields an overidentified equation, that is one with more regression constants than there are structural constants. However, another possibility is available since it follows from (5) that

$$\mu_1 = \lambda \sum_{\theta=0}^{\infty} (1 - \lambda)^\theta E^{-\theta} \mu \tag{21}$$

Accordingly, (20) can be expressed in the form

$$\epsilon = \alpha_1 \gamma E^{-2} \mu_b + \alpha_1(E^{-2} + E^{-1})\sigma + \beta_2 \mu + (\beta_1 - \beta_2)\lambda \sum_{\theta=0}^{\infty} (1 - \lambda)^\theta E^{-\theta} \mu \tag{22}$$

The parameters in this equation could be estimated by varying λ until the proportion of the variance of ϵ accounted for by the equation was maximized. It may well be, however, that the maximum would turn out to be not very well defined; also, even if, as in Britain, λ is of the order of 0·7, it would be necessary to have a series for μ extending some ten to fifteen years back from the starting date of the main body of observations.

It will be noticed that a direct estimate of ω_1^* is not required in (22) but, since γ is estimated in that equation it can always be built up, using (16) and (19). It will also be noticed that if $\alpha_1 \omega_1^*$ in (20) were replaced by $\alpha\omega^*$, then $\alpha_1\gamma E^{-2}\mu_b$ and $\alpha_1(E^{-2} + E^{-1})\sigma$ in (22) would be replaced respectively by $\alpha\gamma E^{-1}\mu_b$ and $\alpha E^{-1}\sigma$. In principle, therefore, it would be possible to distinguish between the hypotheses that the community responds to total wealth or only to its permanent component.

4. APPLICATIONS TO THE PERSONAL SECTOR IN BRITAIN

This section contains the results of a number of calculations relating to the personal sector in Britain. The data, set out in tables I and II at the end of this paper, relate to the years 1949 through 1964 and are taken, except for the figures for ξ, from the 1965 *Blue Book* on national income and expenditure [87].

Four forms of the basic equation were considered, denoted by the letters A, B, C and D. These forms correspond to (10), (12), (11) and (13) of the preceding section except that in each case the appropriate term in ξ is added. Four variants of each form were considered, denoted by the numerals (i), (ii), (iii) and (iv). These variants correspond to subsets of variables in the different forms. The four variants are as follows.

(i) $\varDelta^*\omega$ and $\varDelta^*\mu$ are omitted. This corresponds to the hypothesis that people respond only to the permanent components of wealth and income and are unaffected by the transient components.

(ii) ω and $\varDelta^*\mu$ are omitted. This corresponds to the hypothesis that people respond only to the transient component of wealth and the permanent component of income.

(iii) $\varDelta^*\omega$ is omitted. This corresponds to the hypothesis that people do not respond to the transient component of wealth but do respond to the transient component of income.

(iv) $\varDelta^*\mu$ is omitted. This corresponds to the hypothesis that people do not respond to the transient component of income but do respond to the transient component of wealth.

The regression estimates of the constants in these sixteen equations are set out in table IV at the end of the paper. The derived estimates of the structural parameters are set out in table 1 opposite. The main positive interest of this table lies in the left-hand half which contains the structural parameters derived from the odd-numbered variants A (i) through D (iii); the right-hand half is mainly of negative interest in showing what happens if one insists on trying to introduce the effects of transient wealth.

If we concentrate on the first eight columns we can see that the α's and β's are remarkably constant across the rows, a very satisfactory result. From the value of α_1 we see that an extra £1000 of wealth is accompanied, other things being equal, by an extra £60 of spending, hence, in the same circumstances, by £60 less saving. Correspondingly, from the value of β_1, we see that an extra £1000 of permanent income is accompanied, other things being equal, by an extra £775 of spending, hence an extra £225 of saving. If we consider not income in general but wages and small transfers on the one hand and other forms of income on the other, the extra £775 of spending is replaced by about £790 and £650, respectively. This difference, though not negligible, is perhaps smaller than might be expected; it is interesting, therefore, to look at the effect of transient income. From the value of β_2 we see that an extra £1000 of transient income is accompanied, other things being equal, by an extra £450 or so of spending, hence an extra £550 or so of saving. As can be seen from table IV at the end of the paper, this effect cannot be estimated accurately. When, however, we try to divide it, in B (iii) and D (iii) between the two types of income, we find a striking result. In the case of wages and small

TABLE 1   MODELS FOR THE PERSONAL SECTOR: STRUCTURAL PARAMETERS

	A (i)	A (iii)	B (i)	B (iii)	C (i)	C (iii)	D (i)	D (iii)	A (ii)	A (iv)	B (ii)	B (iv)	C (ii)	C (iv)	D (ii)	D (iv)
α_1	0·059	0·059	0·061	0·061	0·059	0·059	0·060	0·060	—	0·047	—	0·048	—	0·048	—	0·050
α_2	—	—	—	—	—	—	—	—	-1·243	-1·001	-1·229	-1·180	-1·430	-0·778	-1·362	-0·898
β_1	0·772	0·774	—	—	0·776	0·776	—	—	1·008	0·822	—	—	1·007	0·816	—	—
β_{1a}	—	—	0·786	0·795	—	—	0·785	0·789	—	—	1·003	0·839	—	—	0·990	0·828
β_{1b}	—	—	0·665	0·604	—	—	0·698	0·659	—	—	1·033	0·696	—	—	1·087	0·723
β_2	—	0·499	—	—	—	0·436	—	—	—	—	—	—	—	—	—	—
β_{2a}	—	—	—	0·766	—	—	—	0·739	—	—	—	—	—	—	—	—
β_{2b}	—	—	—	0·099	—	—	—	-0·025	—	—	—	—	—	—	—	—
δ	-41·6	-19·1	-48·7	-22·6	-37·8	-21·4	-41·7	-24·8	-19·1	-38·2	-18·9	-44·6	-21·9	-38·0	-21·2	-42·6
λ	0·846	0·648	0·865	0·682	0·821	0·670	0·834	0·703	0·594	0·824	0·593	0·845	0·625	0·814	0·620	0·830
R^2	0·928	0·937	0·930	0·942	0·973	0·975	0·973	0·977	0·937	0·937	0·886	0·939	0·950	0·975	0·951	0·975
d	1·90	2·00	2·00	2·32	1·96	2·04	2·05	2·33	2·00	2·00	1·90	2·13	1·96	2·04	1·89	2·16

transfers the effect of a unit change in transient income is only a little less than the effect of a unit change in permanent income; but for other types of income, the effect of a unit change in transient income is virtually zero. In other words, the distinction between permanent and transient components is practically irrelevant in the case of wages and small transfers but it is highly relevant in the case of other forms of income. Apparently, recipients of income from property and entrepreneurship spend rather less than recipients of wages and small transfers out of an increase in permanent income but virtually nothing out of an increase in transient income. This result seems to me decidedly plausible though, statistically speaking, it cannot be stated with much certainty.

When we look at the values of δ and λ we see that they fall into two groups, depending on whether or not transient income is included in the equation. The inclusion of this variable is accompanied by a smaller negative value of δ and a smaller positive value of λ.

The lower part of the table shows the values of the square of the coefficient of multiple correlation, R^2, and Durbin and Watson's statistic, d, for each of the sixteen models.

The right-hand side of the table shows the consequences of introducing transient wealth into the equation; an increase in transient wealth is apparently accompanied by a more or less corresponding decrease in spending. This result is not at all likely, and the approximately zero value of β_{2b} seems to provide a justification for omitting the term in transient wealth; if people do not spend out of transient income from property and entrepreneurship, they probably do not spend out of transient wealth either. If this argument is accepted we can entirely ignore the right-hand side of table 1.

The results obtained from the subdivision of income open the door to alternative methods of estimation, though I have not thought it worth-while to try these out. For example, if we put $\beta_{2b} = 0$ in variant B (iii), we could introduce the term in $\Delta^*\omega$ and so estimate α_2 at the same time as α_1, β_{1a}, β_{1b} and β_{2a}. Or, again, we might think it useful to simplify the model by putting $\beta_{1a} = \beta_{2a} = \beta_a$, say. However, this would involve a more complicated estimation procedure than the one I have used because it would require the replacement of the terms $\beta_{1a}\lambda\mu_a + \beta_{2a}(1-\lambda)\Delta^*\mu_a$ by $\beta_a\Delta^*\mu_a + \beta_a\lambda E^{-1}\mu_a$. Since λ is estimated separately from the term in $E^{-1}\epsilon$, the new equation would be overidentified and we should have to impose the constraint that the product of the coefficients of $\Delta^*\mu_a$ and $E^{-1}\epsilon$ be equal to the coefficient of $E^{-1}\mu_a$.

5.   DATA REVISION AND STRUCTURAL PARAMETERS

In Britain, as in many other countries, personal saving is not measured directly and the estimates of it in successive issues of the *Blue Book* [87] vary considerably. It is often thought that the parameters in a saving function based on such estimates must be very unstable. Some light on this question is provided by table 2 below. For model C (i) I have calculated the values of the structural parameters from the last three *Blue Books* for the periods 1949–1962 (three equations), 1949–1963 (two equations) and 1949–1964 (one equation). We can therefore observe the effect of revisions on the structural parameters as well as the effect of increasing the number of observations.

TABLE 2   MODEL C (i) FOR THE PERSONAL SECTOR: EFFECT OF REVISIONS ON THE STRUCTURAL PARAMETERS

	1949–1962			1949–1963		1949–1964
	BB 63	*BB* 64	*BB* 65	*BB* 64	*BB* 65	*BB* 65
α_1	0·073	0·063	0·061	0·061	0·060	0·059
β_1	0·721	0·763	0·768	0·764	0·772	0·776
δ	−31·3	−34·8	−37·5	−49·4	−38·8	−37·8
λ	0·778	0·790	0·817	0·860	0·824	0·821
R^2	0·969	0·966	0·968	0·963	0·970	0·973
d	1·76	1·82	1·90	1·81	2·03	1·96

These results seem reasonably encouraging. The change between the 1963 *Blue Book* and the two that followed it seems fairly substantial but, apart from this, the remaining changes are rather small and, in particular, the extreme values of δ and λ that come from *BB* 64: 1949–1963 have been reversed in the latest estimates.

6. APPLICATIONS TO THE COMPANY SECTOR IN BRITAIN

The model of spending and saving that I have been describing, though worked out originally to explain the behaviour of the personal sector, can also be applied to the company sector. In this application, income is disposable income including stock appreciation, spending is spending on dividend payments and saving is undistributed profit. Since in this case there is no subdivision of income, only models A and C are relevant. These two models give similar results and attention here will be restricted to model C, in which the dependent variable is the saving-income ratio. As in the case of the personal sector, the introduction of a term in $\Delta^* \omega$ leads to an apparent negative influence of transient wealth on dividend payments. Consequently only variants (i) and (iii) are tabulated. The data are given in table III at the end of this paper and the regressions are given in table V. The structural parameters appear in table 3 below.

TABLE 3   MODELS FOR THE COMPANY
SECTOR: STRUCTURAL PARAMETERS

	C (i)	C (iii)
α_1	0·022	0·042
β_1	0·154	−0·039
β_2	—	0·087
λ	0·356	0·199
R^2	0·860	0·905
d	1·04	1·45

The structural parameters of these models are very different from those in the corresponding models for the personal sector; but this is not at all surprising since the personal sector saves at most about 10 per cent of income whereas the company sector saves between 50 and 75 per cent. The low values of β_1 and λ will be noted; nevertheless, model C (iii) in particular reproduces the movements in the company saving-income ratio fairly accurately.

7. TRANSIENT AND STEADY STATES

In the past, I have approached this subject from a study of the differential equation connecting the rate of change of wealth, $\dot{\omega} = \sigma$, with ω and μ. However, it has been pointed out to me by my friend H. R. Fisher that it is not only illuminating but also much more in the spirit of the finite-difference approach used so far to express the relationship between spending and disposable income as a ratio of polynomials in the operator E. Once this is done, it is a simple matter to derive similar expressions for the ratios of spending or saving to income and to rewrite the equation so as to show explicitly the consequence of particular expressions for the growth of income.

Let us start with the following form of the basic equation from which the term in $\varDelta^* \omega$ is omitted and in which the term in $\varDelta^* \xi$ is ignored:

$$\epsilon = \alpha_1 \lambda \omega + \beta_1 \lambda \mu + \beta_2 (1 - \lambda) \varDelta^* \mu + (1 - \lambda) E^{-1} \epsilon \tag{23}$$

If we apply the operator $\varDelta^* \equiv (1 - E^{-1})$ to this equation and remember that $\varDelta^* \omega = E^{-1} \sigma = E^{-1}(\mu - \epsilon)$, we find that

$$\epsilon = \frac{[\beta_1 \lambda + \beta_2(1 - \lambda)] + [(\alpha_1 - \beta_1)\lambda - 2\beta_2(1 - \lambda)] E^{-1} + \beta_2(1 - \lambda) E^{-2}}{1 - [2 - (1 + \alpha_1)\lambda] E^{-1} + (1 - \lambda) E^{-2}} \mu \tag{24}$$

Consider now the case in which $E^\theta \mu$ is proportional to $(1 + \pi)^\theta$, where π is a constant. If we substitute for $E^{-\theta}$ in (24), we obtain

$$\epsilon = \frac{\alpha_1 \lambda + (\alpha_1 + \beta_1) \lambda \pi + [\beta_1 \lambda + \beta_2 (1 - \lambda)] \pi^2}{\alpha_1 \lambda + (1 + \alpha_1) \lambda \pi + \pi^2} \mu \qquad (25)$$

from which it follows that

$$\frac{\sigma}{\mu} = \frac{(1 - \beta_1) \lambda \pi + [1 - \beta_1 \lambda - \beta_2 (1 - \lambda)] \pi^2}{\alpha_1 \lambda + (1 + \alpha_1) \lambda \pi + \pi^2} \qquad (26)$$

From (26) we can see that if $\pi = 0$, then $\sigma/\mu = 0$, that is if income does not grow nothing is saved. At the other extreme, as π increases, σ/μ tends to the limit $[1 - \beta_1 \lambda - \beta_2 (1 - \lambda)]$. With the values of the parameters given in table 1 of section 4 above, this limit is not very sensitive to the inclusion or exclusion of a term in transient income. Thus, for models C (i) and C (iii) the limits are 0·36 and 0·34 respectively. Such limits can never be reached, but by taking intermediate values of π we can see that a steady growth of real disposable personal income at 3 per cent a year would be accompanied by a saving ratio of 8 per cent; whereas steady growth at 6 per cent a year would have a corresponding saving ratio of 12 per cent.

Let us now see what happens if we follow the differential approach. We have already seen from (21) that the permanent component can be expressed as a weighted average of all past values of income. An exactly similar equation holds for wealth. If we assume that $E^\theta \mu$ is proportional to $e^{\rho\theta}$, then it follows that

$$\frac{\mu_1}{\mu} = \frac{\lambda}{1 - (1 - \lambda) e^{-\rho}} = \zeta \qquad (27)$$

say. If we denote the rate of change of wealth with respect to time by $\dot{\omega}$ and, as before, omit the term in transient wealth and ignore changes in the government policy variable, we can write

$$\dot{\omega} = \sigma$$
$$= \mu - \epsilon$$
$$= [1 - \beta_1 \zeta - \beta_2 (1 - \zeta)] \mu - \alpha_1 \zeta \omega$$
$$= \phi\mu - \psi\omega \qquad (28)$$

say. The solution of this differential equation is

$$\omega = \kappa e^{-\psi\theta} + \frac{\phi\mu}{\psi + \rho} \qquad (29)$$

where

$$\kappa \equiv \bar{\omega} - \frac{\phi\bar{\mu}}{\psi + \rho} \qquad (30)$$

that is the difference between actual and equilibrium wealth at time $\theta = 0$ for the given growth rate, ρ.

If we differentiate (29) with respect to time, we obtain

$$\dot{\omega} = -\kappa\psi e^{-\psi\theta} + \frac{\phi\rho\mu}{\psi + \rho} \tag{31}$$

which, as a saving-income ratio, can be written

$$\frac{\sigma}{\mu} = -\frac{\kappa\psi e^{-\psi\theta}}{\mu} + \frac{\phi\rho}{\psi + \rho} \tag{32}$$

Thus, apart from the transient term (which takes a non-zero value only if actual initial wealth is not equal to equilibrium initial wealth), the saving ratio is, again, a function of the growth rate. The only difference between (26) and the second, steady-state term on the right-hand side of (32) is that in the former, time is treated as discrete whereas in the latter it is treated as continuous. This can be seen by writing $\phi\rho/(\psi + \rho)$ out in full, using (27) and (28), and approximating e^ρ by $1 + \rho$. The resulting equation is the same as (26) with ρ in place of π. The limits are the same in each case: if $\rho = 0$ there is no saving in the steady-state; as ρ increases, ζ tends to λ and so the limit of the ratio of saving to income is $1 - \beta_1\lambda - \beta_2(1 - \lambda)$ as before.

8. A VISUAL SUMMARY

By way of conclusion, I shall set out some of the results described above in diagrammatic form. The numerical values on which these diagrams are based are shown in tables VI through IX.

First, let us see what year-to-year changes have taken place in consumers' expenditure at constant prices and how well the model is able to account for them. Diagram 1 shows the actual course of these changes together with the regression estimates obtained from models A (i) and B (iii). These changes have followed a wave-like movement of considerable amplitude which is reproduced fairly well by both the models.

Second, let us now look at the position if we take the personal saving-income ratio as the dependent variable. The actual movement of this ratio is shown in diagram 2 together with the movement calculated from models C (i) and D (iii). Naturally, the wave-like movements are still in evidence, but perhaps the most striking feature of the diagram is the strong upward movement in the ratio. In the absence of any model-building, such a movement might be taken as evidence of a change in consumers' behaviour in favour of saving. We know, however, from the models presented, that this trend can be accounted for by responses with constant coefficients to the movements of income and wealth.

DIAGRAM 1 YEAR-TO-YEAR CHANGES IN SPENDING BY THE PERSONAL SECTOR IN BRITAIN, 1948–1949 TO 1963–1964

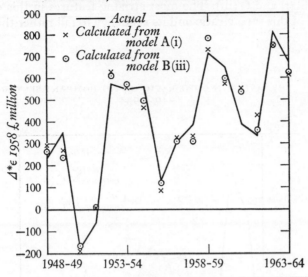

DIAGRAM 2 THE SAVING–INCOME RATIO OF THE PERSONAL SECTOR IN BRITAIN, 1949–1964

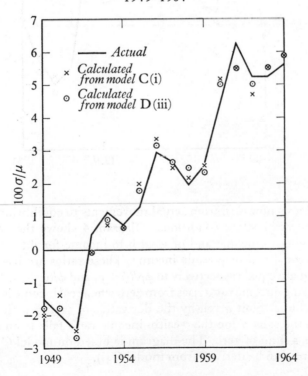

Third, diagram 3 provides for the company sector information similar to that provided in diagram 2 for the personal sector. The models used are again C (i) and C (iii). The most striking features in this case are the high level of this saving ratio and its tendency to fall rather than rise over the period.

DIAGRAM 3   THE SAVING–INCOME RATIO OF THE COMPANY SECTOR IN BRITAIN, 1949–1964

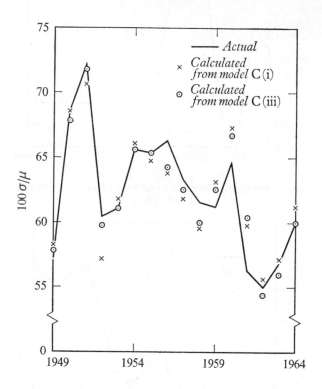

Fourth, let us now turn from actual movements to equilibrium relationships under steady-state conditions. Diagram 4 shows the equilibrium ratios of saving to income and of wealth to income for different growth rates of personal real disposable income. These ratios are based on (29) and (32) and are equal respectively to $\phi\rho/(\psi + \rho)$ and $\phi/(\psi + \rho)$. As we have seen, the saving-income ratio rises from zero when real income is stationary towards an upper limit given by the derivative of saving with respect to income. At the same time the wealth–income ratio falls from a value of ϕ/ψ towards a limit of zero. The diagram is based on model C (iii); very similar figures can be derived from model C (i).

Finally, diagram 5 shows the equilibrium ratios of saving to income and of wealth to income for different growth rates of company real disposable income, based on precisely the same methods as were used in drawing up diagram 4 for the personal sector. In this case it may be illuminating to think not in terms of the wealth–income ratio but in terms of its reciprocal, the rate of return. The results given then show that the higher the growth rate of company real income the higher will be the associated equilibrium rate of return.

DIAGRAM 4   STEADY-STATE RATIOS
FOR THE PERSONAL SECTOR,
BASED ON MODEL C (iii)

DIAGRAM 5   STEADY-STATE RATIOS
FOR THE COMPANY SECTOR,
BASED ON MODEL C (iii)

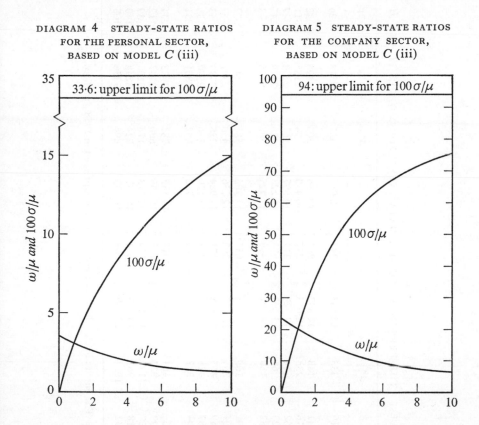

In bringing this paper to a close, I shall mention two aspects of the model that I shall not discuss, as they have been described in the earlier papers referred to [66, 82]. One is that the models can be equally well applied to quarterly data and in this form provide quite usable forecasts for a year or so ahead. Another is that the calculation of equilibrium ratios and a comparison of the resultant saving with investment requirements can be useful in connection with medium-term planning, because recent experience may be a poor guide to what can be expected under equilibrium conditions.

TABLE I THE PERSONAL SECTOR: DATA INPUT FOR MODELS A AND B

Year	$\Delta*\epsilon$	ω	$\Delta*\omega$	μ	$\Delta*\mu$	μ_a	$\Delta*\mu_a$	μ_b	$\Delta*\mu_b$	$E^{-1}\epsilon$	$\Delta*\xi$
1949	238	53 219	−333	12 568	383	10 050	357	2518	26	12 518	0
1950	350	53 031	−188	12 852	284	10 356	306	2496	−22	12 756	0
1951	−177	52 776	−255	12 615	−237	10 430	74	2185	−311	13 106	0
1952	−61	52 462	−314	12 929	314	10 697	267	2232	47	12 929	21·5
1953	575	52 523	61	13 602	673	11 223	526	2379	147	12 868	1·8
1954	548	52 682	159	14 101	499	11 725	502	2376	−3	13 443	−10·7
1955	560	52 791	109	14 755	654	12 306	581	2448	72	13 991	−0·6
1956	131	52 994	203	15 147	392	12 756	450	2391	−57	14 551	25·8
1957	307	53 459	465	15 418	271	12 984	228	2434	43	14 682	2·2
1958	384	53 887	428	15 690	272	13 120	136	2570	136	14 989	−8·8
1959	716	54 204	317	16 553	863	13 752	632	2801	231	15 373	−31·2
1960	648	54 668	464	17 569	1016	14 535	783	3035	234	16 089	6·7
1961	387	55 500	832	18 282	713	15 135	600	3147	112	16 737	3·3
1962	337	56 657	1157	18 421	139	15 313	178	3108	−39	17 124	−5·7
1963	809	57 618	961	19 285	864	16 037	724	3248	140	17 461	−4·3
1964	673	58 632	1014	20 089	804	16 733	696	3356	108	18 270	0

Main source: 1965 *Blue Book*. The entries in all columns except the last are expressed in 1958 £million.

TABLE II   THE PERSONAL SECTOR: DATA INPUT FOR MODELS C AND D

Year	σ/μ	ω/μ	$\Delta^*\omega/\mu$	$\Delta^*\mu/\mu$	μ_a/μ	$\Delta^*\mu_a/\mu$	μ_b/μ	$\Delta^*\mu_b/\mu$	$E^{-1}\epsilon/\mu$	$\Delta^*\xi'/\mu$
1949	−0·014959	4·2345	−0·026496	0·030474	0·79965	0·028405	0·20035	0·002069	0·99602	0
1950	−0·019841	4·1263	−0·014628	0·022098	0·80579	0·023810	0·19421	−0·001712	0·99253	0
1951	−0·024891	4·1836	−0·020214	−0·018787	0·82679	0·005866	0·17321	−0·024653	1·03890	0
1952	0·004718	4·0577	−0·024286	0·024286	0·82736	0·020651	0·17264	0·003635	1·00000	0·0016629
1953	0·011689	3·8614	−0·004485	0·049478	0·82510	0·038671	0·17490	0·010807	0·94604	0·0001323
1954	0·007730	3·7360	0·011276	0·035388	0·83150	0·035600	0·16850	−0·000213	0·95334	−0·0007588
1955	0·013758	3·5778	0·007387	0·044324	0·83402	0·039376	0·16591	−0·004880	0·94822	−0·0000407
1956	0·030699	3·4986	0·013402	0·025880	0·84215	0·029709	0·15785	−0·003763	0·96065	0·0017033
1957	0·027760	3·4673	0·030160	0·017577	0·84213	0·014788	0·15787	0·002789	0·95226	0·0001427
1958	0·020204	3·4345	0·027279	0·017336	0·83620	0·008668	0·16380	0·008668	0·95532	−0·0005609
1959	0·028031	3·2746	0·019151	0·052136	0·83079	0·038180	0·16921	0·013955	0·92871	−0·0018849
1960	0·047356	3·1116	0·026410	0·057829	0·82731	0·044567	0·17275	0·013319	0·91576	0·0003814
1961	0·063286	3·0358	0·045509	0·039000	0·82786	0·032819	0·17214	0·006126	0·91549	0·0001805
1962	0·052169	3·0757	0·062809	0·075457	0·83128	0·009663	0·16872	−0·002117	0·92959	−0·0003094
1963	0·052580	2·9877	0·049831	0·044802	0·83158	0·037542	0·16842	0·007260	0·90542	−0·0002230
1964	0·056996	2·9186	0·050475	0·040022	0·83294	0·034646	0·16706	0·005376	0·90945	0

Main source: 1965 *Blue Book*.

TABLE III THE COMPANY SECTOR: DATA INPUT FOR MODELS C (i) AND (iii)

Year	σ/μ	ω/μ	$\Delta^*\mu/\mu$	$E^{-1}\epsilon/\mu$
1949	0·57429	9·2317	−0·14763	0·45188
1950	0·68661	7·2187	0·26384	0·31339
1951	0·72408	7·0606	0·10686	0·27990
1952	0·60423	12·1490	−0·56067	0·43062
1953	0·61220	11·7920	0·07537	0·36594
1954	0·65963	10·1070	0·18519	0·31599
1955	0·65569	10·3640	0·03746	0·32717
1956	0·66725	10·7620	0·02336	0·33671
1957	0·63451	12·2270	−0·06978	0·35596
1958	0·61765	13·1530	−0·02266	0·37367
1959	0·61486	12·1950	0·11443	0·33860
1960	0·65027	9·9734	0·22141	0·29987
1961	0·56690	11·7790	−0·10874	0·38776
1962	0·55242	12·7690	−0·03431	0·44796
1963	0·57066	12·5650	0·05681	0·42287
1964	0·59835	11·1920	0·14798	0·37714

Main source: 1965 *Blue Book.*

TABLE IV   THE PERSONAL SECTOR: REGRESSION ESTIMATES FOR SIXTEEN MODELS

Model	ω	$\Delta^*\omega$	μ	μ_a	μ_b	$\Delta^*\mu$	$\Delta^*\mu_a$	$\Delta^*\mu_b$	$E^{-1}\epsilon$	$\Delta^*\xi$	R^2	d
A (i)	0·0502±0·0085	—	0·653±0·075	—	—	—	—	—	-0·846±0·107	-6·41±1·75	0·928	1·90
(ii)	—	—	0·599±0·092	—	—	—	—	—	-0·594±0·095	-7·75±2·20	0·886	1·92
(iii)	0·0384±0·0129	-0·505±0·121	0·501±0·146	—	—	—	—	—	-0·648±0·195	-6·74±1·74	0·937	2·00
(iv)	0·0383±0·0129	-0·176±0·146	0·677±0·076	—	—	0·176±0·146	—	—	-0·824±0·107	-6·74±1·74	0·937	2·00
B (i)	0·0529±0·0099	—	—	0·680±0·090	0·575±0·154	—	—	—	-0·865±0·115	-6·57±1·82	0·930	2·00
(ii)	—	—	—	0·595±0·108	0·612±0·197	—	—	—	-0·593±0·100	-7·71±2·34	0·886	1·90
(iii)	0·0419±0·0143	-0·501±0·138	—	0·542±0·162	0·412±0·212	—	—	—	-0·682±0·211	-7·18±1·91	0·942	2·32
(iv)	0·0409±0·0137	-0·183±0·150	—	0·709±0·091	0·588±0·150	—	0·244±0·184	0·031±0·298	-0·845±0·114	-6·94±1·81	0·939	2·13

Model	ω/μ	$\Delta^*\omega/\mu$	$\mu/\mu\equiv1$	μ_a/μ	μ_b/μ	$\Delta^*\mu/\mu$	$\Delta^*\mu_a/\mu$	$\Delta^*\mu_b/\mu$	$E^{-1}\epsilon/\mu$	$\Delta^*\xi/\mu$	R^2	d
C (i)	-0·0482±0·0075	—	0·363±0·064	—	—	—	—	—	-0·179±0·092	6·76±1·66	0·973	1·96
(ii)	—	—	0·371±0·093	—	—	—	—	—	-0·375±0·096	8·22±2·23	0·950	1·96
(iii)	-0·0393±0·0121	0·537±0·129	0·480±0·141	—	—	—	—	—	-0·330±0·186	7·06±1·70	0·975	2·04
(iv)	-0·0393±0·0121	0·145±0·154	0·336±0·071	—	—	-0·144±0·154	—	—	-0·186±0·092	7·06±1·70	0·975	2·04
D (i)	-0·0502±0·0090	—	—	0·345±0·077	0·417±0·138	—	—	—	-0·166±0·099	6·90±1·75	0·973	2·05
(ii)	—	—	—	0·386±0·110	0·326±0·186	—	—	—	-0·380±0·101	8·04±2·40	0·951	1·89
(iii)	-0·0424±0·0135	0·517±0·150	—	0·446±0·155	0·537±0·203	—	—	—	-0·297±0·202	7·37±1·85	0·977	2·33
(iv)	-0·0413±0·0130	0·153±0·160	—	0·313±0·084	0·400±0·140	—	-0·220±0·191	0·007±0·287	-0·170±0·100	7·26±1·80	0·975	2·16

The numbers in the first ten columns represent the regression coefficients for the variables at the head of the column together with the corresponding standard errors. The numbers in the last two columns represent respectively the square of the multiple correlation coefficient and Durbin and Watson's statistic. The basic forms of the models are:

A: $\Delta^*\epsilon = \alpha_1\lambda\omega + \alpha_2(1-\lambda)\Delta^*\omega + \beta_1\lambda\mu + \beta_2(1-\lambda)\Delta^*\mu - \lambda E^{-1}\epsilon + \delta(1-\lambda)\Delta^*\xi$

B: $\Delta^*\epsilon = \alpha_1\lambda\omega + \alpha_2(1-\lambda)\Delta^*\omega + \beta_{1a}\lambda\mu_a + \beta_{1b}\lambda\mu_b + \beta_{2a}(1-\lambda)\Delta^*\mu_a + \beta_{2b}(1-\lambda)\Delta^*\mu_b - \lambda E^{-1}\epsilon + \delta(1-\lambda)\Delta^*\xi$

C: $\sigma/\mu = (1-\beta_1\lambda)\mu/\mu - \beta_2(1-\lambda)\Delta^*\mu/\mu - \alpha_1\lambda\omega/\mu - \alpha_2(1-\lambda)\Delta^*\omega/\mu - (1-\lambda)E^{-1}\epsilon/\mu - \delta(1-\lambda)\Delta^*\xi/\mu$

D: $\sigma/\mu = (1-\beta_{1a}\lambda)\mu_a/\mu + (1-\beta_{1b}\lambda)\mu_b/\mu - \beta_{2a}(1-\lambda)\Delta^*\mu_a/\mu - \beta_{2b}(1-\lambda)\Delta^*\mu_b/\mu - \alpha_1\lambda\omega/\mu - \alpha_2(1-\lambda)\Delta^*\omega/\mu - (1-\lambda)E^{-1}\epsilon/\mu - \delta(1-\lambda)\Delta^*\xi/\mu$

TABLE V   THE COMPANY SECTOR: REGRESSION ESTIMATES FOR TWO MODELS

Model	ω/μ	$\Delta^*\omega/\mu$	$\mu/\mu \equiv 1$	$\Delta^*\mu/\mu$	$E^{-1}\epsilon/\mu$	R^2	d
C (i)	$-0\cdot0079 \pm 0\cdot0032$	—	$0\cdot945 \pm 0\cdot036$	—	$-0\cdot644 \pm 0\cdot113$	$0\cdot860$	$1\cdot04$
C (iii)	$-0\cdot0083 \pm 0\cdot0028$	—	$1\cdot008 \pm 0\cdot041$	$-0\cdot069 \pm 0\cdot029$	$-0\cdot801 \pm 0\cdot116$	$0\cdot905$	$1\cdot45$

The numbers in the first five columns represent the regression coefficients for the variable at the head of the column together with the corresponding standard errors. The numbers in the last two columns represent respectively the square of the multiple correlation coefficient and Durbin and Watson's statistic. The basic form of the model is

$$\sigma/\mu = (1 - \beta_1 \lambda) - \beta_2(1 - \lambda) \, \Delta^*\mu/\mu - \alpha_1 \lambda \omega/\mu - \alpha_2(1 - \lambda) \, \Delta^*\omega/\mu - (1 - \lambda) \, E^{-1} \epsilon/\mu$$

Models B and D do not apply to companies since there is no subdivision by type of income in their case. Model A adds nothing to model C. And models C (ii) and C (iv), involving a term in $\Delta^*\omega/\mu$, lead to the implausible conclusion that an increase in transient wealth discourages spending, just as the corresponding models did in the case of the personal sector.

TABLE VI   THE PERSONAL SECTOR: YEAR-TO-YEAR CHANGES IN
SPENDING, $\Delta^*\epsilon$

(1958 £ *million*)

Year	Actual	Calculated			
		A (i)	A (iii)	B (i)	B (iii)
1949	238	295	298	271	266
1950	350	270	262	250	239
1951	−177	−194	−185	−195	−164
1952	−61	8	27	9	11
1953	575	628	602	637	609
1954	548	556	539	570	574
1955	560	461	475	472	499
1956	131	84	93	98	120
1957	307	325	300	344	310
1958	384	335	328	345	308
1959	716	733	778	739	782
1960	648	572	613	562	599
1961	387	553	552	541	539
1962	337	432	375	425	361
1963	809	751	745	748	751
1964	673	615	623	609	625

TABLE VII   THE PERSONAL SECTOR: PERCENTAGE OF DISPOSABLE
INCOME SAVED, $100\sigma/\mu$

Year	Actual	Calculated			
		C (i)	C (iii)	D (i)	D (iii)
1949	−1·5	−1·9	−1·9	−1·8	−1·8
1950	−2·0	−1·3	−1·3	−1·2	−1·2
1951	−2·5	−2·4	−2·5	−2·4	−2·6
1952	0·5	0·0	0·1	0·0	0·0
1953	1·2	0·9	1·0	0·8	0·9
1954	0·8	0·7	0·8	0·7	0·6
1955	1·4	2·1	2·0	2·0	1·8
1956	3·1	3·4	3·4	3·4	3·2
1957	2·8	2·7	2·8	2·6	2·8
1958	2·0	2·3	2·3	2·2	2·5
1959	2·8	2·6	2·4	2·6	2·4
1960	4·7	5·2	5·0	5·2	5·0
1961	6·3	5·4	5·4	5·5	5·5
1962	5·2	4·6	4·9	4·7	5·0
1963	5·3	5·6	5·6	5·6	5·5
1964	5·7	6·0	5·9	6·0	5·9

TABLE VIII   THE COMPANY SECTOR: PERCENTAGE
OF DISPOSABLE INCOME SAVED, $100\sigma/\mu$

Year	Actual	Calculated	
		C (i)	C (iii)
1949	57	58	58
1950	69	69	68
1951	72	71	72
1952	60	57	60
1953	61	62	61
1954	66	66	66
1955	66	65	66
1956	67	64	65
1957	63	62	63
1958	62	60	60
1959	61	63	63
1960	65	67	67
1961	57	60	61
1962	55	56	55
1963	57	57	56
1964	60	61	60

TABLE IX   BOTH SECTORS: EQUILIBRIUM RATIOS, $100\sigma/\mu$
AND ω/μ, CALCULATED FROM MODEL C (iii) FOR DIFFERENT
GROWTH RATES, ρ, OF REAL INCOME

100ρ	Persons		Companies	
	$100\sigma/\mu$	ω/μ	$100\sigma/\mu$	ω/μ
0	0	3·8	0	24·7
1	3·3	3·3	21	21·0
2	5·8	2·9	35	17·5
3	7·8	2·6	46	15·3
4	9·5	2·4	54	13·5
5	10·8	2·2	60	12·0
6	12·0	2·0	65	10·8
7	13·0	1·9	69	10·0
8	13·9	1·8	72	9·0
9	14·6	1·6	75	8·3
10	15·3	1·5	77	7·7
∞	33·6	0	94	0

A UNITARY INTERPRETATION OF PROFESSOR STONE'S EQUATIONS FOR SAVINGS AND EXPENDITURE

by H. R. FISHER

Professor Stone kindly showed me *Spending and Saving in relation to Income and Wealth* while that paper was being set in type. It occurred to me that there was something disconcerting in his case (iv) regression equations, which apparently indicated a negative value for α_2, the coefficient applying to the transient component of wealth in the equation for expenditure. In two of the cases A there are found coefficients of transient wealth and transient income as in the following extract from table 1:

	Case A (iii)	Case A (iv)
α_2 (applying to transient wealth)	0	−1·001
β_2 (applying to transient income)	0·499	0

the zero values having been assigned beforehand and the others indicated by least-squares regression. The observations support the solutions (iii) and (iv) equally, the two values of R^2 being the same. Since, then, these two solutions appear so different, one is tempted to ask whether the observations can tell us anything useful. The negative coefficient obviously rules out (iv) as describing a plausible model of behaviour. But so also does the zero coefficient in (iii). For if spenders respond substantially to transient income, why should they respond not at all to transient wealth.

These difficulties disappear when it is seen that cases (iii) and (iv) are not two isolated alternatives, but two out of a continuous range of possible solutions all equally supported by the data (in that they lead to the same estimated values of expenditure, and so of R^2), and that in this range there are some solutions that imply entirely plausible values of the coefficients α_1, α_2, β_1, β_2. This possibility of a complete set of plausible coefficients supplies an encouraging confirmation of Professor Stone's model. There are various ways, more or less intuitive, by which one might reach the hypothesis that expenditure is a linear transform of the time-series of income, with perhaps a time-trend built in. The Stone model distinguishes itself from others by the fact that spenders' habitual modes of reaction and adaption are open to explicit description, so that the parameters found to describe these habitual modes can be tested not only for their success in reproducing the data but also for their psychological plausibility. It is encouraging to find, from the analysis below, that this test of plausibility can be passed (contrarily to the first impression given by the values quoted above) and without recourse to a time-trend. As we shall see, there is a certain liberty of choice as to what, in detail, the habit-parameters are; but this does not detract from the attractiveness and usefulness of the model.

The fundamental equation of the model, equation (8), is

$$\epsilon = \alpha_1 \lambda\omega + \alpha_2(1-\lambda)\Delta^*\omega + \beta_1\lambda\mu + \beta_2(1-\lambda)\Delta^*\mu + (1-\lambda)E^{-1}\epsilon \quad (8)$$

As written, this has five terms on the right-hand side. But if one tried to evaluate the constants by regression analysis one would get indeterminate equations, because there holds between the data the identical linear relation

$$-\Delta^*\omega + \mu - \Delta^*\mu - E^{-1}\epsilon = 0 \qquad (9)$$

If, to get over this, one simply drops one of the first four terms in the right-hand side of (8), one commits oneself to the assumption that a selected one of α_1, α_2, β_1, β_2 is zero. But such an assumption is unnecessary. One may instead reach a 4-term expression for ϵ by using (9) to eliminate either $\Delta^*\omega$, μ or $\Delta^*\mu$ (or indeed $E^{-1}\epsilon$). If $\Delta^*\omega$ is eliminated, the equation is

$$\epsilon = \alpha_1\lambda\omega + \{\beta_1\lambda + \alpha_2(1-\lambda)\}\mu + (1-\lambda)(\beta_2-\alpha_2)\Delta^*\mu$$
$$+ (1-\lambda)(1-\alpha_2)E^{-1}\epsilon \qquad \text{8 (iii)}$$

and if $\Delta^*\mu$ is eliminated the equation is

$$\epsilon = \alpha_1\lambda\omega - (1-\lambda)(\beta_2-\alpha_2)\Delta^*\omega + \{\beta_1\lambda + \beta_2(1-\lambda)\}\mu$$
$$+ (1-\lambda)(1-\beta_2)E^{-1}\epsilon \qquad \text{8 (iv)}$$

Now 8 (iii) and 8 (iv) are the same equation. If either is fitted by least squares, precisely the same result will be got—that is the same calculated ϵ, the same R^2 and d. For the μ, $\Delta^*\mu$, $E^{-1}\epsilon$ space is the same as the μ, $\Delta^*\omega$, $E^{-1}\epsilon$ space. And since ω is outside it, the coefficient of ω will be the same in each case (as will also be that of $\Delta^*\xi$ if that variable is used). These equalities may be noted in Table IV to hold between the solutions A (iii) and A (iv), and also between C (iii) and C (iv), except that, doubtless through cumulative rounding-off in the computer, the coefficient of ω comes out as $0\cdot0384$ in A (iii) and $0\cdot0383$ in A (iv). Again, the coefficient of $\Delta^*\mu$ in 8 (iii) is repeated negatively as the coefficient of $\Delta^*\omega$ in 8 (iv), which is confirmed in table IV by $\pm0\cdot176$ in A (iii) and A (iv) and (with another slight computing error) $-0\cdot144$ in C (iii) and $+0\cdot145$ in C (iv). If in these pairs one coefficient is positive, the other can only be negative. From 8 (iv) we see that the negative coefficient applying to $\Delta^*\omega$ in A (iv) does not require that α_2 be negative, but merely that it be less than β_2.

To put the matter another way, the equations A (iii) and A (iv) in table IV, corresponding to 8 (iii) and 8 (iv) above, are (with assimilation of $0\cdot0383$ in A (iv) to $0\cdot0384$)

$$\epsilon = 0\cdot0384\omega + 0\cdot501\mu + 0\cdot176\Delta^*\mu + 0\cdot352E^{-1}\epsilon - 6\cdot74\Delta^*\xi$$

$$\epsilon = 0\cdot0384\omega - 0\cdot176\Delta^*\omega + 0\cdot677\mu + 0\cdot176E^{-1}\epsilon - 6\cdot74\Delta^*\xi$$

but these are the same equation, for the difference between them is

$$0 = 0·176\Delta^* \omega - 0·176\mu + 0·176\Delta^* \mu + 0·176E^{-1} \epsilon$$

which is an identity.

On identifying the coefficients in this regression equation with those required by the parameters of the model, we find, using 8 (iii) or 8 (iv),

$$\left.\begin{array}{l} \alpha_1 \lambda = 0·0384 \\ \beta_1 \lambda + \alpha_2(1 - \lambda) = 0·501 \\ (1 - \lambda)(\beta_2 - \alpha_2) = 0·176 \\ (1 - \lambda)(1 - \alpha_2) = 0·352 \end{array}\right\} \quad \text{or} \quad \left\{\begin{array}{l} \alpha_1 \lambda = 0·0384 \\ (1 - \lambda)(\beta_2 - \alpha_2) = 0·176 \\ \beta_1 \lambda + \beta_2(1 - \lambda) = 0·677 \\ (1 - \lambda)(1 - \beta_2) = 0·176 \end{array}\right.$$

Either of these two sets of equations has solution:

Parameters unlimited: one class of income

	Permanent	Transient
Wealth	$\alpha_1 = \dfrac{0·0384}{\lambda}$	$\alpha_2 = 1 - \dfrac{0·352}{1 - \lambda}$
Income	$\beta_1 = 1 - \dfrac{0·147}{\lambda}$	$\beta_2 = 1 - \dfrac{0·176}{1 - \lambda}$

The regression is essentially incapable of determining all five of α_1, α_2, β_1, β_2, λ. It presents merely a range of possibilities between which the choice (if any) must be made merely on the grounds of plausibility. The range of choice may be shown in a graph with λ as abscissa, as in figure A.

FIGURE A   COEFFICIENTS APPLYING TO WEALTH AND INCOME IN THE EQUATION GIVING EXPENDITURE: PARAMETERS UNLIMITED; ONE CLASS OF INCOME [INCLUDES STONE'S *A* (iii) AND *A* (iv)]

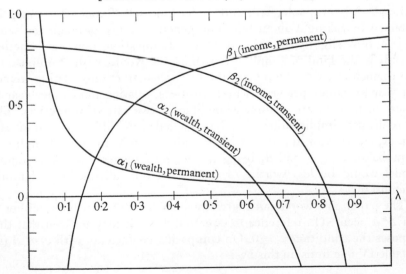

The graph shows that the only admissible range of values of λ is 0·147 to 0·648; for outside this range either β_1 or α_2 would have to be negative. Of the admissible cases, only one of the extreme ones, $\lambda = 0.648$, with $\alpha_2 = 0$, is tabulated in table 1, being case A (iii). But, as noticed at the outset, this case of $\alpha_2 = 0$ can be accepted only with reluctance. If one guesses that probably $\alpha_2 > \alpha_1$ (i.e. that money in the bank or in securities loses with time some of its power to prompt current expenditure) and that probably $\beta_2 < \beta_1$ (i.e. that a rise in income gains with time in its effect on spending) then one might plausibly take λ at about 0·6. But acceptable combinations of coefficients may be found with other values of λ. The choice is academic, because incapable of test with the information available.

To the coefficient $(1 - \lambda)(\beta_2 - \alpha_2)$ in 8 (iii) or 8 (iv) the A-type regression assigns the value 0.176 ± 0.146; and the C-type regression (where the data are all first divided by income μ) gives the value 0.144 ± 0.154. The coefficient is thus barely significant; and if it is assumed zero, so that $\alpha_2 = \beta_2$, the equation takes the form fitted in case A (i). This form, omitting both $\Delta^*\omega$ and $\Delta^*\mu$, is applicable not only when α_2 and β_2 are both assumed zero, as in the case selected for presentation in table 1, but also when they are equal and non-zero. On comparing table IV, case A (i) with either 8 (iii) or 8 (iv) we have

$$\left.\begin{aligned} \alpha_1\lambda &= 0.0502 \\ \beta_1\lambda + \alpha_2(1-\lambda) &= 0.653 \\ (1-\lambda)(1-\alpha_2) &= 0.154 \end{aligned}\right\} \quad \text{and so} \quad \left\{\begin{aligned} \alpha_1 &= 0.0502/\lambda \\ \beta_1 &= 1 - (0.193/\lambda) \\ \alpha_2 = \beta_2 &= 1 - \frac{0.154}{1-\lambda} \end{aligned}\right.$$

as in figure B.

Larger λ is now tolerated, and a plausible set of coefficients may be obtained by taking λ about 0·8. The general picture is much the same and R^2 only slightly diminished. One may question, however, whether $\alpha_2 = \beta_2$ is the kind of simplification that one would wish to impose on the coefficients. For the β's are dimensionless fractions relating money per year to money per year, whereas the α's, relating money per year to a sum of money, are of dimension time^{-1}, as a rate of interest is. The more drastic simplification $\alpha_2 = \beta_2 = 0$ avoids this difficulty, and gives a fair explanation of the data with an ultra-simple model—though the improbability of α_2 and β_2 being in fact zero suggests that this simple model would be less worthy of trust than the full one in unfamiliar circumstances.

The paper also works out regressions labelled (ii), in which neither ω nor $\Delta^*\mu$ occur. On reference to equation 8 (iv) it may be seen that this imposes the condition $\alpha_1 = 0$. On comparing coefficients with case A (ii) in table IV one finds on this basis:

FIGURE B   COEFFICIENTS APPLYING TO WEALTH AND INCOME IN THE EQUATION
GIVING   EXPENDITURE: PARAMETERS   SUBJECT   TO $\alpha_2 = \beta_2$;   ONE   CLASS   OF
INCOME [INCLUDES STONE'S A (i)]

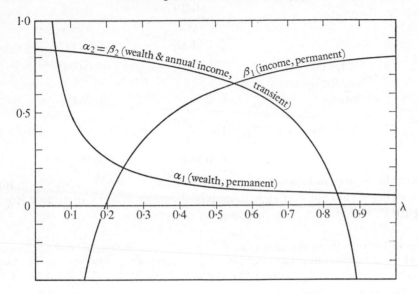

Parameters subject to $\alpha_1 = 0$:

$$\alpha_1 = 0 \qquad\qquad \alpha_2 = 1 - \frac{0 \cdot 911}{1 - \lambda}$$

$$\beta_1 = 1 + \frac{0 \cdot 005}{\lambda} \qquad \beta_2 = 1 - \frac{0 \cdot 406}{1 - \lambda}$$

The particular case of A (ii) quoted in table 1 has $\beta_2 = 0$, $\lambda = 0 \cdot 594$, and so a strongly negative α_2. It is possible to find solutions of type (ii), in which all the parameters are non-negative—for example $\lambda = 0 \cdot 08$, $\alpha_1 = 0$, $\alpha_2 = 0 \cdot 0098$, $\beta_1 = 1 \cdot 0625$, $\beta_2 = 0 \cdot 5587$. But such solutions are hardly acceptable, for to make α_2 positive, one would require $\lambda < 0 \cdot 089$ and so $\beta_1 > 1 \cdot 056$. So this regression is unsatisfactory not only because it gives a distinctly lower R^2 but also because it involves coefficients that could not plausibly arise in the model adopted.

Finally there are the regressions that Professor Stone distinguishes under heads B and D, where income μ is divided between a part μ_a consisting of income from wages and small transfers, and a part μ_b consisting of other income. From his equation (12) it is easy to write down, on the lines of 8 (iii), an equation from which $\varDelta^* \omega$ has been eliminated with the aid of (9), μ having been replaced in (9) by $\mu_a + \mu_b$. On comparing this modification of 8 (iii) with the coefficients B (iii) in table IV we get the parameters indicated below.

Parameters unlimited: two classes of income (with values when $\lambda = 0.657$)

		Permanent	Transient
Wealth		$\alpha_1 = \dfrac{0.0419}{\lambda}$	$\alpha_2 = 1 - \dfrac{0.318}{1-\lambda}$
		$(=0.0623)$	$(=0.0729)$
Wage and small-transfer income		$\beta_{1a} = 1 - \dfrac{0.140}{\lambda}$	$\beta_{2a} = 1 - \dfrac{0.074}{1-\lambda}$
		$(=0.797)$	$(=0.784)$
Other income		$\beta_{1b} = 1 - \dfrac{0.270}{\lambda}$	$\beta_{2b} = 1 - \dfrac{0.287}{1-\lambda}$
		$(=0.589)$	$(=0.163)$

Here the figures in brackets are got by putting $\lambda = 0.657$. The reason for favouring a value of λ of approximately this magnitude will appear from figure C, which shows the full range of possibilities.

FIGURE C   COEFFICIENTS APPLYING TO WEALTH AND INCOME IN THE EQUATION GIVING EXPENDITURE: PARAMETERS UNLIMITED; TWO CLASSES OF INCOME [INCLUDES STONE'S B (iii)]

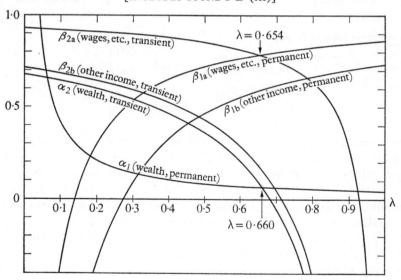

To make all the parameters positive, λ must be in the range 0.270 to 0.682. If, further, we postulate as before that $\beta_{1a} > \beta_{2a}$, then $\lambda > 0.654$. And if we also postulate that $\alpha_1 < \alpha_2$, then $\lambda < 0.660$. Within this narrow range, it is of interest to take for illustrative purposes $\lambda = 0.657$. One thus gets a set of coefficients which, while reproducing the data with $R^2 = 0.942$ and no significant serial correlation, are of absolute and relative orders of magnitude such as one would expect from their function in the model. An extra slice of wage and small-transfer income is spent, early and late, to the extent of nearly 80 per cent. An extra slice of other income is spent to the extent of only one-sixth and later nearly 60 per cent. This spending is supplemented in time through the encouragement supplied by accumulated savings.

In this and the cases treated earlier, the values of the α's and β's (λ being arbitrarily chosen) are evidently not very closely defined by the regression exercise; for considerable standard errors are shown for some of the regression coefficients in table IV. Without knowledge of some of the error co-variances of these coefficients it is not possible to give standard errors for the α's and β's. But if the uncertainties are large, this case seems to be one of the many arising in econometric analysis where, the data being insufficient to *enforce* a particular view of the mechanisms at work, a judgement of inherent probabilities must be used in the choice of an equation for working purposes. But different workers are, of course, entitled to their different judgements.

XI

SOCIAL ACCOUNTING AND
STANDARDIZED NATIONAL ACCOUNTS

1. INTRODUCTION

In this paper I shall first trace the steps by which the estimation of single magnitudes, such as the national income or the gross national product, led gradually to the construction of systems in which these magnitudes were related to each other to form the national accounts as we know them now. I shall then go on to show how the national accounts, having played a most useful, indeed indispensable part in the development of a national and international economic consciousness, are likely to be soon superseded by more detailed systems of social accounts which contain them but are not contained by them. Finally, I shall illustrate by a specific example what I mean by 'social' as opposed to 'national' accounts.

The main difficulty in following the evolution of any body of knowledge is to keep constantly in sight the many, very different factors that influence the growth of ideas and their practical acceptance. In any discussion of economic ideas three influences are of particular importance: the scientific, the political and the administrative. Let us see how these worked in the present instance.

2. THE ORIGINS OF SOCIAL ACCOUNTING

Social accounting is an invention of the last twenty-five years. Some examples will indicate its origins in the late 1930s. In England, Colin Clark brought together in his *National Income and Outlay*, published in 1937 [13], statistics of income, output, expenditure, saving, investment and foreign trade, though he did not set them in an accounting framework which would have enabled their mutual consistency to be tested. At about the same time, Gaathon in Palestine [28] and van Cleeff, in Holland [100, 101] developed systems of national book-keeping. In America, Morris Copeland emphasized the accounting aspect of contemporary work on national income statistics [14, 15]. A rudimentary accounting framework [38] was used from the beginning in the official *White Papers* on national income and expenditure for Britain started in 1941 [92]. In the following year Hicks, in a book intended to provide a new kind of introduction to economics [29], coined the phrase 'social accounting'.

Thus by the end of the last war social accounting was an emerging subject which presented a great intellectual challenge to economists and statisticians. In Britain at any rate, wartime problems of economic and financial policy had stimulated an official interest in the use of statistics of national income and expenditure, and the integrated picture of the economy provided by the *White Papers* and their successors the *Blue Books* on national income and expenditure [87] was found particularly illuminating. At the same time the increased flow of statistics necessary for wartime administration made it possible to improve the accuracy and extend the scope of the estimates as year succeeded year.

In 1944, official talks were held in Washington with the object of bringing the statistics of national income and expenditure in America, Britain and Canada more closely into line. One of the topics discussed at these meetings was a system of social accounts which could be used as a framework for the whole range of economic statistics [16].

In 1945, a subcommittee appointed by the Committee of Statistical Experts of the League of Nations met at Princeton to discuss the problems arising in the measurement of the national income and in the construction of social accounts. In their report, published in 1947 [93], this group recommended that the estimation of the national income be set within a framework of social accounts, and designed a number of accounting formulae 'for the whole economic system and for major sectors of it' which 'are of great utility in practical economic analysis and are also capable of statistical estimation'. This report and its appendix can perhaps be regarded as the first handbook of social accounting.

Shortly afterwards, a new institution was brought into being which has done a great deal to promote the technique of social accounting all over the world. This is the International Association for Research in Income and Wealth, which was founded at the World Statistical Conference held at Washington in 1947. The conference volumes and bibliographies of this Association [30, 31] have greatly helped in fostering among technicians a common point of view, an essential requisite if international cooperation is to be effective.

3.   THE STANDARDIZATION OF NATIONAL ACCOUNTS

In 1949, the newly established O.E.E.C. set up a National Accounts Research Unit at Cambridge. The purpose of this Unit was to promote comparable national accounts statistics among member countries. To do this it was necessary to examine the statistics produced and the methods used by the different countries, design a standard system, and help in the training of economists and statisticians from those countries in which little or no work on national accounts had at that time been done.

In 1950, this Unit issued *A Simplified System of National Accounts* [41], which soon after became *A Standardized System of National Accounts* [42]. published in 1952. In that same year the Unit ceased to have an independent existence and was merged in the Directorate of Statistics and National Accounts in Paris. A short description of the Unit's work is given in [79].

The *Standardized System* was used by the O.E.E.C. in collecting national accounts statistics from member countries, in compiling *Statistics of National Product and Expenditure* [43] and in presenting the regular statistics of national accounts in [47]. The interest of the O.E.E.C. in national accounts statistics was a practical one: the purpose of the Organization was to administer financial aid and encourage economic growth in member countries, and for this it needed systematic information on the economic conditions and economic performance of these countries.

In the summer of 1952, a group of experts appointed by the Secretary General of the United Nations met in New York to formulate a standard system for the U.N., since by then the report of 1947 [93] was somewhat out of date. The resulting document, *A System of National Accounts and Supporting Tables* [94] was published in 1953 and provided the basis for a series of statistical compilations which since 1957 have been entitled *Yearbook of National Accounts Statistics* [96].

From the outset, the systems proposed by the O.E.E.C. and the U.N. were conceptually very close to each other, though they differed slightly in the details of presentation. They were republished with minor revisions in 1958 and 1960 respectively, and at this stage they were virtually identical.

It is often asked how far these systems are of general applicability: granted that they have been conceived largely in terms of mature economies, how do they fare when applied to more primitive ones? On this subject an interesting report dealing with *Systems of National Accounts in Africa* [1] was issued by the O.E.E.C. in 1960.

4.   NATIONAL ACCOUNTS AND INTERNATIONAL COMPARISONS

The standard systems of national accounts described above deal with estimates expressed in the money values of particular times and places. Such information, besides being interesting in itself, is also the first step in making real comparisons over time and over space. By real comparisons I mean comparisons made in terms of a common set of values: over time we can revalue the product flows in different years at the prices of a base year; over space we can revalue product flows in different countries at the prices ruling in one country, or in terms of some other agreed set of values.

The problems of comparisons over time and of the construction of appropriate index-numbers was taken up by the O.E.E.C. in 1952 and a report on the subject was published in 1956 [60]. In the foreword of this report it was stated that 'while a considerable degree of agreement on concepts and methods emerged from the two conferences which dealt with this subject, it was concluded that opinion and practice had not yet reached the point which would make the adoption of international standards practicable'. The hope was expressed that it would eventually be possible 'to reach more formal agreement on the standards to be used in this field'. This hope remains to be realized.

Also in the early 1950s, the O.E.E.C. took up the question of inter-country comparisons, this time not so much to set standards for statistical work in member countries as for the interest of the work itself. A first set of comparisons between five European countries, based on estimates of final expenditure, appeared in 1954 [26]. A second edition of this, revised and enlarged to cover eight countries, appeared in 1958 [27]. Finally, a comparison between Britain and America, based on estimates of net output, was published in 1959 [49].

The aim of these studies was to construct a system of international comparisons over time. This plan was never completed and put on a routine basis, but enough was done to provide a fairly detailed comparative picture of the economies of Western Europe. With the passage of time, however, this picture will fade in relevance and interest unless steps are taken to keep it up to date.

5. FROM NATIONAL ACCOUNTS TO SOCIAL ACCOUNTS

The national accounts as standardized by the O.E.E.C. and the U.N. have many virtues: they are detailed enough to connect together the principal concepts of economic analysis and at the same time simple enough to rest only on general economic and accounting principles; they can actually be constructed from the statistical resources available in a large number of countries, and the distinctions they contain are so broad that a fair degree of international comparability can be reached. They represent therefore an obvious stopping place between the estimation of single magnitudes and the construction of social accounts and provide a set of figures which is always likely to be useful. But they do not integrate all the information we need about the workings of the economic system. For this we must turn to other, allied forms of economic analysis.

For example, in the national accounts there is a single account for production. In input–output analysis this single account is subdivided into numerous branches of production. It was part of the O.E.E.C.'s plan for the coordination of social accounting statistics to extend the national accounts framework to include an input–output table. A memorandum on this subject was submitted by the Organization to a meeting of the Conference of European Statisticians in 1955. Eventually a report was published in 1961 [62]. But this report had a different status from the earlier ones [42, 60] in the national accounts series: it was never discussed at one of the Organization's conferences of national accounts experts and it could not therefore be said to have achieved any degree of official acceptance.

Another question that was raised in connection with these taxonomic studies was the detailed treatment of capital accounts and accompanying balance sheets. This would have involved the integration of flow-of-funds accounts with the national accounts. In the event this step was never taken, although a statistical study relating to the sources and uses of finance was published in 1960 [44].

The last contribution made to social accounting by the O.E.E.C. was a conference held by the European Productivity Agency in 1960 on the subject of regional development within countries. The findings of this conference, which discussed among other things the problems of setting up regional 'national' accounts and input–output accounts, were published in 1961 [45].

The user of economic statistics who would like consistency and uniformity may well regret that these programmes were never fulfilled. He sees national accounting, input–output analysis and flow-of-funds analysis, all essentially branches of a single discipline, carried out within each country by different groups which often have little or no contact with one another. He sees differences in treatment grow up literally by chance in different countries in circumstances where agreement could almost certainly be reached if it were sought. As a consequence, many advantages which flow from comparability are lost. But it is useless to complain. Institutions wax and wane, their interests change. If international organizations have not done all we could have wished for in this field, we should recognize their difficulties, be grateful for what they have achieved and continue where they have left off.

6. AN EXAMPLE: A SOCIAL ACCOUNTING MATRIX FOR BRITAIN

When considering how best to integrate the different branches of economic analysis into a coherent system of social accounts, the first thing to do is to set up a model incorporating all the relationships we wish to examine. The data requirements of the model can then be used to indicate how the accounting system should be elaborated and how the entries in it should be defined and classified. The details of our model will be affected by the type of data that it is possible to collect, by the capacity of the computer at our disposal and by our ability to handle problems in computer programming. Thus, once we have passed the point marked 'national accounts' any further progress is intimately connected with

developments in mathematical economics, econometrics, operational research and computer technology, and is no longer the relatively simple
taxonomic exercise it was up to that point.

It would require a good deal of space to elaborate fully what I have
just said, so I shall content myself with giving a numerical example. This
example has been worked out from a large-scale model of the British
economy by myself and a group of colleagues at the Department of Applied
Economics of the University of Cambridge. This project is being described
in a series of publications entitled *A Programme for Growth*, of which the
first number [6] explains the model we are using and the second number
[7] sets out the accounting framework in the form of a social accounting
matrix for Britain in 1960.

This matrix is drawn up like an input–output table, with money
incomings in the rows and money outgoings in the columns. In place of
the four main categories of the national accounts, namely production,
consumption, accumulation and the rest of the world, there are fifteen
classes, each subdivided into a number of accounts. The whole system
contains 253 accounts and when consolidated so as to provide a single
account for each class appears as in table 1.

It will be noticed that the fifteen classes are divided into four groups
corresponding to the four main categories of the national accounts. In
other words, this matrix is simply an elaboration of the national accounts,
not a different species of system: if we consolidate the fifteen accounts
into the four main groups we obtain the national accounts for Britain in
1960.

For a thorough understanding of this system it is necessary to consult
[7], but one can get a general idea of it by running through the entries
class by class.

Let us begin with the total supply of commodities, or products, class
1, which adds up to £43 252 million. It can be seen from column 1 that
most of this, £40 652 million, is produced by British industries, and a
relatively small part, £2465 million *plus* £135 million of customs duties,
consists of competitive imports. If we now look along row 1 we see in
what proportions this total supply of products is allocated to its different
destinations: 45 per cent of the total, £19 329 million, is absorbed by
industries as intermediate product; 31 per cent, £13 445 million, is
absorbed by private and public consumers; 13 per cent, £5727 million,
is sold for investment in fixed assets and stocks; and 11 per cent, £4751
million, is exported.

Turning to class 2, if we look down column 2 we can see the aggregated
cost structure of the thirty-one industries in SAM: 48 per cent of the
total, £19 329 million, is the cost of the intermediate product; 1 per cent,
£488 million, is the value of indirect taxes, net of subsidies, debited to
industry; 43 per cent, £17 339 million (or 42 per cent, £17 056 million,

TABLE 1   A SOCIAL ACCOUNTING MATRIX FOR BRITAIN, 1960

(£ million)

Type of account	Description of class	Production accounts				Income and outlay accounts		Capital transactions accounts								All accts.	Total incomings
		1	2	3	4	5	6	7	8	9	10	11	12	13	14	15	
Production accounts	1. Commodities	0	19 329	11 917	1 528	0	0	563	1 065	1 845	596	1 320	63	275	0	4 751	43 252
	2. Industries	40 652	0	0	0	0	0	0	0	0	0	0	0	0	0	0	40 652
	3. Consumers' goods and services	0	0	0	0	0	16 214	0	0	0	0	0	0	0	0	215	16 429
	4. Government purposes	0	0	0	0	0	4 189	0	0	0	0	0	0	0	0	0	4 189
Income and outlay accounts	5. Indirect taxes and subsidies	135	488	1 946	44	0	0	1	32	45	100	125	0	0	0	0	2 916
	6. Institutional sectors	0	17 339	728	2 338	2 916	0	0	0	0	0	0	0	0	0	179	23 500
Capital transactions accounts	7. Commodities	0	0	0	0	0	0	0	0	0	0	0	0	0	591	0	591
	8. Industries, replacements	0	1 097	0	0	0	0	0	0	0	0	0	0	0	0	0	1 097
	9. Industries, extensions	0	489	0	0	0	0	0	0	0	0	0	0	0	1 401	0	1 890
	10. Cons. goods, replacements	0	0	696	0	0	0	0	0	0	0	0	0	0	0	0	696
	11. Cons. goods, extensions	0	0	569	0	0	0	0	0	0	0	0	0	0	876	0	1 445
	12. Govt. purposes, replacements	0	0	0	63	0	0	0	0	0	0	0	0	0	0	0	63
	13. Govt. purposes, extensions	0	0	0	70	0	0	0	0	0	0	0	0	0	205	0	275
	14. Institutional sectors	0	−283	0	0	0	3 011	0	0	0	0	0	0	0	0	1	2 729
All accounts	15. Rest of the world	2 465	2 193	573	146	0	86	27	0	0	0	0	0	0	−344	0	5 146
Total outgoings		43 252	40 652	16 429	4 189	2 916	23 500	591	1 097	1 890	696	1 445	63	275	2 729	5 146	

if we add the residual error, which in 1960 was negative) is the cost of primary inputs, namely the income paid by industry to the factors of production, labour and capital; 4 per cent, £1586 million, represents provisions for depreciation valued at replacement cost; and 5 per cent, £2193 million, is the cost of complementary imports of intermediate product.

By looking along rows 3 and 4 we see the total amounts which private and public consumers devote to current expenditure, and by looking down columns 3 and 4 we see, in aggregate, the pattern of these expenditures. For instance, total expenditure by private consumers, both domestic and foreign, adds up in row 3 to £16 429 million; we see from column 3 that 72 per cent of this, £11 917 million, goes to purchases of commodities; 12 per cent, £1946 million, goes in indirect taxes; and the remaining 16 per cent goes in rent, payments for direct services, provisions for the depreciation of consumers' real assets and purchases of complementary imports. The structure of public expenditure, in column 4, is the same but the pattern is different, the largest item being wages and salaries, £2338 million.

Row 5 shows the different amounts of indirect taxes (net) associated with each type of expenditure, whether current or capital.

Row 6 shows the various sources from which income flows into the institutional sectors: apart from indirect taxes it is all income from productive activity, most of it generated in Britain, with a small amount arising from British productive activity abroad. In principle, if we subtract indirect taxes from the total of row 6 we obtain the national income, £23 500 million − £2916 million = £20 584 million. In practice, however, we must add to this the residual error, shown at the intersection of row 14 and column 2, so that the national income is in fact £20 584 million − £283 million = £20 301 million, as in the official *Blue Book* [87: 1962]. Column 6 shows the appropriation of total income to: private and public consumption, £16 214 million and £4189 million respectively; saving, £3011 million; and current transfers abroad, £86 million.

Row 7 shows the value of net investment in stocks and work in progress, and column 7 shows in what measure it is divided between commodities, £563 million, and complementary imports and the associated customs duties, £27 million + £1 million = £28 million.

Rows and columns 8 and 9 show industrial gross investment in fixed assets divided between replacements and extensions. With growing stocks of assets, only part of the provisions for depreciation made in one year is needed to finance the replacement of assets scrapped in that year; the rest contributes to financing extensions to the stock. The estimated value of replacements, £1097 million, appears in row 8 and the corresponding expenditure on products, £1065 million, *plus* purchase taxes, £32 million, appears in column 8. The estimated value of extensions, consisting partly of excess depreciation, £489 million, and partly of the value of net investment, £1401 million, appears in row 9; the corresponding expenditure on products, £1845 million, *plus* purchase taxes, £45 million, appears in column 9.

Rows and columns 10 and 11 deal in exactly the same way with private consumers' gross investment, and rows and columns 12 and 13 do the same for government investment in social capital. If we aggregate the six classes dealing with industrial, private and public investment, we obtain the national total for gross investment in fixed assets, £5466 million. It is worth while to point out that as much as 39 per cent of this total, £2141 million, consists of investment in dwellings and consumers' durables.

To find the value of net investment we must turn to row and column 14. The incomings are saving *plus* the residual error, £3011 million − £283 million = £2728 million, and net capital transfers from abroad, £1 million. The outgoings show the value of net investment divided among: investment in stocks, £591 million; the three groups of investment in fixed assets, £1401 million + £876 million + £205 million = £2482 million; and net lending abroad, which in 1960 was a negative figure, −£344 million. The total, £2729 million, is the net addition to tangible wealth and to claims on the rest of the world, in other words a measure of the increase in the wealth of the country.

The system is closed by row and column 15, which sum up all the transactions which the rest of the world has with Britain. The first four entries in the row, totalling £5377 million, show the distribution of imports among the different classes of production; the sixth, £27 million, shows the value of the increase in stocks of complementary imports; the fifth, £86 million, is net current transfers from Britain; and the seventh, −£344 million, is net lending abroad by Britain. The column shows: British exports, £4751 million; expenditure by foreign visitors to Britain, £215 million; net income paid to Britain, £179 million; and net capital transfers paid to Britain, £1 million.

Even from this short account of our matrix it should be possible to see many of the factors that determine its design. A few examples will illustrate what I mean.

First, at an early stage in the calculations we have to estimate the future composition of private and public consumption. This is best done in terms of the familiar 'shopping list'. But it is then necessary to convert this shopping list into demands for the products of industry and this requires a link between a consumers' classification and an industrial classification. In our model we make this link by means of 'classification converters' connecting classes 3 and 4 with class 1.

Second, even at a moderate level of disaggregation it is impossible to trace a one-to-one correspondence between products and industries. We begin therefore by keeping the two concepts distinct. Furthermore, in our model we represent input–output relationships not in terms of inputs into industries but in terms of inputs into commodities, or products used to make products. With the data at our disposal this calls for a number of assumptions which are discussed in [8].

Third, in input–output analysis it is important that the entries in the rows for the various branches of production should be as homogeneous as possible. This affects the solution of a number of conceptual problems and is largely responsible for the complicated treatment of indirect taxes in our matrix.

Fourth, the treatment of production relationships in the model makes it desirable to distinguish extensions which add to capacity, or the gross stock of assets, from net investment which adds to the future useful life of equipment, or the net stock of assets. Hence our introduction of two capital accounts for each sector.

Fifth, a dynamic treatment of demand which allows for time lags in consumers' adjustment makes it desirable to regard durable consumer goods as assets and to divide consumers' gross investment between consumption (or depreciation) and net investment. Hence our inclusion of consumers' durables in the capital accounts.

Many more examples could be given, but by now the point I am trying to make is probably clear. Once we get past the national accounts, it is difficult if not impossible to build a social accounting system on simple general principles. On the other hand, if we are ready to take some trouble over our basic model, we shall find in such a system an extremely useful tool for a detailed and coherent analysis of economic life.

7. CONCLUSIONS

The conclusions I want to draw from this survey of the development of social accounting can be summed up as follows.

In the first place, the post-war decade saw the replacement of separately estimated magnitudes, such as the national income, consumption, etc., by the estimation of a set of these magnitudes related to each other within an accounting framework. This new approach was intellectually stimulating to many economists and statisticians. The practical side of the work, and certainly the pace of its progress, were largely made possible by the interest and support of national governments and international organizations.

In the second place, once a certain point, represented in practice by the national accounts and supporting tables, had been reached, interest in further developments among those who had promoted this work seems to have waned. For the time being, it would appear, they have got what they wanted.

In the third place, the initiative in this field seems to be passing to the
12

econometric model-builders, who need a framework for their models far
more detailed than that offered by the national accounts. Input–output,
flow-of-funds analysis and even more elaborate and comprehensive social
accounting studies are growing as never before. But unless we keep up
the pressure for international standardization, much valuable effort will
be wasted. At the moment in national accounting we speak a common
language and, if we do not always agree, at least we know what others
are thinking. Ten years from now shall we be able to say the same about
social accounting ?

XII

THE REVISION OF THE SNA:
AN OUTLINE OF THE NEW STRUCTURE

1. INTRODUCTION

After more than three years of work, the proposals for revising the U.N. System of National Accounts (or SNA for short) have reached an advanced stage. Following the meeting of an expert group convened by the U.N. Statistical Office, a first version [97] of the new system was produced in February 1965. After further meetings and consultations in all parts of the world, a second version [98] was produced in June 1966. And a third version [99], produced in August 1967, was considered by the U.N. Statistical Commission early in 1968.

The purpose of this paper is to set out the structure of the new system and to illustrate this structure by means of a numerical example. In doing this I have, with the agreement of the U.N. Statistical Office, drawn heavily on [99], making use of its numerical example and reproducing its second chapter almost unchanged. For further information on concepts, definitions and classifications and on the standard accounts and tables of the system, reference must be made to the report itself, a document of 463 pages.

The original SNA, first published in 1953, was essentially a step on the road to setting out clearly and concisely a framework within which the statistical information needed to analyse the economic process in all its many aspects could be organized and related. But, as its authors recognized, it was only a first step. 'Thus' they wrote in Chapter I, 'if a start is made with a system of national accounts such as is described in this report, the production account could be subdivided so as to display the commodity flows between industries which are the central feature of input–output studies. In a similar way, by a suitable elaboration of the accounts, it would be possible to introduce all relevant financial flows into the same system. The accounting structure could then be completed by adding balance sheets for the different sectors of the economy. Finally, it would be possible to express in constant prices the principal product flows and stocks in the system'.

The new system introduces all these topics and relates them to one another in a much enlarged set of accounts and balances. Requirements for input–output and flows-of-funds are spelt out in detail and standard tables dealing with them are given. National and sector balance sheets are integrated into the system but they are treated much more cursorily, detailed definitions and standard tables being left over for the future. The limited information given on the generation, distribution and use of income is to be supplemented by a complementary system of income distribution statistics on which the U.N. Statistical Office is now working. Two other related topics were considered for inclusion in the new system: regional accounting and accounting for human flows and stocks. But, apart from a table relating to employment classified by kind of economic activity, these topics were also left over for future consideration.

In what follows, I shall start with the four basic accounts of the nation, relating respectively to production, consumption, accumulation and foreign transactions. I shall set out the highly aggregated flows between these accounts in the form of a matrix, on the lines of an input–output table; and shall show how this matrix can be extended to include information on stocks (balance sheet data). I shall then subdivide the categories in this extended matrix so as to introduce the main categories which appear in the new SNA; and, after that, further subdivide these main categories so as to provide an illustration of the complete system. Finally, I shall set out in greater detail the information contained in the system which relates to input–output analysis.

2. THE FOUR ACCOUNTS OF THE NATION

The four accounts of the nation can be set out in a matrix of order 4, with monetary incomings (receipts or revenues) in the rows and monetary outgoing (costs or expenditures) in the columns. In table 1 below a fifth row and column are added to contain the account totals.

The first row of this table shows the incomings into the production account. The total of 309 units is made up of: sales for consumption

TABLE 1   THE FOUR ACCOUNTS OF THE NATION IN MATRIX FORM

	1	2	3	4	Total
1. Production		210	47	52	309
2. Consumption	255		−19	5	241
3. Accumulation		27			27
4. The rest of the world	54	4	−1		57
Total	309	241	27	57	

purposes, 210 units; sales for capital purposes *plus* additions to stocks and work in progress, 47 units; and sales to the rest of the world (exports) 52 units. The first column shows the sources of the supply which meets this demand: domestic production, represented by gross income payments plus indirect taxes, 255 units; and production in the rest of the world (imports) 54 units.

The second row shows the sources of income available for expenditure on consumption: receipts from domestic production as defined above, 255 units; a negative item, −19 units, in respect of the provisions for the consumption of fixed capital, which are included in the receipts just mentioned; and 5 units in respect of net factor income received from abroad. The second column shows the use to which these incomings are put: consumption expenditures, 210 units; saving, 27 units; and net current transfers to the rest of the world, 4 units.

The third row shows the finance provided domestically for making net additions to wealth: saving, 27 units. The third column shows the use of this finance: domestic capital formation in fixed assets and stocks $47 - 19 = 28$ units; and the balance, −1 unit, provided by the rest of the world in the form of net lending to the country we are studying.

The fourth row shows receipts by the rest of the world from the country we are studying: goods and services imported by that country, 54 units; net current transfers from that country 4 units; and −1 unit in respect of net lending from that country. The fourth column shows the corresponding payments by the rest of the world: goods and services exported by the country, 52 units; and net factor income paid to the country, 5 units.

The final row and column contain simply the account totals.

3. THE INTRODUCTION OF BALANCE SHEETS

So far, only transactions (flows) have been accounted for; assets and liabilities (stocks) have been ignored. At the highly aggregated level of the national accounts, it is a simple matter to account for stocks by extending table 1 to include opening and closing balance sheets.

Reduced to its simplest terms a balance sheet shows for a sector or set of sectors such as a national economy: (i) the written-down value of tangible assets held *plus* the excess of financial claims held as assets over financial claims issued as liabilities; and (ii) the net worth of the sector. At any point in time, these two amounts are equal. The entries in the opening and closing balance sheets of a period are connected as follows. Net assets at the end of a period are equal to net assets at the beginning *plus* net investment at home and abroad in the period *plus* revaluations needed to adjust assets previously acquired or liabilities previously issued to the prices holding at the closing date. Similarly, net worth at the close of a period is equal to net worth at the beginning *plus* the new saving available in the period (which will all come from national sources if, as in the present example, capital transfers are ignored), *plus* revaluations as before. Since net worth can only be revalued by applying to it the revaluation calculated from the price movements of tangible assets and financial claims and since saving is equal to net investment, it can be seen that the opening and closing balance sheets are linked by revaluations and by the entries in the capital transactions account.

The extension of the national accounts in this way is set out in table 2.

TABLE 2   THE NATIONAL ACCOUNTS, INCLUDING BALANCE SHEETS, IN MATRIX FORM

	1	2	3	4	5	6	7
1. Opening assets, net				693			
2. Production			210	47	52		
3. Consumption		255		−19	5		
4. Accumulation	693		27			44	764
5. The rest of the world		54	4	−1			
6. Revaluations				44			
7. Closing assets, net				764			

Note: In the columns net assets are balanced by net worth.

In this table, the entries in the transaction accounts of table 1 (apart from the account totals) are reproduced unchanged in the inner rectangle and the information on net assets, net worth and revaluations is shown in rows and columns 1, 6 and 7 which surround this inner rectangle. Opening net assets appear at the intersection of column 4 and row 1, the revaluation of net assets appears at the intersection of column 4 and row 6 and closing net assets appear at the intersection of column 4 and row 7. In a similar way, opening net worth appears in row 4, column 1, the revaluation of net worth appears in row 4, column 6, and closing net worth appears in row 4, column 7.

Table 2 shows the relationship of the balance sheet to the transaction accounts when the system is presented in a highly consolidated, net form. Minor changes are needed if financial claims issued are shown under the heading of liabilities, so that holdings of financial claims are recorded on a gross basis, and if the economy is divided into a number of sectors. The resulting complications are illustrated in the following section.

4. ELABORATING THE BASIC SYSTEM

Additional detail can be introduced into the basic system of table 2 by the simple process of subdividing the seven separate headings shown in the table into categories and subcategories. For example, if financial claims are to be shown gross, then rows 1, 6 and 7 must be divided in two, with separate rows for financial assets and net tangible assets; and the corresponding columns must also be divided in two, with separate columns for financial liabilities and net worth. The rows and columns for financial liabilities can also be subdivided to show holdings and issues of different financial claims. This process is attended with certain consequences. Thus, as soon as any subdivision is made, it has to be remembered that national economies are not closed and that a consolidated balance sheet for the rest of the world must be introduced, in order, for instance, that financial claims held as assets shall be equal in value to financial claims issued as liabilities.

A second example can be taken from production. In table 2, row and column 2 show, respectively, the revenue accruing to production from sales of products to various types of final buyer and the costs, including profit, associated with this production. But for various reasons, analytical as well as statistical, it may be desired to show separately information relating to products (or commodities) and to the productive units (or activities) in which they are made. This information will appear in the system if production is divided into two rows and columns, one relating to commodities and one relating to activities. Once this is done, it is no contradiction of the principle of consolidation to enter in the extended system not only the total value of the commodities used as intermediate input by activities but also the total value of the commodities produced by activities. Once this stage has been reached, it is only another step to introduce full commodity and activity detail by subdividing the rows and columns for commodities and activities according to commodity and activity classifications.

An elaboration of table 2 which incorporates the above examples and carries the description of accounts and balance sheets substantially closer to the new SNA is set out in table 3.

If this table is compared with table 2, it can be seen that the fourth account of table 2, relating to accumulation, has been divided into four and each of the remaining accounts of table 2 has been divided into two. As before, the extended flow accounts are enclosed in an inner rectangle; within this rectangle, the groups of accounts forming the four accounts of the nation are separated from each other by bold lines.

TABLE 3   A PRIMARY DISAGGREGATION OF THE NATIONAL ACCOUNTS, INCLUDING BALANCE SHEETS

Group			1	2	3	4	5	6	7	8	9	10	11	12	13	14	15	16
Opening assets	1	Financial claims										1249		165				
	2	Net tangible assets										661						
Production	3	Commodities				245	166		6	41			50					
	4	Activities			443		44											
Consumption	5	Consumer goods/purposes						210					2					
	6	Income and outlay			14	241						−19	13					
Accumulation	7	Increase in inventories										6						
	8	Fixed capital formation										41						
	9	Financial claims										58		18				
	10	Capital finance	1217	693				27			59				−23	44	1253	764
The rest of the world	11	Current transactions			51	1	2	12										
	12	Capital transactions	197	−32							17		1		0	−2	214	−33
Revaluations	13	Financial claims										−21		−2				
	14	Net tangible assets										42						
Closing assets	15	Financial claims										1286		181				
	16	Net tangible assets										731						

Note: In the columns: opening and closing assets are balanced by opening and closing liabilities; and net tangible assets are balanced by net worth.

No attempt will be made here to explain in detail the entries in table 3. This table should be regarded as a conceptual link between tables 1 and 2 above and table 4 below.

5. THE STRUCTURE OF THE NEW SYSTEM

The purpose of this and of the next eight sections is to describe the conceptual basis of the new system and to illustrate it by extending the numerical example used so far.

A bird's-eye view of the complete system is provided in table 4, in which the matrix given in table 3 is expanded to show all the classes and subclasses of the system. To keep the example manageable (it will in any case contain eighty-two rows and columns) the categories in each class represent aggregations of the categories distinguished in the full system. Thus in table 4 the activity classification is divided into eight categories (rows and columns 13 through 20), four for industries, three for government services and one for the services of private non-profit institutions. In the full system the activity classification has thirty-two main categories, most of which have several sub-categories, so that the total number of items in this classification alone is sixty-seven. This amount of detail is useful for analytical purposes; but when repeated, *mutatis mutandis*, for all the other classes, it would clearly be excessive in an illustrative example.

A glance at the headings of table 4 shows that the seven main headings (opening assets, production, ..., closing assets) are repeated unchanged from table 3. Each of these main headings was already subdivided in table 3, but the division is carried much further in table 4. The following description of the new system is arranged under these seven main headings.

6. OPENING ASSETS AND LIABILITIES

The first main heading of table 4 is divided, as in table 3, between two sub-headings: (i) financial claims held as assets, and (ii) net tangible assets (in the rows); or (i) financial claims issued as liabilities, and (ii) net worth (in the columns). As a consequence of this further subdivision, the single numbers of table 3 are largely replaced either by submatrices or by vectors in table 4.

Let us look first at opening assets (rows 1 through 4 of table 4). It can be easily verified that the single number, 1249, in table 3 is replaced in table 4 by the 3 × 4 submatrix at the intersection of rows 1 through 3 and columns 70 through 73; and that the sum of the elements in this submatrix is equal to 1249. This figure represents the total holding of financial claims as assets by all national sectors at the beginning of the period. The elements of the submatrix show this total divided by type of claim and by sector. For example, non-financial enterprises (corporate and quasi-corporate) hold 23 units of currency and deposits, 32 units of securities and 126 units of other financial assets; conversely, other financial assets are held as to 126 units by non-financial enterprises, as to 120 units by financial institutions, as to 125 units by general government and as to 146 units by households and private non-profit institutions. Similarly, the rest of the world's opening holdings of financial assets, 165 in table 3, is divided between different kinds of claim in the column vector at the intersection of rows 1 through 3 and column 75 of table 4 $(52 + 36 + 77 = 165)$. The opening holding of net tangible assets by national sectors, 661 in table 3, is divided among the different sectors in the row vector at the intersection of row 4 and columns 70 through 73 of table 4 $(304 + 18 + 133 + 206 = 661)$.

If we now turn to opening liabilities (columns 1 through 4 of table 4), we can see that the four numbers, 1217, 693, 197 and −32, which appear in table 3 are replaced in table 4 by: the submatrix at the intersection of columns 1 through 3 and rows 70 through 73; the column vector at the intersection of column 4 and rows 70 through 73; the row vector at the intersection of columns 1 through 3 and row 75; and the single number at the intersection of column 4 and row 75.

This information can be isolated from the other entries in table 4 and brought together in a statement of opening assets and liabilities. This is done in table 5.

In this table we can see more easily the general structure of national and sector balance sheets. In the first place, each sector balance sheet balances, and so does the balance sheet for the rest of the world: in each case the value of financial claims issued as liabilities *plus* share capital *plus* net worth is equal to the value of financial claims and share capital held as assets *plus* the net holdings of tangible assets. In the second place, when the system is closed by including a consolidated balance sheet for the rest of the world, the total issue of any claim as a liability is equal to the total holding of the same claim as an asset; and total net worth is equal to total net holdings of tangible assets. This is not true if only national sectors are considered. Thus, in table 5, national sectors are shown as having issued 296 units of currency and deposits, and the rest of the world is shown as having issued 31 units all of which are held by national sectors. By contrast, the national sectors are shown as holding 275 units of currency and deposits; and, since 31 units of this holding are foreign, 244 units must be national holdings of national currency and deposits. Thus national sectors have issued 296 units of which they hold 244, leaving 52 units to be held by the rest of the world as shown in the table.

The comprehensiveness and simplicity of the relationships just described, which do not depend in any way on adjustment entries, require a common basis of valuation which is uniform throughout the table. The entries in table 5 are valued at current market price or, in the case of most tangible assets, at replacement cost. Certain claims, such as currency and deposits, do not possess a market value different from their nominal value; and in other cases nominal values may have to be used in practice. The measure of net worth, the derived item on any balance sheet, is dependent on the basis of valuation adopted in each case.

TABLE 5   OPENING ASSETS AND LIABILITIES

	Non-financial enterprises	Financial institutions	General government	Household and private non-profit institutions	All national sectors	Rest of the world	Total
Financial assets							
Currency and deposits	23	68	12	172	275	52	327
Securities	32	153	9	263	457	36	493
Other	126	120	125	146	517	77	594
Net tangible assets	304	18	133	206	661		661
Total assets	485	359	279	787	1910	165	2075
Financial liabilities and share capital							
Currency and deposits	8	184	103	1	296	31	327
Securities	235	62	145		442	51	493
Other	151	102	141	85	479	115	594
Net worth	91	11	−110	701	693	−32	661
Total liabilities	485	359	279	787	1910	165	2075

The fact that current values form the basis of table 5 does not mean that other values are not important or that they cannot be incorporated in the system. Thus the current value of claims issued could be divided between the value on issue and the appreciation or depreciation that has taken place since issue. In a similar way, the value of claims held could be divided between the value at which the present holder acquired the claim and the appreciation or depreciation that has taken place since acquisition.

7. PRODUCTION

In table 3, only two rows and columns were shown for production: one relating to commodities and one relating to activities. In table 4, the subdivision of production is carried much further. The commodity account is first divided into two categories so as to show the value of commodities separated into two parts: the value before adding commodity taxes or subtracting commodity subsidies (basic value); and the value of the taxes and subsidies themselves. Each category is then divided into commodities (or commodity groups) defined as the characteristic products of the corresponding industries. The activity account is divided into three categories: industries, which produce commodities, the service activities of general government and the service activities of private non-profit institutions serving households. The last two categories do not, save in exceptional cases, attempt to market the services they produce but themselves meet the cost of these services, which are not regarded as commodities. Each category is then divided into activity groups on the lines of the standard industrial classification of all economic activities, care being taken so to arrange matters that, at the highest level of disaggregation, the services of general government and private non-profit institutions can be identified at the same time with a classification by purpose.

Before examining each of these categories in detail, let us consider briefly some general issues that arise in classifying production flows

First, a distinction is made between commodities and the industries (or, exceptionally, other activities) in which they are produced because it is impossible so to define the elements in the two classifications that there is a one-to-one correspondence between them. This fact is significant, because what can be observed about sales structures usually relates to commodities, and what can be observed about cost structures usually relates to industries. Thus, in analysing the consequences for the productive system of variations in the demand for different commodities, we must recognize that, in general, we cannot observe the cost structures of individual commodities (or commodity groups). The nearest approximation we can find is usually the cost structure of the industry that produces the commodity in question as its characteristic product; but this industry may well produce small quantities of other commodities and several other industries may well produce some of its characteristic products. Since the connection between demand and cost cannot, in general, be observed for individual commodities, any attempt to trace these connections, which is the essence of inter-industry analysis, must rest partly on assumption.

Second, where several conflicting assumptions are possible and where it is difficult to make a choice between them, it is desirable that the role played by assumptions should be reduced as far as possible. It is for this reason that the establishment rather than the enterprise is the unit to be grouped to form industries. In those countries which do not have the practice of setting up enterprises for specific purposes, it can be observed that the output of an establishment is almost always more homogeneous than the output of the enterprise of which it forms a part. Consequently, the grouping of establishments rather than enterprises to form industries will diminish the importance of uncharacteristic production and so will diminish the role played by assumptions in connecting demands and costs. Following this line of argument, it might be supposed that establishments themselves should be divided with the object of further increasing the homogeneity of production. In principle this is correct, but in practice it will rarely be possible to carry out this division without the use of further assumptions in allocating costs to separate departments. In addition, by going too much into detail, there is always the danger of going beyond the commodities which are bought and sold to the technical processes which contribute to their production.

Finally, it may be asked why government services and the services of private non-profit institutions should be separated from industries, since the different types of activity are all designed to fit into a common classification of all economic activities. The reason is to be found partly in the differences in cost structure of activities organized in different ways and partly in the interest which attaches to the cost structures of non-industrial activities and, in particular, to the activities organized by general government.

With this introduction, let us now look first at the accounts for commodities and then at the accounts for activities.

(*a*) *Commodities* (rows and columns 5 through 12). The first four of these rows and columns (5 through 8) relate to the supply and disposal of commodities reckoned at basic values, that is before charging commodity taxes or deducting commodity subsidies. The purpose of showing commodities valued in this way is to ensure that, as far as is practicable, a uniform valuation is obtained throughout each of the rows 5 through 8. This uniformity is important in input–output analysis. The second four rows and columns (9 through 12) relate to commodity taxes and subsidies. When corresponding entries in the two sets of accounts are added together, a commodity flow is obtained which, except in the case of imports, is expressed at the producer's market value, that is to say at the value at which the commodity leaves the producer before transport and distribution charges are added on. These charges are in all cases debited to the purchaser. Imports are valued c.i.f. and to these values customs duties are added in a separate set of entries.

Uniformity of valuation is important for purposes of input–output analysis because the demand for one unit of a commodity by any buyer of that commodity is assumed to stimulate the activity producing that commodity to the same extent. Clearly this will not happen if the valuations are different for different buyers. For example, in a country where tax constitutes four-fifths of the value of a packet of cigarettes sold for domestic consumption but where tax is not charged on export sales of cigarettes, the effect on the tobacco industry of the sale of a packet for domestic consumption would appear five times as great as an export sale if actual values were used. This difficulty is avoided if both packets are valued uniformly and the taxes (or drawbacks) are shown separately where they arise. Similar considerations hold where appliances, such as cookers or refrigerators, are taxed when sold for household use but untaxed when sold for business use; or when a group of commodities, such as petroleum products, is not subdivided and one of these products, such as petrol, is highly taxed while another, such as fuel oil, is lowly taxed. Of course, at the level of aggregation of table 4 this whole issue is of little importance; but it becomes important in many countries at the much more detailed level proposed in the full system.

The treatment of commodities can now be described. In rows 5 through 8 we find the uses to which the supply of the four groups of commodities is put. The consumption by industries appears at the intersection with columns 13 through 16; the consumption by government services and by the services of private non-profit institutions appears at columns 17 through 20; household consumption appears at columns 21 through 23; the inputs into stock-building and into gross fixed capital formation appear at columns 51 through 63; and finally the inputs into exports, that is the values of commodities exported, appear at column 74. The sum of the entries in any row gives the total supply of the commodity group in question.

Correspondingly, in columns 5 through 8 we find the sources of the supply of the four groups of commodities. The outputs of domestic industries appear at rows 13 through 16; any commodities that were produced in the course of rendering government services and the services of private non-profit institutions (for example, reproductions produced by museums or firewood produced by the highway department in pruning the trees under its control) would appear at rows 17 through 20; and imports appear as the sum of the entries at rows 31 and 74, the former relating to protective import duties and the latter to the cost of the imports before these duties are added. The sum of these two last items represents the cost of imported commodities which, in the case of competitive imports, most nearly corresponds to the basic value of the domestically produced article.

As an example let us concentrate on row and column 6, which relate to the commodity group 'manufacturing and construction' expressed at basic values. Column 6 shows the sources of supply: 267 units (at row 14) produced by the manufacturing and construction industries; 2 units (at rows 15 and 16) produced by other domestic industries; and $1 + 29 = 30$ units at (rows 31 and 74) of imports of these commodities valued inclusive of protective import duties, that is duties which tend to raise the cost of the import in relation to the corresponding domestic cost. Import duties (5 units in this example) designed simply to offset similar duties on domestic production appear at the intersection of row 31 and column 10. This distinction serves the purpose of ensuring that, as far as possible, basic values are independent not only of the purchaser but also of the source of supply. Row 6 shows the uses to which the manufacturing and construction commodities are put. The entries of $8 + 118 + 11 + 8 = 145$ (at columns 13 through 16) represent intermediate inputs into industries; the entries of $7 + 3 + 1 = 11$ (at columns 17 through 19) represent intermediate inputs into government services; the entries of $34 + 27 + 5 = 66$ (at rows 21 through 23) represent elements of household expenditure on goods and services; the entries totalling 43 units (at columns 51 through 63) represent elements of capital formation; and, finally, the entry of 34 (at column 74) represents exports.

Commodity taxes, net, are shown in rows and columns 9 through 12; and the same commodity category (involving row and column 10) can be used in explaining their treatment. Looking first at column 10: the entry of 9 (at row 14) represents commodity taxes payable in respect of the domestic output of the products of manufacturing and construction; and, as we have seen, the entry of 5 (at row 31) represents non-protective duties on imports of manufacturing and construction products. The -1 (at row 9) represents a drawback of tax charged on an uncharacteristic input (for example in respect of customs duty charged on the imported raw tobacco embodied in exported cigarettes). This entry in column 10 offsets the entry of -1 in row 10, column 74, which is necessary since the entry in row 6, column 74, is recorded at basic value, that is inclusive of any tax embodied in the value of the producer's raw materials. Turning now to row 10: the entries of 2, 1 and 1 (at columns 14 through 16) represent commodity taxes (other than protective import duties) paid on commodity inputs into industries; the entries of 4, 2 and 4 (at columns 21 through 23) represent commodity taxes payable in respect of household goods and services; and, as we have just seen, the -1 (at column 74) represents a drawback of tax.

The entries in row and column 10 can be added on to the corresponding entries in row and column 6 to yield a valuation of supplies and disposals of the characteristic products of manufacturing and construction after charging commodity taxes and after deducting commodity subsidies. The result of this operation is shown in table 6.

(b) *Activities* (rows and columns 13 through 20). Activities are of two main kinds: industrial activities, which produce commodities; and the

TABLE 6　COMMODITY ACCOUNT FOR THE CHARACTERISTIC
PRODUCTS OF MANUFACTURING AND CONSTRUCTION

Sources of supplies (outgoings)			Destinations of disposals (incomings)		
Domestic manufacturing and construction			Intermediate consumption, industries		
Basic value	267		Basic value	145	
Tax	9		Tax	4	
	—	276		—	149
Other domestic industries			Intermediate consumption, general government services		
Basic value	2				
Tax	0		Basic value	11	
	—	2	Tax	0	
Imports				—	11
C.i.f. value	29		Intermediate consumption, services of private non-profit institutions serving households		
Customs duty	6				
less Drawback	−1		Basic value	0	
	—	34	Tax	0	
				—	0
			Final consumption expenditure in the domestic market by households		
			Basic value	66	
			Tax	10	
				—	76
			Increase in inventories		
			Basic value	6	
			Tax	0	
				—	6
			Gross fixed capital formation		
			Basic value	37	
			Tax	0	
				—	37
			Exports		
			Basic value	34	
			less Drawback	−1	
				—	33
Total		312	Total		312

service activities of general government and private non-profit institutions,
which produce services that are not, in general, marketed. In table 4, the
production accounts for industries are provided by rows and columns 13
through 16; three production accounts (rows and columns 17 through 19)
are shown for the services of general government; and a single production
account (row and column 20) is shown for the services of private non-
profit institutions. Let us look at each of these categories in turn.

(*i*) *Industries.* As an example let us consider the industry group 'manufacturing and construction'. In row 14, this group is shown as selling its
output to the commodity accounts: 267 units of characteristic product

and 1 unit of subsidiary product (at columns 7 and 9). In order to get
the total value of production at producers' values, it is necessary to add
in the 9 units of commodity tax (at column 10). Thus total output is
$267 + 1 + 9 = 277$. The cost structure of the manufacturing and construction industries is shown in column 14. Intermediate inputs of commodities,
whether domestically produced or imported, amount at basic value to

TABLE 7   PRODUCTION ACCOUNT FOR THE MANUFACTURING AND
CONSTRUCTION INDUSTRIES

Costs (outgoings)		Gross output (incomings)		
Characteristic products of agriculture and mining		Characteristic products of domestic industrial activity		
Basic value	19	Basic value	267	
Tax	9	Tax	9	
	— 28		—	276
Characteristic products of manufacturing and construction		Other products of domestic industrial activity		
Basic value	118	Basic value	1	
Tax	2	Tax	0	
	— 120		—	1
Services of transport, communication and distribution				
Basic value	13			
Tax	0			
	— 13			
Other commodities				
Basic value	14			
Tax	0			
	— 14			
Compensation of employees	64			
Operating surplus	23			
Consumption of fixed capital	6			
Indirect taxes, net	9			
Total	277	Total		277

$19 + 118 + 13 + 14 = 164$ (at rows 5 through 8). This total must be
adjusted by adding commodity taxes, net: $9 + 2 = 11$ (at rows 9 and 10).
The remaining items of cost (at rows 28 through 31) amount to
$64 + 23 + 6 + 9 = 102$, representing compensation of employees, operating surplus, provisions for the consumption of fixed capital and indirect
taxes, net. These three groups of costs sum to the value of sales:
$164 + 11 + 102 = 277$.

The information that has just been described can be brought together
in the form of a production account for manufacturing and construction
as in table 7.

13

It will be noticed that the commodity taxes shown in the separation of value of the intermediate inputs on the cost side of the account do not involve any duplication with the indirect taxes, net, shown at the bottom of the account, which are taxes on output. They are balanced by the commodity taxes shown on the opposite side of the account.

(*ii*) *General government services.* These services can be illustrated from the entries in row and column 18 of table 4, which are brought together in the form of a production account in table 8.

TABLE 8   PRODUCTION ACCOUNT FOR HEALTH, EDUCATION AND OTHER SOCIAL SERVICES OF GENERAL GOVERNMENT

Costs (outgoings)			Gross output (incomings)	
Intermediate consumption			Production for own use	16
Basic value	5		Other production	0
Tax	0			
	—	5		
Compensation of employees		10		
Consumption of fixed capital		1		
Total		16	Total	16

(*iii*) *Services of private non-profit institutions.* In the example given in table 4, these services are not of much importance but this will not always be so in practice, particularly where these institutions play an important role in the provision of medical and educational services. The information in row and column 20 of table 4 is brought together in the form of a production account in table 9.

TABLE 9   PRODUCTION ACCOUNT FOR THE SERVICES OF PRIVATE NON-PROFIT INSTITUTIONS

Costs (outgoings)			Gross output (incomings)	
Intermediate consumption			Production for own use	1
Basic value	0		Other production	1
Tax	0			
	—	0		
Compensation of employees		2		
Consumption of fixed capital		0		
Indirect taxes, net		0		
Total		2	Total	2

8. CONSUMPTION

Just as production is divided into a set of accounts for commodities and a set of accounts for activities, so consumption is also divided into two parts: expenditure on the one hand and income and outlay on the other.

The expenditure accounts relate to household goods and services and to the purposes of general government and of private non-profit institutions. In each case the classification is concerned with the use of resources to satisfy the aims of final consumption; and in the revised system, though there are differences in the aims of different sectors, provision has been made for a common purpose classification at all points where these aims overlap. This common classification does not interfere with the classification of household goods and services needed for consumers' demand analysis.

The income and outlay accounts are the current accounts of the institutional sectors. These sectors are conceived of as the centres of financial decisions relating, on current account, to the getting and spending of income and, on capital account, to the provision and use of capital funds. In the example of table 4, three sectors are shown in the current accounts: enterprises (corporate and quasi-corporate); general government; and households and private non-profit institutions serving them. In the capital accounts, these three sectors are expanded to four by dividing the enterprise sector between non-financial enterprises and financial institutions. In the full system, five sectors are distinguished in both types of account (the private non-profit institutions forming one of the sectors), and a number of further subdivisions are made; in particular, the sector for non-financial enterprises is disaggregated on a broad industrial basis.

Since sectors are concerned with financial decisions and since these decisions are usually taken centrally, the units out of which the enterprise sectors are built up are normally aggregations of the smaller units which we encountered in the sphere of production. In the case of industries, the unit was the establishment; in the case of the enterprise sectors the unit is the enterprise. The establishments of which an enterprise is composed may be assigned to different industries in a classification of economic activities: a large chemical combine may control establishments in all branches of the chemical industry and even in other industries, such as food processing, paper manufacture, and so on. It is for this reason that an industrial classification of enterprises must necessarily be more broadly based than an industrial classification of establishments.

It would always be possible to show direct interaction between establishment and enterprise classifications; for example, to classify compensation of employees in corporate and quasi-corporate enterprises simultaneously by industrial activity and by industrial sector. In the present system this is not done and, as can be seen from row and column 28 of table 4, compensation of employees is classified on the one hand by activity (in the row) and on the other by sector of origin (in the column). Although not illustrated in the table, the full system contains a broad industrial classification of enterprises, more specifically non-financial corporate and quasi-corporate units, so that provision is made for the tabulation of compensation of employees and operating surplus according to both kinds of industrial classification. The reason for not proposing the more ambitious treatment is that, while in principle it presents little difficulty, in practice it presents a great deal and in fact up to now has been attempted in only a few countries. Since the routing of income flows forms a central part of any national accounting system and is in no sense an optional extra, as might be said perhaps of the construction of regional accounts or even balance sheets, it seems desirable to formulate the system in a manner accessible in practice to a wide range of countries.

With this introduction, let us look first at the accounts for expenditure and then at the accounts for income and outlay.

TABLE 10   FINAL CONSUMPTION EXPENDITURE ACCOUNT FOR ALL
HOUSEHOLD GOODS AND SERVICES

Purchases (outgoings)			Finance (incomings)	
Characteristic products of agriculture and mining			Final consumption, residents	167
Basic value	17		Direct purchases in the domestic market, non-residents	2
less Subsidy	−1			
	—	16		
Characteristic products of manufacturing and construction				
Basic value	66			
Tax	10			
	—	76		
Services of transport, communication and distribution				
Basic value	38			
Tax	0			
	—	38		
Other commodities				
Basic value	32			
Tax	4			
	—	36		
Services of general government		0		
Services of private non-profit institutions		1		
Direct purchases abroad, residents		2		
Total		169	Total	169

(a) *Expenditure* (rows and columns 21 through 27). The first group in this set of accounts (rows and columns 21 through 23), relates to household goods and services. The single incoming item into each of these accounts is to be found at the intersection with column 50, except in the case of row 23 where a further entry appears (at column 74) in respect of expenditure by foreign visitors. The outgoing items appear mainly at rows 5 through 12, to a minor extent at rows 17 through 20 and, in the case of column 23, there is an entry at the intersection with row 74 in respect of consumers' expenditure abroad.

TABLE 11 ALTERNATIVE FINAL CONSUMPTION EXPENDITURE
ACCOUNT FOR ALL HOUSEHOLD GOODS AND SERVICES

Purchases (outgoings)		Finance (incomings)	
Food, beverages, tobacco		Final consumption, residents	167
Basic value	65	Direct purchases in the	
Tax	3	domestic market, non-residents	2
	68		
Clothing and household goods and services			
Basic value	53		
Tax	5		
	58		
Other goods and services			
Basic value	35		
Tax	5		
	40		
Services of general government	0		
Services of private non-profit institutions	1		
Direct purchases abroad, residents	2		
Total	169	Total	169

If we add together the corresponding entries in rows and columns 21, 22 and 23, we can set up a consumption account for all household goods and services. This is done in table 10.

The derivation from table 4 of the consumption account shown in table 10 is the simplest. But the elements of a matrix can be added up in several ways. Thus, if the entries in rows 5 through 8 and columns 21 through 23, and in rows 9 through 12 and columns 21 through 23 are added up by columns rather than by rows, we obtain the variant shown in table 11.

The second group in this set of accounts (rows and columns 24 through 26) relates to the purpose of general government. As has been said, these are so defined in this system that, at the most detailed level, they are in one-to-one correspondence with government services. At a less detailed level, services and purposes are aggregated differently and the one-to-one correspondence disappears. In table 4, however, the two classifications have been aggregated conformably. As a consequence, an account made from rows and columns 24 through 26 would contain the same entries on each side and will not be exemplified here by a separate table.

In the case of private non-profit institutions, the classifications used in the system in respect of services (row and column 20) and purposes (row and column 27) are identical at both the detailed and more condensed levels. Thus an account made under these classifications will contain the same entries on either side, whether it is derived from table 4 or from the full system.

(*b*) *Income and outlay* (rows and columns 28 through 50). This set of accounts provides links, first, between the activities and the institutional sectors in which value-added originates and, second, between the sector of origin and the sector of receipt of income after allowance has been made for all kinds of current transfers. The term 'sector of receipt' is used here because all flows of property income are shown gross, and are so entered in the income and outlay accounts. Within the structure of the system it is a simple matter to enter flows of property income net. If this were done it would be appropriate to speak of 'sectors of destination', a term more symmetrical with 'sectors of origin'.

(*i*) *Value added.* The four components of value added are shown separately in rows and columns 28 through 31. The first two of these accounts receive, respectively, compensation of employees and operating surplus from the activities in which they arise (rows 28 and 29, columns 13 through 20) and regroup these components of value added in terms of the institutional sector of origin (columns 28 and 29, rows 32 through 34). The third account shows the consumption of fixed capital, transferred positively (row 30, columns 13 through 20) from activities and transferred negatively (row 30, columns 70 through 73) from the capital accounts of the institutional sectors. The first set of transfers show these provisions as an operating cost; the second set contribute to net domestic capital formation appearing on the outgoing side of the sectors' capital accounts. Since the two sets of transfers cancel out, there is no entry to be made in column 30. The fourth account receives indirect taxes, net, from the production accounts (row 31, columns 5 through 16) and pays them directly into the income and outlay account of general government as the ultimate recipient of these taxes (column 31, row 49).

(*ii*) *Sectors of origin.* The purpose of this group of accounts (rows and columns 32 through 34) is to convert the income components of value added originating in sectors into various forms of income. In table 4, compensation of employees in rows 32 through 34 (at column 28) is shown in columns 32 through 34 (at rows 35 and 36) divided between wages and salaries on the one hand and employers' contributions of all kinds on the other. The entrepreneurial income of the unincorporated units in the household sector is shown in the next group of accounts and is distinguished from the operating surpluses of corporate and quasi-corporate enterprises and of general government enterprises – operating surplus n.e.c. – and from the balance of operating surplus arising in the unincorporated private enterprises, which is distributed as property income.

(*iii*) *Forms of income.* Rows and columns 35 through 47 collect together various forms of income and redistribute them to the institutional sectors defined as sectors of receipt. In addition to the income originating from the productive activity that takes place in the sectors, other income arises as a consequence of transfers or in the rest of the world. All this income, however it may arise, finds its destination either in the institutional sectors or in the rest of the world.

In table 4, all wages, salaries and employers' contributions arise in domestic production. Their allocation by sector of origin appears in rows 35 and 36 (at columns 32 through 34) and their allocation by sector of receipt, in this case the household sector, appears in columns 35 and 36 (at row 50). In countries where border workers are important, significant amounts of income in these forms may be received from or paid to the rest of the world. In such cases the flows would appear at the intersection of rows 35 and 36 and column 74 and at the intersection of columns 35 and 36 and row 74 respectively.

In row and column 37, the 18 units of entrepreneurial income arising in unincorporated private enterprises (at column 34) are transferred to the household sector (at row 50).

In row and column 38, the operating surplus of corporate and quasi-corporate enterprises and of general government enterprises is shown transferred from the sectors of origin to the same sectors redefined as sectors of receipt.

In row and column 39, property income is shown, on a gross basis, transferred from various sources to various destinations. In row 39: 4 units are shown (at column 34) as distributed from the operating surplus (after deducting entrepreneurial income) arising in households and private non-profit institutions; 21, 11 and 4 units respectively (at columns 48 through 50) are shown as arising in the institutional sectors as sectors of receipt; finally, 11 units (at column 74) are shown as arising in the rest of the world. In column 39: 16, 4 and 25 units respectively (at rows 48 through 50) are shown as received by the three institutional sectors; and 6 units (at row 74) are shown as received by the rest of the world. The net receipts are obtained by subtracting the payments from the receipts. This operation gives −5, −7 and 21 units respectively for the three sectors and −5 units for the rest of the world.

Row and column 40 relate to direct taxes on income, whether these are payable to the national government or to foreign governments. Enterprises (corporate and quasi-corporate) are shown as paying 10 units, households etc. as paying 21 units and the rest of the world as paying 1 unit. Correspondingly general government is shown as receiving 28 units and foreign governments as receiving 4 units. It can be seen from these numbers that the three resident sectors in all paid $10 + 21 - 4 = 28 - 1 = 27$ units of national tax. If the sectoral division of taxes is to be recorded, then row and column 40 must be divided to show national and foreign taxes separately.

TABLE 12   INCOME AND OUTLAY ACCOUNT FOR ENTERPRISES
(CORPORATE AND QUASI-CORPORATE)

Outgoings		Incomings	
Property income	21	Operating surplus	31
Direct taxes on income	10	Property income	16
Current transfers to households			
etc.	0		
Saving			
Non-financial enterprises 13			
Financial institutions 3			
———	16		
Total	47	Total	47

Row and column 41 relate to social security contributions, and 9 units are shown as paid by households etc. to general government. As was the case with compensation of employees, these flows may also cross national boundaries.

Row and column 42 relate to current transfers made by enterprises. In the example, a token entry is made from enterprises to households.

Rows and columns 43 through 45 relate to current transfers made by general government. Row and column 43 relate to social security benefits, shown as a transfer of 10 units from general government to households. Row and column 44 relate to social assistance grants, shown as a transfer of 4 units from general government to households. Row and column 45 relate to other current transfers by general government: 11 units are transferred, of which 7 are received by government (for example, transfers from central to local government), 3 are received by households and the remaining unit is received by the rest of the world.

Row and column 46 relate to current transfers made by households and private non-profit institutions: 1 unit is shown as transferred to the rest of the world.

Row and column 47 relate to current transfers made by the rest of the world: 1 unit is shown as transferred to households.

(*iv*) *Institutional sectors of receipt.* Rows and columns 48 through 50 show income and its disposal in each of the three sectors. This information is set out in accounting form in tables 12 through 14.

TABLE 13   INCOME AND OUTLAY ACCOUNT FOR GENERAL
GOVERNMENT

Outgoings			Incomings	
Consumption expenditure			Indirect taxes, net	29
	20		Operating surplus	2
	16		Property income	4
	6		Direct taxes on income	28
	—	42	Social security contributions	9
Property income		11	Current transfers by general	
Social security benefits		10	government	7
Social assistance grants		4		
Current transfers n.e.c.		11		
Saving		1		
Total		79	Total	79

TABLE 14   INCOME AND OUTLAY ACCOUNT FOR HOUSEHOLDS AND
PRIVATE NON-PROFIT INSTITUTIONS

Outgoings			Incomings	
Consumption expenditure			Wages and salaries	141
	68		Employers' contributions	11
	58		Entrepreneurial income	18
	41		Property income	25
	1		Current transfers from	
	—	168	enterprises	0
Property income		4	Social security benefits	10
Direct taxes on income		21	Social assistance grants	4
Social security contributions		9	Current transfer from	
Current transfers n.e.c.		1	government n.e.c.	3
Saving		10	Current transfers from the rest	
			of the world	1
Total		213	Total	213

The entries in table 12 are simply the entries in row and column 48 of table 4. For certain purposes it is convenient to show receipts of property income net. If this were done, the first outgoing entry in table 12 would disappear, 21 units would be subtracted from incomings and the total in the account would be reduced to $31 + 16 - 21 = 26$. This total would be exhausted by payments of direct taxes on income, current transfers to households, etc. and saving. In table 12, as in table 4, the saving of enterprises is shown divided between non-financial enterprises and financial institutions. The reason is that this distinction is made in the capital finance accounts although it is not made in the income and outlay accounts.

Table 13 shows the income and outlay account for general government obtained from row and column 49 of table 4. Here again, net property income is negative: as we have seen, $4 - 11 = -7$.

Finally, table 14 shows the income and outlay account for households, etc. obtained from row and column 50 of table 4. Here, net property income is positive: $25 - 4 = 21$.

9. ACCUMULATION

The accounts for accumulation are divided into two sets: a set relating to capital expenditure and a set relating to capital finance. The first set is further divided between stock-building (increase in inventories) and investment in fixed assets (fixed capital formation).

The two sets of accounts play quite distinct roles in the structure of the system. The capital expenditure accounts relate to expenditure on stocks of commodities and on reproducible tangible assets (in effect, all tangible assets other than land, mineral rights, historic monuments and *objects d'art*), and in all cases they are accounts for activities. The capital finance accounts relate to the institutional sectors which finance this expenditure. Thus, for example, column 61 shows (at rows 6 through 8) the commodity structure of fixed capital formation in respect of the health, education and other social services of general government; and row 61 shows (at column 72) the cost of this expenditure debited to the capital finance account of general government. In the case of enterprises (corporate and quasi-corporate), since the capital expenditure accounts are classified by activity whereas the capital finance accounts are classified by institutional sector, all capital expenditure is debited to a dummy account (row and column 64) which is provided with finance by the capital finance accounts. This device avoids setting up an activity × sector matrix in the capital accounts and corresponds to the similar device used in the current accounts to reallocate compensation of employees and operating surplus from activities to institutional sectors.

In table 4, the capital expenditure accounts are not supported by corresponding statements of opening and closing stocks. This could readily be done, however, and would have an important economic meaning. The stock figures relevant here are gross stocks, corresponding to the one-dimensional concept of capital, rather than net stocks, corresponding to the two-dimensional concept. Gross stocks at the end of a period are related to gross stocks at the beginning by gross capital formation, scrappings and revaluations. Thus if the opening stock of fixed assets held by the manufacturing and construction industries were 160 units, say, and if scrapping amounted to −4 units and revaluations to 6 units, say, then we could deduce from column 57 of table 4 that the closing stock was $160 + (10 + 1) − 4 + 6 = 173$. Similarly, if the opening stock of all commodities held by manufacturing and construction were 50 units, say, and if the revaluation (stock appreciation) were 1 unit, say, we could deduce from column 52 that the closing stock was $50 + 5 + 1 = 56$.

Unlike the capital expenditure accounts, the capital finance accounts relate to institutional sectors and it is to these accounts that the sector balance sheets of the system are attached. In these accounts (and in the balance sheets) capital formation (and tangible assets) are reckoned on a net basis.

To sum up: the capital expenditure accounts relate to activities, and in them capital formation is shown gross; and the capital finance accounts relate to sectors, and in them capital formation is shown net, that is as gross capital formation less consumption of fixed capital. The gross stocks (and particularly the gross stocks of fixed assets) which lie behind the capital expenditure accounts (though they are not included in table 4) represent the concept of capital most often used in the analysis of production taking place in the various activities; and the net stocks which lie behind the capital finance accounts (and which are included in table 4) represent the concept of capital most relevant to the financial analysis of sectors.

(a) *Capital expenditure* (rows and columns 51 through 63). As was said above, this set of accounts is divided into two groups, increase in inventories (stock-building) and fixed capital formation.

(i) *Increase in inventories.* Rows and columns 51 through 54 relate to the increase in inventories in the four industry groups, and row and column 55 relate to the increase in inventories in government services. In table 4, only one account is shown for all these services combined; and no account is shown for the increase in inventories in the services of private non-profit institutions.

For industries, expenditure on commodity stocks (columns 51 through 54, rows 5 through 7) is financed by the dummy account for industrial capital formation (rows 51 through 54, column 64). For government, this expenditure, which in the example of table 4 has only negligible entries (column 55, rows 5 through 7), is financed by the capital finance account of general government (row 55, column 72).

(ii) *Fixed capital formation.* Rows and columns 56 through 63 do for gross expenditure on fixed assets exactly what rows and columns 51 through 54 do for inventories. The only differences (which relate to the example rather than to the system itself) are that in this case the government account (rows and columns 60 through 62) is divided between the three services distinguished in the production accounts and that an account is provided for private non-profit institutions (row and column 63).

(*b*) *Capital finance* (rows and columns 64 through 73). The four groups of accounts that fall under this heading are of a diverse character, as was the case with the accounts falling under the heading of income and outlay.

(*i*) *Industrial capital formation, land, etc.* The purpose of the first account in this group (row and column 64) has already been described: it is to collect together the capital expenditure of industries (at rows 51 through 54 and 56 through 59) and re-allocate it over the institutional sectors (at columns 70 through 73). The purpose of the second account (row and column 65) is to show (in the row) net receipts from transactions in land, mineral rights, etc. No entries appear in column 65.

(*ii*) *Capital transfers.* These transfers are shown (in column 66) as net receipts by the national sectors and the rest of the world. No entries appear in row 66.

(*iii*) *Financial claims.* Rows and columns 67 through 69 relate to transactions in financial claims. The entries in the rows relate to net acquisitions of claims as assets by the national sectors (at columns 70 through 73) and by the rest of the world (at column 75). The entries in the columns relate to net issues of financial claims as liabilities by the national sectors (at rows 70 through 73) and by the rest of the world (at row 75). For example, the net issue of currency and deposits by national sectors was 14 units, 11 of which were issued by financial institutions and 3 of which were issued by general government. Of such claims, 8 units were acquired by the rest of the world. At the same time, national sectors acquired, net, 6 units of foreign currency and deposits and an equal amount, $14 - 8 = 6$ units, of national currency and deposits. The distribution of these acquisitions by sector is shown in row 67 (at columns 70 through 73): $-1 - 5 + 2 + 16 = 12$.

(*iv*) *Institutional sectors.* The entries in the financial capital accounts of these sectors are the flow-entries in rows and columns 70 through 73. They are set out as accounts in tables 15 through 18.

The account for non-financial enterprises is shown in table 15. Apart from the entry for net lending, which cancels out within the account itself, the two halves of this account, together with the relevant revaluations, connect net tangible assets (net worth) and financial claims held (issued) on the asset (liability) side of the sector's opening and closing balance sheets. Thus for net tangible assets, $304 + 15 + 0 + 17 = 336$; and for net worth, $91 + 13 + 26 = 130$. Similarly, for financial claims held, $181 + 14 - 2 = 193$; and for financial claims issued, $394 + 16 - 11 = 399$.

The account for financial institutions is shown in table 16. The account for general government is shown in table 17. And the account for households and private non-profit institutions is shown in table 18.

TABLE 15 CAPITAL FINANCE ACCOUNT FOR NON-FINANCIAL
ENTERPRISES (CORPORATE AND QUASI-CORPORATE)

Outgoings			Incomings	
Gross capital formation	28		Saving	13
less Consumption of fixed capital	−13		Capital transfers, net	0
	—	15		
Purchases of land etc., net		0		
Net lending		−2		
Net investment		13	Finance of net investment	13
Currency and deposits		−1	Net lending	−2
Securities		5	Currency and deposits	0
Other financial assets		10	Securities	2
			Other financial liabilities	14
Net acquisition of financial assets		14	Net lending and net issue of liabilities	14

TABLE 16 CAPITAL FINANCE ACCOUNT FOR FINANCIAL
INSTITUTIONS

Outgoings			Incomings	
Gross capital formation	1		Saving	3
less Consumption of fixed capital	−1		Capital transfers, net	0
	—	0		
Purchase of land etc., net		1		
Net lending		2		
Net investment		3	Finance of net investment	3
Currency and deposits		−5	Net lending	2
Securities		4	Currency and deposits	11
Other financial assets		24	Securities	1
			Other financial liabilities	9
Net acquisition of financial assets		23	Net lending and net issue of liabilities	23

TABLE 17   CAPITAL FINANCE ACCOUNT FOR GENERAL GOVERNMENT

Outgoings			Incomings	
Gross capital formation	8		Saving	1
less Consumption of fixed capital	−1		Capital transfers, net	2
	—	7		
Purchase of land etc., net		0		
Net lending		−4		
Net investment		3	Finance of net investment	3
Currency and deposits		2	Net lending	−4
Securities		0	Currency and deposits	3
Other financial assets		7	Securities	5
			Other financial claims	5
Net acquisition of claims		9	Net lending and net issue of claims	9

TABLE 18   CAPITAL FINANCE ACCOUNT FOR HOUSEHOLDS AND PRIVATE NON-PROFIT INSTITUTIONS

Outgoings			Incomings	
Gross capital formation	10		Saving	10
less Consumption of fixed capital	−4		Capital transfers, net	−2
	—	6		
Purchases of land etc., net		−1		
Net lending		3		
Net investment		8	Finance of net investment	8
Currency and deposits		16	Net lending	3
Securities		−6	Currency and deposits	0
Other financial assets		2	Securities	0
			Other financial liabilities	9
Net acquisition of financial assets		12	Net lending and net issue of liabilities	12

10.   THE REST OF THE WORLD

The rest of the world is represented by the entries in two rows and columns (74 and 75). This minimal amount of disaggregation is needed because the rest of the world's balance of payments on current account plays an essential role in the reconciliation of opening and closing net worth as recorded for the rest of the world. This balance is shown in table 4 at the intersection of row 75 and column 74. Had the current account for the rest of the world been divided to show separately an account for production and an account for consumption, the rest of the world's balance of trade would have appeared separately at the intersection of the consumption row and the production column.

The two accounts for the rest of the world are set out in tables 19 and 20.

TABLE 19   CURRENT ACCOUNT FOR THE REST OF THE WORLD

Outgoings		Incomings	
Commodity exports		Commodity imports	
1		15	
$34 - 1 = 33$		29	
11		5	
5		2	
—	50	—	51
Direct purchases in the domestic market, non-resident households	2	Direct purchases abroad, resident households and general government	3
Compensation of employees	0	Compensation of employees	0
Property income	11	Property income	6
Direct taxes on income	1	Direct taxes on income	4
Other current transfers	1	Other current transfers	2
Surplus on current transactions	1		
Total	66	Total	66

TABLE 20   CAPITAL ACCOUNT FOR THE REST OF THE WORLD

Outgoings		Incomings	
Net acquisition of financial assets		Surplus on current transactions	1
		Capital transfers, net	0
		Net issue of liabilities	
8		6	
5		0	
5		11	
—	18	—	17
Total	18	Total	18

11.   REVALUATIONS

Revaluations of existing assets and liabilities, together with the entries in the capital finance accounts of the institutional sectors, provide the link between the entries in the opening and closing balance sheets. These revaluations are shown for financial assets and liabilities in rows and columns 76 and 77 and for net tangible assets and net worth in row and column 78. Currency and deposits, being necessarily recorded at nominal values, are not subject to revaluation and so no revaluation account is shown for them.

The structure of the revaluation entries can be seen clearly from an example; let us take the case of the assets and liabilities of non-financial enterprises. From table 4 we can see that in the example security prices fell and replacement costs rose. In column 70 (at rows 76 through 78), we see that security holdings lost 3 units of value whereas holdings of other financial assets gained 1 unit and net tangible assets gained 17 units. Similarly, from row 70 (at columns 76 and 77), we see that securities issued fell by 13 units and that issues of other claims rose by 2 units. The revaluation of net worth is equal to the revaluation of assets *less* the revaluation of liabilities: $26 = 15 - (-11)$. Each of the revaluation accounts balances. For example, in row and column 76, we see that $-3 - 4 - 18 - 2 = -13 - 2 - 11 - 1 = -27$; in other words, the total of securities recorded in the system was valued 27 units lower at the end of the period than it was at the beginning.

12.   CLOSING ASSETS AND LIABILITIES

Closing assets and liabilities appear in rows and columns 79 through 82. From the information given there, a table similar to table 5 could be made for the end of the period. Here it may be more illuminating to exemplify the relationship between the opening and closing position for all resident sectors taken together. This is done in table 21.

TABLE 21   OPENING AND CLOSING BALANCE SHEETS FOR ALL
RESIDENT SECTORS

	Opening assets	Acquisition of assets	Revaluation of assets	Closing assets		Opening liabilities	Issue of liabilities	Revaluation of liabilities	Closing liabilities
Currency and deposits	275	12		287	Currency and deposits	296	14		310
Securities	457	3	−25	435	Securities	442	8	−26	424
Other financial assets	517	43	4	564	Other financial liabilities	479	37	3	519
Net tangible assets	661	28	42	731	Net worth	693	27	44	764
Total	1910	86	21	2017	Total	1910	86	21	2017

There should be no difficulty in tracing the entries in this table from the entries in rows and columns 70 through 73 of table 4. The only entry that may be terminologically confusing is the one at the intersection of the row for net worth and the column for issue of liabilities. In principle this entry is equal to the sum of saving and capital transfers. In the present example it is in fact equal to saving since net capital transfers to the rest of the world are zero.

13.   THE CONSOLIDATED ACCOUNTS OF THE NATION

In addition to a number of standard accounts, whose relationship to table 4 has been illustrated in the preceding sections, the new system also contains a standard set of consolidated accounts of the nation. These consolidated accounts are in fact nothing other than the four accounts of the nation from which we started, spelt out in considerably greater detail. They are obtained from table 4 by grouping the accounts for production, consumption, accumulation and the rest of the world into four consolidated accounts. In carrying out this consolidation it is desirable to preserve some latitude in the degree to which the entries in table 4 are aggregated and in the side of the consolidated account on which a particular entry is shown. For example, an outgoing item in table 4 can, if desired, be shown as a negative incoming item in the consolidated accounts. With these conventions, the consolidated accounts of the nation appear as in table 22.

Since these accounts are derived from the integrated matrix set out in table 4, it follows that they are completely articulated. Any appearance to the contrary, such as the double reference numbers to items 18 and 22, is due to the fact that in the consolidated accounts the opportunity is taken to show a number of flows on a net basis in one account and on a gross basis in another. If flows were recorded everywhere on the same basis, either gross or net, each item would have a single reference number connecting it with one other item.

The domestic product and expenditure account is concerned with value added in domestic production and the matching composition of expenditures. In the first account of table 22, the entries which emerge from consolidating table 4 are arranged so as to show expenditures in the domestic market and exports and imports of commodities. It will be observed that the flows on the right-hand side of this account can, with the aid of the national disposable income and outlay account, be decomposed and rearranged to show: general government final consumption, 42; private final consumption, $168 + 2 - 2 = 168$; increase in inventories and gross fixed capital formation, $6 + 41 = 47$; exports of commodities *plus* expenditure in the domestic market by non-resident households, $50 + 2 = 52$; *less* imports of commodities, -51, and *less* direct purchases

14

abroad by government services and resident households, $-1 - 2 = -3$, adding up to $-51 - 3 = -54$. The totals obtained by this rearrangement are the same as those shown in table 1.

National disposable income and outlay are set out in the second account of table 22. Here, the single entry for general government final consumption is not reduced by government direct purchases abroad; items 13, 14

TABLE 22   THE CONSOLIDATED ACCOUNTS OF THE NATION
Domestic Product (Value Added) and Expenditure

Outgoings		Incomings	
1. Compensation of employees (17)	152	5. General government final consumption (12)	42
2. Operating surplus (19)	55	6. *less* Direct purchases abroad by government services (−39)	−1
3. Consumption of fixed capital (26)	19	7. Private final consumption expenditure in the domestic market (13)	168
4. Indirect taxes, net (20)	29	8. Increase in inventories (23)	6
		9. Gross fixed capital formation (24)	41
		10. Exports of commodities (32)	50
		11. *less* Imports of commodities (−38)	−51
Gross domestic product (value added) at market prices	255	Gross domestic expenditure at market prices	255

National Disposable Income and Outlay

Outgoings		Incomings	
12. General government final consumption (5)	42	17. Compensation of employees from domestic activities (1)	152
13. Private final consumption expenditure in the domestic market (7)	168	18. Compensation of employees received from the rest of the world, net (34−41)	0
14. Direct expenditure abroad by resident households (40)	2	19. Operating surplus (2)	55
15. *less* Direct expenditure in the domestic market by non-resident households (−33)	−2	20. Indirect taxes, net (4)	29
16. Saving (27)	27	21. Property income from the rest of the world, net (35 − 42)	5
		22. Direct taxes on income and other current transfers from the rest of the world, net (36 − 43)	−4
National outlay	237	National disposable income	237

Capital Finance

Outgoings		Incomings	
23. Increase in inventories (8)	6	26. Consumption of fixed capital (3)	19
24. Gross fixed capital formation (9)	41	27. Saving (16)	27
25. Net lending to the rest of the world (30)	−1	28. Capital transfers from the rest of the world, net (−46)	0
Gross investment	46	Gross capital finance	46
29. Net acquisition of financial assets (47)	17	30. Net lending to the rest of the world (25)	−1
		31. Net issue of liabilities (44)	18
Capital outgoings	17	Capital incomings	17

Rest of the World

Outgoings		Incomings	
32. Purchase of commodity exports (10)	50	38. Sales of commodity imports (−11)	51
33. Direct expenditure in the domestic market by non-resident households (−15)	2	39. Direct expenditure abroad, general government services (−6)	1
34. Compensation of employees (18 + 41)	0	40. Direct expenditure abroad by resident households (14)	2
35. Property income (21 + 42)	11	41. Compensation of employees (34 − 18)	0
36. Direct taxes on income and other current transfers (22 + 43)	2	42. Property income (35 − 21)	6
37. Surplus on current transactions (45)	1	43. Direct taxes on income and other current transfers (36 − 22)	6
Current outgoings	66	Current incomings	66
44. Net acquisition of financial assets (31)	18	45. Surplus on current transactions (37)	1
		46. Capital transfers, net (−28)	0
		47. Net issue of liabilities (29)	17
Capital outgoings	18	Capital incomings	18

and 15 taken together represent private consumption expenditure at home and abroad by resident households; and so on. Correspondingly, items 17 and 18 taken together represent compensation of employees accruing to residents; and so on. The total of this account is closely related to the national income. In fact it is equal to the national income *plus* net unrequited transfers from the rest of the world *plus* net indirect taxes.

The capital finance account is divided into two parts: the top part shows gross investment and its finance; and the bottom part shows the accompanying transactions in financial claims.

The account for the rest of the world is likewise divided into two parts: the top part shows current transactions; and the bottom part shows the accompanying capital transactions.

We have thus come full circle, starting with a simplified version of the four accounts of the nation in section 2 above, subdividing these to show the structure of the new system, as in table 4, deriving from table 4 a number of standard accounts and finally consolidating table 4 so as to return to a more elaborate version of the four consolidated accounts of the nation.

14.   THE INPUT–OUTPUT DATA IN THE SYSTEM

The input–output data contained in the system appear in the rows and columns relating to commodities and industries. In order to explain and illustrate how these data can be used for input–output analysis, a magnifying glass has been applied to the relevant parts of table 4, the number of commodities and industries has been increased from four to thirteen, the unit of measurement has been decreased one hundred fold (so that what appeared as 1 in table 4 now appears as 100) and the results are set out in tables 23 and 24.

Table 23 contains a rearrangement of the kind of information provided in rows and columns 5 through 8 of table 4. In both panels of the table the first eighteen columns relate to commodities and the final column relates to commodity taxes on all the preceding entries of each row. In the upper panel the rows relate to sources of supply: first come the thirteen domestic industry groups; then the services of general government and private non-profit institutions (which in this example do not produce any commodities); and, finally, the rest of the world, represented by imports c.i.f. and the protective import duties levied on them.

The thirteen rows and columns in the top left-hand part of the table indicate the extent of subsidiary production. Commodities, being defined as the characteristic products of industry groups, are naturally mainly produced in their own industry group, and so this part of the table has a pronounced diagonal element. Nevertheless, as can be seen by looking at the rows, every industry produces some commodities characteristic of other industries and every commodity except services is produced by at least one industry as a subsidiary product. It is the existence of subsidiary production, coupled with the fact that cost structures can only be measured

TABLE 23 SOURCES AND DESTINATIONS OF COMMODITY SUPPLIES

Column groups: columns 1–13 = Competitive commodities; columns 14–18 = Complementary commodities; final column = Commodity taxes, net.

Sources of supply	1 Agriculture, forestry, fishing	2 Mining	3 Food, beverages, tobacco	4 Textiles, wearing apparel, leather	5 Rubber, chemicals, petroleum prods.	6 Basic metals	7 Metal products, machinery, equipment	8 Manufacturing n.e.c.	9 Gas, electricity, water	10 Construction	11 Transport and communication	12 Distribution	13 Services	14 Agriculture, forestry, fishing	15 Mining	16 Food, beverages, tobacco	17 Basic metals	18 Manufacturing n.e.c.	Commodity taxes, net
Industries																			
1 Agriculture, forestry, fishing	1695				21	1	1	16	3	1		7							−147
2 Mining		974			5		2	3	1										353
3 Food, beverages, tobacco			3637					1											105
4 Textiles, wearing apparel, leather				2907			9	5	1										63
5 Rubber, chemicals, petroleum products			69	8	2917		58	20	61	1									7
6 Basic metal industries						2639	85	6	54	1									329
7 Metal products, machinery, equipment				3	12	85	7929	21	3	38									85
8 Manufacturing n.e.c.		1		6	8	1	18	2983	8	17									37
9 Gas, electricity, water					7				1187										
10 Construction							6			3151									33
11 Transport and communication		4			109	1	3	13			3313								33
12 Distribution			27	28								3818							77
13 Services							5				1		4920						583
General government services																			
Services of private non-profit institutions																			
Import duties	25	1	26	21	17	3	41	20											1288
Imports, c.i.f.	741	129	592	200	423	151	382	419			558		291	457	423	130	204	116	2824
Total	2461	1109	4354	3173	3519	2882	8454	3507	1318	3209	3872	3825	5211	457	423	130	204	116	2824
Destination of supply																			
Intermediate consumption, industries	942	867	819	1463	2495	2478	3336	2352	707	1000	1668	845	1340	316	423		204	116	1613
Intermediate consumption, general govt. serv.	15	20	26	20	137		534	112	66	197	81	41	385						72
Intermediate cons., services of p.n.–p.i.																			
Final cons. in domestic market, households	1434	192	3266	1257	333		796	621	459	312	981	2800	2862	141		130			1159
Increase in inventories	28	−18	48	46	62	116	204	77	−1		110	29							59
Gross fixed capital formation		9					1865	88	86	1698		11	169						
Exports	42	29	195	387	492	288	1719	257	1	2	1032	99	455						−79
Total	2461	1109	4354	3173	3519	2882	8454	3507	1318	3209	3872	3825	5211	457	423	130	204	116	2824

in terms of commodity and other inputs into industries, that calls for the introduction of assumptions before either a commodity × commodity or an industry × industry input–output table can be constructed.

In the lower panel, the rows relate to destinations of supply. The elements in these rows would appear in an enlargement of table 4 as row sums of the various submatrices strung out along rows 5 through 8. Thus, in table 4, transport, communication and distribution form a single commodity group, and the intermediate use of this commodity by the four industry groups is shown (row 7, columns 13 through 16) as $1 + 13 + 9 + 2 = 25$; in table 23 it is shown in columns 11 and 12 (at the first row of the lower panel) as $1668 + 845 = 2513$ which, apart from rounding, is one hundred times as large as the corresponding entry in table 4. Similarly, the use of this commodity for final consumption by households in the domestic market is shown in table 4 as $15 + 12 + 11 = 38$ and in table 23 as $981 + 2800 = 3781$. Such relationships hold throughout between the entries in tables 4 and 23. They may be obscured by rounding-off errors or by errors introduced into table 4 to compensate for rounding-off errors; but this is a problem that only arises in producing a numerical example which is balanced in each of two different units.

The only new feature in table 23 is the division of commodities into two categories: competitive and complementary. Competitive commodities are those for which there is a domestic industry and which may, therefore, be either home produced or imported. Complementary commodities, on the other hand, are those for which no domestic industry exists, so that if they are needed they can only be obtained as imports. In the example, some of the complementary commodities which contribute most to the totals in columns 14 through 18 are: cotton, maize, oranges, rubber and tobacco under agriculture, forestry and fishing; crude petroleum and non-ferrous ores under mining; coffee and tea under food, beverages and tobacco; non-ferrous metals under basic metal industries; and woodpulp under manufacturing n.e.c.

In input–output analysis it is necessary to distinguish between competitive and complementary commodities because if complementary commodities are needed they must be imported; they cannot be obtained however much domestic production may be stimulated. If the distinction is not made, the analysis will imply that any commodity could be obtained in given proportions from domestic production and imports quite independently of the final product mix. In general, this cannot be true. Different vectors of final demand will imply varying proportions of complementary imports. In a country which mines coal but not oil, the direct and indirect effects on the productive system of a final demand vector implying a given amount of mining products will depend on the proportions in which this required amount is made up of coal and oil.

Table 24 contains a rearrangement of the kind of information provided

TABLE 24 INDUSTRIAL OUTPUTS AND COSTS

		Industries												
		1 Agriculture, forestry, fishing	2 Mining	3 Food, beverages, tobacco	4 Textiles, wearing apparel, leather	5 Rubber, chemicals, petroleum products	6 Basic metal industries	7 Metal products, machinery, equipment	8 Manufacturing n.e.c.	9 Gas, electricity, water	10 Construction	11 Transport and communications	12 Distribution	13 Services
Gross output at basic values		1711	984	3661	2927	3087	2770	8087	3044	1296	3171	3317	3873	4926
Commodity taxes, net		−147	8	353	105	63	7	329	85	37	3	33	77	583
Gross output at producers' prices		1564	992	4014	3032	3150	2777	8416	3129	1333	3174	3350	3950	5509
Intermediate inputs — Competitive commodities														
Agriculture, forestry, fishing	1	76		641	211	14	120	24	102	271	34	41	7	6
Mining	2	3	19	18	25	197			4			32	7	
Food, beverages, tobacco	3	281		473	4	18			69			16		
Textiles, wearing apparel, leather	4	8	6	12	1116	64	4	59	174		8	133	84	16
Rubber, chemicals, petroleum products	5	175	33	143	213	784	164	290	17	1	95	15	121	75
Basic metals	6		28	7	2	24	812	1353	111	93	202	217	3	1
Metal products, machinery, equipment	7	73	44	90	62	104	101	2091	747	14	165	33	78	143
Manufacturing n.e.c.	8	12	30	126	40	90	30	253	59	57	466	7	203	305
Gas, electricity, water	9	12	21	26	28	88	119	98	16	17	7	58	84	71
Construction	10	51	46	11	18	117	15	35	98	85	553	670	114	63
Transport and communication	11	69	36	81	62	57	117	159	100	47	79	55	98	36
Distribution	12	54	20	53	57	117	120	120	155	23	54	76	89	43
Services	13	56	19	100	78		109	303		27	122		121	57
Complementary commodities														
Agriculture, forestry, fishing	14			149	73									
Mining	15					94	73							
Food, beverages, tobacco	16													
Basic metals	17					333	204							
Manufacturing n.e.c.	18							17	97					
Commodity taxes, net		13	12	891	21	19	10	38	24	41	27	116	142	256
Primary inputs														
Compensation of employees		341	570	436	675	464	475	2493	895	295	1061	1353	1616	2073
Operating surplus		367	50	343	172	370	232	592	305	105	256	151	984	369
Consumption of fixed capital		120	50	61	70	95	65	162	71	217	42	344	122	412
Indirect taxes, net		−147	8	353	105	63	7	329	85	37	3	33	77	583
Total costs		1564	992	4014	3032	3150	2777	8416	3129	1333	3174	3350	3950	5509

in rows and columns 13 through 16 of table 4. In both panels of the table the columns relate to industries. In the upper panel the rows relate to the components of gross output at producers' prices: basic values and commodity taxes, net. As in the preceding table, all the figures in this table are related to those in table 4. For example, the gross output at basic values of the transport, communication and distribution industries is shown in table 4 as $1 + 71 = 72$ (row 15, columns 6 and 7) and in table 24 as $3317 + 3873 = 7190$ (in the first row, columns 11 and 12).

In the lower panel, the rows show the cost components of industrial outputs. The first thirteen rows relate to the intermediate inputs of competitive commodities without any separation of imports from domestic supplies. Again, the link with table 4 can easily be traced. For example, the input of transport, communication and distribution commodities into the corresponding group of industries is shown in table 4 as 9 (row 7, column 15) and in table 24 as $670 + 98 + 55 + 89 = 912$ (at the intersections of rows and columns 11 and 12).

The next five rows of table 24 relate to intermediate inputs of complementary commodities. These entries can be compared with those in table 23: the sums of rows 14 through 18 of table 24 are equal to the corresponding column sums of table 23.

The next row relates to commodity taxes, net, and when the entries are added on to those higher up in the panel they provide estimates of total intermediate inputs into the various industries valued at producers' values.

The remaining four rows show the components of value added. In the table these rows are labelled 'primary inputs' but this title is not wholly appropriate in all cases except to distinguish these costs from those of intermediate inputs.

XIII

A COMPARISON OF THE SNA
AND THE MPS

1. INTRODUCTION

The System of National Accounts (SNA) and the Material Products System (MPS) are alternative methods of accounting for the flows and stocks in a national economy. They are different in detail and many of the aggregates that are extracted from them, such as net output (or net value added), are differently defined.

Until a few years ago the two systems lived apart, each surrounded by its devotees. More recently a great deal of work has been done, particularly by the Conference of European Statisticians in Geneva, on links between the two systems. The importance of this work lies not only in the opportunities it gives for comparison, and so for more knowledge about the economic structure of different countries; but also in the possibilities it provides for understanding different views of economic and social processes. Any significant difference of view provides food for thought and may lead, in the end, to a more unified conceptualization of these processes. From time to time it happens in science that alternative conceptualizations, each valid to some extent, prove hard to reconcile: wave and particle theories of matter might be given as a case in point. The existence of apparently irreconcilable alternatives creates an uneasy situation which must, somehow, be resolved. Our problem of alternative accounting systems is in no sense as fundamental as the above example, but it does, nevertheless, lead to a feeling of unease. For most people, the choice lies between ignoring the alternative and understanding it in terms of their own version. Only by making the second choice can we widen the range of experience that is open to us.

The main purpose of this paper is to set out a comparison between the SNA and the MPS in terms of broad categories. Such categories, commodities, activities, consumption, value added, and so on, are common to both systems but their content differs between the two. Thus, in the SNA, commodities are, broadly speaking, marketed products whether these be goods or services; whereas, in the MPS, the concept is restricted to material products and excludes many of the services included among commodities in the SNA. Similarly, in the SNA, activities include not only all industries which produce commodities but also the rendering of services by general government and private non-profit institutions; whereas in the MPS, activities are restricted to industries producing material products and the distributive and transport services associated with them.

Each system can be set out in the form of an accounting matrix with monetary incomings in the rows and monetary outgoings in the columns, exactly like an input–output table expressed in money terms. But, in general, it is impossible to pass directly from one matrix to the other because the content of the corresponding elements is different. For example, in both systems, intermediate product is the value of commodities used up by activities in producing their output; but since the definition of commodities and activities is different in the two systems, the value recorded for intermediate product is necessarily different too. In order to make a proper comparison it is necessary to isolate the differences and make the appropriate adjustments in each case. This process can be represented formally in terms of a super-matrix from which the matrix for each system can be derived by an appropriate grouping of rows and columns.

In section 2, the point that has just been made is illustrated by means of a simple algebraic example relating to the classification of production.

In section 3, the main structure of the two systems is defined in terms of the entries in a set of eleven accounts. In the case of the MPS, one of these accounts is empty because redistributions on both current and capital account are brought together in a single redistribution account. This treatment, it may be noted, corresponds to the total-available-funds approach to the financing of a company in which we ask what total of funds can be made available for the finance of capital expenditure, whether these funds come from provisions for depreciation, retained profits, the sale of financial assets or any other source.

In section 4, the main structure of each system is illustrated, in tables 1 and 2, by rearranging the data given in the numerical example of the preceding paper [XII]. The figures given in table 2 for the MPS can only be approximate, because there are many points of detail that I have ignored in this broad comparison. I have noted some of these and have shown how the two tables have been derived from the original data.

In section 5, a super-matrix is presented, in table 3, from which tables 1 and 2 can be derived by the simple grouping of rows and columns. The grouping matrices are shown in tables 4 and 5. The super-matrix, at least as I have presented it, is a somewhat unwieldy construction of thirty rows and columns. The reason for this is that each element that is treated differently in the two systems must be classified in the super-matrix in a manner appropriate to each system both as a debit and as a credit. The conclusion I draw from this example is that the construction of super-matrices, though useful in simple cases for illustrative purposes, is not to be recommended as a practical aid to comparison. If such a matrix is necessarily highly repetitive in the simple example given in this paper it will certainly become altogether more repetitive if it is to contain the information for a really detailed comparison. Once the general principles are clear, it is probably easier to list the necessary adjustments and go straight to separate tables, like tables 1 and 2.

The paper ends with a brief statement of conclusions.

The versions given of the two systems are to some extent simplified and idealized. The phraseology used is, no doubt, more appropriate to the SNA than to the MPS. In spite of these shortcomings, I hope that my paper will be intelligible and that it will help to focus discussion on the means to be used in comparing the two systems.

2. COMPARING NET OUTPUT AS A WHOLE

We have seen that in the MPS the concept of production is restricted to activities engaged in making material products. It is irrelevant for our present purpose to discuss just what is meant by material products. Apart from goods in the ordinary sense of the word, material production may include, for example, the transport of goods but not of people, or the services of restaurants but not of hotels; but we need not consider such questions here.

In the SNA the concept of production is wider in that it includes the rendering of services as well as the making of material products. As far as value added (or net output) is concerned, it includes the value added that arises in the rendering of services by general government and by private non-profit institutions as well as that which arises in the production of commodities: that is marketed products, whether they be material products or services. The concept of production is, however, also limited in the SNA inasmuch as no value added is associated with amateur activities, housewives' services or the ownership of consumers' durables.

The concept of net output (=national income for a closed economy) can be given a single expression which is appropriate to both systems. It consists of the excess of output over intermediate inputs, that is, inputs which are themselves considered to be part of output. Thus, in the MPS, net output consists of the excess of the value of the output of material products over the value of the input of material products into the production of material products. It includes, therefore, the value of non-material services absorbed in material production as well as the value of primary inputs into material production. By contrast, in the SNA, net output consists of the excess of the value of all production (including services) over the inputs of commodities (including services).

The simplest accounting system which enables us to compare the two concepts is one in which the economy is divided into two main parts, production in the widest sense and everything else (or non-production), and in which production is divided between activities making material products and activities rendering services. We thus need three accounts; one for material products, one for services and one for everything else. Following the familiar arrangement of an input–output table, such a system can be set out in a matrix of order 3 as follows

$$A = \begin{bmatrix} a_{11} & a_{12} & a_{13} \\ a_{21} & a_{22} & a_{23} \\ a_{31} & a_{32} & a_{33} \end{bmatrix} \tag{1}$$

Each element in this matrix has a precise meaning. The first row and column pair relate to material production. In the row we find the destinations of this output: material products absorbed in material production, a_{11}; material products absorbed in the rendering of services, a_{12}; and material products absorbed in everything else, a_{13}. Similarly, in the first column we find the costs associated with material production: material products absorbed as intermediate input, a_{11}; services absorbed as intermediate input, a_{21}; and all other costs, a_{31}. Analogous explanations could be given for the entries in the second row and column, relating to the rendering of services, and for those in the third row and column, relating to everything else.

Net output can be expressed for each system in terms of the entries in (1). Denoting net output (MPS) by α, we have

$$\alpha \equiv a_{21} + a_{31} \tag{2}$$

and denoting net output (SNA) by β, we have

$$\beta \equiv a_{31} + a_{32} \tag{3}$$

Since each row and column pair in (1) is an account which balances, it follows, from the second row and column, that

$$a_{32} - a_{21} = a_{23} - a_{12} \tag{4}$$

Thus $\beta \gtrless \alpha$ according as $a_{23} \gtrless a_{12}$; that is to say net output (SNA) is greater than, equal to or less than net output (MPS) according as the value of services absorbed by non-production in the SNA sense is greater than, equal to or less than material products absorbed by services.

If the only distinction to be made is between production and non-production, then (1) can be reduced for either system, by appropriate grouping, to a matrix of order 2. In the case of the SNA it is the first two rows and columns that must be grouped together since services are included in production. Thus the reduced matrix for the SNA can be expressed in the form $G'AG$ where

$$G = \begin{bmatrix} 1 & 0 \\ 1 & 0 \\ 0 & 1 \end{bmatrix} \tag{5}$$

Thus

$$G'AG = \begin{bmatrix} 1 & 1 & 0 \\ 0 & 0 & 1 \end{bmatrix} \begin{bmatrix} a_{11} & a_{12} & a_{13} \\ a_{21} & a_{22} & a_{23} \\ a_{31} & a_{32} & a_{33} \end{bmatrix} \begin{bmatrix} 1 & 0 \\ 1 & 0 \\ 0 & 1 \end{bmatrix}$$

$$= \begin{bmatrix} a_{11} + a_{21} + a_{12} + a_{22} & a_{13} + a_{23} \\ a_{31} + a_{32} & a_{33} \end{bmatrix} \tag{6}$$

Similarly, in the case of the MPS it is the last two rows and columns that must be grouped together since services are not included in production. Thus the reduced matrix for the MPS can be expressed in the form $H'AH$ where

$$H = \begin{bmatrix} 1 & 0 \\ 0 & 1 \\ 0 & 1 \end{bmatrix} \tag{7}$$

Thus

$$H'AH = \begin{bmatrix} 1 & 0 & 0 \\ 0 & 1 & 1 \end{bmatrix} \begin{bmatrix} a_{11} & a_{12} & a_{13} \\ a_{21} & a_{22} & a_{23} \\ a_{31} & a_{32} & a_{33} \end{bmatrix} \begin{bmatrix} 1 & 0 \\ 0 & 1 \\ 0 & 1 \end{bmatrix}$$

$$= \begin{bmatrix} a_{11} & a_{12} + a_{13} \\ a_{21} + a_{31} & a_{22} + a_{32} + a_{23} + a_{33} \end{bmatrix} \tag{8}$$

By contrasting (6) and (8) it is clear that the two systems cannot be compared in their reduced form since the combinations of entries cut across the basic distinction, which is different in the two systems. Comparison is possible only by going back to (1): the basic principle of this paper.

Given A, net output as defined in either system can readily be derived by matrix operations. Thus if we define

$$j = \begin{bmatrix} 0 \\ 1 \end{bmatrix} \tag{9}$$

and

$$k = \begin{bmatrix} 1 \\ 0 \end{bmatrix} \tag{10}$$

then

$$\alpha = j'H'AHk \tag{11}$$

and

$$\beta = j'G'AGk \tag{12}$$

So much for the simple distinction between production and non-production. Let us now turn to a more detailed, though still highly aggregated, representation of the two systems.

3. THE MAIN STRUCTURE OF THE TWO SYSTEMS

The main structure of the two systems will now be described in terms of the entries in a set of accounts: eleven accounts in the case of the SNA and ten in the case of the MPS. The categories to which these accounts relate are as follows.

(*a*) *Commodities* (account 1). In the SNA, commodities are, in the main, the products of industries, that is to say of producing units which, generally speaking, intend to sell the goods and services which they produce. Although it is understood that commodities may be produced in small quantities in the course of rendering the services of general government and of private non-profit institutions, these service activities are not treated as industries and their main services are not treated as commodities.

In the MPS, commodities are restricted to material products and the concept excludes a number of the 'commercial' services which are included in the SNA.

There is an important difference in the valuation of commodities which appears in the basic tables of the two systems. While provision is made in the SNA for valuation at purchasers' values, the valuation in the basic structure as shown, for example, in table 4 of [XII] is at basic values plus commodity taxes, that is at producers' values. In the MPS, on the other hand, the entries in the commodity rows are expressed at purchasers' values, which means that the rows for trade and transport margins are suppressed and their contents are allocated over the remaining rows. The commodity columns for trade and transport margins are likewise suppressed and the margins on each category of output are shown in a separate row (or rows). Thus, for example, the commodity column for chemicals shows the output of chemicals at producers' values plus, in the separate row (or rows), the trade and transport margins on this output giving, in total, the purchasers' value of chemical output. Accordingly, in the MPS, trade and transport do not appear at all in the commodity rows and columns though they do appear among activities.

For each system, the first account shows, in the row, the uses to which the supply of commodities is put and, in the column, the sources of this supply.

(*b*) *Activities* (account 2). In the SNA, activities include industries, which produce commodities, and the services of general government and private non-profit institutions.

In the MPS, activities are restricted to those branches of industry which are regarded as belonging to the sphere of material production. Among these are goods transport, communications which serve material production, distribution, and services such as those rendered by architects and engineering consultants.

For each system, the second account shows, in the row, the destinations to which the output of activities is disposed of and, in the column, the cost structure of this output. Commodity output is disposed of to the commodity account; in the SNA the services of general government and private non-profit institutions are disposed of directly to the consumption account.

(*c*) *Consumption* (account 3). In the SNA, consumption relates to the expenditure by private households and individuals, private non-profit institutions and general government on goods and services for current use. Services relate to the product of activities and exclude, for example, the direct services of civil servants, the cost of which is debited to the service activity of general government.

In the MPS, consumption relates to material products consumed by private households and individuals and also to the material products used in rendering all kinds of services in the non-productive sphere, whether these are commodities in the sense of the SNA or not. There are a number of minor differences between the two systems: uniforms are debited to activities in the SNA but form part of supplements to wages and, therefore, of consumption in the MPS.

For each system, the third account shows, in the row, the source of finance for consumption and, in the column, the use of this finance to purchase commodities and, in the case of the SNA, to pay for the services of general government and private non-profit institutions.

(*d*) *Net value added* (account 4). In the SNA, net value added represents the payments made for primary inputs plus net indirect taxes; or, in other words, the excess of the value of output over the cost of commodity inputs and depreciation.

In the MPS, the meaning is the same except that output is restricted to the output of material products, and commodity inputs and depreciation are restricted to inputs of material products and depreciation arising in the production of material products. There are differences of allocation in the two systems: employers' contributions form part of supplements to wages in the SNA but form part of transfers, and are therefore not deducted to reach the operating surpluses of activities, in the MPS.

For each system, the fourth account shows, in the row, the receipt of net value added from activities and, in the column, the payment of the same sum to the account for 'incomings and outgoings'.

(*e*) *Depreciation* (account 5). In the SNA, all depreciation is debited to the activity account and debited negatively, that is to say credited, to the capital finance account.

In the MPS, depreciation in respect of material production is debited to the activity account and depreciation arising in the rendering of all kinds of services is debited to the account for incomings and outgoings which, as we have seen, includes the consequences of redistribution on capital account. Total depreciation is debited negatively to the capital finance account. Again, there are differences of detail: provisions for accidental damage are included with depreciation in the SNA but are included in operating surpluses in the MPS.

For each system, the fifth account shows, in the row, the receipt of the above debits and, in the column, nothing, since the debits cancel out.

(*f*) *Redistribution I* (account 6). In the SNA, this account shows the sources and destinations of all transfers on current account. Transfers consist of flows of property income, direct taxes on income, government grants and benefits, and the like.

In the MPS, this account includes, in addition, all receipts and payments arising in respect of the rendering of services in the non-productive sphere and in respect of transactions in financial claims and capital transfers.

For each system, the sixth account shows, in the row, gross transfers received by the economy and, in the column, gross transfers paid. In the case of the SNA, these transfers are restricted to current transfers including transfers of property income; whereas, in the case of the MPS, they cover all transfers.

(*g*) *Incomings and outgoings* (account 7). In the SNA, this account shows the sources and uses of current incomings; that is to say, it is an account for disposable income and outlay except for the fact that current transfers are entered gross.

In the MPS, this account shows the sources and uses of all incomings including those connected with the rendering of services in the non-productive sphere and with transactions in claims.

For each system, the seventh account shows, in the row, the sources of incomings and, in the column, the destination of outgoings. For the SNA, incomings consist of income from productive activity and all current transfers; and outgoings consist of expenditure on consumption, all current transfers and saving. For the MPS, incomings consist of income from productive activity and all transfers; and outgoings consist of expenditure on consumption, all transfers, depreciation in respect of all service activities and domestic finance provided for net capital formation.

(*h*) *Gross capital formation* (account 8). In the SNA, gross capital formation is composed of the value of the physical increase in stocks and all expenditure on the acquisition of fixed assets, including expenditure on such services as those rendered by architects and consulting engineers.

In the MPS, gross capital formation covers the same items but is restricted to expenditure on material products which, as we have seen, includes such services as those just mentioned. Expenditure on services in the non-productive sphere connected with capital formation is treated like any other kind of expenditure on such services, that is as a transfer.

For each system, the eighth account shows, in the row, the source of finance of gross capital formation and, in the column, the capital formation itself.

(*i*) *Redistribution II* (account 9). In the SNA, this account relates to transactions in claims and other capital transfers.

In the MPS, this account does not exist since the transactions to which it relates have already been entered in account 6.

For the SNA, the ninth account shows, in the row, the acquisition of claims and the payment of capital transfers and, in the column, the issue of claims and the receipt of capital transfers.

(*j*) *Capital finance* (account 10). In the SNA, this account relates to the finance of capital formation and the acquisition of claims.

In the MPS, this account relates to the finance of capital formation only.

In each system the tenth account shows, in the row, the sources of finance for capital outlays and, in the column, the capital outlays themselves. In both cases the outlays are net of depreciation. In the SNA, capital outlays include the acquisition of claims; in the MPS, not only is the acquisition of claims excluded but so is any element of gross capital formation consisting of services rendered in the non-productive sphere.

(*k*) *The rest of the world* (account 11). This account contains all transactions with the rest of the world and, generally speaking, is the same for both systems. In the MPS, there are entries for profits in connection with foreign trade which, in this paper, are ignored.

For each system, the eleventh account shows, in the row, the receipts of the rest of the world from the country under study and, in the column, the payments of the rest of the world to that country. As a consequence of the differences of treatment noted above, these transactions are grouped differently in the two systems. Thus, in the SNA, the receipts of the rest of the world are divided between imports of goods and services, receipts from current transfers (including property income) and receipts from the issue of claims and from capital transfers; and the payments of the rest of the world are similarly distributed. In the MPS, imports and exports are restricted to material products and all other transactions appear as transfers in account 6.

This brief comparison of the two systems contains many simplifications but is sufficient to bring out some of the main differences between them. These differences can conveniently be grouped as follows.

15

(i)   Differences in important boundaries. There are two of these. First, the production boundary is drawn differently in the two systems: in the SNA a number of service activities are included within the production boundary which are excluded in the MPS. Second, the SNA recognizes, in connection with finance, a boundary between current and capital transactions. The MPS on the other hand, does not and puts all such transactions through a single set of accounts.

(ii)   Differences of emphasis in questions of valuation. While recognizing the importance of purchasers' values, the basic tables of the SNA are set up in terms of producers' values (basic values plus commodity taxes). The reason for this is that the commodity accounts are thought of mainly in connection with input–output analysis and the treatment adopted helps to achieve price-homogeneity in the valuation of commodities. In the MPS, on the other hand, the uses of commodities are valued at purchasers' values whereas the supplies of commodities are valued at producers' values to which trade and transport margins are then added to give, in total, purchasers' values.

(iii) Relatively minor differences of treatment, some examples of which have been given above: uniforms, employers' contributions, provisions for accidental damage.

Further differences would emerge if we were to consider the detailed classifications of the two systems. In this paper, however, I am concerned only with broad outlines.

4. THE TWO GROUPED MATRICES

Before we come to the derivation of the two systems from a more comprehensive system in the manner of section 2 above, it is convenient at this point to set out the grouped matrices for the two systems following the order of the preceding section. The numerical example that follows is based on an extension of the example given in [XII].

The SNA is set out in table 1 below.

The entries in table 1 and their derivation can be described as follows.

Commodities. We can see from row and column 1 that the total supply of commodities is 511 units, of which 246 units are used as intermediate product by activities (including the services of general government and private non-profit institutions), 166 units are used for consumption purposes by private households and individuals, 47 units are used for gross capital formation and 52 units are exported. Domestic activities provide 457 units and the rest of the supply, namely 54 units, is imported.

The derivation of these figures can be seen most easily by turning to table 3 of [XII]. Two changes have been made: first, import duties have been included in the value of output; and, second, direct expenditures

TABLE 1   THE MAIN STRUCTURE OF THE SNA

	1	2	3	4	5	6	7	8	9	10	11
1. Commodities	0	246	166	0	0	0	0	47	0	0	52
2. Activities	457	0	44	0	0	0	0	0	0	0	0
3. Consumption	0	0	0	0	0	0	210	0	0	0	0
4. Net value added	0	236	0	0	0	0	0	0	0	0	0
5. Depreciation	0	19	0	0	0	0	0	0	0	−19	0
6. Redistribution I	0	0	0	0	0	0	102	0	0	0	13
7. Incomings and outgoings	0	0	0	236	0	103	0	0	0	0	0
8. Gross capital formation	0	0	0	0	0	0	0	0	0	47	0
9. Redistribution II	0	0	0	0	0	0	0	0	0	58	18
10. Capital finance	0	0	0	0	0	0	27	0	59	0	0
11. The rest of the world	54	0	0	0	0	12	0	0	17	0	0

abroad on goods and services in connection with the rendering of government services and the consumption of private households and individuals have been routed through the commodity account. Thus, in terms of table 3 of [XII], the figures shown here are: $246 = 245 + 1$; $166 = 166 + 2 - 2$; $47 = 6 + 41$; $52 = 50 + 2$; $457 = 443 + 14$; and $54 = 51 + 1 + 2$.

Activities. From row 2 of table 1 we can see that the domestic production of commodities amounted to 457 units and that the value of the services rendered by general government and private non-profit institutions amounted to 44 units. From column 2 we can see that the cost structure of all these activities involved an expenditure on intermediate product of 246 units, payments for the services of primary inputs and for indirect taxes of 236 units and provisions for the consumption of fixed capital (depreciation) of 19 units.

The derivation of the new figures in this account can again be obtained from table 3 of [XII]. Thus, $44 = 44$, the figure at the intersection of row 4 and column 5 of that table; 236 = 241 + 14 − 19; and 19 is the figure for total depreciation included in the figure of 241 in table 3 of [XII].

Consumption. Row 3 shows total consumption, 210 = 166 + 44 financed from the account for incomings and outgoings. Column 3 shows expenditure on consumption divided between commodities bought by private households and individuals, 166, and the payments for the services of general government and private non-profit institutions, 44.

Net value added. Row 4 shows the total of net value added received from the account for activities. Column 4 shows the same sum paid into the account for incomings and outgoings.

Depreciation. Row 5 shows depreciation as a credit from the activity account and as a debit to the account for capital finance. Column 5 is empty.

Redistribution I. Row 6 shows current transfers, including transfers of property income and direct taxes on income, received from the account for incomings and outgoings and from the account for the rest of the world. Column 6 shows the same set of transfers paid to the same accounts.

The foreign entries in this account appear in table 3 of [XII] at the intersection of row 6 (11) and column 11 (6).

For the entries in the account for incomings and outgoings we must turn to table 4 of [XII]. The figure of 102 is the sum of the entries in rows 39 through 47 and columns 48 through 50 of that table; and the figure of 103 is the sum of the entries in rows 48 through 50 and columns 39 through 47 less 4 units of property income, included in column 49, which in fact form part of value added and appear in table 4 of [XII] at the intersection of row 39 and column 34.

Incomings and outgoings. Row 7 shows incomings as composed of net value added (domestic income plus net indirect taxes), 236, and gross transfers received, 103. Column 7 shows outgoings as composed of consumption, 210, gross transfers paid, 102, and saving, 27. In [XII], saving can be found either at the intersection of row 10 and column 6 of table 3 or as the sum of the entries at the intersection of rows 70 through 73 and columns 48 through 50 of table 4.

Gross capital formation. Row and column 8 show the finance of gross capital formation and the corresponding expenditure on commodities.

Redistribution II. Row 9 shows the net acquisition of claims by national sectors, 58, and the net acquisition of national claims by the rest of the world, 18. Column 9 shows the net issue of claims by national sectors,

59, and the net issue of claims to national sectors by the rest of the world, 17.

These entries appear in row and column 9 of table 3 of [XII].

Capital finance. Row 10 shows the sources of finance as saving, 27, and the net issue of claims, 59. Column 10 shows the use of these sums in paying for net capital formation, $28 = 47 - 19$, and the net acquisition of claims, 58.

These entries appear in row and column 10 of table 3 of [XII].

The rest of the world. Row and column 11 bring together the transactions with the rest of the world, thus closing the system. These transactions have already been described in connection with accounts 1, 6 and 9.

Let us now turn to the MPS. The same example is set out in terms of this system in table 2 below.

TABLE 2   THE MAIN STRUCTURE OF THE MPS

	1	2	3	4	5	6	7	8	9	10	11
1. Commodities	0	204	157	0	0	0	0	45		0	47
2. Activities	402	0	0	0	0	0	0	0		0	0
3. Consumption	0	0	0	0	0	0	157	0		0	0
4. Net value added	0	184	0	0	0	0	0	0		0	0
5. Depreciation	0	14	0	0	0	0	5	0		−19	0
6. Redistribution	0	0	0	0	0	0	257	0		0	36
7. Incomings and outgoings	0	0	0	184	0	261	0	0		0	0
8. Gross capital formation	0	0	0	0	0	0	0	0		45	0
9. (Redistribution II)											
10. Capital finance	0	0	0	0	0	0	26	0		0	0
11. The rest of the world	51	0	0	0	0	32	0	0		0	0

Note: The single category of redistribution in the MPS is shown in account 6; account 9 is left blank.

The entries in table 2 and their derivation can be described as follows.

Commodities. We can see from row and column 1 that in this case the total supply of commodities (meaning material products) is 453 units, of which 204 units are used as intermediate product by activities (meaning industries producing material products), 157 units are used for consumption purposes (meaning consumption in the rendering of all kinds of services in the non-productive sphere as well as consumption by private households and individuals), 45 units are used for gross capital formation and 47 units are exported. Domestic activities provide 402 units and the rest of the supply, namely 51 units, is imported.

These figures cannot be derived, as were the corresponding figures in table 1, from tables 3 and 4 of [XII]; reference must be made to the more detailed information in tables 23 and 24 of [XII]. Even with this information only an approximate treatment is possible.

The two main difficulties that arise turn on the basis of valuation of product flows. In the SNA, two bases are used: basic values and producers' values, that is, basic values plus net commodity taxes. In the example of [XII], more detailed information is given on basic values than on producers' values. Thus from table 23 we can see that the output of 'services' (row 13) at producers' values is $4926 + 583 = 5509$, or, in the units adopted here, $49 + 6 = 55$ units; and that if imported 'services' are included, this total is increased by a figure of 291, that is by 3 to 58 units. But, from the lower part of the same table, we can see that the destinations of this supply are given only at basic values. For the purpose of this example, therefore, the 6 units of commodity taxes on 'services' were allocated *pro rata* to the different destinations. With a fuller tabulation of commodity taxes than that shown in the final column of table 23, this approximation would not be necessary.

The second difficulty is more important. In the MPS, the uses of commodities are expressed at purchasers' values, that is to say at values which include trade and transport margins on outputs rather than on inputs. The numerical example in [XII] does not provide this kind of information and, to do so, it would be necessary to expand the commodity rows for trade and transport into matrices, as is done in the case of commodity taxes.

This is not the place in which to debate the merits of alternative bases of valuation; but it should be noted that, from the point of view of input–output analysis, the argument that leads to a preference for basic over producers' values also leads to a preference for producers' over purchasers' values. The reason for this is that trade and transport margins, like commodity taxes, lead to substantially different unit values for different classes of buyer: in this case, for those who buy at wholesale prices as against those who buy at retail prices.

In the present example, commodities are not differentiated and so purchasers' values are well approximated if trade and transport are included in commodities. For this reason, only category 13 in tables 23 and 24 of [XII] is transferred to the non-productive sphere. Services consist, therefore, of 'commercial' services (category 13) *plus* the services rendered by general government and private non-profit institutions. By adopting this treatment, some services, such as the services of architects, which in the MPS would be included in material production will, in this example, be included in the non-productive sphere. This difficulty could only be met by a subdivision of category 13.

Let us return now to the derivation of the figures in row and column 1 of table 2 above. We have already seen that the domestic output of 'services' (category 13) transferred to the non-productive sphere amounted to 55 units, leaving $457 - 55 = 402$ units as the output of material products. We have also seen that, in this example, the import of 'services' amounts to 3 units, leaving $54 - 3 = 51$ units as the imports of material products.

The addition of commodity taxes to the figures for the different uses of 'services' shown in the lower part of table 23 of [XII] leads to a figure of 14 units as the value of 'services' used as intermediate inputs. This figure is not changed if the small amount of 'services' used in the production of 'services' is deducted. From table 24 of [XII] it also appears that 'services' use, as intermediate inputs, 10 units of material products and 1 unit of 'services'; and, from table 23, that the services of general government and private non-profit institutions use 13 units of material products and 4 units of 'services'. Thus total intermediate input in table 2 is $246 - 14 - 10 - 1 - 13 - 4 = 204$ units.

Including commodity taxes, the value of 'services' used for consumption purposes by private households and individuals, shown in table 23 of [XII], amounts to 32 units. Hence, material products used for these purposes equal $166 - 32 = 134$ units. To this must be added the material products used in rendering all kinds of services, leading to a figure of $134 + 10 + 13 = 157$ units, as shown in table 2.

Again from table 23 of [XII], we can see that 2 units of 'services' are embodied in gross capital formation (though much of this might disappear if category 13 were subdivided) and that 5 units are exported. Thus in table 2 we find gross capital formation equal to $47 - 2 = 45$ units and commodity exports equal to $52 - 5 = 47$ units.

Activities. The output of activities producing material products, 402 units in row 2 of table 2, is matched in column 2 by the corresponding elements of cost. We have already seen that the cost of intermediate products amounted to 204 units. From tables 24 and 4 of [XII], we can see that net value added in 'commercial' services (category 13) and in rendering the services of general government and private non-profit institutions amount respectively to 40 and 26 units. Since net value added in material production includes the value of 'services' embodied in material products, it follows that in table 2 net value added is equal to $236 - 40 - 26 + 14 = 184$ units.

The depreciation debited to the activity account is calculated by deducting from total depreciation that part which arises in the rendering of 'commercial' services and of the services of general government and private non-profit institutions. These amounts can be seen from tables 24 and 4 of [XII] to amount to 4 units and 1 unit respectively. Hence the entry in table 2 is equal to $19 - 4 - 1 = 14$ units.

Consumption. This account shows the 157 units of material products consumed by private households and individuals or embodied in services in the non-productive sphere to be financed from the account relating to incomings and outgoings.

Net value added. This account shows the 184 units of net value added in material production credited to the account for incomings and outgoings.

Depreciation. The only point to be made in respect of this account is that the 5 units of depreciation arising in connection with the rendering of services in the non-productive sphere are debited to the account relating to incomings and outgoings.

Redistribution. Row and column 6 contain not only the transfers shown in rows and columns 6 and 9 of table 1 but also receipts and payments connected with the rendering of services in the non-productive sphere. The expenditure on these services by national sectors amounts to 97 units since, as we have already seen, 14 units are bought by activities as intermediate product, 5 units are absorbed by services in the non-productive sphere, 32 units are bought by private households and individuals for purposes of consumption, 44 units represent the cost of the services of general government and private non-profit institutions and 2 units are used for capital purposes. Hence, the receipts into this account from the account relating to incomings and outgoings amount to $102 + 58 + 97 = 257$ units. We have also seen that the value of services rendered nationally in the non-productive sphere amounts to 99 units, of which 55 units represent the value of 'commercial' services and 44 units represent the value of services rendered by general government and private non-profit institutions. Hence, the payments from this account to the account for incomings and outgoings amounts to $103 + 59 + 99 = 261$ units. In a similar way the receipts from and payments to the rest of the world amount respectively to $13 + 18 + 5 = 36$ units and $12 + 17 + 3 = 32$ units. The figures 5 and 3 relate respectively to exports and imports of 'commercial' services.

Incomings and outgoings. Row 7 shows total incomings composed of 184 units of net value added and 261 units of gross 'transfers'. Column 7 shows the allocation of this total to consumption, 157 units, depreciation associated with service activities, 5 units, gross 'transfers', 257 units, and finance of net capital formation, 26 units. This last figure is equal to saving plus the excess of claims issued over claims acquired by national sectors less the service element in gross capital formation: $26 = 27 + 1 - 2$.

Gross capital formation. Row and column 8 show the finance of gross capital formation from the capital finance account and the corresponding expenditure on material products.

Redistribution II. Row and column 9 are empty since all capital redistribution is included with current redistribution in account 6.

Capital finance. Row and column 10 show the finance of net capital formation from the account for incomings and outgoings applied to expenditure on gross capital formation less depreciation.

The rest of the world. Row and column 11 bring together the transactions, which have already been described, with the rest of the world, thus closing the system.

5. A SUPER-MATRIX FOR THE TWO SYSTEMS

A super-matrix of order 30, A say, comparable to the little A-matrix of section 2 above, is set out in table 3 below. From it the grouped matrices in tables 1 and 2 can be obtained, in the forms $G'AG$ and $H'AH$, by the application of the grouping matrices, G and H, set out in tables 4 and 5 below.

The A-matrix of table 3 is partitioned according to the eleven categories employed in the preceding section, but I am not at all sure that this partitioning, though it has a certain rationale, is carried out in the best possible way. Nor am I confident that the matrix itself has been set out in the simplest and most economical manner. Thus it will be noticed from table 4 that G does not make use of accounts 2, 11, 12, 16, 22 and 27 of A, and it will be noticed from table 5 that H does not make use of accounts 7, 15, 16, 18, 27 and 29. Accounts 16 and 27 are common to both these series, and it might be supposed, therefore, that it would be possible to dispense with them. I have found it difficult to do so and am content in this paper to present a version of the A-matrix without any suggestion that it is the best version.

Let us now examine the thirty accounts of table 3.

Account 1. This relates to the supply and disposal of material products

TABLE 3 A VERSION OF THE A-MATRIX

		1	2	3	4	5	6	7	8	9	10	11	12	13	14	15	16	17	18	19	20	21	22	23	24	25	26	27	28	29	30
Commodities	1. Material products (ex service use)						204				134													45							47
	2. Material products (service use)											23																			
	3. Material products (service use)																														
	4. Commercial services (ex use in m.p.)								23					32											2						
	5. Commercial services (use in m.p.)						14		5																						5
Activities	6. Material production	379	23																												
	7. Material production (service use)			23																											
	8. Services in the non-productive sphere				41								14																		
	9. Commercial services (use in m.p.)					14									44							134									
Consumption	10. Material products (household use)							23																							
	11. Material products (service use)																														
	12. Commercial services (use in m.p.)																														
	13. Commercial services (household use)									14							32														
	14. Non-commercial services															76															
	15. All services (final use)																						44								
	16. All services (final use)																						76								

Net value added	17. Material production	170								
	18. Services in the non-productive sphere	66								
Depreciation	19. Material production and all services	14	5					−19		13
Redistribution I	20. Current transfers (ex services)				102					
Incomings and outgoings	21. All sectors			170 66	103					
	22. Government services			44						
Gross capital formation	23. Material products							45 2		
	24. Services									
Redistribution II	25. Financial claims and capital transfers						58			18
Capital finance	26. Claims issued					59				
	27. Excess of issue over acquisition of claims						1			
	28. Finance of capital formation (m.p.)				26			1		
	29. Finance of capital formation (services)				1			1		
Rest of the world	30. All accounts	51	3		12	17				

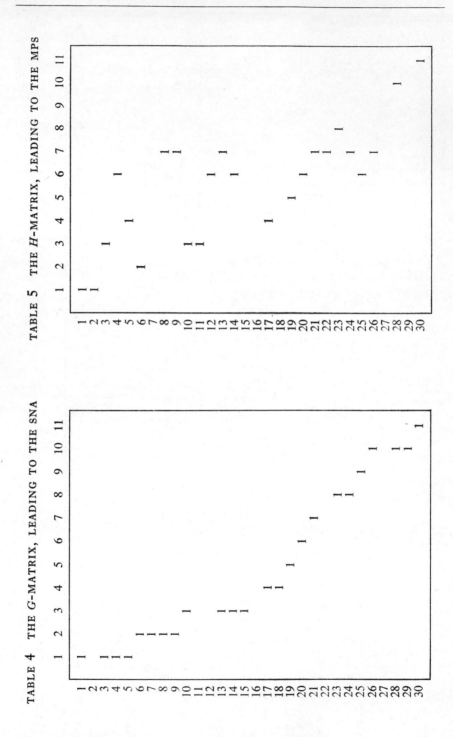

TABLE 4   THE *G*-MATRIX, LEADING TO THE SNA

TABLE 5   THE *H*-MATRIX, LEADING TO THE MPS

except those used up in the rendering of services in the non-productive sphere.

Account 2. This shows the value of material products used up in the rendering of services in the non-productive sphere as received from the consumption account, 11, and paid into the activity account for material production, 6.

Account 3. This shows the same amount as in account 2 received from the activity account for services in the non-productive sphere, 8, and paid into a special account, 7.

Account 4. This relates to the supply and disposal of 'commercial' services except those used up in material production.

Account 5. This shows the value of 'commercial' services used up in material production as received from the activity account for material production, 6, and paid into special account 9.

Account 6. This is the activity account for material production showing, in the row, the disposal of output to commodity accounts 1 and 2 and, in the column, the cost structure of material production.

Account 7. This is a special account relating to material products used up in the rendering of services in the non-productive sphere. The value of these products is received from commodity account 3 and is paid into consumption account 11.

Account 8. This is the activity account for the rendering of services in the non-productive sphere. In the row, it shows the disposal of 'commercial' services to commodity account 4 and to consumption account 12, and of the services of general government and private non-profit institutions to consumption account 14. In the column it shows the cost structure of these activities.

Account 9. This is a special account relating to 'commercial' services used up in material production. The value of these services is received from commodity account 5 and paid into consumption account 12.

Account 10. This relates to material products consumed by private households and individuals.

Account 11. This relates to material products consumed in the rendering of services in the non-productive sphere.

Account 12. This relates to 'commercial' services consumed in material production.

Account 13. This relates to 'commercial' services consumed by private households and individuals.

Account 14. This relates to the consumption of services rendered by general government and private non-profit institutions.

Account 15. This shows the value of services consumed by private households and individuals and by general government and private non-profit institutions as received from account 21 and paid to account 16.

Account 16. This shows the value of services consumed by private households and individuals and by general government and private non-profit institutions as received from account 15 and paid to accounts 13 and 22.

Account 17. This shows net value added in material production (as defined in the SNA) as received from the activity account for material production, 6, and paid into account 21.

Account 18. This shows net value added in the rendering of services (as defined in the SNA) as received from the activity account for services, 8, and paid into account 21.

Account 19. This relates to depreciation.

Account 20. This relates to current transfers as defined in the SNA.

Account 21. This relates to the receipt and disposal of net value added in material production and in the rendering of all kinds of services and of all current transfers as defined in the SNA.

Account 22. This is a special account which transfers the value of government services from one consumption account to another.

Account 23. This relates to the material products component of gross capital formation.

Account 24. This relates to the services component of gross capital formation.

Account 25. This relates to the net acquisition and net issue of financial claims.

Account 26. This shows the finance obtained by the net issue of claims by national sectors as used by these sectors either to acquire financial claims or to make a transfer to account 27.

Account 27. This shows the receipt from account 26 applied to the finance of gross capital formation. The sum involved is equal to net national borrowing from the rest of the world.

Account 28. This shows the material products component of gross capital formation and its finance.

Account 29. This shows the services component of gross capital formation and its finance.

Account 30. This shows all transactions with the rest of the world.

6. CONCLUSIONS

The main conclusions to be drawn from this paper can be summarized as follows.

First, the main structure of the two systems can be presented in terms of a common set of accounts, as exemplified by tables 1 and 2.

Second, since the content of the categories, represented by the accounts, is different in the two systems, corresponding entries in the two sets of accounts will, in general, be different too.

Third, it is impossible to pass directly from one accounting system to the other. This can only be done by isolating all items which are classified differently.

Fourth, once this is done, the set of entries necessary to construct either system can be arranged in a super-matrix, exemplified by table 3. From this matrix either system can be derived by appropriate grouping operations, exemplified by tables 4 and 5.

Fifth, the super-matrix is necessarily somewhat repetitive because each item which is treated differently in the two systems must be classified appropriately to each system both as a debit and as a credit. Though useful for illustrative purposes, the attempt to construct a super-matrix for a really detailed comparison would probably not be very illuminating.

Finally, once a general framework for comparison can be accepted, the next step is to work out the details. Reference has been made to the question of valuation and to minor differences of definition and treatment. There remain questions of classification, particularly of activities and institutions, and the introduction of balance sheet information to supplement the information on flows, with which alone this paper is concerned.

XIV

THE USE OF SOCIAL ACCOUNTING MATRICES IN BUILDING PLANNING MODELS

1. INTRODUCTION

The use of social accounting matrices as a means of organizing and presenting social accounting data has a number of advantages. First, it enables the structure of even a complex system to be grasped as a whole and the connections between different bodies of data and different classifications to be traced.

Second, it enables the data to be arranged systematically and coherently so that all the simple identities of the system are explicit. This is particularly important at a time when computers are coming to be used more and more in data-processing and model-building.

Third, it forces us to think about the connections between the variables we intend to use and the relationships we need to formulate for different kinds of model and ensures a certain measure of consistency among these models.

Finally, it is helpful in laying out complicated calculations and in establishing efficient methods of estimating parameters. When matrix algebra is used, as it very often is, in formulating economic models, it ensures a simple correspondence between the arrangement of the numerical data and the symbolic counterpart of this arrangement.

In what follows I shall try to illustrate these points. In doing this I shall have in mind the structure of flows and stocks envisaged in the proposals for revising the System of National Accounts (SNA) of the United Nations as described in [XII] above.

2. INPUT–OUTPUT STRUCTURE

In the revised SNA, the production accounts are divided into two main classes: those relating to commodities and those relating to activities. The accounts for commodities are themselves divided into two groups: commodity flows valued at producers' values *less* commodity taxes paid directly; and the commodity taxes paid directly on these flows. In a similar way, the accounts for activities are divided into two main groups: those for industries, that is, activities producing commodities, and those for the services of general government and private non-profit institutions, which do not produce commodities except incidentally.

The commodity accounts show the sources and uses of commodities. The purpose of showing commodity taxes separately is to ensure that the unit values in the commodity accounts are reasonably homogeneous without going to the length of expressing these unit values at factor cost.

The sources of commodity supplies are domestic production and imports. In the commodity accounts, imports are valued in two parts: the payment made to the rest of the world; and the payment of protective import duties made to the state. The sum of these two entries is likely to provide a good approximation to the corresponding value of the domestically produced article where this exists. Non-protective import duties, like excise duties on domestic products, appear in the commodity tax accounts.

The activity accounts show sales and the corresponding cost structures. Industries sell the whole of their output to the commodity accounts which then distribute commodities to the various users. The services of general government and private non-profit institutions are sold mainly to general government and private non-profit institutions although purchases, usually small, may be made by other buyers.

Reduced to its simplest terms, the accounting structure just described can be set out as in the following table.

A SCHEMATIC ARRANGEMENT OF DATA ON COMMODITIES
AND ACTIVITIES

	Basic value of commodities	Commodity taxes	Industries	Everything else	Total incomings
Basic value of commodities			U	e	q
Commodity taxes			U^*	e^*	q^*
Industries	V	V^*			g^{**}
Everything else			y'		η
Total outgoings	q'	$q^{*\prime}$	$g^{**\prime}$	η	

In this table a capital letter denotes a matrix, a small letter denotes a column vector and a small greek letter denotes a scalar (a single number). A row vector is denoted by a prime superscript ($'$). Thus q' is simply the column q written out as a row. In what follows we shall also need to

16

transpose (interchange the rows and columns of) matrices, and this operation will also be represented by a prime superscript. Thus, for example, V' denotes the matrix whose rows are the columns of V and whose columns are the rows of V.

The matrix U has commodities in the rows and industries in the columns, that is to say it is of dimension commodity × industry. The element in row j and column k of U represents the input of commodity j into the output of industry k. These inputs of commodities are measured at basic values, that is to say at producers' values less commodity taxes. The matrix U^* relates to commodity taxes on commodity inputs into industries. It is also of dimension commodity × industry and its typical element represents the commodity tax on input j absorbed by industry k. Inputs at producers' values are simply $U + U^* = U^{**}$, say.

In a similar way the vectors e and e^* represent respectively the basic value of the commodities and the associated commodity taxes which enter into net final demand, that is to say into final demand (including the input into the services of general government and private non-profit institutions) *less* all forms of imports. The vectors q and q^* are simply row totals, so that

$$q = Ui + e \tag{1}$$

and

$$q^* = U^*i + e^* \tag{2}$$

where i denotes the unit vector so that, for example, Ui denotes the column of row sums of U.

The matrix V is of dimension industry × commodity and the element in row r and column s represents the amount of commodity s produced by industry r. If, as is often the case, commodities are defined as the characteristic products of industries, then the elements of V will be heavily concentrated on the diagonal, since industries mainly produce their characteristic products. But V will never be a completely diagonal matrix since most industries produce a certain amount of subsidiary products, that is products characteristic of other industries.

The matrix V^*, also of dimension industry × commodity, has as its typical element the commodity tax paid by industry r in respect of its output of commodity s.

Thus from the first two columns of table 1 we have, after transposition,

$$q = V'i \tag{3}$$

and

$$q^* = V^{*\prime}i \tag{4}$$

From the third row of table 1, we can divide the outputs of industries into basic values, g say, and commodity taxes, g^* say. Thus

$$g = Vi \tag{5}$$

$$g^* = V^*i \tag{6}$$

and

$$g^{**} = g + g^* \tag{7}$$

For purposes of input–output analysis, we need to define three coefficient matrices, as follows

$$B = U\hat{g}^{-1} \tag{8}$$

$$C = V'\hat{g}^{-1} \tag{9}$$

and

$$D = V\hat{q}^{-1} \tag{10}$$

In these equations a circumflex over the symbol for a column vector indicates that the elements of that vector are spread out to form a diagonal matrix and the superscript -1 indicates inversion. Thus $\hat{g}^{-1}$ denotes a diagonal matrix of the reciprocals of industry outputs.

On the basis of these relationships four distinct input–output tables can be constructed, all expressed in terms of basic values. The first dichotomy depends on how we choose to treat subsidiary production: should we assume a commodity technology implying that a given commodity requires the same inputs per unit of output in whichever industry it is made; or, alternatively, should we assume an industry technology implying that a given industry requires the same inputs per unit of output whatever commodities it happens to be making. The second dichotomy depends on whether we wish to construct commodity $\times$ commodity or industry $\times$ industry tables.

These various possibilities work out as follows. If we adopt the assumption of a commodity technology then we must combine (1), (3), (8) and (9). From these equations we can write

$$
\begin{aligned}
q &= Ui + e \\
&= Bg + e \\
&= BC^{-1}q + e \\
&= (I - BC^{-1})^{-1}e
\end{aligned} \tag{11}
$$

and

$$
\begin{aligned}
g &= C^{-1}(I - BC^{-1})^{-1}e \\
&= (I - C^{-1}B)^{-1}C^{-1}e
\end{aligned} \tag{12}
$$

where I denotes the unit matrix. Equation (11) expresses commodity outputs, q, as a matrix multiplier times net final demands for commodities, e. The commodity $\times$ commodity input–output coefficient matrix, usually denoted by A, is in this case equal to BC^{-1}. Equation (12) expresses industry outputs, g, as a matrix multiplier times the net final demand for the outputs of industries, $C^{-1}e$. In this case the coefficient matrix is equal to $C^{-1}B$.

If, alternatively, we adopt the assumption of an industry technology, then we must combine (1), (5), (8) and (10). From these equations we can write

$$q = Ui + e$$
$$= Bg + e$$
$$= BDq + e$$
$$= (I - BD)^{-1} e \qquad (13)$$

and

$$g = D(I - BD)^{-1} e$$
$$= (I - DB)^{-1} D e \qquad (14)$$

By comparing (13) and (14) with (11) and (12) we can see that the effect of changing from the assumption of a commodity technology to one of an industry technology is to replace C^{-1} by D. It can also be seen that unless the number of commodities is equal to the number of industries, the assumption of a commodity technology, requiring the inversion of C, cannot be made.

In general (11), (12), (13) and (14) will lead to slightly different tables. Only in the case of the complete absence of subsidiary production, that is when $C = D = I$, shall we find that the four equations reduce to

$$q = g = (I - B)^{-1} e \qquad (15)$$

in which case the coefficient matrix reduces to B and there is no distinction between commodity and industry outputs.

But necessary as it may be to choose between these possibilities, there are two other questions which are likely to be of much greater practical importance. The first concerns the uniformity of valuation of commodities; and the second concerns the distinction between competitive and complementary commodities.

We can examine the first question by adding together corresponding elements in the first two rows and columns of the table. By doing this we express all commodity flows at producers' values and, corresponding for example to (11), we can write

$$q^{**} = (I - B^{**} C^{**-1})^{-1} e^{**}$$
$$= (I - B^{**} C^{**-1})^{-1} E^{**} i \qquad (16)$$

if, in place of the vector of net final demand at producers' values, e^{**}, we write the sum of the demands by different final buyers represented by the columns of the matrix E^{**}.

If we compare (16) with (11) we can see that there are two points of difference. In the first place the input–output coefficient matrices are different, since

$$BC^{-1} = UV'^{-1} \qquad (17)$$

whereas

$$B^{**}C^{**-1} = (U + U^*)(V' + V^*)^{-1} \tag{18}$$

It could happen, therefore, that the coefficient matrices on the two bases of value turned out to be quite different from one another; but experience suggests that this may not be a very serious difficulty. The reason for this is probably connected with the fact that, as a rule, commodities are not taxed differentially according to the industry that uses them as intermediate product.

This is not, however, the situation when we come to final product. Thus it is usual to find that commodities sold to private consumers are highly taxed, the same commodities when sold to business buyers are lowly taxed and when sold abroad are not taxed at all. The consequences can be seen clearly from (16). A single matrix multiplier, $(I - B^{**}C^{**-1})^{-1}$, multiplies all final demands; but a unit of final demand by different buyers may represent widely different amounts of product. Thus, if producers' values are used, £1 spent on cigarettes sold abroad will be deemed to stimulate the tobacco industry and its suppliers to the same extent as £1 spent on cigarettes by domestic consumers, yet the first £1 may buy several times as many cigarettes as the second £1 because exporters can reclaim the very high duty levied on the raw tobacco embodied in their exports. In practice, the shares of different final buyers may not change very much; but if we are always cutting unnecessary analytical corners we have only ourselves to blame if our results are rather disappointing.

The second question is not illustrated by the table but can readily be formulated. It is usual to distinguish between competitive commodities and complementary commodities. In the first case, imports compete with a corresponding domestic product; in the second case, any supplies needed must come from abroad. Thus, for Britain, raw cotton, crude petroleum, non-ferrous ores and raw tobacco are examples of complementary imports.

In the SNA, industries, and therefore commodities, are grouped according to a single international standard classification of all economic activities. But in any particular country, a given industrial category may only be partially represented. In some countries mining means coal mining, the mining of ferrous ores and quarrying. In others it may mean petroleum mining and in yet others it may mean the mining of non-ferrous ores. In each case some mining products are competitive and others are complementary; but they are not the same products in the different cases. In any particular country, therefore, it is important to divide the commodity accounts so as to show at least the main complementary commodities separately. If this is not done, the demand for a complementary commodity will appear to stimulate the domestic industry belonging to the same group although this industry is in fact incapable of producing the particular commodity demanded.

If the separation is made, then the regular input–output calculations are carried out in terms of competitive commodities; and intermediate demands for complementary commodities can be worked out once activity levels are known.

The main purpose of this section has been to bring out the interplay of data-organization and theory in setting up input–output calculations, which are a central feature of all disaggregated models. Since it is commodities that are bought and activities that incur costs, the arrangement described provides a good framework for observation, a framework which can then be consciously modified for the purposes of analysis.

3. PRICES AND COSTS

In the table given in the preceding section the producers' values of commodity flows were divided between commodity taxes and what were called basic values. These basic values are in fact only approximate since, while they exclude commodity taxes paid directly, they do not involve the removal of commodity taxes paid indirectly. As I said, the purpose of this concept is to improve the uniformity of commodity valuation without going to the lengths of an input–output analysis of costs. The concept is somewhat similar to the approximation to factor costs often employed, in which outputs are measured at factor costs and inputs are measured at market prices. The relationships between producers' values, basic values (true and approximate) and factor values (true and approximate) can be seen by examining the price circuit of an input–output system.

From the table we can see that

$$g^{**} = y + U^{**\prime} i$$
$$= y + \hat{g}^{**} B^{**\prime} i \tag{19}$$

where $U^{**} \equiv U + U^*$ and $B^{**} \equiv U^{**} \hat{g}^{**-1}$. If we denote by z the vector of primary costs entering commodity outputs, then, on the assumption of a commodity technology, we can write

$$q^{**} = z + \hat{q}^{**} C^{**\prime-1} B^{**\prime} i \tag{20}$$

where $q^{**} \equiv q + q^*$ and $C^{**} \equiv V^{**\prime} \hat{g}^{**-1}$. If, corresponding to (10), we write $D^{**} \equiv V^{**} \hat{q}^{**-1}$, then, on premultiplying (20) by D^{**}, we obtain

$$g^{**} = D^{**} q^{**}$$
$$= D^{**} z + V^{**} C^{**\prime-1} B^{**\prime} i$$
$$= D^{**} z + V^{**} V^{**-1} \hat{g}^{**} B^{**\prime} i$$
$$= D^{**} z + \hat{g}^{**} B^{**\prime} i \tag{21}$$

and so, by comparing (19) and (21), we see that

$$y = D^{**} z \tag{22}$$

On the assumption of an industry technology, we should find that

$$y = C^{**-1} z \tag{23}$$

Equations (22) and (23) show the relationship between primary inputs into industries and primary inputs into commodities on different assumptions. Let us denote these costs expressed per unit of output by

$$m = \hat{g}^{**-1} y \tag{24}$$

in the case of industries and by

$$n = \hat{q}^{**-1} z \tag{25}$$

in the case of commodities. Then, from the market-price equivalents of (9) and (10), and from (22), (24) and (25),

$$\begin{aligned}
m &= \hat{g}^{**-1} y \\
&= \hat{g}^{**-1} D^{**} \hat{q}^{**} \hat{q}^{**-1} z \\
&= \hat{g}^{**-1} V^{**} \hat{q}^{**-1} z \\
&= C^{**'} \hat{q}^{**-1} z \\
&= C^{**'} n
\end{aligned} \tag{26}$$

whence

$$n = C^{**'-1} m \tag{27}$$

Similarly, if (23) is used in place of (22),

$$n = D^{**'} m \tag{28}$$

In what follows the argument will be carried out in terms of (27).

Let us denote by p the vector of commodity prices at producers' values, assumed for the moment to be uniform for all buyers; and let us denote by m, t and x the vectors of the components of industry costs per unit of output: m denotes the cost of primary inputs (factors of production) per unit; and t and x denote respectively the cost of non-commodity indirect taxes and commodity taxes per unit. Then

$$\begin{aligned}
p &= A' p + C^{**'-1} (m + t + x) \\
&= (I - A')^{-1} C^{**'-1} (m + t + x) \\
&= H(m + t + x)
\end{aligned} \tag{29}$$

where $A \equiv B^{**} C^{**-1}$ and $H \equiv (I - A')^{-1} C^{**'-1}$. If we denote the vector of true basic values per unit of output by b and the vector of true factor costs per unit of output by f, then

$$b = H(m + t) \tag{30}$$

and

$$f = Hm \tag{31}$$

Let us now turn to the approximate measures, denoted by b^* and f^* respectively. By definition

$$b^* = A' p + C^{**'-1} (m + t) \tag{32}$$

and so, since

$$p = b^* + C^{**\prime-1} x \tag{33}$$

it follows that

$$
\begin{aligned}
b^* &= A' b^* + A' C^{**\prime-1} x + C^{**\prime-1}(m+t) \\
&= H(m+t) + A' Hx \\
&= b + A' Hx
\end{aligned} \tag{34}
$$

In other words, b^* exceeds b by the accumulated commodity taxes on inputs into commodities.

Similarly,

$$f^* = A' p + C^{**\prime-1} m \tag{35}$$

and so, since

$$p = f^* + C^{**\prime-1}(t+x) \tag{36}$$

it follows that

$$
\begin{aligned}
f^* &= A' f^* + A' C^{**\prime-1}(t+x) + C^{**\prime-1} m \\
&= Hm + A' H(t+x) \\
&= f + A' H(t+x)
\end{aligned} \tag{37}
$$

In other words, f^* exceeds f by the accumulated indirect taxes of all kinds on inputs into commodities. It can be seen that if all indirect taxes are allocated to commodity tax categories, then $t = \{0,0,\ldots,0\}$, $b = f$ and $b^* = f^*$.

Let us now relax the assumption that prices are uniform to all buyers and attribute this lack of uniformity to differential commodity taxes. In order to see what will happen in this case it is sufficient to postulate an average price, p_a say, and a uniform price on intermediate uses, p_u say, with corresponding commodity taxes per unit, x_a and x_u. Then we can write

$$
\begin{aligned}
p_a &= b^* + C^{**\prime-1} x_a \\
&= A'(b^* + C^{**\prime-1} x_u) + C^{**\prime-1}(m+t+x_a)
\end{aligned} \tag{38}
$$

from which it follows that

$$b^* = H(m+t) + A' Hx_u \tag{39}$$

On comparing (39) with (34) we see that the only difference is that $x \equiv x_a$ in the new notation is replaced by x_u. By substituting for b^* from (39) into (38), we can see that p_a can be written in the form

$$
\begin{aligned}
p_a &= A'(b + Hx_u) + C^{**\prime-1}(m+t+x_a) \\
&= b + A' Hx_u + C^{**\prime-1} x_a
\end{aligned} \tag{40}
$$

This is a perfectly general expression which can be changed to give the price vector for any group of buyers simply by changing the suffixes in the left-hand and ultimate right-hand terms. Thus, if p_d and x_d denote the prices paid by domestic final consumers and the commodity taxes payable directly in respect of these sales by the producing industry, then

p_d is given by substituting x_d for x_a in (40). It follows from this argument that the price paid by intermediate users, p_u, is given by

$$
\begin{aligned}
p_u &= b + A' H x_u + C^{**'-1} x_u \\
&= b + H x_u \\
&= H(m + t + x_u)
\end{aligned}
\tag{41}
$$

which can be compared with (29).

The main purposes of this section are, first, to express various measures of value in terms of the vectors and matrices of the system and, second, to show how these measures are affected by a lack of uniformity in the commodity taxes charged to different buyers. Again, we see that the matrix approach is helpful in providing a precise formulation of different concepts and in distinguishing between true and approximate measures.

4. INDEX-NUMBERS OF PRICES AND QUANTITIES

This section is written in terms of producers' prices on the assumption that they are homogeneous. If they are not, then products sold to different buyers must be recognized as distinct products, each with its own price. Alternatively, the calculations must be carried out with homogeneous unit values, which means substituting p_a, b or f for p in the expressions given below.

In spite of the immense number of formulae that have been proposed for the construction of index-numbers, most numerical work is based on one of three formulae:
(i)   the base-weighted aggregative, or Laspeyres' formula;
(ii) the current-weighted aggregative, or Paasche's formula; and
(iii) the geometric average of (i) and (ii), or Fisher's ideal index-number.

These index-numbers can readily be expressed in matrix form. Let us denote the three price index-numbers by Λ, Π and Φ and the three quantity index-numbers by Λ^*, Π^* and Φ^*. Then the final product system can be written in the form

$$
\Lambda = \frac{p_1' e_0}{p_0' e_0}
\tag{42}
$$

$$
\Pi = \frac{p_1' e_1}{p_0' e_1}
\tag{43}
$$

$$
\Phi = (\Lambda \Pi)^{1/2}
\tag{44}
$$

$$
\Lambda^* = \frac{p_0' e_1}{p_0' e_0}
\tag{45}
$$

$$
\Pi^* = \frac{p_1' e_1}{p_1' e_0}
\tag{46}
$$

$$
\Phi^* = (\Lambda^* \Pi^*)^{1/2}
\tag{47}
$$

In these expressions, p denotes a vector of commodity prices, e denotes a vector of quantities entering into net final demand and the suffixes 0 and 1 denote respectively the base and current periods. Thus, for example, Λ is the ratio of the inner product of the current-period price vector and the base-period quantity vector to the inner product of the base-period price vector and the base-period quantity vector.

If, as before, we denote a commodity × commodity input–output coefficient matrix by A, we can express the fact that the output of each commodity is devoted either to intermediate uses or to net final uses in the form

$$q = Aq + e \qquad (48)$$

where the ** superscripts which might seem appropriate from the earlier notation are now dropped in the interests of simplicity. By substituting for e from (48) into (42) through (47) we see that

$$\Lambda = \frac{p_1'(I - A)q_0}{p_0'(I - A)q_0} \qquad (49)$$

$$\Pi = \frac{p_1'(I - A)q_1}{p_0'(I - A)q_1} \qquad (50)$$

$$\Phi = (\Lambda\Pi)^{1/2} \qquad (51)$$

$$\Lambda^* = \frac{p_0'(I - A)q_1}{p_0'(I - A)q_0} \qquad (52)$$

$$\Pi^* = \frac{p_1'(I - A)q_1}{p_1'(I - A)q_0} \qquad (53)$$

$$\Phi^* = (\Lambda^*\Pi^*)^{1/2} \qquad (54)$$

These expressions will be recognized as net output index-numbers of prices and quantities, and their derivation *via* (48) demonstrates their identity with the corresponding final product index-numbers.

In (49) through (54) the coefficient matrix A in undated. If it changes, it should be given the same suffix as q. This means that in the quantity index-numbers a different A-matrix will appear in the numerator and the denominator. For example,

$$\Lambda^* = \frac{p_0'(I - A_1)q_1}{p_0'(I - A_0)q_0}$$

$$= \frac{p_0'(I - A_0)q_1}{p_0'(I - A_0)q_0} + \frac{p_0'(A_0 - A_1)q_1}{p_0'(I - A_0)q_0} \qquad (55)$$

The second line of (55) illustrates the difference between single-deflation and double-deflation methods. In the first term on the right-hand side of (55), the quantity of each input per unit of output in each industry remains unchanged, and so the ratio of gross output to net output at base-year prices in each industry remains the same. Such changes are brought into account in the second term of (55), but it will be noticed that the numerator of this term may well be small as a result of the cancellation of items in the two sets of cost structures.

The index-numbers (49) through (55) are written out in terms of the net outputs of commodities. They can, however, readily be rewritten in terms of the net outputs of industries. Thus, in these terms, the first line of (55) becomes

$$\Lambda^* = \frac{p_0'(I - A_1) D_1^{**-1} g_1}{p_0'(I - A_0) D_0^{**-1} g_0} \tag{56}$$

It will be recognized that (45), (55) and (56) all yield identically the same value of Λ^*. It is only when these index-numbers for the economy as a whole are divided into their components that the natural differences appear: the components of (45) are net final products; the components of (55) are net outputs of commodities; and the components of (56) are net outputs of activities (strictly, with the notation used, the net outputs of industrial activities).

5. PRODUCTIVITY

In the preceding section we were concerned with measures of final product and net output at constant prices. If we are to measure productivity we must find a way to measure primary inputs as well. The revised SNA is not very explicit on this subject but the framework it provides offers at least a first approximation.

In the analysis that follows only two kinds of primary input are considered: labour and capital. Labour (including as far as possible the self-employed, who are of great importance in such activities as agriculture and distribution) could be measured in terms of heads, or man-hours or, better still, heads or man-hours weighted by average earnings. Capital presents a more difficult problem. The revised SNA contemplates the construction of balance sheets for sectors in which the entries for tangible assets are represented by the net (written down) stock valued at replacement cost. It also contemplates the estimation of gross stocks of tangible assets classified by activities. These estimates would provide a first approximation to the concept of real capital employed. On this basis we could proceed as follows.

Let us define a coefficient matrix, F say, each element of which represents the quantity of a given primary input required per unit of output of a given commodity. Let us also define a vector, r say, each element of which represents the rate of remuneration to a particular primary input. In the notation introduced in section 3 above,

$$F'r = C^{**'-1} m \tag{57}$$

and

$$f = A'f + F'r$$
$$= (I - A')^{-1} F'r \tag{58}$$

Let us now consider a system of Laspeyres' index-numbers in which the basis of valuation is not producers' prices, p, but factor costs, f. If, despite this change, we continue to use Λ^* to denote the quantity index-number then, on transposing the terms in the numerator and denominator, we can write

$$\Lambda^* = \frac{q_1'(I - A_1')f_0}{q_0'(I - A_0')f_0}$$
$$= \frac{q_1'(I - A_1')(I - A_0')^{-1} F_0'r_0}{q_0' F_0' r_0} \tag{59}$$

on substitution for f_0 from (58). The transposition of terms is allowable because the numerator and denominator of (59) are single numbers.

Corresponding to (59), a Laspeyres' index-number of primary inputs, Λ^{**} say, takes the form

$$\Lambda^{**} = \frac{q_1' F_1' r_0}{q_0' F_0' r_0} \tag{60}$$

and so a Laspeyres' index-number of productivity, Λ^{***} say, takes the form

$$\Lambda^{***} = \frac{\Lambda^*}{\Lambda^{**}} = \frac{q_1'(I - A_1')(I - A_0')^{-1} F_0' r_0}{q_1' F_1' r_0} \tag{61}$$

Equation (61) shows how changes in intermediate technology, represented by the elements of A, and changes in primary technology, represented by the elements of F, enter into a measure of productivity. It also shows that if $A_1 = A_0$ and $F_1 = F_0$ there can be no change in productivity. On the other hand, if $A_1 = A_0$ but $F_1 \neq F_0$, then

$$\Lambda^{***}(A_1 = A_0) = \frac{q_1' F_0' r_0}{q_1' F_1' r_0} \tag{62}$$

and if $F_1 = F_0$, but $A_1 \neq A_0$, then

$$\Lambda^{***}(F_1 = F_0) = \frac{q_1'(I - A_1')(I - A_0')^{-1} F_0' r_0}{q_1' F_0' r_0} \tag{63}$$

and so it follows that

$$\Lambda^{***} = \Lambda^{***}(A_1 = A_0) \times \Lambda^{***}(F_1 = F_0) \tag{64}$$

that is to say, the measure of productivity is equal to the product of the two partial measures.

A similar set of equations, leading to the same conclusion, can be derived for the Π-system and, therefore, for the Φ-system as well.

In this section and the preceding one I have tried to set out a system of index-numbers of prices, final product, net output and productivity in matrix form with the help of the terminology of input–output analysis.

Again, it seems to me, the approach is useful in making explicit the many variants that are technically possible even within a very restricted range of index-number forms and in providing a coherent framework within which to lay out sets of consistent calculations.

6. THE ANALYSIS OF PRODUCTION

The information described up to now not only throws a good deal of light on movements in production and productivity but also provides the basic data usually considered necessary for setting up production functions for various branches of industry. The question remains: what kind of production function is appropriate? This problem is particularly acute in the context of medium or long-term planning models, where one of the aims is often to increase the rate of growth of production in relation to the rate of growth of the labour force [51]. Simple forms of production function, such as the Cobb-Douglas function, imply that capital can always be substituted for labour, so that the output of a given labour force can always be increased if only it is given enough capital to work with. This line of thought suggests that great efforts should be made to increase the proportion of income saved, in the belief that the additional saving can and will be devoted to productive investment. But it is not obvious that this belief is altogether justified. In any economically adapted society it is likely that a considerable part of production will be in the hands of firms which are already using as much capital as they know how to use, and that in many other firms the limited use of capital may be due not so much to the difficulty of raising finance as to the attitude of the proprietors and managers to processes and equipment with which they are unfamiliar. Even where there is no indifference or hostility to innovation, much of the potential gain from innovation may be absorbed by the restrictive practices of the labour force, by lack of retraining facilities or an unwillingness to use them, or by difficulties associated with mobility and with the condition of many of the older centres of industrial activity.

Thus while the revised SNA makes provision for a good deal of information about production, altogether more than the original SNA did, it does not contribute very much to the range of problems just outlined. Of these, the one most obviously ripe for attention is the treatment of research and development. In this field there is still a considerable amount of work to be done, despite much admirable pioneer work for example by the OECD, before a generally accepted set of concepts and form of presentation can be said to exist.

7. THE ANALYSIS OF CONSUMPTION

In the revised SNA, household expenditure on consumption is classified by goods and services and the expenditure on consumption by private non-profit institutions and by general government is classified by purpose. In neither case is the classification in one-to-one correspondence with the classification of commodities. Thus a feature of the system is the set of connecting matrices which show how each of the consumer classifications is transformed into the commodity classification. Although, for purposes of input–output analysis, it is usual to reclassify expenditures on consumption in terms of commodities (or of industry outputs), it is less usual to show the detailed transformations explicitly. Yet experience suggests that many uses can be found for this kind of information.

The reason for these distinct classifications of consumption is not simply that the available data on consumption happen to follow classifications different from the one appropriate to industrial commodities, but, more positively, that these classifications are needed for the analysis of consumption. Households and government do not think in terms of a commodity classification and in order to analyse their expenditures effectively we must adopt the classifications that they actually use.

In the case of household demand, analyses have been made using a wide variety of demand equations expressing the market demand for a particular good or service in terms of income, prices and other factors. In building a disaggregated model, it would be useful to have a single, general form of relationship which possessed various properties of consistency. One such form, which we have found useful in Cambridge, is the linear expenditure system, so called because in it expenditure on each good is a homogeneous linear function of total expenditure and each of the prices.

The system can be generalized in a number of ways, as explained in [VIII] above. Applications to British data over the period 1900–60 can be found in [67, 76]. Applications to Belgian data are given by Paelinck in [48] and by Rossi in [53]. The system is not, of course, the only one that could be devised and, despite its merits, it also has shortcomings. One of these is that it is suited to a world of competitive goods and cannot handle complementary or inferior goods. At Cambridge we are now experimenting with a non-linear expenditure system but it is too early to report on the results.

8. SPENDING AND SAVING

Reason suggests and experience seems to confirm [36, X] that any formulation of the aggregate consumption (or saving) function ought to contain a term in wealth as well as in income. Once this is accepted, it may be possible to demonstrate that, after all, spending is nothing but a transform of lagged disposable income; but a glance at equation (24) of [X] shows that this would not be a very enlightening starting point.

Up to now, estimates of wealth (net worth) by sector have rarely been available and so it has been necessary to use an approximate series, such as accumulated real saving. By providing for the inclusion of sector balance sheets, the revised SNA makes a contribution to improving the analysis of spending and saving behaviour. It is true that this part of the SNA is spelt out in much less detail than is the accounting for flows; but the reason simply is that there is less experience and agreement on the details of constructing balance sheets than there is on the details of constructing flow accounts.

The main point of this and the preceding section has been to show the information available in the revised SNA which bears on aggregate spending and saving, on the analysis of aggregate spending for the household sector and on the conversion of consumer categories to industrial categories for all consuming sectors. It does not seem very profitable to consider a set of demand equations for government purposes, though it may well be that the development through time of the components of government consumption could be approximated by a set of equations like (4) in [VIII] above.

9. THE GENERATION, DISTRIBUTION AND USE OF INCOME

In the revised SNA, value added arises in activities. That part of value added which consists of factor income is then reclassified by sector of origin. These incomings into sectors of origin are then paid out as various forms of income. At the same time they are added to by various transfers of income; and there is an overlap in the case of property income which may be paid out either by a sector of origin or, as in the case of national debt interest and consumer debt interest, by a sector of receipt. The essential feature of this system is that as far as possible all income flows are recorded on a gross basis. Companies, for example, not only pay out property income in the form of interest and dividends but also receive it; the rest of the world not only pays taxes on income to the economy under study but also receives taxes on income from it.

As I have tried to show in [XVI] below, this information can easily be rearranged to show all redistributions among sectors and, furthermore, this can be done in such a way as to provide a transition to the more detailed information needed for the socio-economic analysis of redistribution.

10. STOCKBUILDING AND FIXED CAPITAL FORMATION

The revised SNA contains a set of capital expenditure accounts whose purpose is to connect the expenditure by activities on commodities for the purposes of stock-building and fixed-capital formation with the finance obtained from the institutional sectors. In the case of government activities (and of the activities of private non-profit institutions) there is usually no difficulty in tracing the direct finance of the activity to the sector immediately concerned. But with industrial activities the position is different because capital expenditure in any activity, say in the mining industry, might arise in any one of a number of sectors: the personal sector (unincorporated businesses), companies or public corporations (national-ized coal mines). In the revised SNA the link between industrial capital expenditure and capital finance, like the link between the factor income components of value added and income originating, is made by means of one or more dummy accounts in order to avoid activity × sector matrices. Such matrices are difficult to construct and are in fact attempted in only a very few countries. The line taken in the revised SNA is to accept the difficulty of constructing them and the lack of experience in doing so, not to deny their interest.

This part of the system, taken together with the information provided on production, sales and gross capital stocks, provides a basis for studying stock-building and fixed-capital formation. This part of the whole system of relationships is particularly important in short-term models in view of the role played by stock cycles and fluctuations in the formation of fixed capital. In our work at Cambridge we have found it possible to build quite satisfactory stock-adjustment models for major branches of activity, pro-vided that raw material, work in progress and finished products, which respond to different influences, are kept separate.

The main point of this section is to explain the role of the capital expenditure accounts in the revised SNA. Their importance lies in the fact that they relate to activities, in which capital is used, rather than to sectors, which provide the necessary finance.

11. CAPITAL FINANCE

The capital finance accounts of the revised SNA relate to sectors and show the way in which saving, borrowing and capital transfers contribute to the finance of net capital formation and the net acquisition of financial claims. The structure of the system in this respect, and various possibilities for modelling it, are set out in some detail in [XV] below.

12. FOREIGN TRADE AND PAYMENTS

In the revised SNA, the rest of the world is provided with a current account and a capital account; and imports and exports are classified by commodity. Import demand can be studied satisfactorily commodity by commodity, provided that adequate domestic and foreign price series can be obtained. In Cambridge we have recently made a study of the import demand for some fifty commodities distinguished in our model, using as the principal determinants in each case the total demand for the commodity in question and the domestic and foreign price. At this level of disaggregation there appears to be considerable price sensitivity. The form of equation used was mainly log-linear, and it was found that not only was the exponent of relative prices usually greater than one and often as high as two or three, but also that the exponent of total demand was often significantly greater than one. This means that a change in the import ratio can arise simply through a growth in demand even if there is no change in relative prices. As anything but a very short-term phenomenon this is a somewhat disturbing possibility.

In studying a country's exports it seems desirable to look not only at commodities but also at the different regions in which they are sold. There is much to be said for starting from a set of commodity × region matrices and we have made some progress at Cambridge in constructing such matrices for British exports. This is a laborious undertaking, and since similar data must be needed in many countries, it would seem desirable that information of this kind should be compiled centrally, for example as part of the work on foreign trade statistics undertaken by the Statistical Office of the United Nations. A transformation from the international classification to the particular groupings used in different countries would often be necessary but there would be great advantages in the analysis of a common body of data in different countries.

13. MODELS AND MODEL SYSTEMS

We have seen that the various parts of the revised SNA provide a basis for modelling particular aspects of the economic process; for more complete models many of these parts must be brought together and combined. In doing this, the coherence and consistency ensured by the use of accounting matrices is a great advantage, as is illustrated by the analysis of the British economy given in *Exploring 1970* [11]. In that study all the relationships in the circuit for commodity balances are linear and can be represented by a network diagram which makes the structure of the model very easy to follow, as shown in [I] above. Now that we are changing the foreign trade structure of the model to incorporate non-linear import and export functions, the diagrammatic representation is less simple but the changes in the programme needed to handle the more complicated relationships can be set out in a straightforward way.

Beyond a certain point models cannot be elaborated simply by increasing their size, partly because of the difficulties of data processing and partly because the comparatively simple relationships generally used in models of the economic system as a whole may not be suitable in a more detailed study of a part of the system. If a model is to be elaborated by building sub-models, then it is essential that the exchange of information among the members of the model system should work smoothly. Here again the use of matrices can be very helpful.

17

At Cambridge we are at present making a sub-model of the fuel industries. Up to now we have concentrated on the changing demand for different kinds of fuel products in different parts of the economy. As far as the intermediate uses of fuel are concerned, this is simply a study of changing input–output coefficients and we have been able to estimate a large number of these over the last ten to fifteen years. In Britain the most striking change over this period has been the substitution of oil for coal. In order to account for this substitution in the various industries we have used a stock adjustment model in which the desired relative consumption depends on the price ratio. This model accounts well for past movements and suggests that if the price ratio continues to remain constant, as it has been for some years, relative consumption would take about another five years to settle down, with more oil and less coal used than at present. In fact, both are likely to be affected by the advent of North Sea gas.

In addition to this work on demand, we are also developing a production submodel. This model is provided with a set of output levels and final demands by the main model and is required to work out the quantities of different fuels to be produced by different methods. With reliable cost data this problem could be solved by minimizing a cost function subject to any policy constraints that might be imposed. For the moment, however, we have taken policy measures as setting limits to production by most methods and have worked out the required production level of each residual method. In this way, the submodel revises the cost structure of each fuel industry by taking account of likely changes in methods of production. These revised cost structures are then put back into the main model in place of the initial cost structures and the cycle of calculations is repeated. Experience shows that this iterative process is rapidly convergent.

The link between the models is the exchange of information: each model must produce the information needed by the other in the required form. Provided that this condition is met, the models can have different structures and can be operated at different centres. As the model system is extended, more and more information will come from the submodels until the main model becomes largely a regulating device for keeping them all in step.

14.   CALCULATION AND ESTIMATION

The construction and operation of large models involves a very large amount of computing, not only to reach a solution but also to adjust the observations, to estimate the parameters and to carry out sensitivity tests on the results. For all these purposes, matrix manipulation is important and, at Cambridge, Burley has developed a scheme for doing this [5] which we have found immensely useful. It is, of course, necessary to keep calculations within the capacity of the available computer and it is helpful if the size of the model and the form of its relationships can be changed without the need for extensive reprogramming. With a general matrix programme, the size of the various vectors and matrices can be treated as parameters, so that changing the size of the model is simply a question of making suitable changes in these parameters. Problems of machine capacity can largely be met by writing programmes in stages; and problems of changes in the forms of the relationships can often be met by programming in the first place a general method of solution of which the initial linear approximations are only a special case.

A good example of the use of matrices in calculations arises in connection with the adjustment of observations. This is a recurrent problem in national accounting, which is certainly not solved by being ignored, as it usually is. Thus income, output and expenditure can be defined so that they equal one another, but if they are separately estimated the estimates are usually discrepant. Residual errors, statistical discrepancies and unallocated items usually appear at some point in economic accounting publications and, while there is everything to be said for showing the limits of direct observation, they are only a nuisance to the model builder. From his point of view they should be removed and the person best qualified to do this is the compiler of the statistics.

The adjustment of observations is a well-known scientific problem. Some twenty-five years ago an application to national accounting, involving subjective estimates of the variances and covariances of the errors, was given in [77]. The idea has not caught on, partly, no doubt, because of the difficulty of making the estimates, partly because the notion of subjective estimates of error is repugnant to many people and partly because of the formidable computing problems that are involved. But times are changing: the extensions that take place year after year in national accounting have made discrepancies harder and harder to avoid; the development of statistical decision theory has brought home the importance of subjective probabilities; and the use of electronic computers has enormously increased our capacity to carry out complicated calculations.

In order to adjust a system of discrepant observations, it is necessary to construct a variance matrix of the errors, based on the compilers' impressions about the errors in their initial estimates, about the degree to which these errors are related to one another and about the extent to which they would be willing to revise any particular estimate up or down in the interests of balancing the whole system. In other words, having made a set of initial estimates, the compilers should set out their impressions about the accuracy and interdependence of their work in the form of a variance matrix. Perfection cannot be expected in such an exercise, but it is impossible to make a set of estimates without forming impressions about which members of the set are relatively accurate or inaccurate and which are connected or independent. The systematic use of such impressions can only lead to improvements in the set of estimates as a whole. We might start, as in the example below, by setting the variance matrix equal to the unit matrix (which would certainly yield a consistent set of estimates) and then consider how we could improve this version so as to reflect more correctly our beliefs about the accuracy of our initial estimates. We can stop this work where we like, but the more accurately we can assess the relative reliability and connectedness of our initial estimates the more reliable will our final estimates be.

The adjustment procedure can be formalized as follows. Consider a vector, x^* (of type $\nu \times 1$), of initial estimates which contains unbiased estimates of the elements of another vector, x, of true values. Suppose that the elements of x are subject to linear constraints, that is

$$Gx = h \tag{65}$$

where G is of type $\mu \times \nu$ and rank μ and h is of type $\mu \times 1$. Let V^*, of order ν and rank greater than μ, denote the variance matrix of the elements of x^*; and assume that any constraints satisfied by x^* are linearly independent of (65). Then the best linear unbiased estimator, x^{**} say, of x is given by

$$x^{**} = x^* - V^* G'(GV^* G')^{-1}(Gx^* - h) \tag{66}$$

from which it can be seen that the elements of V^* need only be approximated up to a scalar multiplier, since any such multiplier will disappear in the matrix product $V^* G'(GV^* G')^{-1}$. The variance matrix of x^{**}, V^{**} say, is

$$V^{**} = V^* - V^* G'(GV^* G')^{-1} GV^* \tag{67}$$

Thus the final estimates, which satisfy all the constraints, are given by the elements of x^{**} in (66). The variance matrix of these estimates is V^{**} in (67), which differs from V^* in that it takes into account the constraints of the system as well as the initial impressions of the investigator.

It is frequently possible, as is illustrated in the following example, to divide the constraints into two sets, adjust the initial estimates to meet one set and then adjust the partially adjusted estimates to meet the second set. The advantage of this two-stage procedure is that it enables the calculations to be separated so that the largest matrix to be inverted is equal in order to the number of constraints in the larger set.

The method can be extended to the problem of adjusting a series of sets of balance sheets so as to allow for autocorrelated, systematic and proportional errors. It is not a mechanical method, imposing some arbitrary rule of adjustment on the initial estimates, but a means of using the impressions of the investigator systematically to make improvements.

In [62] an example was given of allocating the unallocated items in an input output table by this method. Let us now apply it to the construction of sector balance sheets. To keep the example as simple as possible, consider an economy with two sectors and two assets (liabilities), so that the system of sector balance sheets is characterized by eight entries. Let us suppose that each of these entries can be measured independently by two independent methods but that no independent estimates are available of any totals either for sectors or for assets and liabilities.

In this example there are eleven independent constraints. Eight of these are single-value constraints: there is only one true value of each of the eight entries. The remaining three are accounting constraints, and can be chosen arbitrarily from the four accounting constraints of the system. The fourth accounting constraint adds nothing; it is satisfied automatically if the other three are satisfied. Let us choose as the three accounting constraints to be used:

(i)   the total liabilities of the first sector equal the sector's total assets;
(ii) the total issues of the first claim equal the total holdings of that claim;
(iii) the total issues of the second claim equal the total holdings of that claim.

Finally, let us assume that each of the sixteen estimates are not only independent and unbiased but also have a common variance. This means that we should be willing to revise any initial estimate up or down independently of the others by a fixed amount in the interests of balancing the whole system.

The initial estimates used in this example are given in the following tables:

INITIAL ESTIMATES (A)

	Sectors			Sectors	
Liabilities	85	5	Assets	35	50
	10	130		55	80

and

INITIAL ESTIMATES (B)

	Sectors			Sectors	
Liabilities	80	0	Assets	20	55
	5	140		60	90

In what follows, these estimates are ordered in the vector x^* by successive columns. In other words, when written out as a row,

$$x^* = \{85, 10, 5, \ldots 60, 55, 90\} \tag{68}$$

The matrix G is given by

$$G = \begin{bmatrix}
1 & 0 & 0 & 0 & 0 & 0 & 0 & 0 & -1 & 0 & 0 & 0 & 0 & 0 & 0 & 0 \\
0 & 1 & 0 & 0 & 0 & 0 & 0 & 0 & 0 & -1 & 0 & 0 & 0 & 0 & 0 & 0 \\
0 & 0 & 1 & 0 & 0 & 0 & 0 & 0 & 0 & 0 & -1 & 0 & 0 & 0 & 0 & 0 \\
0 & 0 & 0 & 1 & 0 & 0 & 0 & 0 & 0 & 0 & 0 & -1 & 0 & 0 & 0 & 0 \\
0 & 0 & 0 & 0 & 1 & 0 & 0 & 0 & 0 & 0 & 0 & 0 & -1 & 0 & 0 & 0 \\
0 & 0 & 0 & 0 & 0 & 1 & 0 & 0 & 0 & 0 & 0 & 0 & 0 & -1 & 0 & 0 \\
0 & 0 & 0 & 0 & 0 & 0 & 1 & 0 & 0 & 0 & 0 & 0 & 0 & 0 & -1 & 0 \\
0 & 0 & 0 & 0 & 0 & 0 & 0 & 1 & 0 & 0 & 0 & 0 & 0 & 0 & 0 & -1 \\
1 & 1 & 0 & 0 & -1 & -1 & 0 & 0 & 0 & 0 & 0 & 0 & 0 & 0 & 0 & 0 \\
1 & 0 & 1 & 0 & -1 & 0 & -1 & 0 & 0 & 0 & 0 & 0 & 0 & 0 & 0 & 0 \\
0 & 1 & 0 & 1 & 0 & -1 & 0 & -1 & 0 & 0 & 0 & 0 & 0 & 0 & 0 & 0
\end{bmatrix} \tag{69}$$

and the complete set of constraints takes the form

$$Gx = 0 \tag{70}$$

The variance matrix V^* is given by

$$V^* = I \tag{71}$$

of order 16.

This information yields the matrix product

$$G'(GG')^{-1}G =$$

$$= \tfrac{1}{16} \begin{bmatrix}
11 & 1 & 1 & -1 & -3 & -1 & -1 & 1 & -5 & 1 & 1 & -1 & -3 & -1 & -1 & 1 \\
1 & 11 & -1 & 1 & -1 & -3 & 1 & -1 & 1 & -5 & -1 & 1 & -1 & -3 & 1 & -1 \\
1 & -1 & 11 & 1 & -1 & 1 & -3 & -1 & 1 & -1 & -5 & 1 & -1 & 1 & -3 & -1 \\
-1 & 1 & 1 & 11 & 1 & -1 & -1 & -3 & -1 & 1 & 1 & -5 & 1 & -1 & -1 & -3 \\
-1 & -1 & -1 & 1 & 11 & 1 & 1 & -1 & -3 & -1 & -1 & 1 & -5 & 1 & 1 & -1 \\
-1 & -3 & 1 & -1 & 1 & 11 & -1 & 1 & -1 & -3 & 1 & -1 & 1 & -5 & -1 & 1 \\
-1 & 1 & -3 & -1 & 1 & -1 & 11 & 1 & -1 & 1 & -3 & -1 & 1 & -1 & -5 & 1 \\
1 & -1 & -1 & -3 & -1 & 1 & 1 & 11 & 1 & -1 & -1 & -3 & -1 & 1 & 1 & -5 \\
-5 & 1 & 1 & -1 & -3 & -1 & -1 & 1 & 11 & 1 & 1 & -1 & -3 & -1 & -1 & 1 \\
1 & -5 & -1 & 1 & -1 & -3 & 1 & -1 & 1 & 11 & -1 & 1 & -1 & -3 & 1 & -1 \\
1 & -1 & -1 & 1 & -1 & 1 & -3 & -1 & 1 & -1 & 11 & 1 & -1 & 1 & -3 & -1 \\
-1 & 1 & 1 & -5 & 1 & -1 & -1 & -3 & -1 & 1 & 1 & 11 & 1 & -1 & -1 & -3 \\
-3 & -1 & -1 & 1 & -5 & 1 & 1 & -1 & -3 & -1 & -1 & 1 & 11 & 1 & 1 & -1 \\
-1 & -3 & 1 & -1 & 1 & -5 & -1 & 1 & -1 & -3 & 1 & -1 & 11 & 11 & - & 1 \\
-1 & 1 & -3 & -1 & 1 & -1 & -5 & 1 & -1 & 1 & -3 & -1 & 1 & -1 & 11 & 1 \\
1 & -1 & -1 & -3 & -1 & 1 & 1 & -5 & 1 & -1 & -1 & -3 & -1 & 1 & 1 & 11
\end{bmatrix} \tag{72}$$

the adjusted estimates x^{**} take the form

$$x^{**} = [I - G'(GG')^{-1}G]x^* \tag{73}$$

and the variance matrix of x^{**} is, in this case, equal to the premultiplier of x^*.

The adjusted system of balance sheets is as follows:

FINAL ESTIMATES

	Sectors			Sectors	
	$80\frac{5}{8}$	$1\frac{7}{8}$		$29\frac{3}{8}$	$53\frac{1}{8}$
Liabilities			Assets		
	$6\frac{7}{8}$	$135\frac{5}{8}$		$58\frac{1}{8}$	$84\frac{3}{8}$

The variances of the final estimates are reduced by eleven-sixteenths to five-sixteenths of those of the initial estimates. At the same time the covariances, which were all assumed to be zero for the initial estimates, are obtained by changing the signs of the off-diagonal terms in (72).

As has already been mentioned, the same result is obtained if the adjustment is carried out in stages; we could first adjust the two sets of estimates to their mean values and then adjust these mean values to meet the accounting constraints. If we denote the first eight rows of G by G_1 and the last three rows by G_2, then we can rewrite (70) as

$$\begin{bmatrix} G_1 \\ \cdots \\ G_2 \end{bmatrix} x = \begin{bmatrix} 0 \\ \cdots \\ 0 \end{bmatrix} \tag{74}$$

The first stage consists of putting $G_1 x = 0$. This leads to

$$x^{**} = [I - G_1'(G_1 G_1')^{-1} G_1]x^*$$
$$= \frac{1}{2}\begin{bmatrix} I & \vdots & I \\ \cdots & \vdots & \cdots \\ I & \vdots & I \end{bmatrix} x^* \tag{75}$$

where in the first row of (75) I is of order 16, while in the second row it is of order 8. The second row gives the obvious result that, with equal variances, each adjusted estimate is simply the arithmetic mean of the two initial estimates.

The second stage consists of putting $G_2 x = 0$. This leads to estimates x^{***} say, where

$$x^{***} = [I - G_2'(G_2 G_2')^{-1}G_2]x^{**}$$
$$= [I - G_2'(G_2 G_2')^{-1} G_2][I - G_1'(G_1 G_1')^{-1} G_1]x^* \tag{76}$$

The first term in square brackets in (76) takes the form

$$\begin{bmatrix} I - G'_{21}(G_{21}\,G'_{21})^{-1}\,G_{21} & \vdots & 0 \\ \cdots\cdots\cdots\cdots\cdots\cdots\cdots\cdots\cdots & \vdots & \cdots \\ 0 & & \vdots & I \end{bmatrix}$$

and the product of the two terms in square brackets in that equation is, therefore,

$$\tfrac{1}{2}\begin{bmatrix} I - G'_{21}(G_{21}\,G'_{21})^{-1}\,G_{21} & \vdots & I - G'_{21}(G_{21}\,G'_{21})^{-1}\,G_{21} \\ \cdots\cdots\cdots\cdots\cdots\cdots\cdots\cdots\cdots & \vdots & \cdots\cdots\cdots\cdots\cdots\cdots\cdots\cdots\cdots \\ I & & \vdots\, I \end{bmatrix}$$

where G_{21} denotes the submatrix with 3 rows and 8 columns at the bottom left of G. This submatrix contains the accounting relationships. The final estimates are contained in the first eight rows of (76) and the second eight rows contain only a repetition of the adjusted values after stage 1. The reason for this lies in the particular form given to G; the accounting relationships in the last three rows are applied only to the first set of initial estimates. Since the two sets are equalized at the end of the first stage, nothing can be gained by applying the accounting constraints to the second set as well.

The extreme simplicity of this example, in which all the calculations can be made by mental arithmetic, disappears in more realistic cases. Just because the example is simple, however, it brings out clearly the general nature of the adjustment process though it does not fully demonstrate its power.

The purpose of this section has been to indicate various ways in which the matrix approach can contribute to the solution of problems of calculation and estimation and to show how this approach can be applied to the adjustment of a discrepant set of initial estimates.

15. CONCLUSION

There is little to be said by way of conclusion. I have tried to illustrate the many uses of social accounting matrices in building planning models. As far as possible I have organized the discussion within the framework provided by the revised SNA.

XV

SIMPLE FINANCIAL MODELS BASED ON THE NEW SNA

1. REVALUATIONS AND BALANCE SHEETS

In venturing into the area of revaluations and balance sheets, the revised SNA has done something to correct a serious imbalance in the development of social accounting: the concentration on flows to the exclusion of stocks. Two generations ago there was not much difference in the attention paid to the national capital and to the national income. In the great upsurge of interest that has followed the introduction of national accounting, work on the national capital has been left far behind. The reason for this change of emphasis can hardly be attributed to great disparities in available data or to the much greater conceptual difficulties in accounting for stocks compared with accounting for flows, though these factors may have played a part. The main reason is probably a greater concern, in the immediate postwar years, with problems of production and employment than with problems of finance, coupled with the belief that at the national level financial problems solve themselves. However this may be, the neglect of wealth has had some unfortunate results. From the point of view of statistical compilation, a full set of accounting checks has not been available, with the result that many flows and, in particular, saving have not been measured as accurately as they might have been. From the point of view of econometrics, great efforts have been made to devise consumption functions which do not depend explicitly on wealth as well as income, as if economic systems were always in a steady state with wealth in a fixed ratio to income. In general, the description of the economic system has been left incomplete so that analyses of it are necessarily incomplete too.

In the revised SNA, balance sheets relate to sectors. Assets are divided into four classes: (i) reproducible tangible assets, which have entered the balance sheet through capital formation in the past and which appear in it at written down replacement cost; (ii) non-reproducible tangible assets, the most important items being land and mineral wealth, which are valued, as far as possible, at market value; (iii) intangible assets matched by liabilities, that is financial claims of all kinds, which are valued, as far as possible, at market values whether they are held as an asset or as a liability; and (iv) other intangible assets, such as goodwill, which represent the excess of the value of an economic unit as a going concern over the sum of the preceding items. Since items (i), (ii) and (iii) are all valued at current replacement cost or market value, it is proposed that (iv) should be omitted, at least in the first instance.

The liabilities that match these assets take two main forms: (i) financial claims held as liabilities (corresponding to (iii) above); and (ii) accumulated saving, including net capital transfers received, which can be regarded as liabilities to self. This last item is the only entry in the balance sheet which cannot, even in principle, be revalued directly; its revaluation must be deduced, therefore, from the revaluations of tangible assets and of claims.

The introduction of balance sheets offers great possibilities to model builders. In [X] above, I have shown the effect of a term in wealth on the saving function, and the usefulness of such a term can be illustrated further with the help of the toy model set out in the first essay of this book. If we turn to p. 2 above we can see that if income, μ, were to grow exponentially so that $\dot{\mu}/\mu = \rho$ say, then in the steady state the saving ratio, σ/μ, would be given by

$$\sigma/\mu = \beta\rho/(\alpha + \rho) \tag{1}$$

where α and β denote respectively the coefficients of wealth and of income in the saving function. We can also see that if the extra capital expenditure needed for a unit increase in output is a constant, κ say, then

$$\dot{\omega}/\mu = \kappa\rho \tag{2}$$

By equating (1) and (2) it follows that either $\rho = 0$ or $\rho = (\beta/\kappa) - \alpha$. Thus we can connect the saving supply and the investment demand with the rate of growth of income as shown in the diagram opposite.

On the simple assumptions of the model, the saving ratio is related to the growth rate by the curve, and the investment ratio is related to it by the straight line. Unless it is stationary, an economy rigidly governed by these relationships will grow at the rate $(\beta/\kappa) - \alpha$ and will save a proportion $\beta - \alpha\kappa$ of its income. If, for example, $\beta = 0.25$, $\kappa = 2.5$, and $\alpha = 0.07$ the growth rate will be 0.03 and the saving ratio will be 0.075.

But, apart from such simple uses of information from balance sheets, there are the more complicated problems of the structure of the capital market and the forces leading to transactions in financial claims. The problem of portfolio selection has been analysed by Markowitz [37] and the notion of preferred portfolio patterns has become familiar through the work of Tobin and Watts [85, 102]. In the following section I shall explore some of the more obvious possibilities for using flow-of-funds and balance-sheet data for the purposes of model building. It is not too soon to consider how this kind of information could be used and, in particular,

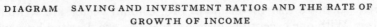

DIAGRAM   SAVING AND INVESTMENT RATIOS AND THE RATE OF
GROWTH OF INCOME

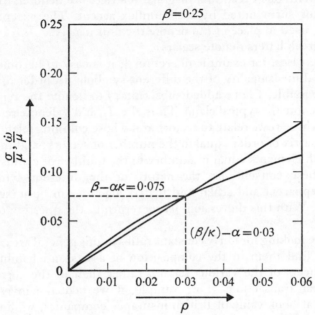

to see if it is at all amenable to the kind of manageable simplifications that have proved so useful in studying the flow of products. Even if the results presented here are not very impressive, we shall at least have developed some techniques and recognized a few blind alleys.

2. MODELLING THE FINANCIAL SYSTEM

The models I shall describe in the sections that follow relate to many sectors and many claims. They can conveniently be set out in a matrix notation of the kind that has become familiar to economists through input–output analysis. Before proceeding, it may be convenient if at this point I summarize the main conventions on which my notation is based.

Capital roman letters denote matrices. Capital greek letters denote operators: Σ for summation; Π for forming a product; Λ for shifting a variable (thus $\Lambda^{\theta} A(\tau) \equiv A(\tau + \theta)$); and Δ for forming first differences (thus $\Delta \equiv \Lambda - 1$).

Small roman letters denote vectors. These are written as column vectors: a row vector is written with a prime superscript, as is the transpose of a matrix. The letter i is used to denote the unit vector: that is, $i = \{1, 1, \ldots, 1\}$ where $\{\ \}$ denotes that the elements of a column vector are written out in a row. With one exception, diagonal matrices are denoted by a symbol for a vector surmounted by a circumflex accent. The exception is the familiar I, used in place of $\hat{i}$ to denote the unit matrix.

Small greek letters denote scalars.

In some cases, for example in section 4, it is easy to become confused about the dimensionality of the different symbols. In order to avoid this as far as possible, I have added subscripts: j to denote the typical sector and k to denote the typical claim. Thus A_{jk}, I_{jj} and i'_k denote respectively: a matrix whose rows relate to sectors and whose columns relate to claims; the unit matrix of order equal to the number of sectors; and the unit row vector with elements equal in number to the number of claims.

With these conventions, the nature of the different symbols soon becomes apparent and scalar and matrix algebra can be mixed without confusion. With this digression, let us return to the question of financial models.

If we are looking for fairly constant ratios in this general area, we should expect to find them in the composition of assets and liabilities in the balance sheets of the various sectors rather than in the corresponding year-to-year transactions. For example, if we take the invested assets measured at book value of British insurance companies, we find that the broad composition remained fairly constant over the years 1955–1963, except that there was a tendency for mortgages to rise in importance and there was a considerable shift from British government securities to ordinary shares. These movements had largely come to an end by 1960 and the portfolio patterns for 1961, 1962 and 1963 were all very alike. Over the same period the composition of balance sheet changes were altogether more variable. This seems to be a fairly general phenomenon and suggests that the estimation of changes in preferred portfolio patterns may be no more difficult than the estimation of changes in input–output coefficients. Equally, though there may be considerable variation, whole sectors seem to have fairly stable patterns of liabilities; in other words, sectors have typical ways of raising outside finance just as they have typical ways of holding that part of their capital that they devote to financial assets.

Accordingly, let us now set up the balance sheets of a closed economy in a standard matrix form, distinguishing on the assets side between financial assets and real assets and on the liabilities side between liabilities to third parties and liabilities to self, that is accumulated saving. For a system of n sectors and m claims, this can be done as shown in table 1.

In this table the first n row-and-column pairs relate to sectors; each row contains a sector's assets and the corresponding column contains its liabilities. The following m row-and-column pairs relate to financial

claims; each row contains the holdings of a particular claim as a liability
and the corresponding column contains the holdings of the same claim
as an asset. The penultimate row-and-column pair relates to the real
assets and accumulated saving in the various sectors and the final row-
and-column pair relates simply to totals.

The degrees of freedom of this system are easily calculated. By simply
counting the symbols we can see that there are $2nm + 4n + 2m + 2$ variables.
These are connected by $2n + 2m + 2$ independent arithmetic identities

TABLE 1   A SYSTEM OF SECTOR BALANCE SHEETS IN
MATRIX FORM

	n sector statements	m financial claim statements	Real asset/ accumulated saving statement	Row totals
n sector statements		A_{jk}	e_j	w_j
m financial claim statements	L'_{jk}			l_k
Real asset/ accumulated saving statement	z'_j			ζ
Column totals	x'_j	a'_k	ϵ	

corresponding to the fact that the entries in each row and column add
up to the relevant total, and by $n + m$ independent accounting identities
since, in a closed system of $n + m + 1$ balancing statements, $n + m$ of
these statements are independent. The number of degrees of freedom is,
therefore, $2nm + n - m$.

If we apply the first-difference operator, Δ, to the entries in the table,
we obtain the flows for the accounting period following the date for which
the balance sheets were drawn up: ΔA_{jk} and $\Delta L'_{jk}$ contain the flow-of-
funds information for this period; the elements of Δe_j are the investments
of the sectors in real assets; and the elements of $\Delta z'_j$ are the saving by the
sectors in the period. The application of Δ does not change either the
number of variables or the number of independent identities, and so in
the flow matrix the number of degrees of freedom remains as stated above.

In what follows I shall assume that we know Δe_j, the sectors' investment
programmes, and $\Delta z'_j$, the sectors' intended saving, and I shall examine
possible methods of calculating ΔA_{jk} and $\Delta L'_{jk}$. On this basis we now have

$2n$ additional variables assumed to be known, so that the degrees of freedom are reduced to $2nm - n - m$, that is to $n(m - 1) + m(n - 1)$.

3. EXOGENOUS AND ENDOGENOUS VARIABLES

I have just said that I propose to take the sectors' investment programmes and their saving intentions as actual or potential exogenous variables, leaving the acquisition and issue of different claims by the various sectors as endogenous variables. The reason for this is that I can imagine the investment programmes to come from another part of the model dealing with continued production and I can imagine saving intentions coming from yet another part of the model dealing with spending and saving behaviour. In a balanced model, total investment would equal total saving and so we should be left, at this stage, with the creation of new assets and liabilities which would enable the financial capital accounts to balance by sector as well as in total. I realise, of course, that all these aspects of the general economic process are interdependent and should, ideally, be solved simultaneously. I see no harm, however, in treating the different aspects separately in the first instance, although I am aware that by dividing the problem in this way I leave the repercussions of financing considerations on the saving and investment of individual sectors for separate treatment later on.

The scope of the exogenous variables I have chosen is, I think, clear but may well not be the most convenient; it might be desirable to include some of the transactions in financial claims among the exogenous variables. Thus, if we are estimating saving, we might at the same time estimate certain types of contractual saving, such as saving through life insurance. If we did this it would seem logical to move the financial claim 'liability to policy holders' into the exogenous part of the acquisition of assets by individuals and into the exogenous part of the issue of additional liabilities by insurance companies.

4. FINANCIAL INPUT–OUTPUT

The arrangement of the balance sheet entries in the table of section 2, which would be more in conformity with the arrangement in the revised SNA if it were transposed, bears a superficial formal resemblance to the account entries in an input–output system where a distinction is made between commodities and industries. Thus, with a change of headings, we could identify e_j with final demands, z'_j with primary inputs, L'_{jk} with intermediate product flows and A_{jk} with the mix of commodity outputs by the different industries. The discrepant element in the analogy is that in the input–output case we should find not e_j but e_k: final demands would be expressed as demands for commodities, not as demands on industries.

In the case of input–output we know that the distinction between industries and commodities leads to the possibility of alternative formulations, as described in [8]. The same is true in the present case. Thus suppose we were to define two coefficient matrices, A_{jk}^{**} and $L_{jk}'^*$, as follows:

$$A_{jk}^{**} = A_{jk}\,\hat{a}_k^{-1} \tag{3}$$

and

$$L_{jk}'^* = L_{jk}'\,\hat{x}_j^{-1} \tag{4}$$

By premultiplying (3) by i_j' we can see that the column sums of A_{jk}^{**} are all equal to 1; and so (3) adds $m(n-1)$ new independent relationships. Similarly, by premultiplying (4) by i_k' we can see that the column sums of $L_{jk}'^*$ are all equal to 1 minus the proportion of the capital of one of the sectors that is represented by that sectors' accumulated saving; and so (4) adds $n(m-1)$ new independent relationships. Thus we have just enough new relationships to enable us to construct a fully determined model. This model takes the form:

$$w_j = A_{jk}^{**}\,a_k + e_j \tag{5}$$

$$l_k = L_{jk}'^*\,x_j \tag{6}$$

$$w_j \equiv x_j \tag{7}$$

$$a_k \equiv l_k \tag{8}$$

from which it follows that

$$w_j = A_{jk}^{**}\,L_{jk}'^*\,w_j + e_j$$
$$= (I_{jj} - A_{jk}^{**}\,L_{jk}'^*)^{-1}\,e_j \tag{9}$$

and

$$l_k = L_{jk}'^*(I_{jj} - A_{jk}^{**}\,L_{jk}'^*)^{-1}\,e_j$$
$$= (I_{kk} - L_{jk}'^*\,A_{jk}^{**})^{-1}\,L_{jk}'^*\,e_j \tag{10}$$

If e_j is taken from the table from which the coefficient matrices were calculated, (9) and (10) will exactly reproduce w_j and l_k in that table and, by the use of the other relationships specified, the whole of the table can be filled in. Similarly, if e_j is replaced by Δe_j, a completely balanced flow table will be obtained.

This flow table may not be very acceptable because of the highly restrictive assumptions of the model. On the liabilities side, the model reproduces in detail for each sector the pattern of financing, including self-financing from accumulated saving, as it appeared in the original table. The total of each kind of financial claim is obtained by summing liabilities to third parties, the elements of L_{jk}', over sectors. These claims are then assumed to be held by the various sectors in fixed proportions, the proportion relevant to a particular claim being given by the elements in the relevant column of A_{jk}^{**}.

It is not very difficult to criticize this model. Bearing in mind that it is intended to apply to sectors and not to the individual transactors of which sectors are composed, it is probably a point in its favour that it recognizes normal patterns in the issue by the various sectors of liabilities to third parties, the relative size of the elements in each of the columns of L'^{*}_{jk}. It seems much less reasonable to assume: (i) that self-financing through accumulated saving will have the same relative importance, sector by sector, in this year's investment programme as it has had, on the average, in all past investment programmes; and (ii) that sectors will be deflected away from the normal composition of their holdings of financial assets merely by the consideration that some one has to hold the claims that they and others choose to issue.

We shall now see that if we try to meet these criticisms by an alternative formulation of the model, we can only do so by destroying what I have described as its more reasonable feature and by replacing one set of dubious assumptions by another.

The alternative model is as follows. Let us define two coefficient matrices, A'^{*}_{jk} and L^{**}_{jk}, as follows:

$$A'^{*}_{jk} = A'_{jk} \hat{w}_j^{-1} \tag{11}$$

and

$$L^{**}_{jk} = L_{jk} \hat{l}_k^{-1} \tag{12}$$

Like (3) and (4) above, (11) and (12) add $n(m-1) + m(n-1)$ new independent relationships. The resulting model is therefore fully determined and takes the form

$$x_j = L^{**}_{jk} l_k + z_j \tag{13}$$

$$a_k = A'^{*}_{jk} w_j \tag{14}$$

$$x_j \equiv w_j \tag{15}$$

$$a_k \equiv l_k \tag{16}$$

from which it follows that

$$x_j = L^{**}_{jk} A'^{*}_{jk} x_j + z_j$$
$$= (I_{jj} - L^{**}_{jk} A'^{*}_{jk})^{-1} z_j \tag{17}$$

and

$$a_k = A'^{*}_{jk} (I_{jj} - L^{**}_{jk} A'^{*}_{jk})^{-1} z_j$$
$$= (I_{kk} - A'^{*}_{jk} L^{**}_{jk})^{-1} A'^{*}_{jk} z_j \tag{18}$$

The story now repeats itself with z_j in place of e_j. If z_j is taken from the table from which the coefficient matrices were calculated, (17) and (18) will exactly reproduce x_j and a_k in that table and the whole of the table can be filled in; and if z_j is replaced by Δz_j, a completely balanced flow table will be obtained.

The two reproductions of the original table will, of course, be the same but, in general, the two flow tables will be different. This will happen unless the exogenous elements of the flow tables are equal to the corresponding elements in the original table multiplied by a constant. Since we can always write

$$\Delta e_j = \hat{b}_j e_j \qquad (19)$$

and

$$\Delta z_j = \hat{c}_j z_j \qquad (20)$$

where b_j and c_j are vectors of constants, the equality of the two flow tables is equivalent to the condition that

$$b_j = c_j = \alpha i_j \qquad (21)$$

where α is a constant.

The assumptions of the second model are different from those of the first, but equally restrictive. On the assets side, the model reproduces in detail for each sector the pattern of asset holding, whether these assets be real or financial, as it appeared in the original table. The total of financial claims is obtained by summing financial assets, the elements of A_{jk}, over sectors. These claims are then assumed to be issued by the various sectors in fixed proportions, the proportions relevant to a particular claim being given by the elements in the relevant column of L_{jk}^{**}.

With a suitable change of words, the criticism of the second model follows the same pattern as the criticism of the first model.

The first model produces a balanced flow table which accords with our initial assumptions about the investment programmes of the different sectors; and the second model does the same in respect of our initial assumptions about the sectors' saving intentions. If we denote these two tables by T^* and T^{**}, we could always obtain a third balanced flow table, T say, defined as

$$T = \lambda T^* + (1 - \lambda) T^{**} \qquad (22)$$

where λ is a constant. As we increase λ from zero to one we shall give less and less weight to our initial assumptions about saving intentions and more and more weight to our initial assumptions about investment programmes.

In a preliminary and formal treatment like the present one it does not seem very useful to go into practical details such as how to treat an open economy, what to do with capital transfers or where to put many forms of land and buildings, in particular, dwellings, shops and offices, which, though real assets, have many of the properties of financial assets. But it does seem worthwhile to make a few points about the idea of normal coefficients in the financial sphere. First, these must clearly be derived from holdings, that is from balance sheets, and not from transactions, that is from accounts. Second, there is no reason why coefficients should be derived unchanged from actual past balance sheets. Just as we know that input–output coefficients change, so we know that portfolio patterns change too; in section 2 we saw an example of this in the gradual switch

18

from British government securities to industrial ordinary shares. Third, there is the whole question of current versus constant prices. As in input–output, though for different reasons, it would seem best to regard normal coefficients as leading to estimates at constant prices which have then to be transformed to current prices

Although the point is perhaps an obvious one, what has emerged from this section is that the structure of assets and liabilities is so interconnected that the use of enough fixed coefficients to yield a fully determined model leads to excessive rigidity. Let us now, therefore, explore the possibilities of systematically changing the coefficients in the interest of achieving a balance while at the same time ensuring, as far as possible, that these coefficients relate to the preferences of sectors rather than to the proportions in which different financial assets are held and different financial liabilities are issued.

5. PREFERRED PORTFOLIO PATTERNS

Let us begin with the sectors' holdings of assets, real and financial, as set out in the first n rows of the table in section 2 above, and let us premultiply these rows by the diagonal matrix $\hat{b}_j$ defined in (19) of the preceding section. The result of the operation can be written in the form

$$
\begin{aligned}
\varDelta w_j &= \hat{b}_j w_j \\
&= \hat{b}_j A_{jk} i_k + \hat{b}_j e_j \\
&= \varDelta A_{jk} i_k + \varDelta e_j
\end{aligned}
\tag{23}
$$

Using the symbol $\varLambda \equiv 1 + \varDelta$ we can write out the equation for the stocks of assets held by various sectors at the end of the period. Thus

$$
\begin{aligned}
\varLambda w_j &= (I_{jj} + \hat{b}_j) w_j \\
&= (I_{jj} + \hat{b}_j) A_{jk} i_k + (I_{jj} + \hat{b}_j) e_j \\
&= \varLambda A_{jk} i_k + \varLambda e_j
\end{aligned}
\tag{24}
$$

If we could now accept $A'_{jk}(i_j + b_j)$ as an estimate of $\varLambda a_k$, then by the RAS technique [8, 64] we could try to construct an estimate of $\varLambda L'_{jk}$ of the form

$$
\varLambda L'_{jk} = \hat{r}_k L'_{jk} \hat{s}_j
\tag{25}
$$

where r_k and s_j are vectors of constants, such that

$$
\begin{aligned}
\varLambda L'_{jk} i_j &= \varLambda l_k \\
&= \varLambda a_k
\end{aligned}
\tag{26}
$$

and

$$
\begin{aligned}
\varLambda L_{jk} i_k &= \varLambda x_j - \varLambda z_j \\
&= \varLambda w_j - \varLambda z_j
\end{aligned}
\tag{27}
$$

where $\varLambda w_j$ is given by (24), and $\varLambda z_j = z_j + \varDelta z_j$ embodies our initial estimates of the intended saving of the various sectors. If every sector issued a wide variety of claims we should undoubtedly succeed in estimating $\Lambda L'_{jk}$ since we know that, subject to very general conditions, the RAS technique converges to a unique solution when applied to non-negative matrices. The small number of types of claim issued by some sectors may, however, lead to a singular situation to which the technique cannot be applied. The problem is apparent if we consider a sector that issues only a single type of claim. In this case, a particular amount will be needed to balance the sectors' balance sheet, but this may not equal the amount of this type of claim that other sectors, following their preferred portfolio patterns, would wish to hold at the end of the accounting period. Since the amount of the holding is fixed there may simply be no way to balance the sector's balance sheet.

If we are successful, we should obtain a completely balanced set of closing balance sheets and holdings of claims as assets and as liabilities. By subtracting the elements of our original table from the corresponding elements of this table, we should obtain a completely balanced system of flows. This system of flows would respect the sectors' investment programmes and also their saving intentions. Each sector would add to its portfolio of assets according to its preferred pattern and what have been made to give in order to balance the system are the quantities of different financial claims issued by the various sectors.

In this case, just as with the input–output models of the preceding section, there is an alternative way of setting up the model. In this alternative, we start with the sectors' liabilities at the end of the period, rather than with their assets, and form the equation

$$
\begin{aligned}
\Lambda x_j &= (I_{jj} + \hat{c}_j)\, x_j \\
&= (I_{jj} + \hat{c}_j)\, L_{jk} i_k + (I_{jj} + \hat{c}_j)\, z_j \\
&= \Lambda L_{jk} i_k + \Lambda z_j
\end{aligned}
\tag{28}
$$

where the diagonal matrix $\hat{c}_j$ is defined in (20).

If we could accept $L'_{jk}(i_j + c_j)$ as an estimate of Λl_k, then by the RAS technique we could try to construct an estimate of ΛA_{jk} of the form

$$
\Lambda A_{jk} = \hat{p}_j A_{jk} \hat{q}_k
\tag{29}
$$

where p_j and q_k are vectors of constants, such that

$$
\begin{aligned}
\Lambda A'_{jk} i_j &= \Lambda a_k \\
&= \Lambda l_k
\end{aligned}
\tag{30}
$$

and

$$
\begin{aligned}
\Lambda A_{jk} i_k &= \Lambda w_j - \Lambda e_j \\
&= \Lambda x_j - \Lambda e_j
\end{aligned}
\tag{31}
$$

where Λx_j is given by (27) and $\Lambda e_j = e_j + \Lambda e_j$ embodies our initial estimates of the sectors' investment programmes.

In this case we are more likely to be successful because sectors hold varied portfolios of financial assets and it is the composition of these portfolios that is made to give in order to achieve a balance.

If we were successful we should again obtain a completely balanced set of closing balance sheets and holdings of claims as assets and as liabilities. By subtraction we could again reach a completely balanced system of flows.

If we denote the two tables of flows by T^* and T^{**}, we can see that any linear combination of these tables, as in (22), would also be a balanced table and, moreover, a table that respected the sectors' investment programmes and their saving intentions. As we increased λ from zero to one, we should be insisting less and less on sectors' preferred patterns in the holding of assets and more and more on their preferred patterns in the holding of liabilities. At the same time, changes would be taking place in the extent to which the wealth (or capital) of the different sectors increased and in the total amount of new financial claims.

In applying the RAS technique we are at liberty to fix some of the entries at the outset, adjust the remainder and add back the entries that have been fixed so as to obtain a complete table. This procedure would be likely to alter some of the account totals and so lead to adjustments in both $\Lambda L'_{jk}$ and ΛA_{jk}. It would be useful in such a case to have a convergent, iterative procedure, a kind of *tâtonnement* that would simulate the adjusting mechanism of the market itself. At the moment I have no practical suggestions as to how this might be obtained.

Some readers may have been bothered by a purely technical point in the description of the models. Why, it may be asked, do we estimate the end-period balance sheets and then obtain the flow tables by difference instead of estimating the flows directly; in other words why do we begin by multiplying the initial balance sheets by Λ rather than by Δ. The reason is that the flow tables may contain negative elements, and the RAS technique is applicable only to matrices with non-negative elements. This means that we should begin by applying Λ rather than Δ to the initial tables. Though at first sight it might appear otherwise, it is not a matter of indifference which we do since, if we accept (25), then

$$\Delta L'_{jk} = \hat{r}_k L'_{jk} \hat{s}_j - L'_{jk} \tag{32}$$

that is $\Delta L'_{jk}$ is not related to L'_{jk} by an RAS transformation.

6. PROGRAMMING AND THE CAPITAL MARKET

The portfolio models of the last section, though less rigid than those of the section preceding it, are still perhaps too rigid for practical purposes. A step in the right direction might be, therefore, to allow portfolio patterns to change in response to market forces rather than to change in a mechanical and one-sided way to meet arithmetic and accounting identities. I cannot claim to have made much progress with this problem but the formulation that follows may show the kind of consideration that we have to take into account.

Consider a matrix, C say, with elements c_{ghk}, where g and h relate to typical sectors and k denotes a typical kind of claim. This matrix shows transactions in claims in a wholly disaggregated form: c_{ghk} denotes the money received by sector g from sector h in respect of parting, either by issue or sale, with a claim of type k. We can conveniently think of the main subsets of row-and-column pairs in this matrix as relating to sectors, and of the elements of each subset as relating to a particular claim. Let us now see if we can devise a linear programme that will determine, or at least circumscribe, the elements in this matrix.

Linear programming consists of maximizing, or minimizing, a linear function of certain variables (the objective function) subject to linear inequalities (the constraints). Let us consider: first, what constraints could reasonably be put on the c_{ghk}; and, second, what function of these elements could reasonably be maximized or minimized.

There are certainly five types of constraint to be considered.

(i) Since there is no netting, all transactions are non-negative. That is

$$c_{ghk} \geqslant 0 \tag{33}$$

for all g, h and k.

(ii) Since no one can part with something he does not possess, there is an upper bound on the sales of each type of asset by each sector. That is

$$\sum_j c_{gjk} \leqslant \bar{c}_{g \cdot k} \tag{34}$$

where j denotes a typical sector, for all g and at least for all k which are not issued as a liability by sector g.

(iii) Since no one can sell without someone else buying, the total amount of each claim sold (or issued) by all sectors must equal the total amount bought (or acquired) by all sectors. That is

$$\sum_g \sum_j c_{gjk} = \sum_j \sum_h c_{jhk} \tag{35}$$

for all k.

(iv) Since the account for each sector balances, the financial assets acquired plus the financial liabilities redeemed plus the real investment of a sector are equal to the financial assets sold plus financial liabilities issued plus the saving of the same sector. That is

$$\sum_j \sum_k c_{gjk} + \Delta e_g = \sum_j \sum_k c_{jgk} + \Delta z_g \tag{36}$$

for all g.

(v) Since sectors have to consider not only the present but also the uncertainties of the future, there are upper and lower bounds to the changes in the composition of their holdings of financial assets and liabilities that they can allow to result from the transactions of a single period. That is

$$a_{g \cdot m} \sum_j \sum_m c_{gjm} \leqslant \sum_j c_{gjm} - \sum_j c_{jgm} \leqslant b_{g \cdot m} \sum_j \sum_m c_{gjm} \qquad (37)$$

where $a_{g \cdot m}$ and $b_{g \cdot m}$ are lower and upper bounding proportions for claim m, held as a liability by sector g, and

$$a_{\cdot gn} \sum_j \sum_n c_{jgn} \leqslant \sum_j c_{jgn} - \sum_j c_{gjn} \leqslant b_{\cdot gn} \sum_j \sum_n c_{jgn} \qquad (38)$$

where $a_{\cdot gn}$ and $b_{\cdot gn}$ are lower and upper bounding proportions for claim n, held as an asset by sector g. For the degree of aggregation of claims that we are likely to use in this kind of analysis, it is probable that (38) will dominate (34): normal patterns will be violated before the complete holding of a particular claim is disposed of.

We come now to possible objective functions. From the point of view of borrowers we should like to minimize the cost of the elements in the matrix since this would minimize the total cost of all borrowing. If we assume, for simplicity, that a certain return, r_k say, is received per unit of claim k independently of the borrowing and lending sectors, then we could denote by s_{ghk} the return received by sector h from sector g in respect of the sale (or issue) of a unit of claim k by sector g to sector h. Then

$$s_{ghk} = r_k c_{ghk} \qquad (39)$$

and from the borrowers' point of view we should want to have

$$\sum_g \sum_h \sum_k s_{ghk} = \min \qquad (40)$$

Correspondingly, from the lenders' point of view, we should want to have

$$\sum_g \sum_h \sum_k s_{ghk} = \max \qquad (41)$$

For a fixed vector $\{r_k\}$, the solution of (40) and (41) subject to (33) through (38) would represent the position if (i) borrowers and (ii) lenders were completely dominant in the market. A linear combination of these solutions with positive weights would represent an intermediate position in which neither borrowers as a whole nor lenders as a whole had their way completely.

Finally, we might seek a vector, $\{r_k^*\}$ say, such that, if it were in force, the solutions of (40) and (41), subject to the constraints, would coincide. This would imply a set of rates of return on different claims at which the interests of borrowers and lenders would be the same.

For the present, I shall not try to go further with this type of model; perhaps I have said enough to show the kind of thing that is involved if we want to get away from the rigidities of the models described in the preceding sections.

XVI

THE GENERATION, DISTRIBUTION
AND USE OF INCOME

1. INTRODUCTION

The aim of this paper is to provide a social accounting framework within which information relating to the generation, distribution and use of income can be arranged. Since, in unfamiliar fields, *pro-forma* tables are much less easy to comprehend than tables that are filled in with figures, I shall illustrate my scheme with the help of recent British statistics.

The paper has some bearing on the discussions centering on the revised system of national accounts (SNA) of the United Nations. Naturally enough, this system contains information on the generation, distribution and use of income, but not in the detail that would be desirable for socio-economic analysis. As a result the Statistical Office of the United Nations is now engaged in formulating a complementary system of income distribution statistics which, while integrated into the system of national accounts, will, so to speak, take up the story at the point where that system leaves off. In what follows, I shall suggest a possible connecting link between the two. My point of departure will be to trace the chain of redistribution among sectors as it appears in a social accounting system and then demonstrate how, at various points and in various ways, the information set out can be elaborated along socio-economic lines with the help of detailed cross-section studies.

2. THE DISTRIBUTION OF FACTOR INCOME AMONG SECTORS

In this paper the word 'sector' is used in the same sense as in the SNA to indicate a group of similar transactors concerned primarily with financing decisions rather than with the technical decisions of production. In the SNA the transactors in the accounts relating to production and to capital expenditure on tangible assets are 'activities' thought of, essentially, as establishments classified according to a standard classification of all economic activities. By contrast, the transactors in the accounts relating to income and outlay and to capital finance are 'sectors' thought of as more-embracing units, enterprises as opposed to establishments, classified along institutional lines. Thus we may speak of the personal sector, the company sector, the central government sector and so on.

In the SNA, domestic factor incomes originate in activities and are then reclassified according to sector of origin. At this stage there are two forms of factor income: 'compensation of employees' consisting of wages, salaries, employers' contributions and other supplements to labour income; and 'operating surplus' consisting of income from enterprises and all types of property. If to the sum of these two forms of income arising in all sectors net factor income accruing to residents from abroad is added, the total obtained is the national income.

The analysis, which begins with table 1, takes as its starting point the two forms of factor income originating in the national sectors and in the rest of the world. The figures relate to Britain in 1965 as set out in the *Blue Book* on national income and expenditure for 1966 [87]. Thus we can see that £1868 million of compensation of employees originated in the personal sector as sector of employment, £13 279 million originated in the company sector, and so on.

But the amount of income originating in a sector has little to do with the amount of the same form of income retained there. Thus all compensation of employees is retained in the personal sector except that, in countries where border workers are important, some of it may flow abroad. In the central panel of the table, relating to redistribution, these movements are shown in the form incomings minus outgoings equal net movement. Thus the personal sector receives all the compensation of employees originating in other sectors, £19 097 million, and each other sector transfers away the compensation of employees originating in it.

When we come to other forms of factor income, here referred to for short in all contexts as 'property income', the position is more complicated. In the first place, each sector may receive property income as well as pay it out; and, in the second place, consuming sectors may pay out interest in respect of consumption loans (national debt interest, consumer debt interest) as well as any interest they may pay out in respect of business borrowing. Redistributions of property income of all kinds are shown in the central panel of the table.

The final panel of the table shows factor income originating plus redistributions of factor income, that is to say factor income retained. For example, while £4694 million of factor income originated in the personal sector, either in unincorporated private enterprises or in the form of income to domestic servants or to the employees of private non-profit institutions, the amount retained was altogether larger. To the amount originating there must be added the £19 097 million of compensation of employees originating in other sectors and the £2566 million of property income transferred, net, from other sectors to the personal sector. By making these additions, the total amount retained by the personal sector can be seen to be £26 357 million.

The total of factor income originating in the sectors plus net factor

TABLE 1 DISTRIBUTIONS AMONG SECTORS: INCOME ORIGINATING AND INCOME RETAINED. BRITAIN, 1965

(£ million)

	Income originating			Redistribution: factor incomes		Income retained		
	Compensation of employees	Property income	Total	Compensation of employees	Property income	Compensation of employees	Property income	Total
Persons	1 868	2 826	4 694	19 097 — 0 = 19 097	3 184 — 618 = 2 566	20 965	5 392	26 357
Companies	13 279	3 667	16 946	0 — 13 279 = —13 279	2 444 — 3 009 = — 565	0	3 102	3 102
Public corporations	2 067	350	2 417	0 — 2 067 = — 2 067	45 — 412 = — 367	0	—17	—17
Central government	1 922	17	1 939	0 — 1 922 = —1 922	592 — 988 = — 396	0	—379	—379
Local authorities	1 829	313	2 142	0 — 1 829 = —1 829	67 — 502 = — 435	0	—122	—122
Rest of the world (net)	0	803	803	0 — 0 = 0	715 — 1 518 = — 803		0	0
Residual error			—332					—332
Total				0	0			
National income			28 609					28 609

TABLE 2 DISTRIBUTIONS AMONG SECTORS: THE CONTRIBUTION AND USE OF RESOURCES. BRITAIN, 1965

(£ million)

	Factor income	Redistribution: current non-tax transfers	Total income*	Redistribution: direct taxes, etc. on income	Disposable income*	Redistribution: indirect taxes, net, on consumption and on net capital formation	Command over resources	Redistribution: net capital transfers and net borrowing	Use of resources	Net contribution	Contribution of resources = factor income
Persons	26 357	2 883 — 165 = 2 718	29 075	0 — 4 943 = — 4 943	24 132	0 — 3 835 = — 3 835	20 297	—157 — 727 = — 884	19 413	6 944	26 357
Companies	3 102	0 — 28 = — 28	3 074	0 — 1 088 = —1 088	1 986	0 — 118 = — 118	1 868	20 — 288 = — 268	1 600	1 502	3 102
Public corporations	—17	0 — 0 = 0	—17	0 — 7 = — 7	—24	0 — 42 = — 42	—66	536 + 102 = 638	572	—589	—17
Central government	—379	0 — 3 976 = —3 976	—4 355	5 708 — 0 = 5 708	1 353	3 263 — 138 = 3 125	4 478	—458 — 107 = — 565	3 913	—4 292	—379
Local authorities	—122	1 248 — 173 = 1 075	953	0 — 0 = 0	953	1 184 — 130 = 1 054	2 007	59 + 792 = 851	2 858	—2 980	—122
Rest of the world (net)		342 — 131 = 211	211	515 — 185 = 330	541	0 — 184 = — 184	357	0 — 104 = — 104	253	—253	
Residual error	—332		—332		—332		—332	332		—332	—332
Total		0		0		0		0		0	
National income	28 609		28 609		28 609		28 609		28 609		28 609

* This term is appropriate to the personal sector but not to others.

income transferred from the rest of the world plus, in the present case, a residual error of —£332 million, is equal to the national income. If it is objected that the figure of £28 609 million shown in the final row of the table is not the figure for the national income shown in the *Blue Book* for 1966, the answer is simple. The figure of net property income from abroad, £473 million, shown in the *Blue Book* as the link between domestic income and national income, includes all transfers of taxes on income. The rest of the world received, net, £330 million from this kind of transfer and so the net movement of property income was £803 million in favour of Britain, as shown in table 1. Since, at a later stage in the analysis, taxes on income form a separate category, it seems desirable to keep them separate from factor incomes right from the beginning.

As its name implies, a redistribution changes the distribution of a total among its components without altering its magnitude, and so the redistributions must in each case sum to zero, as shown in the table.

3. THE CONTRIBUTION AND USE OF RESOURCES BY THE SECTORS

The total of factor income retained by a sector provides a measure of that sector's contribution of resources to the national economy through its labour, enterprise and provision of capital. The next stage of our analysis is to see how far each sector's use of resources exceeds or falls short of its contribution. A sector's use of resources is defined as the factor value of its consumption and net expenditure on domestic tangible assets. There is nothing either honourable or dishonourable in a sector contributing more or less resources than it uses. Governments do not pay their way by contributing resources to production, their function is somewhat different; but to the extent that they do not pay their way, some other sector must obviously pay it for them.

The results of this stage of the analysis are set out in table 2, from which it can be seen that this stage is divided into a number of steps. The starting point is the end point of table 1, that is to say the distribution of factor income by sectors. The first redistribution considered arises from current non-tax transfers. These are largely, but not exclusively, transfers made by the central government in the form of national insurance and assistance grants, non-contributory pensions, family allowances, grants to local authorities and so on. The principal gainer from this form of redistribution is the personal sector. As can be seen from the table, the personal sector gained £2883 million from transfers of this kind, mainly from public authorities but partly from companies and from the rest of the world; and it paid out £165 million, all in the form of transfers to the rest of the world. Anyone interested in the composition of these figures will find an immense amount of detail in the *Blue Book*.

If current non-tax transfers are added on to factor income, there results a total which, from the view point of the personal sector, would be described as 'total income'; in the personal case it is equal to consumption plus direct taxes on income plus saving. For the sectors of general government it does not have this meaning, it is just a total that arises at a particular stage in the process of redistribution.

The second redistribution considered arises from direct taxes on income, including national insurance and health contributions. In the British case, the only beneficiaries at this step are the central government, which in 1965 received £5708 million from this source, and the rest of the world, which received £515 million. Towards these totals, the personal sector contributed £4943 million and the company sector contributed £1088 million.

If direct taxes etc. are added on to the preceding income aggregate, there results a total which, from the point of view of the personal sector, would be described as 'disposable income'; in the personal case it is equal to consumption plus saving.

The third redistribution considered arises from indirect taxes on the goods and services bought by the different sectors either for purposes of consumption or as a net addition to their stocks of tangible assets. A full analysis would require an input–output matrix but, as this is not available in the present case, the calculation has been made with the help of the information given in the *Blue Book* on the allocation of indirect taxes and subsidies to different types of final expenditure. The only item that presents any difficulty is the £457 million allocated to gross domestic capital formation. This figure has been divided *pro rata* between depreciation and net domestic capital formation; the amount attributed to depreciation has then been allocated *pro rata* between personal consumption, government consumption and exports; and the amount attributed to net domestic capital formation has been allocated *pro rata* between the net capital formation of the different sectors. From the table we can see that in 1965 the personal sector is estimated to have paid, directly or indirectly, £3835 million in net indirect taxes, the company sector £118 million, and so on. The net gainers at this stage are, of course, the central government and local authorities.

If indirect taxes, net, are added on to the preceding income aggregate, a new total is obtained which might be called 'command over resources'. The figures in this column, £20 297 million for the personal sector and so on, show the factor services that could have been bought by each sector had it decided to spend all it could on these services without either making or receiving capital transfers or loans of any kind.

The fourth redistribution considered arises because in fact the sectors do not act in the way just envisaged. In passing from their command over resources to their actual use of resources it is necessary to deduct net capital transfers and net loans made. These two net totals are shown as the link; thus the personal sector made net capital transfers of £157 million and net loans of £727 million, so that this sector's use of resources was £884 million less than its command over resources.

If these figures are added on to the preceding aggregate, estimates of resources actually used are obtained. Thus the figure of £19 413 million is equal to consumption plus net domestic capital formation by the personal sector valued at factor cost.

Finally, if these figures are subtracted from the corresponding figures of factor income retained, the result is an estimate of net resources contributed, that is the excess of resources contributed over resources used. Thus, the net contribution of the personal sector was £6944 million. As might be expected, the private sectors make a net positive contribution and the public sectors make a net negative contribution. The only figure in the column which may be difficult to interpret is the one for the rest of the world. If the −£253 million shown at the end of table 2 are added to the £803 million shown at the beginning of table 1, the result, £550 million, is equal to the excess of British imports of products over British exports valued at factor cost.

4. TAXES AND GOVERNMENT TRANSFERS: A SOCIO-ECONOMIC ANALYSIS OF HOUSEHOLD TYPES

I shall now try to show that at least part of the scheme, illustrated in table 2, for the analysis of redistribution among sectors can be applied to the components of a single sector and, in particular, to different categories of household classified in terms of factor income and family composition. If we look back at table 2, we can see that for the personal sector, factor income is reduced by a combination of direct taxes etc. on income and non-tax current transfers to $24\ 132/26\ 357 = 92$ per cent and is further reduced by indirect taxation to $20\ 279/26\ 357 = 77$ per cent. These figures relate to 1965; the corresponding percentages for 1964 are 93 and 79, respectively.

In *Economic Trends* for August 1966 [86] a somewhat similar analysis is given, based on the continuous survey of family expenditure. This analysis relates to private households classified by 'original income' and by family composition. Original income is defined as the sum of the incomes, including income in kind, of all members of the household, before deduction of all direct taxes and before the addition of all direct benefits listed. These direct benefits are similar to the current non-tax transfers of table 2 except that they are restricted to transfers made by the central government and local authorities and have not quite such a wide coverage as in table 2. Direct taxes have the same coverage as in table 2 and indirect taxes are restricted to indirect taxes paid directly or

TABLE 3   THE EFFECT OF GOVERNMENT TAXES AND TRANSFERS ON DIFFERENT TYPES OF HOUSEHOLD.

BRITAIN, 1964

(£'s a year)

Number of households in sample	Range of original income	Household type*	Average original income	Cash benefits	Benefits in kind	National insurance contrib.	Income tax and surtax	Average disposable income	Housing subsidies	Indirect taxes paid directly	Indirect taxes paid indirectly	Average command over resources
12	216–259	1a	234	139·3	24·9	−6·0	−13·9	378	3·9	−65·2	−11·4	305
17		2a	236	284·3	57·4	−6·5	−6·1	565	10·3	−88·0	−19·8	467
10	382–459	1a	417	36·5	18·0	−38·6	−33·1	400	5·8	−74·7	−15·9	315
11		2a	422	215·8	43·4	−36·2	−23·2	622	17·3	−108·8	−23·7	507
27	676–815	1a	728	10·2	14·0	−67·0	−65·0	620	9·9	−109·6	−17·6	503
77		2a	750	83·1	48·0	−67·9	−49·4	764	5·9	−115·5	−26·2	628
46		2a 1c	753	32·4	106·8	−72·5	−23·9	796	6·1	−124·0	−25·2	653
30		2a 2c	766	28·9	161·1	−70·7	−10·1	875	8·6	−129·2	−27·7	727
13		2a 3c	755	69·4	249·2	−67·2		1006	7·6	−131·1	−31·6	851
11	1196–1447	1a	1287	13·9	12·8	−73·4	−164·3	1076	—	−160·3	−22·3	893
99		2a	1323	13·5	30·0	−93·0	−117·2	1156	5·7	−188·5	−33·9	931
72		2a 1c	1315	10·2	104·4	−86·0	−91·8	1252	5·9	−173·4	−36·3	1048
45		2a 2c	1304	27·9	153·2	−82·3	−76·2	1327	6·1	−162·8	−40·5	1130
28		2a 3c	1299	76·2	231·6	−81·4	−51·1	1475	4·6	−170·7	−42·0	1267
23	2122–2565	2a	2348	19·8	30·6	−88·3	−381·6	1929	2·0	−209·2	−42·8	1672
10		2a 2c	2289	25·6	197·3	−68·5	−219·9	2223	—	−280·3	−66·6	1877

* The symbol *a* denotes adult (person 16 and over) and the symbol *c* denotes child (person under 16).

Note: Components do not always add to totals because of rounding-off errors.

indirectly in respect of household consumption. Here again, the difference, namely indirect taxes in respect of the net capital formation of unincorporated businesses, is of minor importance. A selection of the results of this analysis are set out in table 3.

In table 3, households are ordered first by range of original income and, within ranges, by size and composition. The family expenditure survey is comparatively small, covering about 3500 households a year, and results are only given in [86] for household types represented in the sample by at least ten households. The various kinds of transfer are set out in greater detail than in table 2 and, despite the fact that with so small a sample there must be considerable sampling errors, a fairly clear picture emerges of redistributions among family types. None of the households on which table 3 is based is the household of a pensioner.

An abbreviated version of table 3, in which attention is concentrated on percentage gains and losses, is set out in table 4.

TABLE 4   THE EFFECT OF GOVERNMENT TAXES AND TRANSFERS ON DIFFERENT TYPES OF HOUSEHOLD. BRITAIN, 1964

(*Percentages*)

Range of original income	Household type*		Original income = 100	Gain or loss from direct taxes and benefits	Disposable income	Loss from indirect taxes and subsidies	Command over resources
216–259	1a		100	62	162	−32	130
	2a		100	139	239	−41	198
382–459	1a		100	−4	96	−20	76
	2a		100	47	147	−27	120
676–815	1a		100	−15	85	−16	69
	2a		100	2	102	−18	84
	2a	1c	100	6	106	−19	87
	2a	2c	100	14	114	−19	95
	2a	3c	100	33	133	−20	113
	2a	4c	100	46	146	−23	123
1196–1447	1a		100	−16	84	−15	69
	2a		100	−13	87	−17	70
	2a	1c	100	−5	95	−15	80
	2a	2c	100	2	102	−15	87
	2a	3c	100	14	114	−16	98
2122–2565	2a		100	−18	82	−11	71
	2a	2c	100	−3	97	−15	82

* The symbol *a* denotes adult (person 16 and over) and the symbol *c* denotes child (person under 16).

From these two tables some idea can be gained of the extent to which the system of taxes and transfers tends to equalize command over resources as between rich and poor and as between large and small households. At the poorest level shown, the original income is considerably increased on balance and it is increased very much more for households consisting of two adults than for households consisting of only a single adult. At the second level shown, a single adult loses, net, some 24 per cent of his original income mainly through the payment, directly or indirectly, of indirect taxes. At this level, however, households consisting of two adults gain, net, some 20 per cent of their original income since their net gain from direct transfers and taxes far exceeds their loss from indirect taxation. As we go up the scale of income, we find that the net loss tends to increase for small households and that the net gain is gradually turned into a net loss for large households. If we compare households consisting of two adults at either end of the income range, we can see that the original incomes of £236 and £2348 become finally £467 and £1672, respectively. Thus the original tenfold difference becomes finally a difference of between three- and four-fold.

Although the definitions in table 2 and in tables 3 and 4 are not quite the same and although the personal sector in table 2 includes the small subsector of private non-profit institutions, it is of some interest to compare the principal ratios in the two analyses. The average household size in the family expenditure survey is about three persons and the average original income appears to be at the lower end of the top range but one in table 4. Thus, on average, we should expect disposable income to be about 95 per cent and command over resources to be about 80 per cent of original income. These figures compare with the 93 per cent and 79 per cent given at the beginning of this section on the basis of table 2. Thus if the two sources, the *Blue Book* and the *Family Expenditure Survey*, were brought more fully into line with one another, it would seem that the analysis given in this section could be regarded as a true extension of the one given in the preceding section. As it is, for a broad survey, the discrepancies do not seem to be too serious.

5. FORMS OF HOUSEHOLD INCOME: A SOCIO-ECONOMIC ANALYSIS OF CONTRIBUTIONS

The total income of a household may take many forms: wages and salaries, income from self-employment and so on. This income reaches the household from a number of contributors: the head of the household, his wife and other members of the household. In the Report for 1965 on the *Family Expenditure Survey* [91] an analysis of this kind is given for five broad ranges of household income. A rearrangement and slight condensation of this material is given in table 5, where the original figures

TABLE 5 CONTRIBUTIONS TO HOUSEHOLD INCOME. BRITAIN, 1965

(£'s a year and percentages)

Number of households in sample	Number of persons in sample	Persons per household	Persons 16 and over per household	Percentage of persons under 16	Range of household income	Contributors to household income	Wages and salaries	Self-employment income	Income from investments	Income from subletting, etc.	Income n.e.c.	Income from non-state annuities and pensions	State retirement, old age and widows' pensions	Other state benefits	Total	Total in percentages
513	709	1·4	1·3	5·5	Under 520	Head	28·8	4·9	16·0	14·8	15·1	15·6	162·2	46·7	304·0	88·1
						Wife of head	0·5	0·6	0·7	—	0·3	—	28·4	0·4	30·4	8·8
						Others	1·1		0·4	—		—	6·0	2·1	10·5	3·1
						Total	30·4	5·5	17·1	14·8	15·6	15·6	196·6	49·2	344·9	100·0
						Total in percentages	8·8	1·6	5·0	4·3	4·5	4·5	57·0	14·3	100·0	
916	2491	2·7	1·9	30·5	520–1040	Head	461·9	44·1	20·1	20·4	17·6	34·4	56·3	25·9	680·8	85·1
						Wife of head	20·4	1·5	2·2	—	4·3	0·7	19·3	9·6	58·1	7·2
						Others	45·5	1·5	0·8	—	2·0	0·8	7·7	3·1	61·6	7·7
						Total	527·8	47·2	23·1	20·4	24·0	35·8	83·4	38·7	800·4	100·0
						Total in percentages	65·9	5·9	2·9	2·6	3·0	4·5	10·4	4·8	100·0	
1039	3393	3·3	2·2	32·8	1040–1560	Head	808·9	52·3	17·9	28·9	14·4	17·7	22·4	11·7	974·2	75·9
						Wife of head	112·3	4·5	3·7	—	6·7	1·7	4·1	12·1	143·4	11·2
						Others	142·9	3·4	1·5	—	4·9		8·5	3·3	166·1	12·9
						Total	1064·2	60·2	23·2	28·9	25·9	19·3	35·0	27·0	1283·7	100·0
						Total in percentages	82·9	4·7	1·8	2·3	2·0	1·5	2·7	2·1	100·0	
515	1854	3·6	2·7	25·5	1560–2080	Head	1003·4	56·9	22·6	36·8	12·6	19·0	18·1	9·2	1178·6	66·2
						Wife of head	192·9	4·7	6·0	—	5·8	—	3·6	10·3	223·3	12·6
						Others	326·6	4·8	3·9	—	14·6	6·6	16·7	3·9	377·2	21·2
						Total	1523·0	66·5	32·5	36·8	32·9	25·7	38·4	23·4	1779·1	100·0
						Total in percentages	85·6	3·7	1·8	2·1	1·9	1·4	2·2	1·3	100·0	
409	1601	3·9	3·1	19·9	Over 2080	Head	1175·7	390·2	144·0	57·7	21·8	36·5	18·3	8·3	1852·4	63·9
						Wife of head	234·5	10·7	36·8	—	14·5	1·3	3·9	8·5	310·1	10·7
						Others	642·6	25·9	16·3	—	21·7	9·1	15·5	5·2	736·4	25·4
						Total	2052·8	426·8	197·2	57·7	58·0	47·0	37·6	21·9	2898·9	100·0
						Total in percentages	70·8	14·7	6·8	2·0	2·0	1·6	1·3	0·8	100·0	
3392	10 048	3·0	2·2	26·9	All households	Head	671·0	84·4	34·2	29·1	15·9	24·4	51·6	20·0	930·5	72·6
						Wife of head	97·6	3·8	7·2	—	5·9	0·3	11·8	8·9	135·5	10·6
						Others	183·3	5·4	3·3	—	6·9	2·8	10·0	3·4	215·2	16·8
						Total	951·9	93·5	44·6	29·1	28·8	27·5	73·3	32·4	1281·2	100·0
						Total in percentages	74·3	7·3	3·5	2·3	2·2	2·2	5·7	2·5	100·0	

Note: components do not always add to totals because of rounding-off errors.

have been multiplied by 2·6 to convert them from shillings a week to £'s a year.

In table 5, households are arranged by broad ranges of income and, within ranges, the contributions of the different types of contributor are shown separately. The forms of income shown at the head of each column make up income before deduction of income tax, national insurance contributions and any other deductions from income at source. The concept of income used here, however, excludes income in kind and employers' contributions to national insurance and health services. Income n.e.c. is mainly composed of transfers such as trade union and friendly society benefits, alimony and gifts between persons.

In this case the lowest income group is heavily weighted with the households of pensioners, as can be inferred from the relatively small contribution of wages and salaries and the relatively large contribution of retirement, old age and widows' pensions paid by the state. On average these households are very small and almost wholly composed of adults. Although in this group of households about 50 per cent of income comes, on average, from the pension of the head of the household, still a number of other forms of income are also important. In this group, the proportion of household income contributed by the head of the household is at its highest, doubtless because so many of the households in it consist of only one member.

When we pass to the next income group the importance of wages and salaries and of income from self-employment rises sharply and the importance of state pensions and other benefits falls sharply. At the same time the average household size doubles and the proportion of children (persons under 16) increases six-fold. As we progress further up the scale of household income, the average household size rises and the proportion of children first rises and then falls. The proportion of income contributed by the head of the household falls steadily until, in the highest income group, it is only 63·9 per cent of household income. The contribution of the wife of the head of the household is fairly steady but in the two top income groups the contributions of other members of the household assume considerable importance. In the top group, income from self-employment and from investments is beginning to supplant wages and salaries as a source of household income.

6. CONCLUSIONS

In setting up a framework which links the information on the generation, distribution and use of income shown in the SNA with the much more detailed information needed for a socio-economic analysis of these phenomena, I have tried to bring out, by means of numerical illustrations, the complex nature of household income formation and the modifications

19

which it undergoes as a consequence of the system of government taxes and transfers. The analyses of sections 4 and 5 owe nothing to me but are simply taken over from British official publications. They do, however, illustrate the possibilities of passing from a broad analysis by sectors as envisaged in the SNA to the much more detailed analysis called for in the discussion of socio-economic policy. It is for this reason that I thought that the framework proposed and the illustrations I have given of a more detailed treatment based on British experience would hold some interest for an international audience.

XVII

MATHEMATICAL MODELS IN
EDUCATIONAL PLANNING:
A VIEW OF THE CONFERENCE

1. THE SETTING

The papers in this volume [46] examine from various points of view the possibilities of applying a number of related techniques, such as mathematical model building, simulation, systematic control theory, in short, systems analysis, to the problems of educational planning. Even in the countries where it can be said to exist at all, educational planning is a very recent development arising from the transformation of the scale of educational endeavour, which in many countries of Europe amounts to little less than an educational revolution. The diverse and often conflicting aims of education, the complex structure of the educational system itself and the great cost of educational programmes mean that if desired results are to be achieved efficiently the educational system must be looked at as a whole. Day-to-day administrative decisions must somehow be co-ordinated within the framework of a consistent policy. And such a policy cannot be shaped unless a longer and broader view is taken of the functioning of the educational system in relation to social and economic needs on the one hand and human and financial resources on the other.

Those who attended the conference at which these papers were discussed combined the belief that the methods described hold great promise for the future, with the recognition that much more work is needed before they can be said to have passed from the pilot to the operational stage. In this introductory paper an attempt is made to recapitulate the general consensus of opinion which emerged clearly from the discussions, partly to show research workers the possibilities of an important new field of research and partly to show educators, educational administrators and educational planners the possibilities of new methods which only now are beginning to be applied to educational problems.

2. SYSTEMS AND SYSTEMS ANALYSIS

According to Webster's dictionary the most general meaning of the word 'system' is: an aggregation or assemblage of objects united by some form of regular interaction or interdependence; a natural combination, or organization of part to part, conceived as formed by a process of growth or as due to the nature of the objects connected; an organic whole. We need not go beyond some such description as this in order to understand the meaning of the term the 'educational system'.

The study of any system can be divided into a number of distinct stages. First, we must isolate and define the system itself according to the purpose of our study; thus we may speak of a system of railways, but for some purposes this may be regarded simply as part of the transport system in general. Second, we must describe the system in such a way that we can analyse it and so be in a position to draw conclusions about those aspects of it that interest us. Third, having specified the variables that enter into our description, we must collect information about them so as to secure the data for analysis. Fourth, we must formulate the relationships that we think connect the variables and we must estimate the parameters that enter into these relationships.

Up to this point we have a model of the system ready for application. But, fifth, if we want to use this model to help us to plan, we must specify our aims in terms of the variables we have used to describe the system. We can then try to discover whether these aims can be realized with the present operating characteristics of the system. If so, is there more than one way to do this, and can there be said to be a 'best' way? If not, how could we modify the system so that the aims could be realized, and is there a 'best' way of doing this?

Finally, we must establish some means of regulating the system so that its performance comes close to our aims. In a physical system we should try to design a control device, like the governor of a steam engine, which would enable the system to regulate itself. In more complicated cases, like the present one, such automatic devices are likely to play a limited role and more reliance must be placed on human decisions in controlling the system; indeed, it must be recognized that there may be features of the system which can be controlled only within limits or cannot be controlled at all with the means of control that are considered acceptable.

This ordered catalogue of steps is useful only for expository purposes. In real life, models, aims and controls interact, and, wherever we begin our investigation, we must recognize that at the outset our knowledge of the other steps will be incomplete. We must begin to collect and arrange data without knowing all about our aims which, even if fully specified, would almost certainly have to be modified when we spelt out some of their implications in terms of cost and indirect effects. We must begin to specify aims without being sure initially that they are attainable or even, in the final analysis, desirable. We must begin to regulate the system without having enough information about its operating characteristics to design efficient control devices. What is important is that we should keep all these aspects of the problem in mind and gradually develop an analytical tool for educational decisions which can make systematic use of all relevant data, allows for imperfect information and incorporates a learning mechanism capable of responding promptly and effectively to experience and calculation.

At the conference all these topics were discussed. Let us now look at them in greater detail.

3. DESCRIBING THE SYSTEM

The authors who presented numerical descriptions of their countries' educational systems concentrated on formal education in schools, colleges and universities to the exclusion of part-time vocational and professional training undertaken after formal education has ceased. The reason for this concentration was simply that a start has to be made somewhere and that the obvious starting point is formal education. At the same time it was recognized that informal education is important, since one aspect of educational planning relates to the needs of the economy, and it was considered necessary to get more information about this aspect. It was emphasized that in advanced countries nowadays the length of life of a particular occupational skill might in many cases be as short as fifteen years, so that retraining in adult life was becoming a matter of necessity for a growing proportion of the labour force. This tendency, it was thought, was likely to react on the nature of formal education, where it would be necessary to place more emphasis on adaptability and general education and less on rigid and specialized education which would tend to freeze the student at a particular stage of a rapidly developing subject.

Having isolated the system of formal education as the subject to study first, the authors divided this system into a number of branches and concentrated on the flow of students through this disaggregated system and on the stocks of students in different parts of it. In addition to a statement of student flows and stocks, it would also be necessary to set out a corresponding statement of economic flows and stocks, namely of the teachers, materials, equipment and buildings necessary to operate the different branches of the system. This double system of flows and stocks, demographic and economic, would provide a quantitative picture of the educational structure as it is. A model based on this structure would help us to estimate the scale of different educational activities implied by the growth of the population or needed to ensure that the future composition of leavers, or 'graduate mix', accorded with the aims set for the system's performance.

This work on student flows, which can be formalized in what may be called a demographic accounting system, was compared with the economic accounting systems for whole economies which have been developed in most countries in the last twenty years. These economic accounting systems have proved an indispensable framework for national economic policies and have been expanded, from small and relatively inaccurate beginnings, in the light of policy needs mediated through theoretical considerations and statistical possibilities. The view was expressed, and generally accepted, that a complementary system of social accounting for education was an indispensable first step which should be given top priority by educational model-builders. Without a well-defined picture, that can easily be kept up to date, of the existing educational structure, it is impossible, it was argued, to consider modifications of this structure on anything but a piecemeal basis, looking at one problem after another without being able to trace their interactions.

The limitations of existing data were discussed and a number of specific problems emerged, some of which call for action on the part of educational statisticians.

First, at present there is a general lack of statistics on flows of students; with few exceptions, flows have to be derived from information about stocks. In many cases a reasonable approximation can be reached by recognizing that many possible flows are unlikely to be more than trickles and can therefore be ignored, and by making full use of the arithmetical and accounting identities which a systematic organization of the data reveals. However, this is not always so and, since flow statistics enter so largely into descriptive models, it would be helpful if a greater statistical effort could be concentrated on them.

Second, it is often found that published information sufficient to build up a detailed picture of student flows is only available for recent years, perhaps only for two or three years at the most. Here the collection of new data cannot help in providing a picture of the past, but research into existing records might enable at least parts of the picture to be filled in. Since a knowledge of the changing structure of education would be useful, this subject might repay investigation by institutes devoted to educational research.

Third, the available statistics are usually highly aggregated: they relate to categories rather than to individuals. There is a growing recognition that individual data systems are in many ways desirable, particularly where administrative action is concerned with individuals as well as with categories, as in the case of teachers, and where age, location, qualifications and other characteristics of the individual are at least as significant as the broad class in which the individual is classified. Since individual data systems, for students as well as teachers, cannot be introduced quickly, it was thought that their potential value in educational planning was such that the time had come for an appraisal of their merits and of the problems of instituting them in any country seriously interested in educational planning.

A number of other questions relating to data were discussed in connection with estimating the parameters in the models described at the conference. These questions are easier to understand when something has been said about the kind of relationships that enter into these models, and so a discussion of them will be deferred to section 5 below.

4. THEORIES

Theories relate to the way in which we propose to connect variables to one another, to our aims and to possible instruments of control. It is convenient to distinguish two kinds of theory, both of which were represented in the papers given to the conference. The first kind starts from a set of observations and asks how these observations can be related. This kind of theory usually takes it for granted that the first attempts at relating the observations will be only approximate and looks to experience to suggest improvements, which may be needed as much in the data and the way they are organized as in the theory itself. Such theories may be called 'theories for application'.

By contrast, the second kind starts with a problem and asks how in principle it could be solved even if, initially, no data are available. This kind of theory is usually concerned with the character of the solution under fairly general conditions. The problem is usually posed in a highly abstract manner which offers some hope of solution if sufficiently advanced methods are used. Such theories may be called 'theories for insight'.

The first kind of theory was illustrated by the papers at the conference which were designed to organize information about flows of students. The general idea in this case was that the educational system can be represented as a set of branches through which students flow. We can observe that the students in any branch in one period distribute themselves over branches in the next period in given proportions. If these proportions were fixed, the future activity levels of all the branches would depend partly on the present numbers in the different branches and partly on the new entrants to the system from births and migration. Given the future course of these demographic variables, therefore, the future activity levels of each branch of the system could be calculated and so could the system's future final product, that is the numbers of students leaving the system altogether from one or other of its different branches.

This model is conceptually and algebraically simple, and the problems that have to be solved before it can be applied are mainly the taxonomic and data problems discussed in the preceding section. Its merit, shared with its economic counterpart input–output analysis, which in many respects it resembles, is that it enables a very large body of data to be processed systematically to give quantitative answers to important questions. The answers will be approximate, however, because the relationships of the model are simple and because the information used to estimate its parameters, the transition proportions, are, in practice, likely to be biased in various ways. In addition, as with economic input–output, there are the problems of changing parameters and of the introduction of new processes and new products.

The second kind of theory was illustrated by a model designed to distribute the fifty-year period from the end of compulsory education to retirement among full-time education, part-time education and full-time earning by reference to the earning prospects which would follow from different distributions. This model, too, has an economic counterpart in Ramsey's theory of saving, which is concerned with the rate of saving that a community should adopt if it wishes to maximize the satisfaction it can expect to obtain by consuming less or working harder now in order to be able to consume more or work less in the future. Both problems are extremum problems, but whereas Ramsey was able to formulate his so that it was accessible to the classical methods of the calculus of variations, the present problem could not be formulated in this way. It was solved, however, by an application of Pontryagin's maximum principle and, in discrete form, would have been accessible to Bellman's technique of dynamic programming. Though formulated and solved at a rather high level of abstraction, the author indicated ways in which many of his assumptions could be relaxed. One of these related to the introduction of different kinds of education into the model. It was suggested in discussion that if the distinction were made between general and vocational education, it would be interesting to see how the model would react to the high obsolescence rate of many specific skills which was mentioned earlier. With these additional features, the model might shed some light on the desirability of a general education, favouring adaptability, in youth, followed by spells of highly specialized education at various stages of adulthood, as opposed to a relatively specialized education in youth followed by little, if any, further education in adulthood, which is the prevalent pattern today.

As has been said already, the distinction between theories for application and theories for insight is one of convenience: there is no suggestion that the former can give no insight or that the latter cannot be applied to real problems. They are, however, superficially very different and it is important to recognize that each has its contribution to make.

In the discussion a number of points were made.

First, there was a considerable similarity in the models of student flows presented to the conference. It was thought that an international organization could help greatly by providing opportunities for model-builders to keep in touch and by encouraging uniformities of treatment where this was desirable. In this way it would be easier to compare the experience of different countries, and results achieved in one country could be replicated in another.

Second, models of economic inputs into education were not much discussed, but the link provided by the fact that the educational system produces its own major input, teachers, was emphasized. Economic input-output tabulation and analysis offers a pattern which could readily be applied to the educational system. It was thought that more information was desirable on the effect of grants in influencing the choices of students.

Third, the models of student flows divided the educational system up into branches but did not try to get inside the branches and see what was going on there: in other words the educator and the psychologist were left out of the models. This defect would have to be remedied because existing educational techniques could not be taken for granted in planning the great expansion of education that was now beginning to take place.

Fourth, and this point is closely related to the preceding one, more attention should be paid to the concept of productivity in education: an impartial look at existing curricula and their effectiveness is much needed. It was recognized that to do this new concepts and methods of measurement would have to be developed. It was also recognized that many educators associated high productivity with bad education and were generally suspicious of productivity studies. It was thought, however, that the inputs of resources needed by present and prospective educational programmes were so high that the problem could not be neglected for much longer.

5. ESTIMATION

The main topic discussed under this heading was the estimation of transition proportions, the parameters in the student-flow models. At present these are based on past observations, exactly like input–output coefficients in many economic investigations, and it was agreed that this was the only practical way to get a first approximation to these proportions. It was pointed out, however, that the economic analogy of supply and demand analysis ought to be kept in mind; the proportions based on past data reflected partly the demand of students to move from one branch to another in the educational system and partly the supply of places in those branches. To the extent that supply limitations were important, especially in the higher branches of the system, estimates based on the past would give a distorted picture of student demands if they were in a position to exercise their first preferences; not only would the demand for the more preferred branches be underestimated, but the demand for the less preferred branches might be overestimated since the demand for them comes in part from the exercise of second or third preferences by those who have failed to find a place in their preferred branch.

A number of suggestions were made for handling this problem. In the first place, institutions would usually know how many applications they received as well as how many students they admitted, and might be able to divide the difference between these numbers between the applicants who did not reach their standard and the applicants who had to be rejected owing to the limit on the number of places available. This kind of information would be useful. But it might still be the case that the general knowledge that places were limited discouraged application by weak but suitable candidates. It was suggested that sample surveys of student preferences and attainments might help to get closer to transition proportions based on demand; and the possibility of trying to model the determinants of student demand was also mentioned.

Apart from the question of estimating a set of transition proportions, consideration was also given to the estimation of changes in this set. This problem is familiar to economists in the context of input–output coefficients. Something could be gained by constructing a series of tables of student flows, but these would all be subject to the difficulties just mentioned, due to limitations of supply. Here again it was suggested that it would be necessary to model the determinants of student demand. For example, it might be helpful to regard the wish to reach successively higher rungs on the educational ladder as analogous to a multiple epidemic process in which the change in the transition proportion between any two stages depended partly on the proportion who had made the move in the previous period and so tended to infect others to follow their example, and partly on the proportion who had not made the move in the previous period and so might be susceptible to infection. Again it might be helpful to regard the choice of course at any stage as analogous to a learning process in which the existing distribution over courses is compared with a distribution based on an assessment of their prospects, and students tend continually to move away from the first distribution towards the second at a given speed.

It was generally agreed that educational modelling was still in its infancy and offered immense scope for further research.

6. AIMS

The discussion of the aims of educational policy tended to base these aims on the usual, rather limited, considerations: the apparent needs of the productive system; and the apparent preferences of those being educated. It could be argued that there are educational aims over and above these: namely, to bring every individual up to the educational level suited to him and so enable him to enjoy what education can contribute to a happy and adjusted life. This aim, if realized, might bring about large changes in the supply of different economic skills, and so in the prices of these skills, with the result that the apparent demands forecast by the productive system would be wide of the mark if these price changes were not taken into account. This aim might also conflict with individual attitudes, or at least actions, as historically determined. However, it was recognized: (*a*) that most individuals must earn their living and that the educational system should help them to do this to their satisfaction; and (*b*) that within any system of inducements that may be offered, individuals should be free to follow the courses that appeal to them. These considerations suggest that the needs of the productive system are important but that the productive system may have to adapt itself to individual attitudes.

From the discussion on educational aims a number of points emerged on which there was general agreement.

First, there are many different educational aims and the weight that should be assigned to each is a problem for the policy-maker rather than the model-builder. However, the model-builder can play an important role in the process of policy formation in so far as he is able to work out problems of feasibility and cost, and can compare the alternative paths by means of which different aims can be realized.

Second, many aims are uncertain, partly because we know relatively little about social and economic dynamics. For example, even if we ignore the possibility of the kind of major adjustment contemplated at the beginning of this section, it is still a difficult matter to estimate future manpower needs, since these depend on future output levels, technology, labour mobility, restrictive practices and many other factors. These subjects can be, and are being, studied. In this case the educational model-builder must get together with the economic model-builder.

Third, aims may be diametrically opposed to one another because of conflicts of interest which must be resolved before a coherent statement of aims can be made. The theory of games was mentioned as a technique which might be useful in this difficult area.

7. CONTROLS

Any system that is to operate satisfactorily must have some form of control to prevent imbalances from building up and to keep it on its intended course. The distinction between automatic controls and controls operated by human agents is not as obvious and clear-cut as it may seem. The thermostat on the one hand and the driver of a motor-car on the other are examples of the two extremes. The price mechanism working under the assumption of universal perfect competition is something between the two, for in this case the economic system is controlled by human agents who have, however, an automatic response to price changes: a rise in price will stimulate supply and curtail demand, and a fall in price will have the opposite effect. In general, the self-interested responses of human agents to price movements are supposed to converge towards an equilibrium solution and so re-establish a balance that has been upset by crop failures or other natural occurrences. Even with this simple model, however, it is not difficult to state conditions under which the human responses to a departure from equilibrium will lead not to convergence but to oscillation: the feed-stock cycle is an example of this.

The subject of systematic control has been deeply studied in recent years in connection with engineering control problems. Two of the papers presented to the conference dealt with control from this point of view, not in order to reduce the problems of controlling a programme of educational development to the automatic methods appropriate to controlling, say, a chemical plant, but in order to introduce the general philosophy of the problem of control as it has been developed in control-system engineering. These ideas fit easily into the framework of the discussion given so far, and can be summarized in four propositions: (*a*) from a knowledge of the operating characteristics of the system and the aims it is intended to serve, suitable control variables must be found; (*b*) control relationships connecting these variables with the system must be designed in such a way that they act with the speed and intensity, neither too much nor too little, necessary to keep the system close to its intended path; (*c*) the whole exercise must be based on conditions and knowledge as they are, and not on hypothetical conditions and 'perfect' knowledge; (*d*) the control mechanism should be adaptive, that is to say it should embody a learning process which enables it to adjust itself as new experience is gained. This statement of the problem, which is as relevant to systems controlled by human agents as to automatic-control systems, provides some insight into the fundamental nature of control.

In the discussion, a number of points were made.

First, any human system is likely to be only partially controllable, because there may be human responses which are not amenable to any acceptable control variable. This does not, of course, imply that control is unimportant in such systems.

Second, more work is needed on the concept of control variables as applied to educational systems. For example, suppose an improvement in the pay and status of teachers is needed to secure adequate recruitment and retention; how are potential teachers likely to react to specific proposals? Or again, how can administrative arrangements, which themselves form a system, be better adapted to their tasks? And finally, how far does effective control involve changing the attitudes of students and their parents, so that those parts of the system which are not amenable to controls now become self-regulating?

Third, emphasis was placed on the difficulty of designing control systems. Some of the reasons for this are: (*a*) the control function which specifies the changes in the control variables in response to the performance of the system must be tractable as well as effective, and it is not easy to satisfy both conditions; (*b*) the objective function to be maximized or minimized is rarely single-peaked and it is often difficult to find the true maximum or minimum rather than some local peak or trough; (c) controls must operate at the appropriate speed and intensity if they are not to lead to oscillations or ineffectiveness.

8. CONCLUSIONS

Those who attended the conference left it with the feeling that the ideas presented held much promise and that the achievements in building quantitative educational models, though modest to date, pointed to important new techniques which would be helpful in the formulation and control of educational programmes. They saw a number of new areas where research is urgently needed, and commended these alike to those engaged in research and to those who support research. They expressed the hope that, even at this early stage, the papers presented in this volume would come to the notice of educators, educational administrators and educational planners, without whose understanding and help educational model building could easily become separated from the very activity it was designed to assist. They thought that at a later stage, when educational model-building was a little further developed, there would be a strong case for another kind of conference at which a wider range of interests would be represented.

XVIII

INPUT–OUTPUT AND DEMOGRAPHIC ACCOUNTING: A TOOL FOR EDUCATIONAL PLANNING

1. INTRODUCTION

We are all familiar with the idea of accounting for sums of money, of arranging transactions expressible in terms of money in a system of interlocking statements in each of which total incomings are equal to total outgoings. We know that in a closed system of n accounts the entries are not unrelated but are connected by $n - 1$ independent accounting identities, and that further arithmetical identities appear if we give separate symbols to the totals in the accounts. By adopting an accounting habit of thought, therefore, we force ourselves to keep in mind a number of inescapable connections between the concepts we use, connections which must as far as possible carry through into any measurements we make of the empirical correlates of these concepts. Within an accounting framework we can build models in the certain knowledge that these connections will be respected. Input–output analysis is the most obvious example of this kind of model-building.

There is, however, no reason why the application of accounting ideas should be restricted to concepts expressible in terms of money; concepts expressible in any other homogeneous unit will do equally well. In this paper elementary accounting ideas will be applied to demography, with its obvious unit the individual human being, and to education, with its equally obvious unit the student. The point of this exercise is to present in an orderly manner the vast mass of material relating to human resources. If we wish to plan our educational system in a rational way, we need first of all an integrated body of demographic information which will enable us to trace the flows of individuals with various characteristics into various activities, to show in detail the structure of the population at any one time, and to project into the future the way in which this structure can be expected to change under the impact of individual choice, or may be required to change if certain social and economic aims are to be achieved.

In an earlier article [69] I set out a model of the educational system which brought together the human inputs into the system, namely the flows of students through its various branches, and the economic inputs, namely the costs of the teachers, buildings and equipment needed to carry out the functions of these branches. But I did not place clearly in focus the common accounting structure appropriate to both types of input, nor the formal similarity but essential difference of the models appropriate to each type. Here I try to repair these defects. First I discuss economic input–output and describe an accounting structure leading to a model which, given the usual assumption of fixed input coefficients, allows for time-lags in production. I then establish a formally identical structure for demographic flows and show that in this case the appropriate model is obtained by fixing the output coefficients, thought of as transition probabilities, rather than the input coefficients. Finally I indicate what the categories in a demographic matrix should be, with particular reference to educational categories.

2. ECONOMIC INPUT–OUTPUT

In economic input–output analysis the productive system is divided into a number of branches, or industries. Each industry is defined as producing a particular product or group of products, which constitutes its output. Within a given time-period, this output has two main destinations: it can either be absorbed at once by the productive system as an intermediate input, to be used in the fabrication of some other product; or it can flow out of the system as final product. Final product in its turn has three destinations: most of it goes to satisfy the demands of consumers; some goes to replace and extend the capital equipment of industries; and a small part does not leave the system altogether but forms a stock of products, some unfinished, which will flow back into production for intermediate use in the future. Producing goods and services for final use is the principal function of the industries. In order to perform this function, each industry, besides the materials, fuels and business services which constitute its intermediate inputs, needs the services of labour and capital. These primary inputs flow into production from outside the productive system.

This in a nutsehll is the economic system as seen from the point of view of input–output analysis. The purpose of this type of analysis is to study the interdependence of the industries and their connections with the other parts of the economy. If we want to apply input–output theory to the study of a particular economy we must of course bring imports and exports into the picture. But in what follows I shall ignore foreign trade, which would raise complications irrelevant to the object of this paper, and shall consider only a closed economy.

Before setting out the basic input–output model, let us look at the facts that have to be modelled. These are the inputs and outputs that flow within a given time-period between the branches of production and between these branches and the rest of the economy, which we may designate collectively as non-production. The whole set of flows and their totals can conveniently be arranged in a table, or matrix, with outputs in the rows and inputs in the columns. The entries in this table can be expressed in terms of money, in which case each row-and-column pair can be regarded as an account which balances: the revenues realized from the sale of the outputs are equal to the cost of the inputs. Reduced to its simplest terms, such a table can be represented as follows:

TABLE 1   A SIMPLE ECONOMIC ACCOUNTING MATRIX

	Production	Non-production	Total
Production	W	f	q
Non-production	y'	0	$y'i$
Total	q'	$i'f$	

In this table the row and column for production are to be thought of as divided into many rows and columns, equal in number to the industries we wish to distinguish. The symbol W denotes a submatrix of intermediate product-flows between the industries: the element at the intersection of row j, say, and column k, say, of this submatrix shows the amount of the product of industry j absorbed by industry k during the period to which the table relates. Continuing along the first row of the table, the symbol f denotes a column vector of final products: the jth element of f shows the amount of final product made by industry j. And the symbol q denotes a column vector of total outputs: the jth element of q shows the total output of industry j. If we add together all the elements in a row of W and add on the corresponding element of f, we obtain the corresponding element of q.

Turning now to the first column of the table, we can see the costs that make up the value of output. Part of these consists of the costs of intermediate inputs, the elements of W, and the remainder consists of the costs of primary inputs, represented by the elements of the row vector y'. If we add together the elements of W and y' by columns we obtain the elements of q', which is simply a row vector with the same elements as q.

The static, open input–output model for a closed economy is based on two premises. The first is the arithmetical identity which tells us that the total output of a period is absorbed either in intermediate or in final uses; that is

$$q \equiv Wi + f \tag{1}$$

where i denotes the unit vector, so that Wi denotes the row sums of W. The second is an assumption about the technology of production, which says that the inputs of intermediate products are related in fixed proportions to the output into which they enter; that is

$$W = A\hat{q} \tag{2}$$

where the circumflex on $\hat{q}$ means that the vector q is spread out to form a diagonal matrix; and where A denotes a matrix of input–output coefficients in which the element at the intersection of row j and column k measures the amount of input j needed to make one unit of output k.

The simplest input–output model comes from substituting for W from (2) into (1). Thus

$$\begin{aligned} q &= A\hat{q}i + f \\ &= Aq + f \\ &= (I - A)^{-1}f \end{aligned} \tag{3}$$

where I denotes the unit matrix and $(I - A)^{-1}$ is usually called the matrix multiplier because it is the matrix analogue of the scalar multiplier which plays such an important part in Keynes' theory of income determination. Since each industry needs primary inputs in addition to intermediate inputs, the column sums of A are less than one. As a consequence, A is convergent: A^θ approaches the null matrix as θ increases, with the result that $(I - A)^{-1} \equiv (I + A + A^2 + A^3 + ...)$ has finite elements. From this identity we can see that the outputs needed to meet final demand, f, can be divided into three parts: If, the production of f itself; Af, the inputs needed directly to produce f; and $(A^2 + A^3 + ...)f \equiv A^2(I - A)^{-1}f$, the inputs needed indirectly to produce f.

The model given in (3) is termed 'open' because it does not generate all its variables but depends for its solution on a variable, f, which must be estimated exogenously. Its purpose is to enable us to calculate the amount of total output, q, which must be produced in order to satisfy a given level of final demand, f; and hence to work out what would happen to q if f were to change.

But this model is much too simple. Among other things, it implies that all the intermediate product used this year is made in the course of the year. We know, however, that part of the final product of any period goes to form a stock of intermediate products for use in the succeeding period; in other words, that f includes additions to stocks and work in progress. From this it follows that some of this year's W must have been part of last year's f; in other words, that some of the intermediate product used this year must have been made last year. In order to deal explicitly with this time-lag, therefore, we must treat additions to stocks and work in progress as a separate entity and think of exogenous final product as composed only of consumption goods and capital equipment.

With this modification in mind, let us consider a productive system in which all the intermediate product used this year was made last year and in which all the intermediate product made this year will be used

20

next year, so that provision must be made in advance for any expected change in final demand. This state of affairs is shown in table 2 below.

TABLE 2   AN ECONOMIC ACCOUNTING SYSTEM WITH SIMPLE
TIME-LAGS

| | | Production | | | Non-production | Total |
		Last year	This year	Next year		
Production	Last year		W			
	This year			ΛW	e	q
	Next year					
Non-production			y'			
Total			q'			

In this table production is divided into three periods, last year, this year and next year, but the table is filled in only for this year. The intermediate product absorbed this year, W, is shown as coming from last year, and the intermediate product made this year, ΛW, is shown as carried forward to next year. The symbol Λ denotes the lag operator (often written as E) which advances by one time-unit the variable to which it is applied. In a growing economy any difference between ΛW and W represents an excess of products made over products used, that is to say represents stock-building. The symbol e, therefore, denotes final product redefined to exclude stock-building.

The model of this situation is built up from two elements:

$$q \equiv \Lambda Wi + e \qquad (4)$$

corresponding to (1); and

$$\Lambda W = \Lambda \Lambda \hat{q} \qquad (5)$$

corresponding to (2). By substitution we see that in this case

$$
\begin{aligned}
q &= \Lambda \Lambda \hat{q} i + e \\
&= \Lambda \Lambda q + e \\
&= (I - \Lambda \Lambda)^{-1} e \\
&= \sum_{\theta=0}^{\infty} \Lambda^{\theta} \Lambda^{\theta} e \qquad (6)
\end{aligned}
$$

In the third row of (6) the solution is expressed as a dynamic matrix multiplier, that is, a multiplier which combines the lag operator Λ with the parameter A; this device is of great convenience in giving formal expression to the solution of more complicated cases [6: p. 80]. Its effect can be seen in the fourth row of (6), where Λ^θ advances the variable to which it is applied by θ time-units, so that $\Lambda^\theta e$ represents the value of e in θ years' time; thus this year's output, q, is no longer given simply in terms of this year's final demand but in terms of a weighted sum of present and future demands, the weights tending to zero with time. This result is easily obtained by applying successive values of Λ^θ to the second row of (6) and substituting these values in the preceding equation of the series.

The second row of (6) can also be written as

$$q = Aq + A\Delta q + e \qquad (7)$$

where $\Delta \equiv \Lambda - 1$. Here the productive system is explicitly represented as: (i) replacing, for use next year, the intermediate product, Aq, which it is using up for current production and which was carried forward from last year; (ii) adding to stock a supplementary amount, $A\Delta q$, needed to sustain the increment of output from this year to next year; and (iii) satisfying this year's final demand for consumption goods and capital equipment, e. If we put $f = A\Delta q + e$, then (7) becomes the same as (3).

Let us now get a bit nearer to the real world and consider a system which gets this year's supplies of intermediate product partly from last year's production and partly from this year's, and produces intermediate product partly for this year and partly for the next; but what it must consume within a year and what it can carry forward from one year to the next is rigidly determined. This state of affairs is shown in table 3 below.

TABLE 3   AN ECONOMIC ACCOUNTING SYSTEM WITH PARTIAL
TIME-LAGS

		Production			Non-production	Total
		Last year	This year	Next year		
Production	Last year		W^{**}			
	This year		W^{*}	ΔW^{**}	e	q
	Next year					
Non-production			y'			
Total			q'			

Here the intermediate product absorbed this year is divided into two parts, W^{**}, which was made last year, and W^*, which is made this year. Also, the intermediate product made this year is partly absorbed this year, W^*, and partly carried forward for use next year, ΛW^{**}. Otherwise table 3 is the same as table 2.

The model of this situation is built up from three elements. First, the arithmetical identity

$$q \equiv W^* i + \Lambda W^{**} i + e \tag{8}$$

and, second and third, the technical assumptions

$$W^* = A^* \hat{q} \tag{9}$$

and

$$W^{**} = A^{**} \hat{q} \tag{10}$$

where $A^* + A^{**} = A$. From these we obtain

$$
\begin{aligned}
q &= A^* q + A^{**} \Lambda q + e \\
&= (I - A^*)^{-1} (A^{**} \Lambda q + e) \\
&= (I - A^*)^{-1} A^{**} \Lambda q + (I - A^*)^{-1} e \\
&= \{I - [(I - A^*)^{-1} A^{**} \Lambda]\}^{-1} (I - A^*)^{-1} e \\
&= (I - A^*)^{-1} \{I - [A^{**}(I - A^*)^{-1} \Lambda]\}^{-1} e \\
&= (I - A^*)^{-1} \sum_{\theta=0}^{\infty} [A^{**}(I - A^*)^{-1}]^{\theta} \Lambda^{\theta} e
\end{aligned}
\tag{11}
$$

corresponding to (6)

By analogy with (7), the first row of (11) can also be written as

$$
\begin{aligned}
q &= A^* q + (A^{**} q + A^{**} \Delta q) + e \\
&= (A^* + A^{**}) q + A^{**} \Delta q + e \\
&= Aq + A^{**} \Delta q + e
\end{aligned}
\tag{12}
$$

which is the same as (7) except that the matrix of current coefficients, A, and the matrix of stock-building coefficients, A^{**}, are different.

Like (7), the statement expressed in (12) presupposes perfect foresight: in each year the amount of intermediate product made but not used is precisely equal to the needs of the succeeding year which cannot be met from that year's production. Its purpose is to illustrate a particular dynamic scheme, not to suggest that the real world is in a perpetual state of equilibrium.

Many things could be done to improve this simple model. For example, in the same way as the model generates the necessary amount of stock-building, it could be made to generate the necessary amount of fixed capital investment, leaving only consumption to be estimated exogenously. But such elaborations are not relevant to my present purpose, which is to show that an identical accounting framework and a very similar analysis can be used to describe and model demographic flows.

3. DEMOGRAPHIC INPUT–OUTPUT

If we want to apply input–output methods to the analysis of demographic flows, the first thing to do is to define our categories in terms of the social, as opposed to the economic, system. Thus the unit, instead of being the pound, will be the human individual; and the main categories within which these units will be grouped, instead of being industries and products, will be age-groups and, within age-groups, activities or occupations. I shall say more about these categories in the next section, but first let us be clear about the flow equations of the system and their solution.

We can see that table 2 provides the basic accounting framework in its simplest dynamic form; all that is necessary is to reinterpret the symbols. If we think of total output, q, as the total population of a country during a given period; of intermediate product, W, as the surviving part of this population; of final output, e, as deaths and emigrations; and of primary inputs, y, as births and immigrations; then we can write the table more appropriately as table 4.

TABLE 4   A DEMOGRAPHIC ACCOUNTING MATRIX

| | | Our country | | | Elsewhere | Total |
		Last year	This year	Next year		
Our country	Last year		$\Lambda^{-1} S$			
	This year			S	d	p
	Next year					
Elsewhere			b'			
Total			p'			

In this table the sources of p', the population vector, are partly the survivors from last year, the elements of $\Lambda^{-1} S$, and partly the births and immigrations of this year, the elements of b'. Correspondingly, the destinations of p are partly the survivors into next year, the elements of S, and partly the deaths and emigrations of this year, the elements of d. If we sum the elements of the matrix S across the rows, we obtain a vector of the living population at the end of the year, that is, $Si \equiv p - d$.

In order to build from table 4 a demographic model analogous to the economic model we built from table 2, we must reverse the roles of inputs and outputs. In the economic model it was assumed that while output patterns change with changes in final demand, the input patterns in the different industries are fixed. In the demographic case it seems more reasonable to make the opposite assumption, namely that input patterns may change with changes in the number of births and immigrations, but that the output patterns, or transition probabilities, for the different age-groups and activities are fixed: if out of 1000 science graduates aged 21, say, 500 go on to further training, 300 get jobs in industry, 100 go into teaching, 50 become civil servants and 50 emigrate or die, we assume that if the number of science graduates aged 21 were 1200, then 600 of them would go on to further training, 360 would get jobs in industry, 120 would go into teaching, 60 would become civil servants and 60 would emigrate or die.

This assumption means that instead of fixing the coefficients by columns, as we did in the economic model, we must fix them by rows. Also since the determining variable is no longer the vector of final demands but the vector of primary inputs, we must take the building blocks for our model not from this year's row, as we did in the case of production, but from this year's column: we must ignore S and d and concentrate on $\Lambda^{-1}S$, b' and p'. In manipulating these variables, however, we shall find it convenient to transpose them, that is turn b' and p' into column vectors so that they become b and p, and interchange the rows and columns of S so that it becomes S'. Then we can write, corresponding to (4) and (5),

$$p \equiv \Lambda^{-1} S' i + b \tag{13}$$

and

$$\Lambda^{-1} S' = C\Lambda^{-1} \hat{p} \tag{14}$$

where $\Lambda^{-1} S' i$ denotes the column sums of $\Lambda^{-1} S$ written out as a column vector; and C denotes a matrix of transition probabilities (or output coefficients). By substituting for $\Lambda^{-1} S'$ from (14) into (13), we obtain

$$p = C\Lambda^{-1} p + b \tag{15}$$

corresponding to the second row of (6). But whereas in (6) the coefficient matrix is applied to the future, in (15) it is applied to the past: the intermediate constituent of q is determined by next year's needs; the intermediate constituent of p is determined by last year's performance.

It is interesting to note here that Ghosh has considered a static economic model based on row rather than column coefficients, which he terms an allocation model [25]. Broadly speaking, his idea is that practical limits are set to the use of resources partly by input coefficients and partly by output (allocation) coefficients. In the context of production he does not press the claims of the allocation model very strongly; but given a dynamic form, this model seems to find a natural application in the context of demography.

From (15) we can calculate what the composition of p is likely to be in τ years' time. If we apply the operator Λ to (15), substitute for p into the new equation from (15), carry out this operation $\tau - 1$ times and apply Λ to the final equation of the series, we obtain

$$\Lambda^\tau p = \sum_{\theta=0}^{\tau-1} C^\theta \Lambda^{\tau-\theta} b + C^\tau p \tag{16}$$

corresponding to the last row of (6). Equation (16) expresses the numbers in the various categories of the population (the elements of p) τ periods hence in terms of the present numbers and of all future births and immigrations up to and including those taking place in period τ. Like its economic counterpart, A, the matrix C has non-negative elements. Also, since people die at all ages, its column sums are less than one, so that C^τ approaches zero as τ increases. In fact, since people cannot become younger, C is upper-triangular and $C^\tau p = \{0, 0, \ldots, 0\}$ if τ exceeds the human life-span.

We can now compare the economic and demographic models. The last row of (6) shows output levels this year expressed in terms of present and future values of e: present output depends on present and future demand. By contrast, (16) shows the future population in terms of its present value and of future values of b: future output depends on present and future supply. The solution of the economic model is based on the assumption that the input patterns, the elements of A, remain constant over time; by contrast, the solution of the demographic model is based on the assumption that the transition probabilities, or output patterns, the elements of C, remain constant over time.

These two points of contrast raise two important practical questions. First, how are we to estimate the future values of e in one case and of b in the other? Second, if we want to allow for changes in the coefficients, whether of inputs or of outputs, as in the real world we should, how can we introduce such changes in our models?

An answer to the first question for the economic model will be found in *Exploring* 1970 [11] and in my paper with Alan Brown and D. A. Rowe [76]. For the demographic model, if we are prepared to ignore for the time being the highly erratic element of immigration and concentrate on births, we can invoke a well-known piece of population mathematics [35] to express future values of p simply in terms of its present value, as follows.

Since it is reasonable to relate the number of births of either sex to the age composition of the female population, consider a vector of the female population grouped by year of age, f^* say, ranging from birth to the end of the female reproductive span. Then consider a matrix, H say, whose rows and columns are equal in number to the elements of f^*: the first row of H contains the rates at which females are born to females of different ages; the diagonal below the leading diagonal contains the survival rates of females at the different ages; all the other elements of H are zero. From this we can write

$$\Lambda^\theta f^* = H^\theta f^* \qquad (17)$$

Now consider another matrix, $\mathcal{J}$ say, whose rows are equal in number to the elements of p and whose columns are equal in number to the elements of f^*: the top left-hand corner of $\mathcal{J}$ contains a one; the rest of the first row contains the rates at which males are born to females of different ages; all the other elements of $\mathcal{J}$ are zero. From this we can write

$$\Lambda^{\tau-\theta} b = JH^{\tau-\theta} f^* \qquad (18)$$

where the first element of $\mathcal{J}$ picks out the first element of $H^{\tau-\theta}f^*$, that is, the female births in year $\tau - \theta$; and the age-specific male birthrates in the rest of the first row of $\mathcal{J}$ calculate and add together the male births in year $\tau - \theta$. If we now substitute for $\Lambda^{\tau-\theta}$ from (18) into (16), we obtain

$$\Lambda^\tau p = \sum_{\theta=0}^{\tau-1} C^\theta JH^{\tau-\theta} f^* + C^\tau p \qquad (19)$$

It will be noticed that in (19) the demographic model, from being an open model with one exogenous variable, b, has become a closed model, that is a model which generates all its variables endogenously from given initial conditions.

Turning now to the second question, we know that the assumption of fixed coefficients is only one of those simplifications to which we are forced to resort in the early stages of building a model. In the real world input patterns and transition probabilities change and so we must be ready to allow for such changes. Estimating them may not be easy, and this is not the place to discuss how to do it; a rough method for dealing with changes in input patterns is given in [6, 8] and a suggestion for treating changes in the transition probabilities as a multiple epidemic process is given in [69]. The point I want to make here is that, once we have succeeded in estimating these changes, it is not difficult to introduce them into our original models. The way to do this for the economic model is indicated in [6, 73]. For the demographic model, if we let C change with successive values of Λ^θ, then we can rewrite (16) as

$$\Lambda^\tau p = \Lambda^\tau b + \sum_{\theta=1}^{\tau-1} \left(\prod_{\lambda=\tau-1}^{\tau-\theta} \Lambda^\lambda C \right) \Lambda^{\tau-\theta} b + \left(\prod_{\theta=\tau-1}^{0} \Lambda^\theta C \right) p \qquad (20)$$

where Π denotes the operation of forming a product. From the middle term on the right-hand side of (20) we can see that the multiplier of $\Lambda^{\tau-\theta} b$ is $[\Lambda^{\tau-1} C \times \Lambda^{\tau-2} C \times \ldots \times \Lambda^{\tau-\theta} C]$ in place of C^θ as in (16).

There is one further matter to be settled in this section. Just as in the economic case table 3 added something that was missing from table 2, so in the demographic case something is missing from table 4 and should now be added. In dealing with production we saw that intermediate products might be made and used within the year; similarly, in the case of population we might want to account for changes of activity within the year. For example, a boy who flows in from the preceding year as a schoolboy may go to a university in the course of the year and thus flow out into the succeeding year as an undergraduate; or a woman who flows in as a typist may get married in the course of the year and flow out as a housewife. To deal with this we must introduce a new matrix, S^* say, at the intersection of the row and column for this year, and replace S by S^{**}. When this is done, the demographic accounting system will appear as in table 5 below.

TABLE 5 A DEMOGRAPHIC ACCOUNTING SYSTEM WITH
INTRA-YEAR TRANSITIONS

		Our country			Elsewhere	Total
		Last year	This year	Next year		
Our country	Last year		$\Lambda^{-1} S^{**}$			
	This year		S^*	S^{**}	d^*	p^*
	Next year					
Elsewhere			b'			
Total			$p^{*'}$			

The function of the new matrix, S^*, can best be explained by an example: when an individual moves from category j to category k in the course of the year, this movement is represented in S^* by a -1 at the intersection of row j and column j, balanced by a 1 at the intersection of row j and column k. Thus the sum of the elements of S^* is zero, since in the aggregate all the transfers cancel out. From this it follows that the matrices $\Lambda^{-1} S^{**}$ and S^{**} do not differ in the sum of their elements from $\Lambda^{-1} S$ and S; they do differ from them in the arrangement of their elements, however, because each survivor now enters next year from the activity in which he leaves this year and not from the activity in which he had entered this year. For the same reason the vectors d and p now become d^* and p^*. The vector of primary inputs, b, is, of course, not affected.

Like its economic counterpart, the model of this situation is built from three elements. First, the arithmetical identity

$$p^* \equiv \Lambda^{-1} S^{**\prime} i + S^{*\prime} i + b \tag{21}$$

and, second and third, the demographic assumptions

$$S^{*\prime} = C^* \hat{p}^* \tag{22}$$

and

$$S^{**\prime} = C^{**} \hat{p}^* \tag{23}$$

From these we obtain

$$p^* = C^{**} \Lambda^{-1} p^* + C^* p^* + b \tag{24}$$

whose solution for year τ is

$$\Lambda^\tau p^* = \sum_{\theta=0}^{\tau-1} \{ [(I - C^*)^{-1} C^{**}]^\theta (I - C^*)^{-1} \Lambda^{\tau-\theta} b \} + [(I - C^*)^{-1} C^{**}]^\tau p^* \tag{25}$$

corresponding to the last row of (11).

By an extension of the method used to reach (20) we could also allow for changing values of $\Lambda^\theta C^*$ and $\Lambda^\theta C^{**}$.

4. THE CATEGORIES IN A DEMOGRAPHIC MATRIX

A preliminary survey shows that in Britain, at any rate for recent years, there exists a considerable amount of relevant statistical material, and suggests that the construction of demographic accounting matrices may be no more difficult than the construction of their economic counterparts. In order to do this, however, it is necessary to have a clear idea of how we are going to define our categories and then find a means of reconciling the classifications used in the different statistical sources with each other and with our own.

In a demographic matrix the primary classification, as I said above, should be by age and the secondary classification should be by activity. Dividing all information into uniform age-groups is not quite so simple as it sounds. An obvious standard to choose would be age last birthday at the end of the calendar year. Much educational information is already available on this basis. But in other cases flows are recorded by the age at which they take place; for example, first employment is recorded by age on entry, death by age at death, and so on. Endless adjustments have therefore to be made; in principle, they could be avoided by retabulating the basic statistics, since information on exact age is usually recorded too.

As concerns the classification by activities, it should be drawn up on the following lines. With minor exceptions, the newly born enter the home of their parents and remain there until, at age two, a few of them begin to go to nursery school. Accordingly, at this age we must establish a new category, requiring a separate row and column in the matrix, so as to distinguish between two-year-olds who go to nursery school and two-year-olds who stay at home. Apart from the children of immigrants, all two-year-olds come from the one-year-olds of the year before, all of whom are classified under 'home' since no one goes to school at age one. When we get to age three the supply, again apart from immigrants, comes from two sources: two-year-olds who went to school and two-year-olds who stayed at home. With the data available in Britain, it is not possible to tell how many children return to the category 'home' after a first year at nursery school nor how many go to school for the first time when they are three; it is therefore necessary to make the assumption that all the children who were at nursery school at age two continue in it at age three, and that only the additional three-year-old school-goers come directly from 'home'. With increasing age more and more children go to school until, when the age of compulsory school attendance is reached, the category 'home' becomes virtually empty. Even at this early age it would be possible to distinguish different administrative types of school (independent, direct grant, etc.); but from an educational point of view there would not be much advantage in doing so. An argument for making such distinctions would obtain only if there were significant differences in the economic inputs (teachers, buildings, equipment) used in the different types of school.

Around the age of 11 or 12 most children pass from primary to some form of secondary education. Here again, a purely administrative classification of schools is of only minor interest. It is more useful to group schools into academic types (grammar, secondary modern, comprehensive, etc.) which offer substantially different curricula.

At the age of 15 compulsory education comes to an end and the majority of children leave school and seek employment. Even when employed, however, they may continue to receive education, mainly technical or professional, on a part-time basis. The minority who remain at school normally take public examinations and if successful pass on to a more specialized kind of education in the sixth form. So, from the age of 15 on, it becomes important to distinguish, among those who have left the educational system, between those who attend part-time courses and those who do not; and among those who remain in the educational system, between those who concentrate on science, those who concentrate on the humanities and those who continue to follow a mixed curriculum.

Those who remain at school after the age of 15 gradually drop out of it either into employment or into some other institution of advanced education, such as a technical college or a university. By the age of 25–30 even the longest type of formal education, such as medical training or postgraduate work at university, is over and virtually the whole of the male and a large part of the female population is engaged in gainful occupation. From this point we can follow them throughout their working life until, at retiring age, their home or some institution becomes the centre of such activity as is left to them. At age 100 or so the accounts close.

The accounting structure just described relates to a cross-section of human vintages alive in a particular year. In econometric terms, it provides a basis for cross-section analysis of the kind described above under 'demographic input–output'. If we could compile a set of tables like table 5 stretching over 100 years, we could pick out the information relating to successive ages in each table and thus obtain the elements for a time-series analysis of a particular human vintage.

But we are far from being able to undertake such an exercise; indeed, with the statistics as they are now, it is hard to know how best to classify the population once all regular education has ceased. Fortunately, for the immediate purpose of building models of the flow of students through the educational system this does not matter: the matrices can be partitioned at any age and the analysis concentrated on the earlier ages, on which we have fairly detailed information.

5. CONCLUSION

In this paper I have tried to bring together various forms of input–output accounting and analysis suited to dynamic problems. In the usual, static accounting system, the entries all relate to a single time-period and the set of accounts is completely closed. In the alternative, dynamic system suggested here, the inputs for a given period come, either in whole or in part, from the preceding period and the outputs go, either in whole or in part, to the succeeding period.

Two types of model can be built within the framework of this dynamic accounting structure: the conventional input–output model, in which the input coefficients are fixed; and an allocation model, in which the output coefficients are fixed. The conventional model is appropriate to the analysis of production flows; the allocation model to that of demographic flows.

These two models provide us with the main building blocks for an educational model, since as far as the human inputs are concerned the educational system is simply a partition of the demographic system, and as far as the economic inputs are concerned it is a partition of the productive system. A first attempt at combining the two was described in [69].

XIX

AN EXAMPLE OF DEMOGRAPHIC ACCOUNTING: THE SCHOOL AGES

1. INTRODUCTION

Demographic, educational and manpower statistics are usually treated as three separate subsystems in the statistical universe. Here an effort is made to connect them, and to do it in such a way as to enable us to trace through time the gradual transformation of human stocks and flows. In economics, the power of an accounting framework in co-ordinating information on flows and stocks has been increasingly recognized over the past generation. In demography, an accounting approach offers a comparable means of collating data in a way useful for analysis.

The basic building-block in our system of accounts, the population accounting matrix, with its unit of measurement, the human being, brings out clearly, in quantitative terms, the pattern of activities of the people in different age-groups and the way in which this pattern changes within a given period. As a tool for educational planning, it makes it easy to measure the flows of children and young people into, through and out of the educational system and to see how they are related to each other. The direction and volume of these flows do not stay constant through time; and even if they did, one might nevertheless wish to change them in order to obtain, let us say, more trained teachers, more mathematicians or simply a better educated population. Following this line of thought, there are three things one can do. First, one can construct a series of accounting matrices covering a sequence of years and observe how the direction and volume of the flows change from year to year. Second, one can try to understand the factors that cause the changes and so gain more insight into what would happen if circumstances were different. Finally, one can try to use this knowledge, in combination with data on costs, educational technology and available resources, to bring about desirable changes in the circumstances.

Thus in constructing population accounting matrices we have two aims in mind, one general, the other specific. The general aim is to develop a framework within which demographic, educational and other social and economic statistics can be organized into a consistent whole. The specific aim is to provide a basis for projection models of the kind elaborated in [69, XVIII].

In what follows we work up from the simplest schematic presentation of what we mean by a population accounting matrix (table 1) to a detailed numerical example relating to the school-age group in 1963–64 (table 8). The figures given in this example are provisional: they represent our first attempt to set up part of a system of demographic accounts with the help of the published information that is readily available. This information, though voluminous, is far from ideal for our purposes, so that assumptions and special knowledge are needed at many points, even to get as far as we have. But now that a start has been made the results can undoubtedly be improved, partly through discussions with people more knowledgeable than we are about the facts and partly by extending the same detailed treatment to a series of years. In this respect our work has a great deal in common with the construction of economic input–output tables.

Until we have refined and extended our estimates we shall not be in a position to use them for our specific aim, that of making projections. However, we have begun to programme the models given in [XVIII] so as to be ready to use them as soon as we can trust our figures. A trial run with our preliminary estimates has confirmed our expectations, but the figures on which it was based were too rough to make it worth publishing.

2. THE POPULATION ACCOUNTING MATRIX

As we have said, the population accounting matrix, which we shall call PAM for short, is a numerical statement of the changes that take place in the pattern of activities of the inhabitants of a given country during a given period. The first step in the construction of the matrix is to divide the population by age-group and, within each age-group, by activity: being at home, being at school, being in employment, being retired, etc. The information thus classified is then arranged as an interlocking set of rows and columns showing in what formation each age-group enters the period and how it redistributes itself among the various activities in the course of the period.

In accounting terminology this matrix is a statement of flows, not a balance sheet. These flows have two dimensions, space and time: they run not only from one activity to another and between 'our country' and 'the outside world', but also from one period into the next. Thus last year's population flows out partly along space into the outside world through death and emigration and partly along time into this year through survival. And this year's population flows in partly along space from the outside world through birth and immigration and partly along time from last year through survival.

Table 1 below shows the conceptual framework of the matrix for any one year in its simplest symbolic form.

It can be seen from this table that the destinations of $\Lambda^{-1}p$, last year's population, are partly last year's deaths and emigrations, $\Lambda^{-1}d$, and partly the survivors into this year, $\Lambda^{-1}S$, and that the sources of this year's

TABLE 1 SYMBOLIC PAM

		Outside world	Our country		Total flows
			Last year	This year	
Outside world				b'	
Our country	Last year	$\Lambda^{-1}d$		$\Lambda^{-1}S$	$\Lambda^{-1}p$
	This year				
Total flows				p'	

Note: The meaning of the symbols is as follows:

p = the vector of population flows;
b = the vector of births and immigrations;
d = the vector of deaths and emigrations;
S = the matrix of survivors;
Λ = the lag operator which shifts in time the variable to which it is applied; thus if p = this year's population flows, $\Lambda^{-1}p$ = last year's population flows and Λp = next year's population flows.

The above vectors are defined as column vectors and the addition of a prime superscript (') indicates the corresponding row of vectors.

The blank column for 'last year' and the blank row for 'this year' are not part of the matrix and are put in only to emphasize the time-lag.

population, p', are partly the survivors from last year, $\Lambda^{-1}S$, and partly the births and immigrations of this year, b'. If we imagine the row for last year subdivided into as many rows as there are age-groups and activities distinguished in the system, and the column for this year subdivided into a corresponding number of columns, we see that, to use the language of economics, this is simply a dynamic input–output table, with last year's outputs in the rows and this year's inputs in the columns. Death and emigration correspond to final output; birth and immigration correspond to primary inputs; and the matrix of survivors which links the two years together can be thought of as the matrix of intermediate products, the outputs of one stage in life being the inputs into the next.

And this brings us to the specific purpose of the exercise. As was explained in [XVIII], given the data to construct a matrix such as that summarized above, it is possible to derive from it a matrix of transition coefficients showing in what proportions each age-group has distributed itself among the various activities during 'this year'. Assuming these proportions to be fixed, the coefficient matrix can be used to forecast the distribution of the population by age and activity at any period in the future connected to the present by a series of births, death and migrations.

These proportions are not fixed, however: every year more people continue at school instead of taking a job at 15; more people go on to further education; more people move from agriculture to manufacturing; and so on. In order to estimate these trends with some accuracy it is therefore necessary to construct a chain of PAMs stretching back over several years.

Thus a single PAM is insufficient as a tool for projection. It is also incomplete from an accounting point of view in that it tells only half the story for each year, so to speak: it shows the flows out of last year but not the flows into it, and the flows into this year but not the flows out of it. If we want to close the accounts for either year, we must expand the framework to include another year. For example, let us suppose that we want to close the accounts for this year; then table 1 will become table 2 below.

TABLE 2   TWO CONSECUTIVE SYMBOLIC PAMS

| | | Outside world | Our country | | | Total flows |
			Last year	This year	Next year	
Outside world				b'	$\Lambda b'$	
Our country	Last year	$\Lambda^{-1}d$		$\Lambda^{-1}S$		$\Lambda^{-1}p$
	This year	d			S	p
	Next year					
Total flows				p'	$\Lambda p'$	

Here it can be seen, from the row and column for this year, that the sources of p' are the same as in table 1, and that the destinations of p are partly the deaths and emigrations of this year, d, and partly the survivors into next year, S. Arithmetically, the flows into this year are equal to the flows out of it, or the elements of p' equal the elements of p; that is, inputs and outputs balance.

It will be noticed that with the introduction of a new matrix the inputs into next year have automatically made their appearance. If we want to complete the accounts for next year we must introduce yet another matrix, carrying next year's survivors, ΛS, into 'the year after next'. Conversely, if we want to complete the accounts for last year we must introduce a matrix, $\Lambda^{-2}S$, showing the flow of survivors into last year from 'the year before last'. And so on, as far back as the statistics go and as far forward as our powers of projection take us.

So much for the theory of our work. When it comes to applying this theory to the real world, it is obvious that collecting and collating the data necessary for a full numerical statement of the distribution by age and activity of all the inhabitants of a country is not an easy task. We have made a start by constructing fairly detailed matrices for the youngest age-group, that is, for the under-twenties, in the population of England and Wales in five consecutive years, taking the official statistics of population and education as our point of departure. Naturally we should have liked to do this for the whole of Britain, but we had to exclude Scotland and Northern Ireland because their educational statistics are less detailed than the English ones and somewhat differently classified. In the remaining sections of this paper we shall explain the taxonomic criteria we have followed, develop a numerical example for one year and describe the statistical derivation of our figures.

3. TAXONOMY

As we said at the beginning of the preceding section, the first step in constructing a PAM is to divide the population by age and draw up a classification of activities appropriate to the different ages. In our case, since for the moment we are concerned only with the population up to the age of 19, the principal activities we must concentrate on are learning activities.

Full-time formal learning takes place first in schools—primary and secondary—and later in institutions of further education, such as universities, technical colleges, teacher training colleges, and so on. A large number of young people, however, do not continue in full-time education beyond school-leaving age but take a job, which may or may not carry with it a certain amount of part-time formal education. Thus up to school-leaving age the classification is fairly simple, consisting only of types of school; but after 15 the range of activities widens considerably and the statistical difficulties become altogether more serious.

The figures we present in our numerical example give details only for full-time formal education in primary and secondary schools; all other activities are treated in a summary way. The population is divided into twenty ages, from 0 to 19. Up to the age of 15 the activities are divided into six categories: (0) 'not at school', and five types of school, namely,

21

(1) nursery and primary, (2) secondary modern, (3) grammar, (4) comprehensive and (5) a heterogeneous group, partly composed of special schools for handicapped children, called 'other'. In theory, during the years of compulsory education, that is, between the ages of 5 and 15, the entries under the heading 'not at school' should be zero; in practice there always is a small number of children who are not at school, either for family reasons or for reasons of health. After the age of 15 category (0), 'not at school', is divided between (a) 'home and employment' and (b) 'full-time further education'; category (1), nursery and primary, disappears; and each type of secondary school is divided into two sub-groups, (c) 'under sixth form' and (d) 'sixth form'.

This is as far as we go in this paper. The next stage, on which we are working at the moment, is to expand full-time further education, at the same time extending each matrix to the age of 25. Given our specific aim, the age-group 15–25 is perhaps the most important, and we hope, when we have succeeded in tracing the flows from school into the main branches of further education, to be able to include information about subjects studied and intermediate qualifications obtained.

When this is done, we should like to divide all young people who are not receiving full-time education between those in employment (with or without part-time education) and those at home, the latter category being particularly important in the case of women; then to subdivide employment into a number of industrial categories; and finally to extend each matrix to include the whole population up to the age of 100 and over.

But this is looking a good way into the future. To return to what we have done so far, we have constructed 10 accounting matrices for the school population of England and Wales in the years 1960–61 to 1964–65, five for boys and five for girls. Each matrix shows the flows of children through the various types of school during a year. The two matrices we have been able to develop in the greatest detail are those for 1963–64, and we shall accordingly choose one of these as our example.

4. A NUMERICAL EXAMPLE

In order to show how the detailed matrix fits into the framework discussed above, we shall take as our starting-point table 1. Before going any further, however, one important point, which applies to all the numerical examples given in this paper, must be made. Notionally, the row for 'last year' should contain emigrations as well as deaths; in fact, the official statistics of migration are still rather rough, so that the best we can do with the figures at our disposal is to treat migration as a residual, that is, as the difference between the population at the beginning of the year and the population at the end, making allowance for births and deaths. This difference is entered as net immigration and added to births in the column for 'this year'. This means, of course, that all the totals in our matrices are smaller than they should be: the row totals are smaller because one output, emigrations, is missing; and the column totals are smaller because one input, immigrations, is reduced. Indeed, as we shall see later, in some cases emigrations exceed immigrations, so that this input actually becomes negative. This is regrettable but, for the moment, inevitable.

Let us now rewrite table 1 numerically, with 1963 and 1964 taking the place of 'last year' and 'this year', England and Wales taking the place of 'our country' and totals for the male population taking the place of the symbols. Then table 1 becomes table 3 below.

TABLE 3   BABY PAM FOR ENGLAND AND WALES, 1963–64.

MALES

(*thousands*)

		Outside world	England and Wales		Total flows
			1963	1964	
Outside world				485·3	
England and Wales	1963	292·4		22 937·7	23 230·1
	1964				
Total flows				23 423·0	

Here we should explain that the figures in this and in all subsequent tables are given to the nearest 100, not because we have any means of achieving this degree of accuracy as a general rule but because, when we get down to the more detailed tables, many of the entries would be needlessly rough and might even disappear if we did not adopt this unit. The problem is familiar to national accountants: no one supposes that the figures for, say, the national income are accurate to the final digit shown; but if a smaller number of digits were employed for the large totals, these totals would not be equal to the sum of their components, many of which are very small.

It can be seen from table 3 that the flows of male population through 1963 ($\Lambda^{-1}p$) totalled 23·2 million people, of whom 292 thousand died during the year ($\Lambda^{-1}d$) and 22·9 million survived into 1964 ($\Lambda^{-1}S$); and that the flows through 1964 (p') totalled 23·4 million, of whom 22·9 million were the survivors from 1963 ($\Lambda^{-1}S$) and 485 thousand were the births and net immigrations of 1964 itself (b').

If we expand these accounts to take in one more year, as in table 2, we obtain table 4 below, which brings out clearly the balance of inputs and outputs within 'this year', 1964.

If we write down the whole chain of Baby PAMs for the five years under study, 1960–61 to 1964–65, we obtain table 5 below. In this table

TABLE 4   TWO BABY PAMS FOR ENGLAND AND WALES, 1963–64
AND 1964–65. MALES

(*thousands*)

		Outside world	England and Wales			Total flows
			1963	1964	1965	
Outside world				485·3	477·8	
England and Wales	1963	292·4		22 937·7		23 230·1
	1964	274·8			23 148·2	23 423·0
	1965					
Total flows				23 423·0	23 626·0	

TABLE 5   FIVE BABY PAMS FOR ENGLAND AND WALES, 1960–61
TO 1964–65. MALES

(*thousands*)

		Outside world	England and Wales					Total flows
			1961	1962	1963	1964	1965	
Outside world			564·7	530·6	475·2	485·3	477·8	
England and Wales	1960	269·2	22 225·6					22 494·8
	1961	280·8		22 509·5				22 790·3
	1962	285·2			22 754·9			23 040·1
	1963	292·4				22 937·7		23 230·1
	1964	274·8					23 148·2	23 423·0
Total flows			22 790·3	23 040·1	23 230·1	23 423·0	23 626·0	

TABLE 6 FIVE LITTLE PAMS FOR ENGLAND AND WALES, 1960–61 TO 1964–65. MALES

(thousands)

		Outside world	1961		1962		1963		1964		1965		Total flows
		Deaths	Age 0–19	Age 20+	Age 0–19	Age 20+	Age 0–19	Age 20+	Age 0–19	Age 20+	Age 0–19	Age 20+	
Outside world	Births		417·8		431·6		438·5		451·1		443·2		
	Net Immigrations		38·8	108·1	28·2	70·8	7·8	28·9	−0·5	34·7	5·5	29·1	
1960	Age 0–18	14·9	6709·3										6 724·2
	Age 19	0·3		274·0									274·3
	Age 20+	254·0		15 242·3									15 496·3
1961	Age 0–18	13·9			6837·7								6 851·6
	Age 19	0·3				314·0							314·3
	Age 20+	266·6				15 357·8							15 624·4
1962	Age 0–18	14·5					6952·6						6 967·1
	Age 19	0·4						330·0					330·4
	Age 20+	270·3						15 472·3					15 742·6
1963	Age 0–18	14·4							7022·1				7 036·5
	Age 19	0·4								362·0			362·4
	Age 20+	277·6								15 553·6			15 831·2
1964	Age 0–18	14·1									7124·2		7 138·3
	Age 19	0·4										334·0	334·4
	Age 20+	260·3										15 690·0	15 950·3
Total flows			7165·9	15 624·4	7297·5	15 742·6	7398·9	15 831·2	7472·7	15 950·3	7572·9	16 053·1	

the blank input column for the first year in the series, 1960, and the blank output row for the last year, 1965, are omitted, since they are an unnecessary waste of space now that our point about the time-lag has been made.

If we now divide the male population into two age-groups, '0–19' (the school-age population) and '20 and over' (the rest) and separate births from net immigrations, table 5 becomes table 6 on page 309.

In table 6 we begin to see how our concept of flows and time-lags actually works. Let us ignore for the moment the boxes enclosing some of the figures, the function of which will become apparent later on, and let us look at the table as a whole. It will be noticed at once that the matrices are partitioned non-conformably: in the rows, group 0–19 is divided into two subgroups, 0–18 and 19. The reason for this is that all the survivors of group 0–18 stay within group 0–19 in the succeeding year, whereas the 19-year-olds pass in the succeeding year into the 20+ age-group and thus flow out of the school age, which alone concerns us at present.

In order to avoid possible confusion we shall give a step by step description of how the flows within a matrix are related to each other. The matrix we shall take as our example is that for 1963–64.

Starting with the first row for 1963, we see that the number of children aged 0–18 who flowed out of the year totalled 7 036 500, of whom 14 400 died within the year and 7 022 100 survived into 1964, becoming a year older in the course of that year. From the next row we see that the flow of people aged 19 totalled 362 400, of whom 400 died and 362 000 survived, becoming 20 in 1964. And from the third row, that the flows of people aged 20+ totalled 15 831 200, of whom 277 600 died and 15 553 600 survived, becoming 21+ in 1964.

Turning now to the first column for 1964, we find what appears to be a contradiction in terms: the flow into age 0, namely, the births of the year, 451 100, and the flows into ages 1–19, namely, the survivors from the preceding year, 7 022 100, add up to more than the total flow shown at the bottom of the column, 7 472 700. This anomaly is due to the negative figure of −500 for net immigrations and brings out clearly what we said at the beginning of this section about the regrettable consequences of having to treat migration as a net figure. Finally, if we look at the second column for 1964 we see that the flows into the 20+ age-group totalled 15 950 300, of whom 34 700 were net immigrations, 362 000 were the people aged 19 in 1963 who became 20 in 1964, and 15 553 600 were the people aged 20+ in 1963 who became 21+ in 1964.

The elements in each submatrix add up to the figure in the corresponding submatrix in table 5. The deaths of 1963 are $14·4 + 0·4 + 277·6 = 292·4$ thousand. The survivors into 1964 are $7 022·1 + 362·0 + 15 553·6 = 22 937·7$ thousand. And the births and net immigrations of 1964 are $451·1 − 0·5 + 34·7 = 485·3$ thousand.

Let us now concentrate on the boxes in the first row for 1963 and the first column for 1964. If we put a magnifying glass over the boxes, that is, if we divide them by years of age and subdivide each age between those 'not at school' and those 'at school', we obtain table 7 opposite.

Basically, table 7 is set out like all the preceding tables: for each age we find along the rows the deaths of 1963 *plus* the survivors into 1964, adding up to the total flows out of 1963; and down the columns we find the births and net immigrations of 1964 *plus* the survivors from 1963, adding up to the total flows into 1964. In addition, we find a first, rudimentary subdivision by activity, showing in what formation the survivors of each age flowed out of 1963 and how they rearranged themselves during 1964. For example, if we look at the survivors of age 4 into age 5, we see, row-wise, that $8 \cdot 9 + 264 \cdot 7 = 273 \cdot 6$ thousand children aged 4 were not at school when they flowed out of 1963, while $102 \cdot 4$ thousand were already at school; and, column-wise, that during 1964, when these children became 5, although a small number, $8 \cdot 9$ thousand, stayed at home, the vast majority, $264 \cdot 7 + 102 \cdot 4 = 367 \cdot 1$ thousand, went to school. Another feature of table 7 which does not appear in the preceding tables is the population stocks, that is, the totals of survivors, presented age by age as the excess of flows over deaths.

The derivation of the figures is given in some detail below, but a short summary may be useful here. The stock totals for ages 0 and 1 were calculated by us from the figures for births and deaths given in *The Statistical Review* [89]. The stock totals for ages 2–19 are simply the Government Actuary's age-by-age estimates of the population as published in *Statistics of Education* [88]; our estimates of net immigrations are derived from them, making allowance for deaths. The numbers 'at school' are derived from the age-by-age count of the school population from 2 to 19, also published in [88]. And the numbers 'not at school' are the difference between the total population and the school population. In two cases (1963, row for age 11, and 1964, column for age 11) the numbers in the school count exceed the Government Actuary's figure for the total population and this surplus is entered as a negative figure in the row and column for 'unallocated'.

Finally, let us relate table 7 to the boxes in table 6: the column for the outside world adds up to $14 \cdot 4$ thousand; the column for 'total flows 1963' adds up to $7036 \cdot 5$ thousand; the column for 'total population stocks 1.1.1964' adds up to $7022 \cdot 1$ thousand; the row for the outside world adds up to $451 \cdot 1 - 0 \cdot 5 = 450 \cdot 6$ thousand; and the row for 'total flows 1964' adds up to $7472 \cdot 7$ thousand.

The final development of PAM reached in this paper is given in table 8, in which each age is represented by a separate submatrix.

The submatrices in table 8 are arranged in exactly the same way as table 7, except for an additional row and column giving the school population for each age. In each submatrix from age 1/2 upwards the category 'at school' is divided into different types of school, and from age 14/15 upwards, further subdivided between 'under sixth form' and 'sixth form'. Again from age 14/15 upwards, the category 'not at school' is divided between 'home or employment' and 'full-time further education'.

TABLE 8   BIG PAM FOR ENGLAND AND WALES, 1963–64.
MALES: FLOWS AND STOCKS BY YEAR OF AGE

(thousands)

	Outside world	1964 Age 0 / 0
Outside world		
Outside world		451·1
Total flows 1964		(451·1)
Less 1964 deaths		−8·9
Total pop. 1.1.65		(442·2)

KEY TO SYMBOLS

0 Not at school	a Home and employment
1 Nursery, primary, etc.	b Full-time further education
2 Secondary modern	c Under sixth form
3 Grammar	d Sixth form
4 Comprehensive	
5 Other schools	

		1964 Age 1 / 0	Total flows 1963	*Less* 1963 deaths	Total pop. 1.1.64
Outside world					
1963 Age 0	0	9·1	429·4	(438·5)	−9·1	(429·4)
Total flows 1964		(429·4)			
Less 1964 deaths		−1·4			
Total pop. 1.1.65		(428·0)			

		1964 Age 2			Total flows 1963	*Less* 1963 deaths	Total pop. 1.1.64
	Outside world	0	1	5			
Outside world		−0·2					
1962 Age 1	0	1·6	419·2	1·3	0·2	(422·3)	−1·6	(420·7)
Total flows 1964		419·0	1·3	0·2			
Less 1964 deaths		−0·5					
School pop. 1.1.65			1·5				
Total pop. 1.1.65		420					

TABLE 8 (*continued*)

		Outside world	1964 Age 3			Total flows 1963	*Less* 1963 deaths	School pop. 1.1.64	Total pop. 1.1.64
			0	1	5				
Outside world			−0·7						
1963 Age 2	0	0·5	395·4	11·1	0·1	407·1	−0·5	} 1·4	} 408
	1			1·3		1·3			
	5				0·1	0·1			
Total flows 1964			394·7	12·4	0·2				
Less 1964 deaths			−0·3						
School pop. 1.1.65				12·6					
Total pop. 1.1.65				407					

		Outside world	1964 Age 4			Total flows 1963	*Less* 1963 deaths	School pop. 1.1.64	Total pop. 1.1.64
			0	1	5				
Outside world			−0·8						
1963 Age 3	0	0·3	284·6	97·5	0·2	382·6	−0·3	} 12·7	} 395
	1			12·5		12·5			
	5				0·2	0·2			
Total flows 1964			283·8	110·0	0·4				
Less 1964 deaths			−0·2						
School pop. 1.1.65				110·4					
Total pop. 1.1.65				394					

		Outside world	1964 Age 5			Total flows 1963	*Less* 1963 deaths	School pop. 1.1.64	Total pop. 1.1.64
			0	1	5				
Outside world			0·2						
1963 Age 4	0	0·2	8·9	264·1	0·6	273·8	−0·2	} 102·4	} 376
	1			102·0		102·0			
	5				0·4	0·4			
Total flows 1964			9·1	366·1	1·0				
Less 1964 deaths			−0·2						
School pop. 1.1.65				366·9					
Total pop. 1.1.65				376					

TABLE 8 (*continued*)

	Outside world	1964 Age 6			Total flows 1963	*Less* 1963 deaths	School pop. 1.1.64	Total pop. 1.1.64
		0	1	5				
Outside world		0·2						
1963 Age 5 0 1 5	0·2	3·1	1·9 363·5	0·6 0·9	5·6 363·7 0·9	−0·2 }	364·4 }	370
Total flows 1964		3·3	365·4	1·5				
Less 1964 deaths			−0·2					
School pop. 1.1.65			366·7					
Total pop. 1.1.65			370					

	Outside world	1964 Age 7			Total flows 1963	*Less* 1963 deaths	School pop. 1.1.64	Total pop. 1.1.64
		0	1	5				
Outside world			−0·8					
1963 Age 6 0 1 5	0·2	2·9	1·4 354·3	0·9 1·5	4·3 355·4 1·5	−0·2 }	356·7 }	361
Total flows 1964		2·9	354·9	2·4				
Less 1964 deaths			−0·2					
School pop. 1.1.65			357·1					
Total pop. 1.1.65			360					

	Outside world	1964 Age 8			Total flows 1963	*Less* 1963 deaths	School pop. 1.1.64	Total pop. 1.1.64
		0	1	5				
Outside world			−0·8					
1963 Age 7 0 1 5	0·2	0·2	2·0 341·3	1·1 2·4	2·2 342·6 2·4	−0·2 }	344·8 }	347
Total flows 1964		0·2	342·5	3·5				
Less 1964 deaths			−0·2					
School pop. 1.1.65			345·8					
Total pop. 1.1.65			346					

KEY TO SYMBOLS

0 Not at school	a Home and employment
1 Nursery, primary, etc.	b Full-time further education
2 Secondary modern	c Under sixth form
3 Grammar	d Sixth form
4 Comprehensive	
5 Other schools	

TABLE 8 (*continued*)

		Outside world	1964 Age 9				Total flows 1963	*Less* 1963 deaths	School pop. 1.1.64	Total pop. 1.1.64
			0	1	3	5				
Outside world				−0·9						
1963 Age 8	0	0·2	0·2	1·6			1·8	−0·2 ⎫	330·2 ⎫	332
	1			326·1	0·1	0·9	327·3	⎬	⎬	
	5					3·1	3·1	⎭	⎭	
Total flows 1964			0·2	326·8	0·1	4·0				
Less 1964 deaths				−0·1						
School pop. 1.1.65				330·8						
Total pop. 1.1.65				331						

		Outside world	1964 Age 10				Total flows 1963	*Less* 1963 deaths	School pop. 1.1.64	Total pop. 1.1.64
			0	1	3	5				
Outside world				0·1						
1963 Age 9	0	0·1	0·6	0·8			1·4	−0·1 ⎫	333·6 ⎫	335
	1			327·8	0·8	0·9	329·6	⎬	⎬	
	3				0·1		0·1			
	5					4·0	4·0	⎭	⎭	
Total flows 1964			0·6	328·7	0·9	4·9				
Less 1964 deaths				−0·1						
School pop. 1.1.65				334·4						
Total pop. 1.1.65				335						

		Unallocated	Outside world	1964 Age 11						Total flows 1963	*Less* 1963 deaths	School pop. 1.1.64	Total pop. 1.1.64
				0	1	2	3	4	5				
Unallocated				−2·4									
Outside world					−0·3	−0·3	−0·1	−0·1	−0·1				
1963 Age 10	0	−2·4	0·1		0·8	1·0	0·4	0·1	0·2	0·1	−0·1 ⎫	337·9 ⎫	338
	1				107·4	129·6	48·8	18·6	27·6	332·1	⎬	⎬	
	3						1·1			1·1			
	5								4·8	4·8	⎭	⎭	
Total flows 1964				−2·4	107·9	130·3	50·2	18·6	32·5				
Less 1964 deaths					−0·1								
School pop. 1.1.65					339·4								
Total pop 1.1.65					337								

TABLE 8 (*continued*)

	Unallocated	Outside world	1964 Age 12: 0	1	2	3	4	5	Total flows 1963	Less 1963 deaths	School pop. 1.1.64	Total pop. 1.1.64
Unallocated			−0.6						−0.6			
Outside world			0.1									
1963 Age 11 — 0	−0.6	0.1	1.0	8.8	57.2	21.0	8.4	9.6	106.0			
1					127.1	0.1	2.7	2.2	132.2			
2						50.0			50.0	−0.1	333.6	333
3							14.8		14.8			
4												
5								30.7	30.7			
Total flows 1964			0.5	8.8	184.3	71.1	25.9	42.5				
Less 1964 deaths					−0.1							
School pop. 1.1.65					332.5							
Total pop. 1.1.65					333							

	Outside World	1964 Age 13: 0	1	2	3	4	5	Total flows 1963	Less 1963 deaths	School pop. 1.1.64	Total pop. 1.1.64
Outside world				−1.0			0.1				
1963 Age 12 — 0		0.7			0.3	0.7	0.5	2.2			
1			3.1		5.8		0.1	9.0			
2	0.1			186.1	0.1	3.8	3.4	193.5	−0.1	333.8	336
3					70.8			70.8			
4						21.2		21.2			
5							39.4	39.4			
Total flows 1964		0.7	3.1	185.1	77.0	25.7	43.5				
Less 1964 deaths				−0.1							
School pop. 1.1.65				334.3							
Total pop. 1.1.65				335							

	Outside world	1964 Age 14: 0	1	2	3	4	5	Total flows 1963	Less 1963 deaths	School pop. 1.1.64	Total pop. 1.1.64
Outside world		−0.1		−0.4	−0.1		−0.2				
1963 Age 13 — 0		3.0						3.0			
1			0.1		3.3	0.1		3.5			
2	0.1			190.6	0.1	4.0	3.4	198.2	−0.1	342.0	345
3					76.8	0.5		77.3			
4						21.4		21.4			
5							41.7	41.7			
Total flows 1964		2.9	0.1	190.2	80.1	26.0	44.9				
Less 1964 deaths				−0.2							
School pop. 1.1.65				341.1							
Total pop. 1.1.65				344							

TABLE 8 (*continued*)

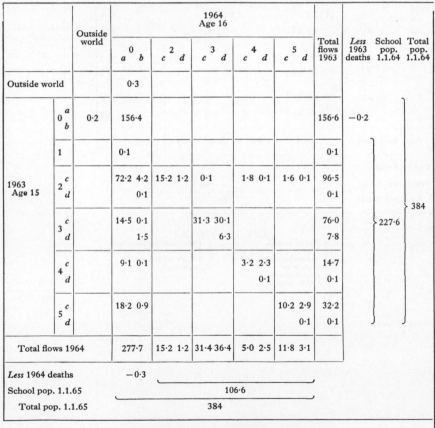

1964 Age 15

	Outside world	0 a	0 b	2 c	2 d	3 c	3 d	4 c	4 d	5 c	5 d	Total flows 1963	*Less* 1963 deaths	School pop. 1.1.64	Total pop. 1.1.64
Outside world		0·2													
1963 Age 14 0		4·8										4·8			
1	0·2	0·3										0·3			
2		102·5	5·1	92·1	0·0	0·1		4·2		3·5		207·7	−0·2	356·2	361
3		2·6	0·2			72·3	7·8					82·9			
4		9·0	0·1					12·7	0·1			21·9			
5		13·6	0·5							29·3	0·2	43·6			
Total flows 1964		138·9		92·1	0·0	72·4	7·8	16·9	0·1	32·8	0·2				

Less 1964 deaths −0·2

School pop. 1.1.65 222·3

Total pop. 1.1.65 361

1964 Age 16

		Outside world	0 a	0 b	2 c	2 d	3 c	3 d	4 c	4 d	5 c	5 d	Total flows 1963	*Less* 1963 deaths	School pop. 1.1.64	Total pop. 1.1.64
Outside world			0·3													
1963 Age 15	0 a / b	0·2	156·4										156·6	−0·2		
	1		0·1										0·1			
	2 c		72·2	4·2	15·2	1·2	0·1		1·8	0·1	1·6	0·1	96·5		227·6	384
	2 d			0·1									0·1			
	3 c		14·5	0·1			31·3	30·1					76·0			
	3 d			1·5				6·3					7·8			
	4 c		9·1	0·1					3·2	2·3			14·7			
	4 d									0·1			0·1			
	5 c		18·2	0·9							10·2	2·9	32·2			
	5 d											0·1	0·1			
Total flows 1964			277·7		15·2	1·2	31·4	36·4	5·0	2·5	11·8	3·1				

Less 1964 deaths −0·3

School pop. 1.1.65 106·6

Total pop. 1.1.65 384

KEY TO SYMBOLS

0 Not at school
1 Nursery, primary, etc.
2 Secondary modern
3 Grammar
4 Comprehensive
5 Other schools

a Home and employment
b Full-time further education
c Under sixth form
d Sixth form

TABLE 8 (*continued*)

		Outside world	1964 Age 17										Total flows 1963	*Less* 1963 deaths	School pop. 1.1.64	Total pop. 1.1.64
			0		2		3		4		5					
			a	b	c	d	c	d	c	d	c	d				
Outside world			1·4													
1963 Age 16	0 a / b	0·3	312·9										313·2	−0·3		
	2 c / d		11·5 0·6	1·4	1·3	0·5 0·4			0·2	0·1	0·2	0·1	13·8 / 2·5		112·1	425
	3 c / d		13·3 2·7	4·6			3·3	17·2 32·8					33·8 / 40·1			
	4 c / d		2·0 1·1	0·3					0·5 1·3	1·6			4·1 / 2·7			
	5 c / d		8·0 0·5	0·8							1·6	1·8 2·4	11·4 / 3·7			
Total flows 1964			361·1		1·3	0·9	3·3	50·0	0·7	3·0	1·8	4·3				

Less 1964 deaths	−0·4
School pop. 1.1.65	65·3
Total pop. 1.1.65	426

KEY TO SYMBOLS

0 Not at school	a Home and employment
1 Nursery, primary, etc.	b Full-time further education
2 Secondary modern	c Under sixth form
3 Grammar	d Sixth form
4 Comprehensive	
5 Other schools	

TABLE 8 *(continued)*

		Outside world	0 a	0 b	2 c	2 d	3 c	3 d	4 c	4 d	5 c	5 d	Total flows 1963	*Less* 1963 deaths	School pop. 1.1.64	Total pop. 1.1.64
Outside world			1·4													
1963 Age 17	0 a / b	0·3	335·5										335·8	−0·3		
	2 c		0·8		0·1								0·9			
	2 d		0·5	0·3	0·2					0·1			1·1			
	3 c		3·3				0·3						3·6		58·5	394
	3 d		12·7	12·6				19·6					44·9			
	4 c		0·1						0·1	0·1			0·3			
	4 d		1·0	0·4						1·1			2·5			
	5 c		1·2								0·3	0·1	1·6			
	5 d		0·8	1·3								1·5	3·6			
Total flows 1964			371·9		0·3		0·3	19·6	0·1	1·3	0·3	1·6				
Less 1964 deaths			−0·1													
School pop. 1.1.65							23·5									
Total pop 1.1.65							395									

TABLE 8 (*continued*)

	Outside world	1964 Age 19 – 0 *a*	0 *b*	3 *c*	3 *d*	4 *c*	4 *d*	5 *c*	5 *d*	Total flows 1963	*Less* 1963 deaths	School pop. 1.1.64	Total pop. 1.1.64
Outside world		2·4											
1963 Age 18 — 0 *a* / *b*	0·4	314·0								314·4	−0·4		
2 *c* / *d*		0·1								0·1			
3 *c* / *d*		2·4 11·7		1·7						15·8		18·0	332
4 *c* / *d*		0·3 0·3				0·2				0·8			
5 *c* / *d*		0·5 0·6						0·1		1·2			
5 *d*									0·1	0·1			
Total flows 1964		332·3		1·7		0·2		0·1	0·1				
Less 1964 deaths		−0·4											
School pop. 1.1.65				2·1									
Total pop. 1.1.65				334									

On the whole, the flows shown in the submatrices are easy to interpret. By this we do not mean, of course, that they are all accurate, but only that they seem fairly consistent with each other. Wherever the marginal totals left us some choice in the arrangement of the flows between schools, we have made use of what inside knowledge we had and, failing that, of our common sense to allocate these flows realistically; an example of this are the flows between grammar schools, secondary moderns and comprehensives.

Here and there, however, the constraints imposed by the marginal totals give rise to obvious inconsistencies. For instance, at age 11/12 the figure of −600 unallocated, due to the excess of the school population over the total population, has forced us to leave the cell at the intersection of row-and-column 0, 'not at school', empty and to show a flow of 1000 children leaving school at the age of 12, which seems improbable and indeed does not tally with the pattern of flows in the contiguous ages.

The submatrices for ages 14/15 upwards are not quite complete: the four cells at the intersection of rows and columns 0 (*a*) and 0 (*b*) are spanned by a single figure. This is due to the fact that, while we know the destination of school leavers into either further education or other activities in the year in which they leave school, we have not followed their progress beyond that. When we have completed our study of further education we shall be able to show the year-by-year transitions from one stage of further education to another and between further education and other activities.

Before closing this section we should say that, although we have already talked about our work with our friends in the Department of Education and Science, they bear no responsibility for our figures. In this paper we are following our usual practice of making a first shot with the information available so as to have something definite to discuss with the people who are expert in the different areas we cover. At the next round, when we come to revise our provisional estimates, we hope to learn much from this expertise and to improve our estimates accordingly.

5. NOTES ON THE DERIVATION OF THE FIGURES

(a) *The definition of age.* In all our tables, age is reckoned in each year as *age at 1 January of the following year*. For example, the children in the columns headed '1964, age 2' arc all the children who are recorded as being aged 2 on 1 January 1965. The logic of this is obvious: the children born in 1964 will still be aged 0 on 1 January 1965, those who have their first birthday during 1964 will still be aged 1 on 1 January 1965, those who have their second birthday during 1964 will still be aged 2 on 1 January 1965, and so on.

(b) *Births and deaths.* The figures for births are taken directly from [89], which gives the number of live births in each calendar year. The figures for deaths are derived from the same source with one adjustment. In [89], deaths are recorded by age at death. Our figures relate to age at 1 January. For age 0 the adjustment, which as far as children are concerned is important only in infancy, has been made by taking, quarter by quarter, appropriate proportions of the deaths recorded at various periods of the first year of life. This gives an estimate of the number of deaths occurring among children born within the calendar year (our age 0), and the remaining number of 0-year-old deaths is transferred to our age 1. Similarly, some of the 1-year-old deaths are transferred to our age 2, and so on.

(c) *Population.* For ages 0 and 1 the population is estimated by us from the statistics of births and deaths from 1959 (needed to calculate the 1-year-olds in 1960) to 1965. For ages 2–19 it is taken directly from the Government Actuary's end-of-year estimates published in [88]. For the age-group 20 and over it is calculated by us by first adjusting the Registrar General's mid-year estimate for 1963 to the end of that year and then

22

combining this figure with the series of deaths and migrations of the age-group to generate figures for other years with the help of the accounting constraints.

(d) *Migration.* No official estimates of migration are published for ages 0 and 1. For ages 2–19 each of our figures of net immigration is obtained as a residual from the Government Actuary's estimates of population in [88], making allowance for deaths. The figures for the 20 and over age-group are obtained by subtracting net immigrations in the age-group 2–19 from total net immigrations as calculated by us on the basis of the Registrar General's estimates in [89]. For most years these estimates take the form of a single total for both sexes, but in the estimate for 1962–63 the sexes are distinguished and we have used this information to calculate the proportion of males in the other years.

(e) *Category 0, 'not at school'.* For ages 0 and 1 this category covers the whole population. For ages 2–19, it is the excess of the Government Actuary's estimates of total population over the Department of Education's count of the school population, both given age by age in table 6 of the 1964 issue and table 11 of the 1965 issue of [88, pt. 1].

(f) *Unallocated.* In the two years with which we are concerned, the figure for the school population of age 11 exceeds the figure for the total population of the same age. This excess is entered as an 'unallocated' negative figure against category 0 in our submatrices for ages 10/11 and 11/12.

(g) *School categories.* All our figures for primary, secondary and further education are derived from [88]. The basic information on the number of children in primary and secondary education is taken from tables 6 in the 1964 issue and 11 in the 1965 issue. These tables give an annual count of all children in primary and secondary schools, classified by age at 1 January and by type of school. In them, schools are grouped under administrative headings: maintained by local educational authorities, direct grant, independent recognized as efficient, other independent. We have preferred to group them according to their educational character, namely: (1) nursery and primary, (2) secondary modern, (3) grammar, (4) comprehensive and (5) other. The correspondence between our classification and the official one is as follows:

1. Nursery and primary
    Schools maintained by local education authorities:
    Infants
    Junior with infants

Junior without infants
All-age (ages 2–10)
Nursery
Direct grant schools:
Nursery
Lower grammar
Independent schools recognized as efficient:
Nursery
Primary
Primary and secondary (ages 2–10)
Other independent schools:
Nursery
Primary
Primary and secondary (ages 2–10)

2. Secondary modern

Schools maintained by local education authorities:
Modern

3. Grammar

Schools maintained by local education authorities:
Grammar
Direct grant schools:
Upper grammar
Independent schools recognized as efficient:
Secondary
Primary and secondary (ages 11 and over)

4. Comprehensive

Schools maintained by local education authorities:
Comprehensive

5. Other

Schools maintained by local education authorities:
All-age (ages 11 and over)
Technical
Bilateral and multilateral
Other secondary
Special (other than hospital)
Special (hospital)
Direct grant schools:
Special (other than hospital)
Special (hospital)
Institution and technical

Other independent schools:
Secondary
Primary and secondary (ages 11 and over)

Primary education normally goes up to age 11, and so we have included all-age schools and schools spanning both primary and secondary education in category (1) for all children up to the age of 10 inclusive. For children aged 11 and over these schools are included in one of the secondary school categories. However, some children whose eleventh birthday occurs late in the year are unlikely to move until the following year, and we intend to make an adjustment for this later on.

(*h*) *School flows.* The flows into, through and out of our five types of school are calculated as follows. The school categories in table 6 (11) of [88] are regrouped as shown in subsection *g* above and the numbers of children in each age added up according to our classification. Thus we obtain the total number of children of each age in each of our five categories at 1 January 1964 and 1 January 1965. This gives us the marginal totals for a 1963 × 1964 matrix of survivors. We then compare, category by category, the number of children in each age at January 1964 with the number in the succeeding age at January 1965: the number of 12-year-olds at grammar school, say, at January 1964 with the number of 13-year-olds at grammar school at January 1965. The smaller number is taken to represent those children who have remained in the same category from one year to the next. The difference indicates a flow to or from the other categories: if the first-year number is the smaller, then during the second year there must be an input from one or more of the other categories; if it is the larger, then there must be an output into the other categories.

The flows are of necessity net flows, and we have tried to establish their directions on as rational a basis as possible, bearing in mind the changes that are taking place in school nomenclature, the most obvious being the change from secondary modern to comprehensive.

(*i*) *School leavers.* The most detailed information available on school leavers comes from the school-leaver survey published in *Statistics of Education.* This survey is based on a 10 per cent sample of schools and records the numbers leaving different school categories in each term of the academic year by age at leaving. By combining the leavers in the spring and summer terms of the academic year 1963–64 with those in the autumn term of the academic year 1964–65, we can derive a total for the calendar year 1964 for each school category except other independent schools and special schools, which are not included in the survey. These totals, of course, will refer to age at time of leaving.

However, for the two broad categories 'all maintained schools' and 'all schools' the information in the survey is retabulated so that it is possible to work out how many children in each age-group had a birthday between 1 January and time of leaving. For the first of these categories in 1964 we can set out the information as follows.

BOYS LEAVING ALL MAINTAINED SCHOOLS IN 1964

	15	16	17	18	19	20	Total
(1) Age at leaving	203 310	64 060	24 250	22 980	5 380		319 980
(2) No birthday between 1 Jan., 1964, and leaving	72 050	23 380	9 720	8 270	1 850		115 270
(3) Birthday between 1 Jan., 1964, and leaving	131 260	40 680	14 530	14 710	3 530		204 710
(3) Age at 1 Jan. 1965: row (2) at age $x-1$ plus row (3) at age x	131 260	112 730	37 910	24 430	11 800	1 850	319 980

Thus, if we look at the first column, we see that of the 203 310 leavers who were aged 15 at time of leaving, only 72 050 were already aged 15 at 1 January 1964, and 131 260 had their fifteenth birthday after that date. Conversely, to obtain leavers classified by age at 1 January 1965, we have to add together information from adjacent columns: the 112 730 leavers aged 16 at 1 January 1965 are made up of 72 050 who were still aged 15 when they left and 40 680 who were already 16 when they left.

Information of this kind is not available for detailed school categories, but net information can be obtained by comparing successive school counts. If we use this source we obtain information on our standard definition of age but we cannot take account of children who change their category of school. Thus we obtain a figure of leavers which is too high for any category of school from which children are on balance transferring to other categories, and too low for any category to which children are transferring from other categories.

For some school categories transfers in and out are small and any discrepancy between the survey and the count can be attributed to sampling errors in the survey and the figures adjusted to agree with those in the count. This is the position in the case of the large category 'all maintained schools' but it is not the position with the components of this category. For example, we found by comparing successive counts that we were getting too many 'apparent' leavers from secondary modern schools and too few from comprehensives and other maintained schools. We dealt with this problem by transferring boys from each age group in the correct proportions for an average secondary modern school to the other categories. Having done this we then made the necessary adjustments to yield our standard definition of age.

As regards direct grant schools and independent schools recognized as efficient, the differences between the survey and the count were so small that we again attributed them to sampling errors. The survey does not cover other independents and special schools and in their case we have, for the moment, applied to the count the same analysis of birthdays as that made for other maintained schools.

(*j*) *Destination of leavers.* The school-leaver survey in [88] gives information on the destination of leavers under the following headings:

> University
> Colleges of advanced technology
> Colleges of education
> Other full-time education
> Temporary employment (pending entry into full-time further education not later than September/October of the following year)
> Other employment

For the moment we are not using all these distinctions but have simply divided leavers into two categories: (*a*) home and employment and (*b*) full-time further education.

The information about the destination of leavers in the survey relates to academic years and not to individual terms. As a consequence we have had to assume that the distribution of leavers between full-time further education and employment is the same for the calendar year 1964 as for the academic year 1963–64, and have applied it to the estimates of leavers derived from the school count. Although from the age of 15 upwards we can introduce a new activity, full-time further education, for the moment we can channel into it only the leavers of 1964. In other words, we can show where leavers go when they leave, but until we have studied the flows through and out of further education we cannot say anything about the present activity of past leavers.

(*k*) *Sixth form.* From the age of 15 upwards we have divided each type of secondary school into two subgroups: (*c*) under sixth form and (*d*) sixth form. In [88] there are two tables relating to sixth-form pupils, one giving the number of pupils by age, the other the number by subject and year of course. It should be explained that year of course does not necessarily mean year in sixth form; that is, it is quite possible to have spent two years in sixth form but to have completed only one year of course. For the moment, however, since there is no cross-tabulation of sixth-formers by year of course and year of age, we have taken year of course to be synonymous with year in sixth form.

This lack of cross-tabulation also makes it difficult to say anything very definite about drop-out rates. We have tried various ways of estimating these, and although a method was devised for calculating transition ratios from one year of course to the next at different ages, it was not generally applicable because of the transfers between schools, about which we have no information. So, while we have used these ratios wherever possible, we have had to rely on more subjective assessments to fill in many of the cells in the rows and columns for sixth form within the arithmetical and accounting constraints of PAM.

As we have no information on the destination of sixth-form leavers as opposed to under-sixth-form leavers, we have assumed that sixth-formers are more likely than under-sixth-formers to go on to further education. So, having calculated the number of leavers going on to further education, we have made up that number wherever possible from sixth-form leavers.

6. CONCLUSIONS

The experience reported in this paper suggests a number of conclusions on a range of topics which can be summarized as follows.

(*a*) *Definitions and classifications.* Every subject has its problems of definition and classification and this one is no exception. For example, if we were asked 'what is a sixth form?' our reply would be that for all practical purposes it is anything so described in [88]. Looking at the matter from a more critical point of view we should say that sixth-form work is essentially the preparation for A-level examinations. If we look at [88] we can see that the majority of sixth-formers are indeed engaged on A-level work but that there is a minority who are not. The proportions, however, vary considerably from one type of school to another, so that for some of the less academic schools the term 'sixth form' is associated more with the age of the students than with the work they are doing. We also know that A-level work can be done in establishments of further education, which are not technically 'schools'. All this is reminiscent of the definition of income as 'what the tax authorities regard as such'. In this and many other cases there is room for making definitions more precise, granted all the difficulties of choosing between an institutional and a functional classification.

Another kind of problem arises where a classification must serve more than one purpose. For example, we have grouped schools into five broad categories which are intended to reflect academic rather than administrative distinctions. But when, at a later stage in our work, we come to look into the cost structures of different educational establishments, we may find our decision an embarrassment, because financial data are likely to be based on administrative distinctions. In so far as data ultimately come from educational establishments, it may be possible to solve this difficulty be retabulation. But we cannot say anything constructive until both aspects of the problem have been studied.

(*b*) *The period of account.* Largely because in England and Wales the school count relates to January of each year, we have chosen to record flows over the ends of calendar years. Our task is eased by the fact that, although the population estimates made by the Registrar General relate to mid-year, for the population of school age the Government Actuary makes estimates relating to end-year. From an educational point of view it would be better to switch to academic years and to some extent we shall suffer from the choice we have made when we come to integrate statistics of further education into our matrix. But from other points of view the choice of an academic year would not be ideal: manpower statistics usually relate to mid-year; the national economic accounts relate to calendar years and so do national wealth estimates, at any rate for Britain [52]; the government financial accounts start from the second quarter of the year; and so on. In the end, no doubt, we shall be driven to quarterly estimates. But for the moment we propose to stay with our original choice, without excluding the possibility of producing alternative accounts for academic years.

(c) *The recording of age.* A recurrent problem in our work has been the need to convert all the data we have used to a uniform definition of age. We have chosen age at 1 January, which is also the definition adopted for the school count in [88]. However, many of the other data in [88], and most data in other publications, are classified by the age at which something happens: somebody leaves school, or receives a first employment book, or dies. The technical difficulties of making these adjustments are usually not very great but, as there is a large number of them to be made, an enormous amount of time could be saved if a standard definition of age were more widely adopted in statistical tabulations.

(d) *Ages and grades.* Until the sixth form is reached, British school statistics contain only information about ages and none about grades. For purposes of demographic accounting this is the better way round because it provides a direct link between demographic and educational data. This link would be much more difficult to forge if, as in many countries of continental Europe, school statistics were classified by grade with no information about age.

(e) *Incomplete tabulation.* Cases arise where the data collected are not fully tabulated, so that the missing information has to be estimated. For example, the data on sixth-form pupils are given in [88] in two separate tables, each drawn up on a different classification: the numbers in each age without reference to stage and the numbers at each stage without reference to age, and this forces us into a lot of uncertain calculations. A more complete tabulation would greatly contribute to the accuracy of the estimates.

(f) *Types of information.* Speaking generally, there are three types of information that can be used in demographic accounting:

(i)   Statistics of stocks from which only net flows can be inferred. The obvious example in our case is the annual school count. Such information combined with accounting constraints is hardly ever sufficient to determine even the distribution of net flows, and reliance must usually be placed on a knowledge of what flows are possible and which are likely to be large and which small.

(ii) Statistics of stocks in which the activity of members a year ago is also recorded. Such information would resolve most of the difficulties inherent in (i). It should be fairly easy to obtain for school populations, and its existence would greatly increase the accuracy of the transition coefficients that we are trying to measure.

(iii) Individual-data systems, in which the important events in the career of each individual are brought together in a single record. This type of information is the ultimate ideal, since it permits individual characteristics to be introduced into the classification system and retained at points in a series of matrices that are not directly connected. This is of some consequence because, with existing statistics, categories have a way of disappearing before they are really useful. For example, in educational statistics school leavers are classified by type of school, but in manpower statistics new entrants are classified with no reference to their education, so that this particular characteristic, which is so important both from a social and an economic point of view, is lost for ever.

These are some of the problems that we think will have to be resolved if demographic accounts are to achieve the accuracy now expected of economic accounts. Fortunately, statistical systems are everywhere on the move, and before long we may expect to see great strides forward in the subject-matter of this paper.

A LIST OF WORKS CITED

In every essay except essay IX, which has its own bibliography, the roman numerals in square brackets refer to the other essays in this book, and the arabic numerals refer to the entries in the following list.

1. ADY, Peter, and Michel COURCIER. *Systems of National Accounts in Africa.* O.E.E.C., Paris, 1960.
2. AITCHISON, J., and J. A. C. BROWN. A synthesis of Engel curve theory. *The Review of Economic Studies*, vol. XXII, no. 57, 1954–55, pp. 35–46.
3. AITCHISON, J., and J. A. C. BROWN. *The Lognormal Distribution.* Cambridge University Press, 1957.
4. BODEWIG, E. *Matrix Calculus.* North-Holland Publishing Co., Amsterdam, 1959 (p. 217).
5. BURLEY, H. T. A programming language for linear algebra. *Computer Journal*, vol. 10, no. 1, 1967, pp. 69–73.
6. CAMBRIDGE, DEPARTMENT OF APPLIED ECONOMICS. *A Computable Model of Economic Growth.* No. 1 in *A Programme for Growth.* Chapman and Hall, London, 1962.
7. CAMBRIDGE, DEPARTMENT OF APPLIED ECONOMICS. *A Social Accounting Matrix for 1960.* No. 2 in *A Programme for Growth.* Chapman and Hall, London, 1962.
8. CAMBRIDGE, DEPARTMENT OF APPLIED ECONOMICS. *Input–Output Relationships, 1954–1966.* No. 3 in *A Programme for Growth.* Chapman and Hall, London, 1963.
9. CAMBRIDGE, DEPARTMENT OF APPLIED ECONOMICS. *Capital, Output and Employment, 1948 to 1960.* No. 4 in *A Programme for Growth.* Chapman and Hall, London, 1964.
10. CAMBRIDGE, DEPARTMENT OF APPLIED ECONOMICS. *The Model in Its Environment: a Progress Report.* No. 5 in *A Programme for Growth.* Chapman and Hall, London, 1964.
11. CAMBRIDGE, DEPARTMENT OF APPLIED ECONOMICS. *Exploring 1970: Some Numerical Results.* No. 6 in *A Programme for Growth.* Chapman and Hall, London, 1965.
12. CAMBRIDGE, DEPARTMENT OF APPLIED ECONOMICS. *Exploring 1972, with Special Reference to the Balance of Payments.* No. 9 in *A Programme for Growth.* Chapman and Hall, London, 1970.
13. CLARK, Colin. *National Income and Outlay.* Macmillan, London, 1937.
14. COPELAND, M. A. National wealth and income – an interpretation. *Journal of the American Statistical Association*, vol. XXX, no. 190, 1935, pp. 377–86.
15. COPELAND, M. A. Concepts of national income. In *Studies in Income and Wealth*, vol. 1, pp. 3–63, and especially p. 63. National Bureau of Economic Research, New York, 1937.
16. DENISON, Edward F. Report on tripartite discussions of national income measurement. In *Studies in Income and Wealth*, vol. 10, pp. 3–22. National Bureau of Economic Research, New York, 1947.

17. DURBIN, J. A note on regression when there is extraneous information about one of the coefficients. *Journal of the American Statistical Association*, vol. 48, no. 264, 1953, pp. 799–808.

18. DURBIN, J., and G. S. WATSON. Testing for serial correlation in least squares regression, I and II. *Biometrika*, vol. 37, pts. 3 and 4, 1950, pp. 409–28, and vol. 38, pts. 1 and 2, 1951, pp. 159–78.

19. DUVAL, A., E. FONTELA, and G. McNEIL. *Explor 80: A Computable Model for Europe*. Paper presented at the European Econometric Society meeting, Brussels, 1969. Mimeographed.

20. EUROPEAN ECONOMIC COMMUNITY, STATISTICAL OFFICE. *Input–Output-Tabellen für die Länder der Europäischen Wirtschaftgemeinschaft*. E.E.C., Brussels, 1964.

21. FONTELA, E., and A. DUVAL. *Changes in Relative Prices and Technical Coefficients*. Mimeographed, October 1967.

22. FORSYTH, F. G. The relationship between family size and family expenditure. *Journal of the Royal Statistical Society, Series A (General)*, vol. 123, pt. 4, 1960, pp. 367–97.

23. FRISCH, Ragnar, and Frederick V. WAUGH. Partial time regressions as compared with individual trends. *Econometrica*, vol. 1, no. 4, 1933, pp. 387–401.

24. GEARY, R. C. A note on 'A constant-utility index of the cost of living'. *The Review of Economic Studies*, vol. XVIII, no. 45, 1949–50, pp. 65–6.

25. GHOSH, A. *Experiments with Input–Output Models*. Cambridge University Press, 1964.

26. GILBERT, Milton, and Irving B. KRAVIS. *An International Comparison of National Products and the Purchasing Power of Currencies*. O.E.E.C., Paris, 1954.

27. GILBERT, Milton, and associates. *Comparative National Products and Price Levels*. O.E.E.C., Paris, 1958.

28. GRUENBAUM (GAATHON), Ludwig. *National Income and Outlay in Palestine, 1936*. Economic Research Institute of the Jewish Agency for Palestine, Jerusalem, 1941.

29. HICKS, J. R. *The Social Framework*. The Clarendon Press, Oxford, 1942: 2nd edition, 1952.

30. INTERNATIONAL ASSOCIATION FOR RESEARCH IN INCOME AND WEALTH. *Income and Wealth Series*. Bowes and Bowes, London. Series I to IX appeared between 1951 and 1961.

31. INTERNATIONAL ASSOCIATION FOR RESEARCH IN INCOME AND WEALTH. *Bibliography on Income and Wealth*. Bowes and Bowes, London. Volumes I to VI, covering the years 1937–1954, appeared between 1952 and 1958.

32. KENDALL, M. G. *The Advanced Theory of Statistics*, vol. II. Griffin, London, 1946.

33. KLEIN, L. R., and H. RUBIN. A constant-utility index of the cost of living. *The Review of Economic Studies*, vol. XV, no. 38, 1947–48, pp. 84–7.

34. LEONTIEF, Wassily. Inter-regional theory. In *Studies in the Structure of the American Economy*. Oxford University Press, New York, 1953.

35. LESLIE, P. H. On the use of matrices in certain population mathematics. *Biometrika*, vol. XXXIII, pt. III, 1945, pp. 183–212.

36. LYDALL, H. F. Saving and wealth. *Australian Economic Papers*, December 1963, pp. 228–50.

37. MARKOWITZ, Harry M. *Portfolio Selection*. Cowles Foundation, monograph 16. John Wiley, New York, 1959.

38. MEADE, J. E., and Richard STONE. The construction of tables of national income, expenditure, savings and investment. *The Economic Journal*, vol. LI, no. 202–3, 1941, pp. 216–33.

39. MENDERSHAUSEN, Horst. Annual survey of statistical technique: methods of computing and eliminating changing seasonal fluctuations. *Econometrica*, vol. 5, no. 3, 1937, pp. 234–62.

40. NICHOLSON, J. L. The general form of the adding-up criterion. *Journal of the Royal Statistical Society, Series A (General)*, vol. 120, pt. 1, 1957, pp. 84–5.

41. ORGANISATION FOR EUROPEAN ECONOMIC CO-OPERATION. *A Simplified System of National Accounts.* O.E.E.C., Paris, 1950; reprinted, 1951.

42. ORGANISATION FOR EUROPEAN ECONOMIC CO-OPERATION. *A Standardised System of National Accounts.* O.E.E.C., Paris, 1952: *1958 Edition*, 1959.

43. ORGANISATION FOR EUROPEAN ECONOMIC CO-OPERATION. *Statistics of National Product and Expenditure: 1938, 1947 to 1952.* O.E.E.C., Paris, 1954; no. 2 (to 1955), 1957.

44. ORGANISATION FOR EUROPEAN ECONOMIC CO-OPERATION. *Statistics of Sources and Uses of Finance, 1948–1958.* O.E.E.C., Paris, 1960.

45. ORGANISATION FOR EUROPEAN ECONOMIC CO-OPERATION. *Regional Economic Planning.* O.E.E.C. (E.P.A.), Paris, 1961.

46. ORGANISATION FOR ECONOMIC CO-OPERATION AND DE-VELOPMENT (formerly O.E.E.C.). *Mathematical Models in Educational Planning.* O.E.C.D., Paris, 1967.

47. ORGANISATION FOR ECONOMIC CO-OPERATION AND DE-VELOPMENT. *General Statistics.* O.E.C.D., Paris, monthly.

48. PAELINCK, Jean. *Fonctions de consommation pour la Belgique, 1948–1959.* Facultés Universitaires N-D de la Paix, Namur, 1964.

49. PAIGE, Deborah, and Gottfried BOMBACH. *A Comparison of National Output and Productivity of the United Kingdom and the United States.* O.E.E.C., Paris, 1959.

50. PRAIS, S. J., and H. S. HOUTHAKKER. *The Analysis of Family Budgets.* Cambridge University Press, 1955.

51. PYATT, G. A production functional model. In *Econometric Analysis for National Economic Planning.* Butterworths, London, 1964.

52. REVELL, Jack, and others. *The Wealth of the Nation.* Cambridge University Press, 1967.

53. ROSSI, Sergio. Stime di modelli con metodi alternativi mediante calcolatore elettronico. In *Modelli Econometrici per la Programmazione.* Scuola di Statistica dell' Università, Firenze, 1965.

54. SAMUELSON, Paul A. Some implications of 'linearity'. *The Review of Economic Studies*, vol. XV, no. 38, 1947–48, pp. 88–90.

55. SCHUMACHER, H. Das input-output-system des Statistischen Amtes der Europäischen Gemeinschaften. *Statistische Informationen*, no. 2, 1964, pp. 13–36.

56. SOLARI, L. *Sur l'estimation du système linéaire de dépenses par la méthode du maximum de vraisemblance.* Centre d'Econométrie, Université de Genève, 1969. Mimeographed.

57. SOLARI, L. *Expériences récentes sur l'estimation du système linéaire de dépenses.* Centre d'Econométrie, Université de Genève, 1969. Mimeographed.

58. SOLARI, L. *Sur l'estimation des fonctions de consommation semi-agregées.* Centre d'Econométrie, Université de Genève, 1969. Mimeographed.

59. STONE, Richard. Linear expenditure systems and demand analysis: an application to the pattern of British demand. *The Economic Journal*, vol. LXIV, no. 255, 1954, pp. 511–27.

60. STONE, Richard. *Quantity and Price Indexes in National Accounts*. O.E.E.C., Paris, 1956.

61. STONE, Richard. A dynamic model of demand (in Polish). *Przeglad Statystyczny*, vol. VII, no. 3, 1960, pp. 255–70. English version published in [71].

62. STONE, Richard. *Input–Output and National Accounts*. O.E.E.C., Paris, 1961.

63. STONE, Richard. Social accounts at the regional level: a survey. In *Regional Economic Planning: Techniques of Analysis*. O.E.E.C., Paris, 1961. Reprinted in [71].

64. STONE, Richard. Multiple classifications in social accounting. *Bulletin de l'Institut International de Statistique*, vol. XXXIX, no. 3, 1962, pp. 215–33. Reprinted in [71].

65. STONE, Richard. Models of the national economy for planning purposes. *Operational Research Quarterly*, vol. 14, no. 1, 1963, pp. 51–9. Reprinted in [71].

66. STONE, Richard. Private saving in Britain, past, present and future. *The Manchester School of Economic and Social Studies*, vol. XXXII, no. 2, 1964, pp. 79–112. Reprinted in [71].

67. STONE, Richard. The changing pattern of consumption. In *Problems of Economic Dynamics and Planning*. Polish Scientific Publishers (PWN), Warsaw, 1964. Reprinted in [71].

68. STONE, Richard. Transitional planning. In *On Political Economy and Econometrics*. Polish Scientific Publishers (PWN), Warsaw, 1964. Reprinted in [71].

69. STONE, Richard. A model of the educational system. *Minerva*, vol. III, no. 2, 1965, pp. 172–86. Reprinted in [71].

70. STONE, Richard. The Cambridge Growth Project. *Cambridge Research*, October 1965, pp. 9–15.

71. STONE, Richard. *Mathematics in the Social Sciences and Other Essays*. Chapman and Hall, London, 1966.

72. STONE, Richard, J. AITCHISON, and J. A. C. BROWN. Some estimation problems in demand analysis. *The Incorporated Statistician*, vol. 5, no. 4, 1955, pp. 165–77.

73. STONE, Richard, and J. A. C. BROWN. Output and investment for exponential growth in consumption. *The Review of Economic Studies*, vol. XXIX, no. 80, 1962, pp. 241–5.

74. STONE, Richard, and Alan BROWN. Behavioural and technical change in economic models. In *Problems in Economic Development*. Macmillan, London, 1965.

75. STONE, Richard, Alan BROWN, Graham PYATT, and Colin LEICESTER. *Economic Growth and Manpower*. British Association for Commercial and Industrial Education, London, 1963.

76. STONE, Richard, Alan BROWN, and D. A. ROWE. Demand analysis and projections for Britain, 1900–1970: a study in method. In *Europe's Future Consumption*. North-Holland Publishing Co., Amsterdam, 1964.

77. STONE, Richard, D. G. CHAMPERNOWNE, and J. E. MEADE. The precision of national income estimates. *The Review of Economic Studies*, vol. IX, no. 2, 1942, pp. 111–25.

78. STONE, Richard, and Giovanna CROFT-MURRAY. *Social Accounting and Economic Models*. Bowes and Bowes, London, 1959.

79. STONE, Richard, and Kurt HANSEN. Inter-country comparisons of the national accounts and the work of the national accounts research unit of the O.E.E.C. In *Income and Wealth, Series III.* Bowes and Bowes, Cambridge, 1953.

80. STONE, Richard, and Colin LEICESTER. The methodology of planning models. In *National Economic Planning.* National Bureau of Economic Research, New York, 1967.

81. STONE, Richard, and D. A. ROWE. The market demand for durable goods. *Econometrica,* vol. 25, no. 3, 1957, pp. 423–43.

82. STONE, Richard, and D. A. ROWE. A post-war expenditure function. *The Manchester School of Economic and Social Studies,* vol. XXX, no. 2, 1962, pp. 187–201.

83. STONE, Richard, and others. *The Measurement of Consumers' Expenditure and Behaviour in the United Kingdom, 1920–1938,* vol. I. Cambridge University Press, 1954.

84. THONSTAD, Tore. *Education and Manpower.* Report no. 4 of the Unit for Economic and Statistical Studies on Higher Education. Oliver and Boyd, Edinburgh and London, 1969.

85. TOBIN, James. The theory of portfolio selection. In *The Theory of Interest Rates.* Macmillan, London, 1965.

86. U.K. CENTRAL STATISTICAL OFFICE. *Economic Trends.* H.M.S.O., London, monthly.

87. U.K. CENTRAL STATISTICAL OFFICE. *National Income and Expenditure.* H.M.S.O., London, annually.

88. U.K. DEPARTMENT OF EDUCATION AND SCIENCE. *Statistics of Education.* H.M.S.O., London, annually.

89. U.K. GENERAL REGISTER OFFICE. *Statistical Review of England and Wales.* H.M.S.O., London, annually.

90. U.K. MINISTRY OF AGRICULTURE, FISHERIES AND FOOD. *Domestic Food Consumption and Expenditure: 1960.* H.M.S.O., London, 1962.

91. U.K. MINISTRY OF LABOUR. *Family Expenditure Survey.* H.M.S.O., London, periodically.

92. U.K. TREASURY. *An Analysis of the Sources of War Finance and an Estimate of the National Income and Expenditure in 1938 and 1940.* H.M.S.O., London, 1941.

93. UNITED NATIONS. *Measurement of National Income and the Construction of Social Accounts.* Studies and Reports on Statistical Methods, no. 7. United Nations, Geneva, 1947.

94. UNITED NATIONS, DEPARTMENT OF ECONOMIC AND SOCIAL AFFAIRS, STATISTICAL OFFICE. *A System of National Accounts and Supporting Tables.* Studies in Methods, series F, no. 2. United Nations, New York, 1953; rev. 1, 1960; rev. 2, 1964.

95. UNITED NATIONS, DEPARTMENT OF ECONOMIC AND SOCIAL AFFAIRS, STATISTICAL OFFICE. *A System of National Accounts.* Studies in Methods, series F, no. 2, rev. 3. United Nations, New York, 1968.

96. UNITED NATIONS, DEPARTMENT OF ECONOMIC AND SOCIAL AFFAIRS, STATISTICAL OFFICE. *Yearbook of National Accounts Statistics.* United Nations, New York, annually since 1957.

97. UNITED NATIONS, ECONOMIC AND SOCIAL COUNCIL. *A System of National Accounts (Proposals for the Revision of the SNA 1952).* E/CN.3/320, February 1965. Mimeographed.

98. UNITED NATIONS, ECONOMIC AND SOCIAL COUNCIL. *A System of National Accounts (Proposals for the Revision of the SNA 1952).* E/CN.3/345, June 1966. Mimeographed.

99. UNITED NATIONS, ECONOMIC AND SOCIAL COUNCIL. *A System of National Accounts* (*Proposals for the Revision of the SNA 1952*). E/CN.3/356, August 1967. Mimeographed.

100. VAN CLEEFF, Ed. Nationale boekhouding: proeve van een jaaroverzicht Nederland 1938. *De Economist*, no. 7/8, 1941, pp. 415–24.

101. VAN CLEEFF, Ed. Beteekenis en inrichting eener nationale boekhouding. *De Economist*, no. 11, 1941, pp. 608–23.

102. WATTS, Harold W., and James TOBIN. Consumer expenditures and the capital account. In *Consumption and Saving*, vol. II. University of Pennsylvania, 1960.